The

Jamestown
Project

The

Jamestown Project

Karen Ordahl Kupperman

The Belknap Press of Harvard University Press

Cambridge, Massachusetts · London, England

First Harvard University Press paperback edition, 2008.

Library of Congress Cataloging-in-Publication Data
Kupperman, Karen Ordahl, 1939–
The Jamestown project / Karen Ordahl Kupperman.
p. cm.
Includes bibliographical references and index.
ISBN 978-0-674-02474-8 (cloth : alk. paper)
ISBN 978-0-674-03056-5 (pbk.)
1. Frontier and pioneer life—Virginia—Jamestown. 2. Colonists—
Virginia—Jamestown—Biography. 3. Indians of North America—
Virginia—Jamestown—Biography. 4. Jamestown (Va.)—History—17th century.
5. Virginia—History—Colonial period, ca. 1600–1775. 6. Jamestown (Va.)—
Biography. 7. Virginia—Relations—Great Britain. 8. Great Britain—
Relations—Virginia. 9. Jamestown (Va.)—History—17th century—Sources.
10. Virginia—History—Colonial period, ca. 1600–1775—Sources. I. Title.
F234.J3 K87   2007
973.2'1—dc22   2006052185

Contents

Acknowledgments

Many friends and institutions have contributed to *The Jamestown Project*. Much of the writing was done while I was the Mellon Distinguished Scholar in Residence at the American Antiquarian Society in 2003–04, and that year of writing and research was also supported by a fellowship from the John Simon Guggenheim Foundation. A fellowship at the Institute for Advanced Study of Religion at Yale University in 2000–01 allowed me to undertake research in recent climate reconstruction scholarship and in the response, especially the religious response, of early modern people to the harsh conditions that characterized the late sixteenth and early seventeenth centuries. The Folger Library hosted my National Endowment for the Humanities seminar for college and university teachers on "Texts of Imagination and Empire: The Founding of Jamestown in Its Atlantic Context," in summer 2000. Colleagues in all these institutional settings were immensely important in shaping the way I conceived this project, and I value the many conversations and close readings they have afforded me. Alison Games, Peter Mancall, Daniel Richter, and Thad Tate read the entire manuscript and made many valuable suggestions.

New York University has been generous in allowing me leave time to complete research and write *The Jamestown Project*. The NYU Atlantic history workshop has been the invaluable ground of all my thinking on the interconnections that developed between peoples and lands in this period. All the participants—faculty, students, and invited guests—have shaped my thinking on the construction of the early modern Atlantic.

Many colleagues have helped me to understand the period broadly, and Jamestown specifically, more fully. Discussion with others who are engaged in Jamestown studies, including Tom Davidson, James Horn, Bill Kelso, Martha McCartney, Helen C. Rountree, and Crandall Shifflett, have been particularly valuable. Jean Howard and Nabil Matar opened my eyes to the way English audiences were fascinated by the Muslim East, and Joe Miller and the various projects he has sponsored allowed me to understand Europe's engagement with Africa. I also continue to learn from Mark Peterson, David Harris Sacks, Stuart Schwartz, and Tom Cogswell. The Omohundro Institute of Early American History and Culture, with which I have had a long and satisfying relationship, hosted two conferences that were very important to me. One was on Jamestown and the Atlantic World; the other was in Istanbul, and concerned relationships between the Ottoman and Atlantic Empires. Both brought together wonderful groups of scholars with a wide range of perspectives and areas of expertise. Researching and writing *The Jamestown Project* has taken me back to familiar scholarly territory as well as to areas that were new to me. All these colleagues and institutions have helped me to see the early modern world in new ways.

The
Jamestown
Project

Introduction: Creation Myths

IN MAY 1607 a party of just over a hundred men and boys landed on the James River in Virginia and planted the colony they named Jamestown in honor of the English king. The little colony struggled through a horrible first decade in which it barely held on before the settlers began to find their footing on the path that would lead to stability and, eventually, success. Jamestown has always occupied an equivocal position in American history. It is celebrated as the first permanent English settlement in the territory that would become the United States. These colonists planted the tiny seed from which would grow a powerful nation where all the world's people would mingle.

And yet Jamestown makes us uncomfortable. The portrait of it that has come down to us depicts greedy, grasping colonists in America and their arrogant backers in England. The settlement's first years were marked by belligerent intrusions on the Chesapeake Algonquians which manifested mainly the ignorance of the English. Within Jamestown, life degenerated into a shambles of death and despair. When John Rolfe finally developed a marketable crop—tobacco—the colonists exploited the land and one another in the scramble for profits. Ultimately they would institute slavery for imported Africans in their insatiable search for profits. This is the creation story from hell.

America

Who gets to choose

Americans prefer to think of Plymouth colony in New England as our true foundation. This 1620 settlement, also composed of just over a hundred people, was a puritan foundation; about half of the settlers were separatists, that is, puritans who considered the Church of England so hopelessly corrupt that they separated themselves from it completely. By contrast, the puritans who settled Massachusetts Bay a decade later remained nominally within the established church. The Pilgrims at Plymouth, in our agreed-upon national story, are portrayed as the direct opposites of the Jamestown group. They were humble people who wanted only a place to worship God as they saw fit, and they lived on terms of amity with one another and with the neighboring Indians, relationships memorialized in the First Thanksgiving. They occupied family farms and were content with self-sufficiency. These are the forebears we prefer to acknowledge.

The good origins versus bad origins dichotomy is a false one based on a whole series of faulty premises. *The Jamestown Project* reconstructs America's origin story by placing the Virginia colony within its true context. By examining the maelstrom of previous plans and experiences that converged on the James, we can see the genuine accomplishment that emerged from the apparent wreckage wrought by the planters, and the efforts of the rank and file who largely brought it about.

In fact, through a decade's trial and error, Jamestown's ordinary settlers and their backers in England figured out what it would take to make an English colony work. This was an enormous accomplishment achieved in a very short period of time, a breakthrough that none of the other contemporaneous ventures was able to make. The ingredients for success—widespread ownership of land, control of taxation for public obligations through a representative assembly, the institution of a normal society through the inclusion of women, and development of a product that could be marketed profitably to sustain the economy—were beginning to be put in place by 1618 and were in full operation by 1620, when the next successful colony, Plymouth, was planted.

Thus the Pilgrims were able to be relatively successful (after a disastrous first year) because they had studied Jamestown's record and had learned its lessons. Jamestown was not just the earliest English colony to survive; its true priority lies in its inventing the archetype of English colonization. All other successful English colonies followed the Jamestown model.

England was a laggard in overseas ventures. By 1606, when the Virginia Company was organized and plans for the colony were laid, English merchants in collaboration with political leaders had begun to establish a role for their nation in the newly opening trades around the Atlantic, the Mediterranean, and in the East. In these endeavors they were attempting to emulate, and often intrude on, the Spanish and Portuguese, united under the Spanish crown since 1580, who were the pioneers in creating the connections and bases through which trading operations were carried on.

New Spain was almost a century old when Jamestown was founded, and French traders had established firm partnerships with Indian nations in the fur trade along the St. Lawrence to the north. Spanish ships had scouted Chesapeake Bay repeatedly before concluding that the region would not repay the effort required to sustain settlement. The Spanish had planted St. Augustine on the Florida coast, and this, not Jamestown, was actually the first permanent European colony within the future United States; it was settled in 1565, almost half a century before Jamestown. And Santa Fe in New Mexico was founded shortly after Jamestown.

By 1607 English fishermen had been visiting the Newfoundland Banks and the New England coast for a century or more, and they built temporary settlements there, but no permanent English presence existed. In the last decades of the sixteenth century, a time when England and Spain were at war, English ships participated enthusiastically in privateering—licensed piracy against Spanish fleets traveling from the Caribbean to Seville. In the 1580s Sir Walter Ralegh's colony at

Roanoke, within the Outer Banks of North Carolina, was initially designed to serve as a base for those patriotic privateers.

The first group of settlers sent to Roanoke in 1585 conformed to the classic model: a group of young men under military authority. Their governor was Captain Ralph Lane. As always with such a design, Lane found the settlers, whom he characterized as the "wylde menn of myne owene nacione," hard to control and motivate. By the end of the colony's first winter, relationships with the coastal Carolina Algonquians, on whom they depended for food, had broken down completely. They deserted the site early the next summer, and Lane scorned the whole enterprise, writing that "the discovery of a good mine by the goodnesse of God, or a passage to the Southsea, or someway to it, and nothing els can bring this country in request to be inhabited by our nation."[1]

Ralegh and his associates did not give up on Roanoke. In fact, they were the first to try the successful model. In 1587 they sent a new colony composed of families under civil government, and each family was promised a large estate to own in the new land. They were intended to settle on Chesapeake Bay near where Jamestown would eventually be planted; the Lane colony's explorations had convinced them that this would be a better location from which good commodities could be produced. But this plan had no lasting influence, for the colony was abandoned, and the planters became famous as the Lost Colonists of Roanoke. Ralegh, meanwhile, was overwhelmed by other commitments and, ultimately, by loss of his favored status at court. So although Roanoke's failure only temporarily dampened English enthusiasm for establishing American colonies, Jamestown had to learn its lessons anew.

England's late entry into the American sweepstakes spawned myriad ventures. The stark dichotomy of Jamestown and Plymouth would have been unintelligible to contemporaries. Virginia was one of many attempts, now largely forgotten, all up and down the coast as far north as the Arctic Circle and south into the Caribbean, floated by English promoters in the last years of Queen Elizabeth's reign and the early years under James I, who succeeded her in 1603. But colonization was expensive and had to be financed by private enterprise. In the absence of any sure source of return on that investment, America took last place in most promoters' minds, after endeavors in the Mediterranean, Africa, and the East, where profits were much more certain. The voyages actually sent out were a fraction of the number of schemes proposed by that class of people who became known as "projectors"— those who made a career out of spinning projects.

English venturers were very conscious of being newcomers in all these places where they sought a foothold, and the keynote of their activities was improvisation. Everywhere they went, they necessarily employed trial and error—and error often predominated. Promoters laid plans, but the ordinary people who carried them out, often very young men and women, were the ones who had to deal with realities on the ground and who ultimately founded a successful colony. Many involved in early-seventeenth-century America—Indians, Europeans, and Africans—had had experience of other Atlantic and Mediterranean regions before they came together on the James River. Often their experience was as captives, or as individuals left behind when the ships on which they had arrived departed hurriedly in the face of dangers ranging from armed resistance to violent Atlantic storms. Those who could improvise were the ones who survived. And the knowledge of transatlantic others gained from these people informed planning and responses on all sides when Europeans attempted to create bases in America. All players brought vast experience, some relevant and some irrelevant, to the changed situations that European ventures created; and they drew on this experience, for good or ill, when confronted by the necessity of making choices.

When James I came to the throne and inaugurated a policy of reconciliation with Spain that ended the lucrative privateering war, prominent policy makers and merchants decided that they would try to sustain a permanent foundation across the Atlantic in the form of a Chesapeake colony. England's being a latecomer meant that its colonists had to take the parts of North America that were left, the places that other countries had rejected as less promising for the kinds of rich products that made the expensive project of colonization worthwhile. Backers knew that the region was not the best choice for the goals they had in mind; at about the same time Jamestown was founded, other companies attempted to plant colonies in Guiana, on various islands in the Caribbean, and in Newfoundland, as well as a colony in Maine. Other locations had been tried in the last decades of the sixteenth century in addition to Roanoke. Jamestown did not stand out in people's minds as a uniquely important venture, as we might expect it to have done.

Jamestown's site, on a peninsula jutting out into the James River some fifty miles upstream from Chesapeake Bay, was chosen with defense against Spanish attack in mind. As far as the Spanish were concerned, the colony was within their territory. They had attacked and eliminated an earlier French settlement on the southern coast. Although Spain and England were officially at peace in 1607, no one expected it to last, and the Virginia Company believed that its little plantation would be a natural target. Although planners were concerned about the response of the Indians on whom they would intrude, their main fear lay in the rivalry with Spain.

The Spanish did make constant efforts to find out what was going on in Jamestown—much of the surviving information available today is actually in Spanish correspondence—and several times seriously considered mounting an attack. Expectations of such an assault also contributed to the composition of the early contingents and plans for governing them. Like Roanoke's backers, the Virginia Company assumed that a group of young men under the command of high-ranking governors was the structure that would work best in the uncertain world of American ventures. After all, such an arrangement would most closely resemble the English society from which they came. But these hierarchical arrangements did not survive the transatlantic passage well, primarily because the colony could not replicate the social relationships on which they traditionally rested. Just as Roanoke's governor, Ralph Lane, found dealing with English savages his biggest problem, ultimately the company deemed brute force under martial law necessary to keep the Jamestown colonists in line.

It was the Chesapeake Algonquians who allowed Jamestown to become established as well as it did at the outset. The land on which the English settled belonged to the Paspahegh tribe, and the Paspaheghs, not surprisingly, deemed their presence unwelcome. Slowly the newcomers came to understand that many polities around Chesapeake Bay were under the influence of one great overlord, whom they came to know as Powhatan. The colonists called him an emperor, the closest European equivalent, but Powhatan was actually his title; eventually they were told that his given name was Wahunsenacawh. His daughter, whom we know by her nickname Pocahontas, became a principal intermediary between the cultures. Later the English learned two given names for her: Amonute and Matoaka.

Wahunsenacawh knew a great deal about Europeans in 1607. The Indians had seen many transatlantic voyagers over the course of the preceding century and understood well their strengths and weaknesses, and their aspirations and fears. They knew that Europeans, because they were so vulnerable, tended to overreact when they felt threatened, so American leaders had developed a series of strategies for handling them. Not only had these people encountered many ships that had sailed in and out of the bay in the sixteenth century, but also at least one man, Paquiquineo, had lived in Spanish colonies and even in Spain for a decade before returning in 1570 to his home at Paspahegh, the site of Jamestown. There is no question that the ram-

shackle Jamestown colony would have been cut off had the Indians decided to eliminate it. During the early years the men were dependent
on the region's native people for their food supply, and relationships
with the hard-pressed Indians grew increasingly tense, replicating the
pattern at Roanoke.

The problems in the early years at Jamestown stemmed from actors
on all sides drawing inappropriate lessons from previous encounters.
Wahunsenacawh and his advisers did not foresee the eventual growth
of the colony; they assumed that it would always be easy to manipulate this motley group, and that the little settlement could serve as
a valuable source of tools, weapons, and other European manufactured goods. For their part, Jamestown's leaders, who were increasingly
drawn from men with military experience in Europe's religious wars,
believed that they could construct a society by enforcing sufficiently
strict discipline, as they had done with English troops abroad. In the
event, they were all wrong. Instead, the outcome grew from the trial-
and-error efforts of the many ordinary people, most lost to the records,
who found a way to build a society.

Only by examining the experience of all these people from around
the Atlantic can we understand how and why Jamestown, however
imperfectly, managed to hold on until it found the formula for recreating a successful version of English society abroad. Once that formula
was devised, then all other colonies, beginning with Plymouth, had a
much easier time of it and gained stability much more quickly. Jamestown's contribution was to develop the model for a true English colony, one that would actually work in America. This plan evolved out
of the welter of failed experiments, false starts, and blind violence that
characterized these early years. No one could say in 1607 how to make
an English plantation in America function or even why investment in
such a project was worthwhile. In the space of about a decade, some
people, mainly those actually in Virginia, figured out what it would
take and how to raise the revenue necessary to sustain English backers'

interest. The results continued to be messy, and many people suffered. But the outlines of a genuinely American society, with all its virtues and defects, first emerged along the James.

So, why does Virginia look so bad? One reason was its site, which proved to be a very poor choice for promoting the well-being of the people who tried to live there. The period during which both Roanoke and Jamestown were founded was a time of environmental crisis that made establishing thriving settlements even more difficult than it should have been. Alonso Suárez de Toledo urged Spain's King Philip II not to worry about other Europeans trying to settle on North America's east coast: "What would happen to foreigners there who must bring their subsistence from a great distance to an inhospitable coast? The land itself would wage war on them."[2] Jamestown was notoriously unhealthy, and the colonists made it more unwholesome by the way they operated their little society. The Spanish never attacked them. and their relationships with Chesapeake area Indians were crucial to the life of the settlement.

Another reason for Jamestown's bad reputation lies in the nature of the records, which consist largely of complaints, special pleading, and excuses sent by colonists back to their patrons in England. Most of the surviving records, not surprisingly, were produced by leaders on both sides of the Atlantic. The migrants had been sent over with notoriously unrealizable goals: to find a good source of wealth, preferably precious metals, or a passage to the Pacific and the riches of Asia. Prominent men in the colony, faced with the problem of explaining why they were not sending back the rich products investors demanded, or why they had not found the passage to the Pacific, could not speak the simple truth: that getting started is extremely difficult, and they would need support for many years just to become established before any valuable products could be expected. Investors in the seventeenth century looked to the next quarterly report as much as those in the twenty-first, and they had the choice of many other potential ventures from which the returns were more secure. Had they known that Virginia would absorb money over many years with no profit, the colony would have been abandoned at the outset—as so many others were. From the company's point of view, the colony was nothing but a drain on its resources, eating up huge amounts of money in supplies and new settlers without ever repaying the backers' investment, much less returning a profit.

The colonists, for their part, desperately wrote letter after letter explaining that colonization was hard, that they had to get set up before they could become self-sustaining, and that they needed support while they did that. Once they were established, then there would be time to make the efforts required to find a source of profit; but it was foolish and counterproductive to pressure them to do it at the beginning. One unspoken message ran through all these reports: Please do not abandon us. Unable to tell the truth in the early struggling years—or even to be sure what the truth was—colonial leaders blamed one another, and especially the rank and file, who were characterized in much of the correspondence as "the scum of the earth." Elites did not know how to organize and motivate them for the necessary work; they simply blamed the men for not acting as they wanted them to. Difficulties in controlling the colonists exacerbated the worsening relationship between the settlers and the Indians on whom they depended, though the leaders blamed the Indians on whom they had intruded for not supporting the colony with food as they wished.

But these same records, if we read beyond the surface noise of complaint and charge and countercharge, demonstrate that some people on the ground were drawing on the Atlantic and Mediterranean experience many had brought to the colony and were improvising relationships with the people and the land that finally achieved a measure of stability and growth in the colony. Often it was just this sort of improvisation, undertaken by ordinary people, that made elites nervous and brought forth their accusations of malfeasance. Whereas many of the leaders whose vitriol figures so prominently in the records left the Chesapeake to promote and participate in other ventures after a few years, ordinary colonists were the ones who set about the task of building families and family farms. The other ventures attempted in the first decade of the seventeenth century all failed. The truly remarkable thing about Jamestown is that it somehow survived through years of hardship and discouragement until a few settlers finally embarked on the course to success at the end of the 1610s. This book is an examination of the various kinds of experiences and backgrounds that came together in the Jamestown project to make this improbable survival—and the evolution of the successful archetype—possible.

I

Elizabethan England Engages the World

EUROPEANS SAW THEIR relationship with America as one act in a huge world-historical drama. Christians commonly believed that they were living in the last days, the culmination of history that was fore-told in the prophetic books of the Bible, especially Daniel and the Revelation of Saint John. Events such as the fall of Constantinople to the Ottomans in 1453 were seen by many as the kinds of turning points figured as the breaking of the Seven Seals and the pouring out of the Seven Vials in Revelation. Scholars argued that the disclosure of the Americas and of previously unknown species of plants and ani-mals fulfilled the prophecy concerning the last days in Daniel 12:4: "But thou ô Daniel, shut up the wordes, and seale the boke til the end of the time: many shal runne to and fro, & knowledge shalbe in-creased." Certain religious thinkers came to be known as gifted inter-preters of the prophecies, and their interpretations were avidly sought by those seeking to read God's will in events.[1]

One task that had to be accomplished as part of the divine plan's culmination was preaching the Gospel to the whole world, and this took on urgency especially for those who subscribed to the widespread view that the American Indians were the descendants of the Ten Lost Tribes of Israel. Not only would Jews and heathens be gathered in during the last days, but all knowledge would be recovered. Adam had had complete knowledge of the world and its nature, but this had been lost through the corruption of ensuing ages. Now European natural historians rushed to try to comprehend the species and the environment of this newly revealed different world in order to achieve the understanding that was part of God's plan.

The timing of God's allowing Old World peoples to know of the existence of what they "more commonlie than properlie called the New Worlde" was seen as significant in every way.[2] Some Spanish writers even argued that revelation of the mission fields of America would make up for the horrible split in Christendom caused by the Reformation; in effect, the conquests of Cortés compensated for the depredations of Luther.[3] For their part, English Protestant commentators argued that God had kept America hidden until after the Reformation so that the true reformed Christianity, not the corruptions introduced in the Middle Ages, would be preached to its people.

Christianity had moved steadily westward from its inception in the eastern Mediterranean, and America was seen as God's next intended venue. The anonymous author who wrote about Jacques Cartier's second voyage up the St. Lawrence in 1535 dedicated his account to the French king, Francis I, writing that God "in His divine goodness" had so designed human history that the spirit of Christianity would move from east to west as the sun does. From its origin in "the Holy Land, which is in Asia to the East of our Europe," the light of the Gospel had progressed steadily westward.[4] And the Spanish Augustinian friar Antonio de la Calancha argued that Jesus himself had prophesied the westward movement of his message, facing west toward America as he died on the cross. Some in Mexico even believed that the pope and the center of the church would ultimately relocate to America when they were driven out of Europe by the "forces of evil."[5]

English Protestants, like their Spanish Roman Catholic counterparts, celebrated the westward advance of Christianity, highlighting especially the Romans, who had brought conversion to Britain. As William Strachey wrote, vividly depicting the savagery of his own ancestors, if the Romans had not invaded the British Isles with force and taught the inhabitants "to know the powerfull discourse of divine Reason (which makes us only men, and distinguisheth us from beasts . . . we might yet have lyved overgrowne Satyrs, rude, and untutred, wandring in the woodes, dwelling in Caves, and hunting for our dynners, (as the wyld beasts in the forrests for their prey,) prostetuting our daughters to straungers, sacrificing our Children to our Idolls, nay eating our owne Children, as did the Scots in those dayes."[6] English Protestants, too, saw America as a potential place of refuge: "If it should please God to punish his people in the Christian countries of Europe, for their coldness, carnality, wanton abuse of the Gospel, contention, etc., either by Turkish slavery, or by popish tyranny," wrote the separatist puritan Robert Cushman in Plymouth colony, "here is a way opened for such as have wings to fly into this wilderness."[7]

For all European Christians, America was central to the divine cosmic drama they believed was entering its final stages as the events foretold in the Book of Revelation played out. Just as the Romans had brought Christianity to Britain, now European Christians were charged with converting the newly revealed inhabitants of the Americas. Robert Johnson, a member of the Virginia Company in London, wrote that "God hath reserved in this last age of the world, an infinite number of those lost and scattered sheepe, to be won and recovered by our means." Johnson, like many others, pointed out that although the Romans had conquered Britain with the sword, the British had been the true winners through the precious gift of Christianity.[8] Earlier, Edward Hayes had written about the conversion of the Indians in very similar terms, arguing that God had ordained "in this last age of the world (or likely never) the time is compleat of receiving also these Gentiles into his mercy." Hayes agreed that the English were to be

God's special agents in this work, and he echoed Spanish authors who saw Christianity moving from east to west, adding that in America as in Europe it would also move from south to north.[9] To encourage investment in the colonization of Cape Breton (which he tried to name New Galloway), Robert Gordon of Lochinvar wrote that "all the Divines" agreed "these are the latter dayes." It was essential that Christians work to convert all those who were "captivate in Ethnick Darkness." (Originally the word "ethnic" was comparable to "pagan" or "heathen"; pre-Christian philosophers such as Plato and Aristotle were known as "the Ethnics.")[10]

The work of conversion could not be carried out, however, unless English people settled permanently among the Indians. John Rolfe, after his marriage to Pocahontas, wrote that no good Christian could regard the Virginia Algonquians without pity for their ignorance of Christianity. Not only were the English charged with responsibility to bring their knowledge of God to Virginia's people, but also they were therefore "a peculier people marked and chosen by the finger of God to possess it." ("Peculiar" in this period meant "set apart" or "special.") Sir William Alexander, writing to promote colonization of Newfoundland, argued that the project of planting settlements in America replicated the "infancie of the first age."[11]

American projects grew out of Old World aspirations. Transatlantic colonization was undertaken in the atmosphere of religious conflict that touched everything Europeans did. Many thinkers believed that Europe—Christendom, as they called it—was in decline and that the great Muslim world might eventually dominate all. Riches from abroad, especially from America, could right the balance and restore the unity of Christian Europe under the pope. Restored, Europe would have the courage and strength to resist the expansive Ottoman Empire. For their part, Protestants hoped that newfound wealth could strengthen their cause and allow them to support the true religion in the face of Roman Catholic tyranny. Although they disagreed on the hoped-for outcome, all Europeans saw the revelation of the Americas as a divine move meant to have momentous consequences. These sentiments built through the century after Columbus's first voyage and came to a head as the sixteenth century entered its last decades. Spain was at the pinnacle of its power, and England then first began its attempts to create colonies in America. It looked as though the fate of Europe and of Christianity would be decided in the 1580s and 1590s, the waning years of Queen Elizabeth's long reign. And America increasingly came to occupy a central role in the drama.

Christian Europe had been rent asunder in two ways. Before Europe existed, there was Christendom, stretching from Scandinavia and Britain in the West to the Byzantine Empire in the East. Despite the occupation of much of the Iberian peninsula by Muslims from North Africa, the great variety of peoples, customs, and governments in what we call Europe were brought together under this hazy notion of a shared faith and purpose in the world from about the seventh century on.[12] In 1453 the expansive Ottoman Empire shattered the unity of Christendom when it seized Constantinople, separating the Eastern Byzantine Christians from those in the West, whose center was at Rome. Not only was the connection with the Byzantine Christians severed, but also the Holy Land was controlled by the Muslim Ottomans. The flood of scholars streaming out of Constantinople, now Istanbul, in the wake of the conquest, bringing with them many of the ancient texts that Western Christians had lost over the centuries of the medieval period, made possible the restoration of much knowledge and understanding, but western Europeans mourned the vanished unity of Christendom.

Christendom was fractured a second time when, in 1517, Martin Luther distributed his Ninety-five Theses from his post in Wittenberg, challenging the teachings of Roman Catholicism. Although he was not the first to pose such questions publicly, or even to draw followers, the movement that began then attracted much attention and ultimately grew into the Protestant Reformation. This second shattering of Christendom was even more fundamental than the first. Over the course of the sixteenth and seventeenth centuries, the implications of these changes would be tested and regularized. In a world in which the religion of the monarch determined the religion of the people, lines quickly hardened, especially as reformers pushed Protestant rulers and churches to strip away the ceremonies and doctrines they associated with Roman Catholicism.

Even time was affected. Christian doctrine and the calendar had both been standardized by the Council of Nicaea in 325; from its deliberations Europe adopted the Julian calendar, named for Julius Caesar. Slowly over the centuries the calendar became increasingly out of tune with the progression of the seasons. So in 1582 Pope Gregory endorsed a reformed calendar that corrected the Julian calendar's errors, partly by regularizing the occurrence of leap years. In order to make up for the accumulated regression, ten days were omitted; thus October 4 was followed by October 15. The Gregorian calendar went into effect in Roman Catholic countries, but those controlled by Protestants refused to accept this popish manipulation of time. John Dee, Queen Elizabeth's science adviser, offered a version that improved on the Gregorian calendar, but it did not attract support. The English continued to begin the year on Lady Day, March 25, even after most European countries, including Scotland in 1600, accepted January 1 as New Year's Day. Despite widespread adoption of the new calendar over the course of the seventeenth century, England and its American colonies did not accept it until 1752, by which time the gap had become eleven days. As early as 1587 an almanac for England and Ireland presented both the Julian and Gregorian calendars for its users, and sophisticated English correspondents in the seventeenth century took to signing their letters with a dual date, especially if they were written between January and March.[13]

Europe's situation was crystallizing around 1570, hardening the fault lines that lay along religious divides. Increasingly leaders looked to American projects as a way to gain the resources required to defend their own positions at home. Roman Catholic Ireland was in rebellion in the 1560s against control from Protestant England, and France, which was split between Roman Catholics and Protestants, saw open religious warfare at that time. Then in 1572 Roman Catholic forces made a concerted attack on the French Protestants, called Huguenots, in the devastating Saint Bartholomew's Day massacre. Several hundred English Protestants responded to the call to go to France and help liberate the Huguenots in the besieged city of La Rochelle.

Meanwhile, much of Spain and Portugal had been occupied by North African Muslims and Jews from the eighth century on, and the Reconquista, the long struggle to push the Moors and Jews out of the Iberian peninsula, had culminated in 1492 with the fall of Granada. Through the sixteenth century the Inquisition sought to root out remnants of the forbidden religions. In the province of Andalucia, Moriscos, people of North African descent, rose up in 1568 against newly promulgated restrictions on their language, dress, and gatherings. The reaction to this rebellion was a campaign to uproot them from their land and resettle them in thinly populated regions of the country, a plan that was carried out in 1570.

In England, which had in the course of the sixteenth century been Roman Catholic, then Protestant, then Roman Catholic, and was now Protestant again, tighter controls seemed increasingly necessary. Mary, Queen of Scots, a Roman Catholic with a claim to the throne that made her Elizabeth's rival, was the focus of the hopes of many who longed for one more turn of the religious wheel. In 1568 Mary fled Scotland and entered England, where she was detained under house arrest. The next year a group of northern nobles with Roman Catholic sympathies, led by the earl of Northumberland, mounted a rebellion, which was thoroughly crushed. In 1570 Pope Pius V issued a bull ex-

Crispin van de Passe created this engraving on the death of Queen Elizabeth in 1603 from a miniature by Isaac Oliver. When it was republished in 1618, the printer included Virginia among her domains. By permission of the Folger Shakespeare Library.

communicating Queen Elizabeth and relieving her subjects of the requirement to obey her, despite the religious oath of loyalty they had
sworn. Spain's Philip II and his councilors, urged on by Pius's successor, Pope Gregory XIII, considered an invasion of England, possibly by
way of Ireland, in the 1570s. Those who favored invasion argued that a
relatively small force would be needed, as the English people, who secretly longed for the restoration of Roman Catholicism, would rise up
to greet the invaders as liberators. Fears ran high at the English court.
In 1576 Dr. William Allen, formerly of Oxford University and now a
cardinal, organized the English College at Rome, and soon specially
trained English Jesuits began to infiltrate their home country.

Across the narrow sea separating England from the continent, the
Protestant Low Countries rose up in rebellion against Spanish rule in
the person of the repressive duke of Alba in 1568, initiating the inter-
mittent campaign that became known as the Eighty Years' War. Influential leaders in England thought that their government should aid
the Protestant Dutch as they struggled to free themselves, and many
ambitious Englishmen accepted Dutch commissions either for fighting
in the Netherlands itself or for privateering. Many English veterans of
these campaigns would later participate in American ventures, and
would bring with them lessons learned in these cruel religious wars.

National leaders' aspirations for American ventures were conditioned
by the religious conflict in Europe. Everyone knew that Spain had
been transformed from a divided and relatively poor country in the fifteenth century to the strongest power in western Europe in the sixteenth by the infusion of American riches. And now the Spanish were
employing that power to try to reverse the Reformation and force European Protestants to again recognize the authority of the pope. The
vise was perceptibly tightening on England toward the end of the century, culminating in the attack by the great Spanish Armada in 1588.
The English had only to look across the channel to the beleaguered

Dutch to see what was in store for them. Elizabeth's advisers increasingly pointed to transatlantic ventures as the way to gain resources sufficient to resist Spain and protect the Protestant cause.

The split within Christendom loomed large; but Europeans were also acutely aware of the earlier split and of the great Ottoman Empire that controlled so much of the circum-Mediterranean lands. Although its nations were slowly reorienting the continent toward the Atlantic, in a very real sense Europe existed on the margins of the great Islamic world, and in this orientation England was on the margins of Europe.[14] Experience of the Mediterranean and of the Muslims who controlled so much of it helped to shape perceptions of other cultures, and many of the English who ventured to America drew parallels between the people they encountered there and what they knew of Eastern cultures either from personal experience or from their reading.

Under Süleyman the Magnificent in the sixteenth century, the Ottoman Empire was the largest in Europe. As the successor to the Byzantine Empire it was a European state, but it was also much more, as it stretched from its center at Constantinople (now Istanbul) into the Balkans and Hungary and around the Mediterranean, encompassing client states across North Africa to Morocco in the west, including what was known as the Barbary Coast. In the east the empire incorporated parts of modern Syria, Egypt, Saudi Arabia, Iraq, Kuwait, and Israel, and even extended into Russia. The great sultan died in 1566, but his campaign continued, and many in western Europe responded to calls for Christians to resist this Muslim presence.[15] Much of the Ottoman fleet was destroyed in the battle of Lepanto in the Mediterranean in 1571, but it was soon rebuilt, and the threat of the "terrible Turk" was felt throughout western Europe. The Ottomans continued to expand westward into Europe, and their armies several times laid siege to Vienna. Europeans were keenly aware of the Ottoman Empire as the greatest power in Europe and watched events there closely.

As it grew, the empire incorporated many non-Muslim people. Its policies became an object of wonder and admiration in a Europe torn by wars pitting Christians against Christians. Whereas each western European nation recognized only one version of Christianity and allowed no others, the Ottoman rulers adopted an official policy of flexibility, even tolerance, in order to govern their diverse population. Administrators of conquered territories took account of local practice. Not only did the empire incorporate a broad interpretation of Islam, but also Judaism and Christianity were particularly tolerated in recognition of their joint genesis with Islam in Abrahamic faith. Although they had to pay a special tax to the empire and practice their religion in private, Christian and Jewish communities were permitted to create courts in which their own traditions determined justice, and European resident traders in the port cities ran their own courts.[16]

Europeans were astonished at such toleration. Stephen Parmenius, a young Hungarian scholar who attended Oxford University (and who died on a voyage to America in 1583), wrote of his origins, "Although I was born in the servitude and barbarism of the Turkish empire, my parents were, by the grace of God, Christians, and I was even educated for some part of the time."[17] Learned western Europeans understood the complexity of the Ottoman Empire. In the sixteenth century Jean Bodin, the "famous Lawyer, and a man of great Experience in matters of State," wrote, "The great emperour of the Turkes doth with as great devotion as any prince in the world honour and observe the religion by him received from his auncestours, and yet detesteth hee not the straunge religions of others; but to the contrarie permitteth every man to live according to his conscience." Bodin's work was translated into English by Richard Knolles and published in 1606 just as the Virginia Company was being organized. Travel by Muslims into Europe or Christians into Muslim countries was not uncommon. Families or associates of captives on both sides traveled to arrange ransoms; others traveled as diplomats or on business. Some traveled purely for pleasure or education. Many Sephardic Jews migrated to the tolerant Netherlands after their expulsion from Spain, but an even larger number went to the Ottoman Empire, where they were valued for their trade ties and knowledge of production in Europe. Some Protestants also sought refuge within Ottoman territories in the seventeenth century. Turkey was the place where Europe's religious refugees found succor. Sir Henry Blount summed up the popular fascination with the Ottomans and the way they ran their empire; for him, they were "the only moderne people."[18]

If western Europe felt itself overshadowed by the powerful and united Ottoman Empire, England was peripheral to Europe. England's leaders were keenly aware that they were lagging behind in Europe's engagement with a wider world. Not only was the nation relatively poor, but also it lacked the technical knowledge to compete on the world stage. Although some among Elizabeth's counselors and leading merchants advocated American ventures as a way toward greatness for England, most still hoped to enter the established older trades with other parts of the world. American ventures were speculative and apt to require a great deal of investment before yielding any returns, but the Eastern and African trades were well established. Because they were relatively late arrivals on the scene, however, English merchants were always trying to break into trading relationships established first by other nations. In the 1550s English merchants organized companies to initiate trade with Morocco and with Guinea on the west coast of Africa, hoping to penetrate the Portuguese monopoly there. Another company was founded to pioneer a route to Muscovy as a means of gaining access to the East and its commodities. Knowledge gained and lessons learned in these efforts would later be transferred to American enterprises.

English merchants believed that Morocco was one African nation whose trade was open to them, and there they began to learn the intricacies of such relationships. Morocco, facing the Mediterranean and the Atlantic, had achieved its independence from both the Ottoman and the Iberian empires. Trade with the country the English called Barbary began tentatively in the 1540s, exchanging English products, particularly textiles, for gold and sugar; one ship in the early 1560s was said to have carried Bibles and other books in Hebrew for the Jewish community of Morocco. English representatives of merchant groups, called factors, were resident in Morocco from at least the end of the 1550s, and in 1577 Queen Elizabeth sent Edmund Hogan as an ambassador to Mulai Abd el-Malek, whose name Hogan rendered as "Mully Abdelmelech Emperour of Maroccus, and king of Fes and Sus." Hogan wrote of waiting on board ship until he was formally invited to disembark by a guard of honor, and he described the opulence of his welcome. He had brought "a great base Lute" for the sultan, who asked him to send musicians from England for his court. In his turn Mulai Abd el-Malek gave Hogan a jewel-encrusted dagger. Hogan was thoroughly impressed, both by the rich possibilities of the trade and by the majesty of the court. He wrote that the sultan knew both the Old and New Testaments well; moreover, he "liveth greatly in the feare of God" and respected the English for their religious beliefs, which, presumably unlike the Roman Catholicism of the Spanish and Portuguese, "forbiddeth worship of idoles." Hogan concluded ambiguously: "The Moores called him the Christian king."[19]

Africans had acquired understanding of a larger world and experienced its influence over the course of several centuries. The African trades originally coursed over the great sea of sand, the Sahara, and focused therefore on the continent's interior rather than the Atlantic coast. Islam had a strong presence in west and central Africa, having entered along the active trade routes as early as the eleventh century; as Ross E. Dunn writes, "From a global perspective the trans-Saharan trade routes were north-south branch lines of the hemispheric Muslim network that extended right across northern Africa and Asia to the ports of the South China Sea."[20] The rich fields of West Africa were the source of most of the world's gold by the fourteenth century, and the peoples engaged in the trade had become Muslims. The introduction of Islam was swiftly followed by the growth of a literate class needed for the conduct of both worship and law.

Many African rulers spoke at least one European language and readily displayed their knowledge of international diplomatic forms. Like Islam, Christianity had an established presence in Africa. The rulers of the kingdom of Kongo had formally adopted Christianity early in the sixteenth century. As it had previously in Europe, Christianity in Kongo absorbed many indigenous forms and spiritual entities, but Kongo's Christianity was recognized by the pope, who received its embassies and consecrated African priests and even bishops. Both Islam and Christianity thrived in part because adherents were able to continue their traditional practices within them.[21]

African states and merchants, who had created long-distance networks centuries before Europeans were active there, dominated trade in West Africa in the sixteenth and early seventeenth centuries. The Portuguese were the earliest Europeans to establish trade with merchants in coastal Africa, having made connections in the 1440s. As the newsgatherer John Pory noted, the currents along the coast made sailing extremely difficult, and these challenges were first understood and managed by Portuguese navigators, "to the unspeakable gaine" of that nation.[22] Europeans sought gold, pepper, hides, ivory, dyewoods, and other goods, and for those lucky enough to get in on the ground floor, it was an immeasurably rich trade. Africans imported textiles, metals in the form of utensils and iron bars, and other goods from Europe to add to their own manufactures in these fields; European traders also facilitated exchange of African-made products and brought items from India and America.[23] The currency of Benin consisted of cowrie shells from the Indian Ocean, and Europeans noted the use of precise weights in measuring gold on the Gold Coast. As they began to look across the Atlantic, English merchants hoped for comparable trading relationships with American Indian nations.

In both Europe and Africa the reorientation of attention toward the Atlantic in the sixteenth century enhanced the position of formerly marginal nations. Just as England gained prominence, so small coastal African states that had previously been on the edge of the great inland commercial routes developed partnerships with the European new-comers, and all the trades increased in volume. Tiny fishing villages grew into large and cosmopolitan cities by the seventeenth century, with populations of Africans and Europeans and people of mixed de-scent. All three populations drew on their knowledge of the many forms and customs by which coastal commerce operated, and their work was facilitated by their knowledge of various languages. Those of mixed descent could claim multiple linkages, and they often predomi-nated. Over time a lingua franca developed, made up of elements of European languages, particularly Portuguese, and several African lan-guages, and this "Guinea Speech" or "Black Portuguese" came to be used all along the coast and throughout the Atlantic.

Guinea was especially important as a source of gold. Overland trade in gold with Muslim merchants from North Africa had been thriving for centuries before the Portuguese learned how to sail in the danger-ous coastal currents of West Africa and inaugurated African-European seaborne commerce. The English made repeated efforts to break into this trade but found it difficult to compete with the already established Portuguese. The early attempts of English merchants to initiate West African trade in the 1550s were awkward and uncertain. The first of these voyages, in 1553, traded for gold at the River Sess on the Malagueta coast in what is now Liberia, and then, despite the misgiv-ings of experienced mariners in the crew, moved on to Benin. A party of merchants traveled inland to the city of Benin in the Niger delta, where they were graciously received by its ruler, the Oba. He spoke Portuguese, having learned the language in childhood, and was clearly sophisticated in the realm of international trade. He offered to sell the merchants a great quantity of pepper, and stipulated that he would establish a line of credit for them, indicating that the merchandise they had brought with them was not good enough for this. While the merchants enjoyed the Oba's hospitality, the mariners on the coast fared badly in the hot environment, and many died. Ultimately the ships sailed away, leaving the merchants stranded in Benin. They never returned to England.[24]

A second voyage the next year became embroiled in controversy with the Portuguese on the Guinea coast. After some tense clashes, Martin Frobisher, a boy of about fifteen, was handed over to African authorities at a town the English called Samma (Shama) and then to the Portuguese in their castle of São Jorge da Mina as a hostage to ensure English good behavior. The published account of these transactions asserted that Frobisher had volunteered: "Martine, by his owne desire, and assent of some of the Commissioners that were in the pinnesse, went a shore to the towne." He later bragged that he had assumed an active role in trading with Africans during his captivity: "Thay were gladd sondry tymes to use hym to make dyvers journayes to those, that dwelt a myle or two of from the said castell, to gett victualls, as goates, pultry, and other, for to supplye thair necessitie; for that they themselves durst not, for perill of their lyves, doo it." After about nine months, Frobisher's captors sent him to Portugal, and he was back in England in 1558, four years after his abandonment on the African coast. By the early 1560s he had set himself up as a privateer. His first attempt along those lines had been a projected 1559 assault on the Mina castle where he had been held hostage, but the expedition was forestalled by the English government's imprisonment of his partner in this project, a notorious pirate named Henry Strangways.[25] A decade later, in the 1570s, Frobisher led three expeditions to America in search of gold and a northwest passage.

While the young Martin Frobisher was being handed over as a

pledge, Robert Gainsh, master of the *John Evangelist,* one of three ships in the expedition, seized "5. Blacke Moores," described as "tall and strong men," near Mina on the Guinea coast. The English, perhaps remembering the fate of their sailors on the Benin coast, were convinced that the Africans would fare better in England than Englishmen did in coastal Africa's penetrating heat: "The colde and moyst ayre doth somewhat offend them. Yet doubtlesse men that are borne in hotte Regions may better abide colde, then men that are borne in colde Regions may abide heate, forasmuch as vehement heate resolveth the radicall moysture of mens bodies, as colde constraineth and preserveth the same."[26]

These rash seizures had repercussions, as the next English voyage to the Guinea coast learned: "None of them would come neere us, being as we judged afrayed of us: because that foure men were taken perforce the last yeere from this place." The English learned that one of the men seized by Gainsh was the son of the region's ruler. William Towerson, the new expedition's leader, was required to leave one man ashore as a pledge during the time they were there. In 1556 he returned with some of the captives, landing at a town the English called Hanta, where "our Negros were well knowen, and the men of the towne wept for joy, when they saw them." The Africans asked about the other men, named Anthony and Binne, and were told that they were in "London in England, and should bee brought home the next voyage." Then Towerson's expedition moved on to Shama, the captive Africans' home, where their relatives "received them with much joy."

Many people with cross-cultural knowledge lived on the African coast frequented by European ships. Not only were Portuguese factors long established in mixed communities of Africans and Europeans, but also Africans who had been to Europe, such as the men Towerson brought back, often played intermediary roles in the trades after their return. Pieter de Marees, a Dutch man who wrote in 1602 about his

African experiences, recorded a long conversation in Ghana with an African who had lived with a monk in the Portuguese castle at Mina. De Marees noted the many Portuguese who were permanent residents on the coast, and he mentioned that much of the trade, especially in textiles, was actually carried on by African women.[27]

Africans controlled the terms of all exchanges and at times encouraged English merchants seeking to break the Portuguese monopoly in trading. For example, Towerson's men were warned when a Portuguese fleet was coming to attack them and were assured that they would always be welcome. But at other times African merchants frankly told the English that their goods were not fine enough. A ruler they knew as King Ebaane, whose capital city at Eguafo in what is now Ghana was as large as London, invited the English to build a trading castle but stipulated that they must bring tailors "and good wares."[28]

Ebaane's invitation to establish an English presence in his territory was not followed up despite various efforts to do so, but after these tentative early contacts, John Hawkins attempted to break into the trade in enslaved Africans in three voyages between 1564 and 1569. Demonstrating how little the English understood about these relationships, Hawkins tried to seize captives in raids on coastal villages. Only on his second and third voyages did he understand that he had to work through local African rulers and resident Portuguese factors to bargain for captives as more established European traders did. In aspiring to a role in the transatlantic trade in slaves, Hawkins had to confront Iberian control in two regions: from the Portuguese in Africa and the Spanish in the West Indies, where he attempted to sell his cargoes despite Spanish monopoly control of the trade. His third voyage ended in a disastrous battle with a Spanish fleet at San Juan de Ulua in Mexico; so many of his ships were lost that he was forced to set a hundred of his sailors ashore on the Gulf Coast to fend for themselves. For most of the next two decades English merchants abandoned the effort to gain a footing in the African trades, and English ships were not active in the slave trade until the middle of the seventeenth century.[29]

In nations all along the Atlantic's eastern shores, the growing competition in trade and mounting religious and national rivalries culminated in the last years of the sixteenth century in ways that raised the stakes for everyone involved and forced America onto the agenda. Morocco, the African country where English merchants had established an entrée, was one place where all these interests collided. Events there reached a dramatic climax in 1578 in the disastrous battle of Alcazarquivir (El-Ksar el-Kebir), which changed the course of European, North African, and even American history. King Sebastian of Portugal intervened in a Moroccan dynastic conflict, seeking to establish his authority in this key territory overlooking the entrance to the Mediterranean. Three monarchs died in this Battle of the Three Kings—Mulai Abd el-Malek of Morocco, Mulai Muhammad al-Mutawakkil, who also had a claim to the throne of Fez, and Sebastian—together with the leading nobles of Portugal. Mulai Ahmad al-Mansur, brother of Muhammad al-Mutawakkil, ruled in Morocco from 1578 until his death in 1603 (al-Mansur means "the victorious"). For Europeans the consequences of this battle were stunning: Portugal and all its overseas possessions were taken over by Philip II of Spain, who claimed that country's empty throne for himself. All those bases and carefully constructed relationships, as well as the unparalleled technological knowledge of the Portuguese, were added to Spain's power.[30]

Rivalries intensified after Alcazarquivir. The last two decades of the sixteenth century saw a hardening of positions and more overt challenges between antagonists. In 1578, the year of the great battle, Pope Gregory XIII decreed that it was no sin to kill a heretic such as England's Elizabeth, who persecuted so many Catholics, and soon the flow of covert Jesuits into England began. A series of suspected and genuine plots against Elizabeth's life led finally to the execution of Mary, Queen of Scots, Elizabeth's imprisoned Roman Catholic rival for the throne, in 1587. Spain and England took up the leadership, respectively, of the Roman Catholic and the Protestant causes in Europe, and a dramatic confrontation seemed inevitable. English leaders established contact with the ousted claimant to the Portuguese throne, Dom Antonio, who had fled to Paris with his court, including Portugal's renowned cartographers, so for the first time the English had access to the most accurate knowledge about America.

England may have proclaimed for itself the grandiose role of protector of Protestantism, but its leaders were acutely aware of their nation's relative poverty and weakness. Increasingly they advocated American ventures as an avenue to strength and riches. What Spain had accomplished, the English could do also. But in America, as in Africa and the Eastern trades, they were intruding on places and relationships in which Spain had preceded them, and they were learning through trial and error.

War was England's first sustained activity in the Americas. In 1585 the Spanish government seized English merchant ships in Spain's harbors, thus initiating open hostilities. The English government began issuing large numbers of licenses for privateering, and English seamen converged on the West Indies, where the conflict was carried on by legalized piracy from 1585 until Elizabeth's death in 1603. There was no question of her government's launching a true royal navy maintained by the state.[31] Instead, individual shipowners and groups of merchants were granted authorization, called letters of marque or letters of reprisal, to attack Spanish ships at sea and to bring them and their contents home as prizes. The government received a fifth of the value of the cargo from these privateering captures, and the rest was divided up among the investors and sailors; sailors got no wages in privateering voyages but served for their share of the booty. In theory a merchant applied for letters of marque when he could demonstrate that a ship of his had been captured by the enemy. The license only allowed his mariners to take an equivalent amount from the Spanish; but in practice, once letters of marque were in hand, privateers could carry out unlimited attacks. Often ships of other nations were attacked as well. Some privateers ventured into the Mediterranean and threatened the legitimate trade of the English Levant Company.

England's first real American colony, Roanoke, was planted as an adjunct to the privateering war. Crossing the stormy Atlantic was considered too dangerous except during the spring and early summer, so the season for privateering was short. If there were an English base where crews could safely reprovision and refit their ships, privateers could operate in the Caribbean year-round. So in 1584, just before the privateering war began, a young courtier named Walter Ralegh sent out a reconnoitering voyage to find a good site, one conveniently located near the Caribbean yet protected from Spanish attack. On the basis of the reconnaissance report, Ralegh sent a company of just over a hundred young men to establish a fort on an island within the Carolina Outer Banks in 1585. Here, as on the coast of Africa, many lessons had to be learned through trial and error, and good intelligence gathering was crucial.

Roanoke was indeed protected by the Outer Banks, but the waters around it were so shallow that the expedition's flagship ran aground, and all the food the men had brought with them was soaked by seawater and spoiled. Thus the Roanoke Indians came under intense pressure to feed all these extra people through the winter. Tensions accumulated, culminating in a preemptive strike by Ralegh's men in the spring of 1586 in which the Roanoke chief, Wingina, was killed. The Englishmen put his head on a pole, the treatment for traitors at home. When Sir Francis Drake arrived with his large fleet, fresh from a successful privateering voyage and ready to inaugurate Roanoke's role as a refitting base, he found the colony in such disarray that he agreed to take the men back to England. In America, as on the African coast,

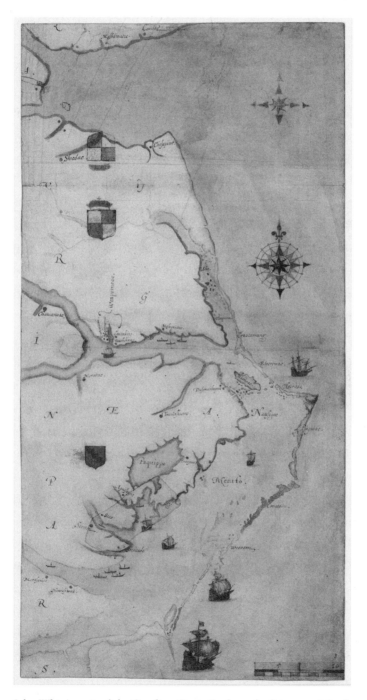

John White's map of the Carolina Outer Banks and adjacent mainland.

error seemed to predominate in their trials. In 1587 Ralegh sent a second group to found another colony—this one composed of families—but he was unable to sustain it; these became the famous Lost Colonists of Roanoke.

Privateering was an enormously lucrative practice, by some estimates accounting for 10 percent of England's imports in the 1590s; in the wake of Roanoke's failure as a base, English seafarers found that they could stay in the Caribbean year-round without one. This period of endeavor contributed mightily to the technical knowledge of English mariners. In the sixteenth century the great majority of seamen employed dead reckoning and other ancient navigational techniques, which required keeping in sight of land. English captains routinely relied on captured Spanish or Portuguese pilots to guide them through American waters. By the early seventeenth century, English mariners had accrued enough knowledge and skill to allow them to drop that dangerous practice, and English captains and pilots commonly knew the elementary trigonometry necessary to use celestial navigation and nautical charts.[32] Much of this transforming knowledge came from abroad; for example, Anthony Ashley received a government commission to translate two volumes of charts and sailing directions that had been created by a Dutchman, Lucas Jansson Wagenaer. Ashley titled his 1588 translation *The Mariners Mirrour*. So crucial was this source of information that even two centuries later, seamanship manuals were called "Waggoners" in England. Capital—both in money and knowledge—accumulated during the privateering war helped make possible English merchants' bids to expand their involvement in worldwide trades.[33]

While the privateering war was in full swing, the English government initiated a plan to confront the nation's vulnerability to Spanish invasion through Ireland, where leaders feared the Roman Catholic population might be sympathetic to Spanish aspirations. The plan was to control the Irish province of Munster through colonization, plant-

Title page of Anthony Ashley, The Mariner's Mirrour, *showing all the kinds of expertise that went into overseas ventures.* Courtesy of the John Carter Brown Library at Brown University.

ing English families on land confiscated from Irish Roman Catholics condemned as rebels. England also sent armed forces to the Netherlands, where the Protestant William of Orange had been assassinated in 1584, to aid the Dutch in their defiance of Spanish Hapsburg rule. Rumors flew that Elizabeth was in conversation with the Ottoman sultan about forming a massive joint Anglo-Turkish fleet to attack the Spanish.[34] The privateering war and England's aid to the Dutch rebels prompted Philip II to undertake the invasion that he had thought about and rejected in the 1570s. In 1588 the great Spanish Armada, sent out at a ruinous cost of thirty thousand ducats a day, threatened to destroy Protestant England until it was itself brought to a disastrous end. The Privy Council had mobilized all available ships to prepare for the impending attack, including those Ralegh had assembled to resupply his second Roanoke settlement, so although Spain did not succeed in conquering England, the armada did bring England's first attempt at founding an American colony to an end.[35]

Robert Payne, who described himself as an "undertaker," or agent, in Ireland for his twenty-five English business partners, argued shortly after the collapse of the Spanish Armada that the Irish had grown to hate the Spanish, as evidenced by the executions of sailors from the Spanish ships who were cast up in Ireland. "Most of the better sort of the Irish," he explained, "have read of their monsterous cruelties in the west Indians." Payne here referred to *The Spanish Colonie*, published in 1583, which offered the English reading public a translation of Bishop Bartolomeo de Las Casas's indictment, first published in 1552, of the Spanish record in America. Las Casas had written to force the Spanish government to control its colonists' treatment of American natives, and had provoked a full-scale debate about his country's policies; comparable self-examinations are notably absent among other colonizing powers. Las Casas's report was avidly consumed in Protestant countries as evidence that the Spanish were somehow uniquely vicious, and that Europeans who opened their doors to Spanish infiltrators would receive the same treatment as the Indians. Payne advised his readers: "If you have not the said booke of the Spanishe cruelties, I praye you buy it, it is well woorth the reading, I have forgotte the title, but it is of a smal volume in quarto: it is written by a learned Bishop of their owne country about forty yeeres sithens [since, ago] in the Castalian toonge, and dedicated to theire king for reformation of those cruelties: afterwardes translated into English and divers other languages, to make their monstrous tirannie knowen to the world." Payne praised the natural intelligence of the Irish and argued that, knowing about Spanish cruelty in America, they would always reject any overtures made by Spain against England: "The Irish is as wise as the Spaniard is proud, and there is no grife more to the wise man then to live in bondage to the proud man."[36] In the heightened atmosphere of the sixteenth century's last decades, English and Dutch propagandists built on Las Casas's book to create the Black Legend of Spanish cruelty and rapacity in America, and their work, reprinted and generalized over the centuries, endures today.

The last two decades of the sixteenth century, despite growing dangers and hatreds, also presented new opportunities. The Levant, as contemporaries called the lands of the eastern Mediterranean, was the source of opulent commodities from Far Eastern regions as well as its own goods, and exotic people lived around its shores. English merchants had been largely cut out of this trade, but by the end of the sixteenth century, they were determined to try to gain a foothold. Entrée into trade with the powerful Ottoman Empire, a principal goal, was achieved in the early 1580s. In order to increase their effectiveness, leading London merchants combined the Turkey and Venice companies to form the Levant Company in 1592. The East India Company was created in 1599 by members of the Levant Company to extend their reach directly into the rich East by the sea route around Africa.[37]

The English government saw special opportunities after Alcazar-

quivir in the changed situation at the western opening of the Mediterranean Sea, and leaders were entirely comfortable with the prospect of
collaborating with Muslim governments against Christian Spain. In
1582 the crown formally chartered the Barbary Company for trade
with Morocco.[38] A renewed approach at the ambassadorial level was
made in 1585, the same year Ralegh sent a contingent to plant England's first American colony. Master Henry Roberts, Elizabeth's ambassador, spent three years at the court of "Mully Hamet Emperour
of Marocco, and king of Fes, and Sus." On his way to court, Roberts dined with the resident European merchants, including English,
French, Flemish, "and divers other Christians." In Marrakesh he was
given lodgings in "a faire house in the Judaria or Jurie, which is the
place where the Jewes have their abode, and is the fairest place, and
quietest lodging in all the citie." Throughout his three years there, he
was always graciously received by "the Emperour," and the language in
which they communicated was Spanish. Roberts obtained a decree declaring that no English person "should bee molested or made slaves in
any part of his Dominions." Queen Elizabeth wrote fulsomely to Mulai
Ahmad in 1587 offering great promises of trade and presents to come
and asking particularly that the king punish an English rebel named
John Herman, who had been apprehended and imprisoned in Morocco. The letters were published soon after they were exchanged, indicating the importance of this relationship to the English government, and Mulai Ahmad's letters were carefully preserved in official
archives.[39]

A great Moroccan embassy visited England in 1600. This was marked
by publication of the English version of the *Geographical Historie of Africa*. Its author, al-Hasan ibn Muhammad al-Wazzan, was a Moroccan
diplomat who had been born in Spain but grew up in Fez after the
Spanish conquest of Granada in 1492. He was captured in 1518 on
one of his frequent diplomatic trips in the Mediterranean; the well-
connected Spaniard who seized him, realizing that he was no ordinary

captive, gave him to Pope Leo X. When al-Hasan al-Wazzan was baptized, the pope gave him his own name, christening him Joannes Leo de Medici, so he was known in Europe as Leo Africanus. He was renowned in Italy for his wide learning and especially valued for his knowledge of Arabic. John Pory, who later went to Jamestown and wrote the official report of the first meeting of the General Assembly, compiled the English version of his book and timed its publication to coincide with the Moroccan embassy. Pory's title page said that the book was "written in Arabicke and Italian by Iohn Leo a More, borne in Granada, and brought up in Barbarie," and his dedication to the queen's adviser Sir Robert Cecil pointed out that Morocco was extensively described in the book. The Moroccan ambassador, Abd el-Ouahed ben Messaoud ben Mohammed Anoun, presented his portrait to the queen as they discussed the possibilities of an alliance. Elizabeth agreed to sell munitions supplies to Morocco, and she and Mulai Ahmad al-Mansur talked on and off about mounting a joint operation against the Spanish before both died in 1603.[40]

The special circumstances of western European merchants in Turkey were formalized in the later sixteenth century in treaties between the Ottomans and chartered trading companies such as England's Levant Company, which under English law had monopoly control of that trade.[41] England's first ambassador, chosen by the Levant Company, was William Harborne. He first went to Constantinople in 1578; the next year Sultan Murad III initiated a correspondence with Queen Elizabeth, both sides writing in Latin. Soon after, the first in a series of envoys was sent from Istanbul to England. As envoys from rival European countries wrote home anxiously of this rapprochement, in 1580 Murad granted trading privileges to the Levant Company through its representative, "VilHelmūsh Kharbūrawunush"—William Harborne.

At the same time a manuscript account of the Americas, mostly from Italian translations of Spanish sources, was compiled for the use of Ottoman rulers. For centuries this remained the only Turkish

Portrait of the Moroccan ambassador presented to Queen Eliza-beth. The University of Birmingham Collections.

book about America. The manuscript was called "Hadis-i nev," which means "fresh new," but when it was published in 1730 it was given the title *Tarih-I Hind-I Garbi*, "A History of the India of the West." Twice in the manuscript the author expressed the hope that someday the Dar ul-Islam would extend even to the New World.[42]

In his correspondence with Elizabeth, Murad emphasized that Islam and Protestantism had much more in common than either did with Roman Catholicism, as both rejected worship of idols, and he suggested that an alliance between the Ottoman Empire and England would be welcome. He addressed the English queen as "the pride of women who follow Jesus, the most excellent of the ladies honoured among the Messiah's people, the arbitress of the affairs of the Christian community, who trails the skirts of majesty and gravity, the queen of the realm of Ingiltere, Queen Elīz'āde." When Harborne was named England's official ambassador in 1583, he addressed Murad as the worthy successor to the Roman emperors, calling him "the most august and benign Caesar." As the Europeans called all Muslims Turks, so the Ottomans called all Protestants Lutherans; thus the English envoy was known as "the Lutheran ambassador" into the seventeenth century.[43]

To the dismay of Roman Catholic Europe, England willingly supplied the Ottoman Empire with tin and lead, raw materials for casting cannon and ammunition. It was particularly galling that the lead was "the scrap-metal resulting from the upheavals of the Reformation," especially "the roofs of ecclesiastical buildings, old bells, and broken metal statuary."[44] In 1585, with the outbreak of open warfare between England and Spain, Queen Elizabeth and Sultan Murad III seriously discussed joining forces in a Muslim-Protestant campaign. Elizabeth's principal minister, Sir Francis Walsingham, wrote to Ambassador Harborne to suggest talking points he could use to persuade Turkish leaders to concentrate their military efforts on confronting the common enemy: "And you may show how that he [Philip II] is already the greatest monarch of Christendom, possessing the whole country of Spain, the realm of Portugal with the riches thereof being lately fallen into his hands, the richest provinces in Italy and Germany, the whole Indias both east and west whence he draweth infinite treasures, the sinews of war." Not only did the king of Spain exert political control, but also, according to Walsingham, the pope was "his creature," adjusting doctrine to further Spain's agenda. If the Iberians were forced to fight strong enemies in both the west and the east, Walsingham instructed Harborne to tell the Ottomans, Spain's might would collapse. In the event, the Ottomans, fully engaged in war against the Persians, declined to collaborate with England against Spain.[45]

As the sixteenth century and the long reign of Queen Elizabeth drew to an end, England had great aspirations and also great fears. The nation's leaders thought they knew the possible avenues to greater power and independence of action, but how to proceed was still unclear. So merchants and statesmen launched ventures in as many directions as possible in the hope that some of them would succeed in bringing England into the rich relationships they saw other nations enjoying. The established trades to the east and south were alluring and raised high hopes but were hard to break into. America increasingly drew leaders' attention. The question was whether the English would find gold as Spain had done, or would be able to develop a lucrative trade in furs or other commodities. English ships already visited the Newfoundland Banks every year, as did ships from all over western Europe, for the splendid fishing; but fish, though essential in protein-hungry Europe, did not produce the kinds of riches England's leaders looked for. Many of Elizabeth's advisers were convinced that America would be one key to making their nation powerful enough to stand up to Spain, but no one yet knew how that might come about or what part of America they should target.

Adventurers, Opportunities, and Improvisation

WHILE ENGLISH STATESMEN and merchants looked to engagement with Africa, the East, and America as a way to wealth and power for themselves and their nation, many who were less highly placed sought positions in this newly open and fluid world of overseas ventures. Thousands of English men and some women traveled to exotic locales and mingled with people of many cultural backgrounds. Some traveled by choice, even taking up an early form of the grand tour. Others saw openings for their own advancement if only they could get the right backing. Still others found themselves placed involuntarily in cross-cultural situations—often at radically different destinations from those they intended—where the ones who survived lived by their wits. The ability to read cues in the environment and respond to changing circumstances marked those who succeeded; presumably the countless unknown others who are lost to history were either unlucky or slow to adapt. Many of these travelers, like Martin Frobisher on the coast of Guinea, were remarkably young. And, like Frobisher, most were forced to improvise in situations they had not chosen. Many whose first experiences along these lines were in Africa or the eastern Mediterranean later turned their acquired skills to American ventures.

The period spawned the class of people known as "projectors," who constantly appealed to the court or wealthy backers for support for one or another pet scheme that would, ostensibly, enhance the nation's economy or security or both while enriching the projector. Early modern monarchs were constantly bombarded with pleas for funding or warnings about what other powers were doing. In fact, much of our understanding of the times comes down to us through government interrogations of people who claimed to have special knowledge and great plans. The evidence that survives provides a window into a world in which leaders desperately sought information, and we can see what they could not: that much of it was bogus, ill-informed, or misguided. Actually, the leaders knew that a lot of what they were told was wrong, but they could not easily separate the true from the false. The historian Geoffrey Parker pictures Philip II of Spain as "drowning in a sea of paper."[1]

Active young men saw the newly opened world as a theater for their own advancement. Although the rhetoric was often bloodthirsty and absolute, the lines along which venturers conceived their allegiances were much less clear-cut than the rhetoric suggested. Many who came to America had traveled widely in the Old World beforehand and had served in a variety of causes. The sixteenth and seventeenth centuries saw an explosion of opportunities for people with great aspirations but limited means to make their way in the world, and many ventured out to seek glory and status. In the process they sometimes caused havoc both for their own country and for others. One writer castigated the ambitious men who, "for the conquering of 40. or 50. miles here and there, and erecting of certaine fortresses," imagine themselves "Lordes of halfe the world."[2]

People who thought they could become lords of half the world were prominent in this period, and they often had the ears of monarchs and other leaders to whom they peddled their schemes. Many of the men who sought greatness through overseas exploits, involvement in colonization, or other development projects came from family backgrounds that gave them an elevated sense of their own station but not the means to realize that status. One such man who did achieve eminence was Sir Walter Ralegh. He, like his fellow adventurers, was able to attract the support of powerful people, even Queen Elizabeth herself, and his ventures promised so much that many were willing to back them.

Many were less successful than Ralegh. One of these men who was celebrated in his own day but is almost completely unknown in ours was Sir Thomas Stukeley. As a young man Stukeley, who was born about 1525, fought in the European wars. Rumor had it that while fighting in France he had served as a double agent for England's Queen Mary. He became known as a "useful" man, perhaps because of his chameleon-like qualities. After engaging in various illegal or semilegal activities back in England, he escaped imprisonment by returning to Europe, this time fighting against France on the Hapsburg side. But he was soon in England again, where he received favored positions from highly placed men at court; he also married a very wealthy young woman.

Queen Elizabeth herself selected Stukeley for an important commission in which she was personally concerned. French Protestants had founded a colony, Charlesfort, in La Florida—modern South Carolina—in the 1560s. The colony's sponsors, Jean Ribault and René de Laudonnière, both Protestants, had come home to a France dangerously rent by religious warfare; Ribault escaped the fighting in France by going to England, which was bolstering the Protestant Huguenot cause with troops. Having previously worked in England for almost a decade, Ribault quickly found support for an effort, this time an Anglo-French attempt, to save the colony he had planted on the Carolina coast. Funds and five ships, one of which was contributed by Queen Elizabeth herself, were raised in England for the project. This renewed venture exemplifies the tangled relationships, and the lack of clarity, in these early overseas exploits.

Elizabeth chose Stukeley to lead the rescue fleet. Then, in a series of maneuvers, Stukeley turned the resources gathered for the Anglo-French colony, even the queen's ship, to his own purposes. He took control, and just in case anyone doubted who was in charge, he rechristened the five ships the *Anne Stucley*, the *Thomas Stucley*, the *William Stucley*, the *Trenite Stucley*, and the *Fortune Stucley*. None of these ships went to America.

Bizarre as it may seem, Stukeley actually kept the Spanish ambassador in London informed about the Anglo-French plans for reinforcing the colony, which was within the territory the Spanish claimed in America, and apparently offered to subvert the venture. Spanish ambassador Alvarez de Quadra wrote home to his government: "Some days since Stukeley sent to me to say that these people were sending him on a bad and knavish business, but that he would be with me and would show me how to play them a trick that would make a noise in the world." The ambassador was unconvinced, adding, "He is quite capable of doing this, and, so far as his position is concerned, a good deal more, but is not much to be trusted."[3]

Stukeley had previously been suspected of secretly working for the French government. But the Spanish king, Philip II, was interested in his offer and told Quadra to keep the channels of communication open. In a face-to-face conversation before the fleet embarked, Stukeley told the ambassador that he wanted to be "known as an adherent" of Philip's, and that he was departing from England "discontentedly and almost desperately." Quadra, still doubtful, wrote that "his visit to me was nothing but cunning" and predicted that, with his well-armed ships, "Stukeley is bent rather on committing some great robbery than discovering new lands." The ambassador sent an official complaint to the English government about the intended expedition.

Quadra was right. Ultimately Stukeley took the ships privateering off the coast of Spain. He made no effort to aid the French Protestant colony for which the fleet had been assembled, though ironically his privateers encountered remnants of it. The twenty-six men left in America by Ribault and Laudonnière had held out for more than a year in their rough wooden fort before giving up and abandoning America. One of the ships Stukeley's privateers seized and boarded happened to be carrying the stragglers from Charlesfort, who were attempting to make their way home in a boat they had built themselves and rigged with Indian-made ropes of bark fibers. One of Stukeley's sailors, who had been in the fleet that had carried the men to Charlesfort, recognized them and learned their story. Their eastward voyage had been grueling. When Stukeley encountered them, only about twenty were still alive, and they had a disturbing story to tell; Laudonnière reluctantly included it in his history of the colonies. Having had no food or water for many days, they had "eaten up their shooes and their leather jerkins" and were reduced to drinking seawater or "their owne urine." In their "extreme despaire certaine among them made this motion that it was better that one should dye, then that so many men should perish." They all agreed; a man named Lachere was killed, and "his flesh was devided equally among his fellowes: a thing so pitifull to recite," said Laudonnière, "that my pen is loth to write it." The survivors, along with their former leader Ribault, were detained in England as hostages while the winds of Europe's religious conflicts continued to fluctuate.

The departing French had left a fifteen-year-old boy, Guillaume Rouffin, behind as Martin Frobisher had been left in Africa. Rouffin lived with Guale Indians for two years and married a daughter of the Edisto chief Orista before he was found by a Spanish expedition sent to seek evidence of French occupation of the coast. In this case, as in so many others, information survives because Europeans in America recorded the activities of rival Europeans so assiduously. Rouffin's career amply demonstrates the nimble adaptability of the survivor. When the Spanish first heard of Rouffin, he was living in a village called Usta. They asked the Indians they met to send for him, giving them "a piece of wood with a cross made upon it . . . as proof that there were Christians in the land." When he came the next day, Rouffin, who was "clothed like the Indians of that country, . . . declared himself to be a Frenchman." He was initially removed to Havana as a prisoner, but soon returned to the coast of La Florida with the Spanish as "Guillermo the interpreter." Rouffin told the Spanish that he had refused to accompany the departing migrants because he did not think that any of them was sufficiently well versed in navigation to complete the voyage. Further evidence of the crossing of national barriers is provided by Guillaume's interrogator, Martín Pérez, who, despite his service as a sailor traveling with the Spanish, also "said he was French." Rouffin confirmed the Spaniards' worst fears when he told them that the purpose of the French post had been to provide a base from which privateers could attack the Spanish treasure fleet. He led the Spanish to the settlement's ruins, a site they had been unable to find.[4]

If Spanish authorities in America gained by the addition of young Guillermo, Spanish merchants on the other side of the Atlantic lost heavily by Stukeley's decision to ignore the queen's instructions for his fleet. To judge by the charges circulating after Stukeley's privateering voyage, the prizes his ships seized were very lucrative. His ability to attack Spanish and other shipping while maintaining his relationships with Spanish authorities is emblematic of the tangled world in which these actors moved. Quadra's successor as ambassador, Guzmán de Silva, angrily demanded that Stukeley be punished and be forced to make restitution, but he also wrote to Philip II the year after Stukeley's voyage that by becoming involved in the Anglo-French project, Stukeley had acted as "a faithful servant of your Majesty." Silva believed Stukeley's claim that he was really a Roman Catholic. On the English side, Stukeley remained a useful man to many, and he was able to lie low in Ireland until the storm had largely passed.[5]

After his hijacking of the Anglo-French La Florida venture, Stukeley had forged a relationship with the great Irish leader Shane O'Neill and sought a career in Ireland. But Queen Elizabeth, having been deceived once, refused to trust him with the offices and lands he desired. So Stukeley again turned to Spain, presenting himself as a man persecuted by the Protestant English government for his Roman Catholicism. He also encouraged rumors that he was an illegitimate son of Henry VIII and therefore had a claim to the throne of England. No one was certain where his true loyalties lay—or even if he was capable of genuine loyalty to any cause other than his own advancement. He continued to have powerful friends in government circles in London. At a banquet at the earl of Leicester's house, Stukeley's cousin Sir Humphrey Gilbert defended him so vehemently that Gilbert's friends had to step in and stop him from going too far. He reportedly declared that if it was true that Stukeley had gone to Spain, "the reason was to be found in the help he could give against the Moors," a blanket term for Muslims. Gilbert was himself on the threshold of a career as a military leader in Ireland. He was a promoter of American exploits, and his younger half-brother, Walter Ralegh, would take up those projects after Gilbert's death on an American voyage in 1583.[6]

We know about Gilbert's defense of Stukeley through the reports that filtered back to the Spanish government about what was going on in England; they are in the Spanish and the Vatican archives. At the banquet where he defended Stukeley, Gilbert also promised that if his cousin's rumored plans to raise a fleet in Spain to attack Ireland proved true, he himself would take the lead in fighting against him. According to some of the reports, that was exactly Stukeley's design. He left Ireland in a heavily armed ship bound ostensibly for England, but actually for the port of Vivero in northern Spain, where he arrived in the spring of 1570. According to the reports, he sailed as the representative of a group of Roman Catholic Irish leaders.

Upon his arrival in Spain, Stukeley, presenting himself as a Catholic who had been persecuted for his religious steadfastness, sent word to Philip II proposing a joint enterprise to free Irish Roman Catholics from the Protestant queen's control. For his part, the Spanish king was distrustful of Stukeley and made him wait in Vivero, an expensive proposition given the huge company Stukeley had brought with him that had to be maintained there. Meanwhile, the king sought as much information as he could get about Stukeley's true motives and allegiances, and about the kinds of support an invading force could expect in Ireland. At the same time, reports filtered back to the English government, creating real fear of a possible Spanish invasion through Ireland; these reports also claimed that Stukeley was living in grandeur in Spain. In reality the Spanish king was far more concerned about the revolt in the Netherlands and put Stukeley off.

Stukeley went on to Rome, where he won the support of Pope Gregory XIII, who tried to get Philip to invade Ireland as Stukeley proposed. Stukeley wanted the pope to bestow the title "Archduke of Ireland" on him. With meager support and one ship, Stukeley set out from Italy but got only as far as Portugal, where in 1578 he joined the expedition led by King Sebastian to invade Morocco and depose Mulai Abd el-Malek. Stukeley joined the three kings Mulai Abd el-Malek, Mulai Muhammad al-Mutawakkil, and Sebastian in death at Alcazarquivir, though in his case rumor said that the fatal shots were fired by his own disgruntled men. Richard Hakluyt, who devoted his life to compiling accounts of the exploits of the English abroad, included a very brief passage on Stukeley's voyage "into Barbary." His source had styled Stukeley "Marquis of Ireland," so Hakluyt included an indignant marginal note: "Thomas Stukeley was wrongfully indued with this title."[7] In 1580 Philip II did send armies to aid the Irish rebels as Stukeley and others had proposed; they were defeated and slaughtered by English forces at Smerwick.

The projector's life, and the ways in which self-promotion splintered allegiance, is exemplified by the career of Ralph Lane, governor of Sir Walter Ralegh's first Roanoke colony in 1585. Lane spent twenty years at court after having been elected to Parliament in 1563, and during those two decades he was involved in a number of military campaigns: putting down the Roman Catholic northern rebels in Britain in 1569, and fighting Hapsburg control in the Protestant Netherlands in the early 1570s. Then in 1574 he sought permission to raise a regiment of one to two thousand men to join the Hapsburg army then forming to fight the Turks in eastern Europe. But he also put forward various ideas for confronting the Hapsburg Spanish in Ireland, in the Netherlands, and at sea, asking for the title "General of the Adventurers" for the last of these in 1579. At the same time he proposed a diplomatic role for himself, requesting the post of ambassador to "the Kings of Fez and Algiers." Finally, at the end of his resources, he accepted a commission from the queen "in Her desolate Kingdom of Ireland" in 1583. Elizabeth recalled him in 1585 to serve as governor of Ralegh's Roanoke colony, which Lane hoped would become an important base against the Spanish, "the swoorde of that Antychryste of Rome and hys sect." After his group abandoned the American colony, Lane served for the next several years in England, including playing a role in the defense against the Spanish Armada. Ultimately he returned to Ireland, where he was finally reduced to asking for the post of chief bell-ringer.[8]

Perhaps the most stunning story was that of Captain John Smith, the man who by his own account (and in the estimation of many others) saved the Jamestown colony from certain ruin. Plain John Smith was not wellborn enough to rise to the ranks of projectors; he had the ear of no one at court. Smith was born in 1580 to a yeoman farmer in Lincolnshire, a man of property but below the gentry class from which colonial leaders and elite travelers were drawn. At the very end of his life he wrote and published an autobiography, *The True Travels, Adventures, and Observations of Captaine John Smith* (London, 1630), one of the very first books in this genre, and he revealed an early life of great adventure.[9] The book is confusing to read, and therefore the events are hard to put in order, but he tells us that he was apprenticed to a merchant in Kings Lynn after a grammar school education. His schoolmaster may have been Francis Marbury, father of Anne Hutchinson, whose strict interpretation of the Calvinist doctrine of Grace and the large following she attracted in Boston in the 1630s led to her expulsion from the Massachusetts Bay colony.[10] When his father died and he discovered that his merchant master would not be sending him to sea, the sixteen-year-old Smith abandoned his apprenticeship and made his way to Europe, where, he says, he served for three or four years in an English regiment fighting in the wars between Protestants and Roman Catholics. Smith was still a teenager when he returned to England.

He went back to Europe the next year as an escort to the sons of the local lord of the manor, Robert Bertie, Lord Willoughby, but soon returned to Britain, this time to Scotland, where contacts made in France had led him to expect some kind of post. His expectations were disappointed, however, so Smith returned to Lincolnshire, where he self-consciously set out to prepare himself for command. He wrote that he "retired himselfe into a little wooddie pasture"; there he built "a Pavillion of boughes" and read "Machiavills Art of warre, and Marcus Aurelius." His "friends" introduced him to "one Seignior Theadora Polaloga," and Smith learned much from him. Although Smith identified him as "a noble Italian Gentleman," Theodore Paleologue was in fact descended from the last ruling family of the Byzantine Empire, now under Ottoman control, and he had come to England as riding master to the earl of Lincoln. Paleologue taught Smith riding, but also "Languages and good discourse." He may also have interested Smith in the possibilities of the East and the danger posed by the Ottoman Empire. As Smith wrote of himself, "Long these pleasures could not content him, but hee returned againe to the Low-Countreyes." The year was 1600, and he was now twenty years old.[11]

Smith argued that he had learned all he could in England. He was "desirous to see more of the world, and trie his fortune against the Turkes, both lamenting and repenting to have seene so many Christians slaughter one another" in Europe's religious wars. After many adventures and lucky escapes in France, he boarded a ship bound for Italy. When it encountered stormy weather in the Mediterranean, the other passengers fixed on Smith as the problem. His account illustrates both how the English were perceived and the extreme religious tensions in Europe: "Here the inhumane Provincialls, with a rabble of Pilgrimes of divers Nations going to Rome, hourely cursing him, not only for a Hugonoit [Huguenot], but his Nation they swore were all Pyrats, and so vildly railed on his dread Soveraigne Queene Elizabeth, and that they never should have faire weather so long as hee was aboard them; their disputations grew to that passion, that they threw him over-board."[12]

He washed up on a little island and was rescued by a French ship, on which he sailed to Egypt, where the crew delivered "their fraught," and then through the eastern Mediterranean to Italy. As they approached the Adriatic Sea, they were engaged in a "desperate Sea-fight" with a ship from Venice. After fifteen men were killed on Smith's ship and twenty on the Venetian, the latter surrendered and was plundered; privateering was the risk all shipping ran in this period. Smith was impressed: "The Silkes, Velvets, Cloth of gold, and Tissue, Pyasters, Chicqueenes and Sultanies, which is gold and silver, they unloaded in foure and twentie houres, was wonderfull." Smith was awarded "five hundred chicqueenes, and a little box God sent him worth neere as much more" for his part in the battle. He next set out to travel through Italy, spending time in Rome, "where it was his chance to see Pope Clement the eight, with many Cardinalls, creepe up the holy Stayres, which they say are those our Saviour Christ went up to Pontius Pilate." Smith heard the pope say mass and met "Father Parsons, that famous English Jesuite." He finally ended up in Austria, where he found a place in the Christian coalition of armies fighting against the expansive Ottoman Empire.[13]

As Smith described it, he made vital contributions to strategy and tactics from his very first battle. A Turkish army had laid siege to a town Smith called "Olumpagh." There he demonstrated a system of communication by torches, which he had derived from an appendix to the translation of Machiavelli's *Arte of Warre* he had read in England, whereby the townspeople could be in contact with the army that had come to save them.[14] He also suggested stringing ropes with pieces of burning cord attached to make the enemy forces think that they faced a numerous army—soldiers equipped with the matchlock muskets of the time carried a smoldering piece of rope, a match with which to ignite the powder that propelled the ball out of the barrel—and to divert them from the true direction of attack. After heavy losses, the Turks withdrew; Smith's studying had paid off. He was given command of a cavalry unit of 250 men.

When augmented armies on both sides renewed the conflict, Smith improved upon his earlier stratagem. At the siege of Szekesfehervar (Alba Regalis), Hungary's coronation city, which had been in Ottoman hands since 1543, he directed the creation of "fiery Dragons," little earthen pots filled with gunpowder and musket balls and covered with layers of cloth soaked in highly flammable materials such as linseed oil, turpentine, and brimstone (sulfur). These were placed in slings and hurled, burning, into the enemy's city at night with spectacular effect: "It was a fearfull sight to see the short flaming course of their flight in the aire, but presently after their fall, the lamentable noise of the miserable slaughtered Turkes was most wonderfull [awe-inspiring, astonishing] to heare." Moreover, fire broke out in several places, and the enemy had to divert forces to fight it, ultimately losing the town.[15]

By the spring of 1602, Smith was serving in the forces of Szigmond

Báthory, the Transylvanian prince who was "caught between the Ottoman and Holy Roman Empires."[16] The army, commanded by Mózes
Székely (Smith called him Lord Moses), settled down for a long siege
of a large town in Transylvania that Smith called Regall; contemporaries also called it Alba Julia. The forces within the town taunted the
besiegers. Eventually, to relieve the boredom and "to delight the Ladies, who did long to see some court-like pastime," the commander,
whom Smith called Lord Turbashaw, challenged any champion from
the other side to meet him in single combat. Lots were drawn among
the various captains, and the choice fell on Smith. The two armies
called a truce for the event. "Turbashaw entred the field well mounted
and armed; on his shoulders were fixed a paire of great wings, com-
pacted of Eagles feathers within a ridge of silver, richly garnished with
gold and precious stones." Smith came onto the field much more mod-
estly. But when the charge was sounded, he moved swiftly forward and
forced his lance through the grill of Turbashaw's helmet, killing him
instantly. Smith cut off the Turk's head and carried it back to his commander. The next day Turbashaw's friend Grualgo demanded satisfac-
tion and similarly lost his head in single combat with Smith.

After some days passed, Smith, "to delude time," sent a message to
the ladies of the town saying that "he was not so much enamoured of
their servants heads" and offering the chance for a third Turkish champion to come and take back the first two heads, as well as Smith's head
into the bargain, "if he could winne it." The challenge was taken up by
a man Smith called Bonny Mulgro. This time Smith found the going
harder, but he eventually prevailed and added a third head to his collection. The army then assaulted the town, and the garrison surrendered and asked to negotiate for terms. Notwithstanding their surren-
der, "Prince Moyses" ordered the beheading of everyone capable of
bearing arms, whose heads were displayed on stakes around the city
walls. The army then sacked that city and three others, carrying away
a great deal of wealth.

John Smith's coat of arms with the motif of three Turks' heads.
Courtesy of the John Carter Brown Library at Brown University.

Báthory came to inspect the army. Hearing of the great service done by Captain John Smith, "hee gave him three Turkes heads in a Shield for his Armes, by Patent, under his hand and Seale, with an Oath ever to weare them in his Colours, his Picture in Gould, and three hundred Ducats, yearely for a Pension." For Szigmond Báthory the victory was short-lived, as he was soon overthrown; but plain John Smith was now officially a gentleman with a coat of arms.[17]

Smith's fortunes were soon to change. The army moved south, encountering a large force of Tatars from the Crimean (Smith called them Crym-Tartars and said they numbered forty thousand) who had come to the assistance of the Ottomans.[18] A huge and bloody battle ensued at Rotenturm in the autumn of 1602. Smith recorded the names of eight Englishmen and a Scot who died that day; he himself was left on the field of battle among the dead and dying till he was picked up by "the Pillagers." They cared for him until his wounds were healed and then took him to a market on the Danube, where the prisoners "were all sold for slaves, like beasts in a market-place." He was bought by "Bashaw Bogall" who decided to give Smith to his "faire Mistresse for a slave." The captives marched, chained together at the neck, to Istanbul, where Smith was presented to the "noble gentlewoman" he knew as Charatza Tragabigzanda, which means "girl from Trebizond." Smith recorded that he and she conversed in Italian and that she was deeply interested in him and his background. Fearing that her mother might sell Smith, she sent him to her brother, an army officer commanding a small territory near the Black Sea, who would teach the Englishman how to operate within the Ottoman system.[19]

Smith believed that his mistress hoped for his eventual freedom and that his sojourn with her brother was to be only until "time made her Master of her self"—until she came of age and was able to make her own choices. But her brother "diverted all this to the worst of crueltie." Smith was immediately stripped, his head shaved, and an iron ring with an attached sickle-shaped "stalke" riveted around his neck. He found himself among many Christian slaves, as well as Moorish and Turkish galley slaves, "and he being the last, was slave of slaves to them all."

It is possible that Smith's intended destiny was a place in the janissary corps, an infantry composed of captives from other countries who served directly under the sultan. Because they came from outside the empire, they were free of competing local loyalties, although janissaries were sometimes rewarded with land in conquered territories, as apparently was the case with Charatza's brother. The Ottoman janissary corps expanded dramatically in the later sixteenth and early seventeenth centuries, at just the time Smith was in Turkey.[20]

Smith, who would later provide one of the most influential accounts of Virginia Indian life from Jamestown, interrupted his account after the arrival on the Black Sea to include a brief ethnographic discussion of Turkish life. He began with food: "Their best drink is Coffa, of a graine they call Coava, boiled with water"; they also drank "Sherbeck, which is only honey and water." The better sort ate pilaf which included choice bits of meat, but slaves were given minced animal entrails and "Cuskus."[21]

His description of Crym-Tartar life was much fuller. He dealt with the people's moveable houses and their decoration, their government and the great state and authority of "their Princes," relations within families, and food and feasting. Their religion, Islam, and their legal system came from the Turks; Smith admired the "integrity and expedition" with which justice was executed "without covetousnesse, bribery, partiality, and brawling." The Tatars were clients of "the Great Turke," and their "Chan" went to war only with his permission; they were bound to come to the aid of the Ottomans if requested to do so. One goal of war was to take captives, who were distributed among the armies; those of good family or position were ransomed, and the others became slaves. Smith thought little of their armaments; still, the "mischiefe" those "tattertimallions" were able to do "in Christendome is wonderfull [awe-inspiring]." Smith attributed their successes to their hardiness and habits of obedience as well as the official policy of rewarding "any memorable service in the face of the enemy" with honors and distinctions regardless of how humble the person was.[22]

After this digression Smith returned to his own story. He despaired of ever achieving release from slavery; his only hope was the love of Tragabigzanda, "who surely was ignorant of his bad usage"; other Christians with whom he conversed told him they had been captives for a long time. As he related it, God opened a way for Smith. He was set threshing one day in a field far from the main house, and his master came to see him work. The man so maltreated him that Smith rose up and smashed his master's skull with the threshing tool. Smith hurriedly put on the dead man's clothes, hid the body, and set out "wandring he knew not whither." He had to escape notice, because the

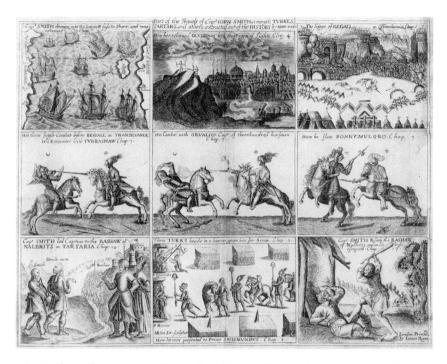

John Smith's exploits in eastern Europe from his True Travels, Adventures, and Observations. *Courtesy of the John Carter Brown Library at Brown University.*

engraving on his iron collar would immediately tell anyone who found him whose estate he had escaped from. He traveled for sixteen days before he came upon a Muscovite camp on the River Don. The commander listened to his story and took pity on him; Smith "thought himself new risen from death." Relieved of his iron ring, and with a safe conduct pass, he journeyed through a bewildering number of places until he arrived back in Transylvania, where he found the land poor and "the Countries rather to be pitied, then envied." Their principal weapons, he noted, were bows and arrows.[23]

Smith found many good friends in Transylvania, and finally was reunited with "the most gracious Prince Sigismundus," who confirmed the honors he had received and gave him "fifteene hundred ducats of gold to repair his losses." He then traveled around Europe, seeing Dresden and many towns in Germany, then Paris and on to the chief

cities of Spain, including "the admired monasterie of the Escuriall"
and Valladolid. Next, being "thus satisfied with Europe and Asia," he
crossed from Gibraltar to "Barbarie." Smith told the story of dynastic
wars among the three sons of Mulai Ahmad IV, el Mansur, the victor
at the battle of Alcazarquivir, whose name he rendered as "Mully
Hamet, or the Great Zeriff of Barbarie." He corrected those who supposed that "King Mully Hamet" was black, saying he and his subjects
were rather "Molata, or tawnie." He described Mulai Ahmad as "everie
way noble, kinde and friendly, verie rich and pompous in State and
Majestie, though he sitteth not upon a Throne nor Chaire of Estate,
but crosse legged upon a rich Carpet, as doth the Turke, whose Religion of Mahomet, with an incredible miserable curiositie they observe." However much English travelers might admire the cultures
they encountered, strict adherence to any religion but Christianity
could be portrayed only as intellectual or spiritual slavery. Smith noted
the many highly paid English artisans at Mully Hamet's court and emphasized in a marginal note "His great love to English-men."[24] Smith
returned from his captivity and his travels to find planning for the
projected colony in Virginia under way, and he signed on for the venture.

Smith's captivity narrative struck a familiar chord, as stories of such
forced boundary crossing became ever more common. The English
were fascinated by the question of the fate—spiritual and physical—of
Christians who became captives in Muslim countries. Forced conversion was one concern, although many who wrote about Islam testified
that conversion was acceptable only if it was voluntary. Even more riv-
eting was the issue of Islam's magnetic allure for Christians. The image
of the "Christian turn'd Turk" was a popular icon on the stage and in
ballads. Travelers' reports were studded with references to Muslims
who had been born European Christians, and it was this phenomenon
that audiences and readers wanted to experience vicariously. Sex and

religion were intertwined in these images; beautiful women were often portrayed as the agents of the Christian's conversion.

Europeans who sought to enter the lucrative trades available throughout the Mediterranean always ran the risk of encountering Muslim corsairs, and the possibility of capture and enslavement for everyone on board. Moreover, the Mediterranean was a dangerous place for anyone who ventured into it, Christian, Jew, or Muslim. Like the Caribbean, it was a world with few rules. Bands of corsairs from the North African coast, the Barbary pirates, attacked shipping throughout the Mediterranean. Their activities increased in the later sixteenth century, and in the first decades of the seventeenth century they moved out into the Atlantic. Whereas privateers from western Europe mostly aimed to seize goods and ships and an occasional skilled pilot, the Barbary corsairs were intent on capturing people. The fortunate among the captives were ransomed by friends or religious societies. Several nationwide collections to raise ransoms were conducted in England beginning in the late sixteenth century, and the ransom infrastructure became increasingly well organized as the seventeenth century progressed. The unlucky or friendless either were sold as slaves within the societies of North Africa or suffered the terrible fate of becoming oarsmen in the galleys.

Many ships bound for America were captured by North African corsairs, and all who set sail were conscious of the danger. The corsairs also attacked coastal regions of Europe and abducted people from villages and farms. Although the greatest number of captives were from countries bordering the Mediterranean on the north, the pirates became so bold over time that they raided Ireland and the west coast of England and captured ships within sight of the shore, even in the English Channel; in the 1640s corsairs actually entered the Thames. Captives were seized from as far away as Iceland.[25] In 1603 Richard Knolles published a 1,400-page *Generall Historie of the Turkes*; the preface to the second edition in 1610 lamented "the infinite number of wofull Christians (whose grievous groanings under the heavie yoke of infidelitie no tongue is able to expresse)."[26]

Relatively young boys and girls were often considered more expendable and malleable than adults, and their captivity was more acceptable. This pattern was continued in America, where European venturers, and sometimes Indian leaders, routinely handed over children to serve as hostages and to learn as much about the other culture as possible. Modern readers cannot help being struck by the nonchalance with which such transactions were recorded. For example, in a sermon he was invited to give to the Virginia Company in 1622, the Reverend Patrick Copland evoked the experience of a Virginia-bound ship, the *Tyger*, recalling that although the passage to Jamestown was normally "out of the walke of the Turkes, and cleere and safe from all Pyrates," the ship had been caught in a storm and captured. Ransomed by the passengers of another ship, all on board were saved and made it to America, "two English boyes onely excepted, for which the Turkes gave them two others, a French youth and an Irish." Copland saw the hand of God in this delivery and expressed no qualms about the two English boys who remained with their Muslim captors.[27]

English people who traveled in the Ottoman Empire constantly remarked on the large numbers of converts they encountered and the centrality of those converts to Turkish life. In 1599 Queen Elizabeth sent Sultan Mehmet III an organ; although it was the queen's gift, the Levant Company paid for it. Thomas Dallam, who built the organ and went to Istanbul to install it, wrote a vivid account of his experiences at the sultan's court and of the many Christians turned Muslim he encountered. As he was brought into the sultan's presence, the sight "was very wonderfull unto me." Mehmet "satt in greate state, yeat the sighte of him was nothinge in Comparrison of the traine that stood behinde him, the sighte whearof did make me almoste to thinke that I was in another worlde." The sultan was surround by two hundred pages, richly dressed, with their heads shaved except for two tails behind

their ears, "all verrie proper men, and Christians Borne." Dallam had
several tricky moments. Once the organ was completed, he was summoned to play it for Mehmet; in order to do that he not only had to
turn his back on the ruler, which he had been told was an offense pun-
ishable by death, but the space was so constructed that he also touched
the monarch's knee with his breeches. He wrote that, far from being
angry, the sultan gave him a large amount of gold. The English ambassador, Sir Henry Lello, was pleased to see Mehmet "rejoysinge greatly"
at the queen's gifts.[28]

While Dallam was in Istanbul, he was placed in the care of two men
he identified as "Jemoglans." These were *adjemoglans*, meaning sons
of strangers, *adjemi*, and they were Christian-born. Through them
Dallam was promised two concubines of his own choosing if he would
agree to stay; he lied in reply, saying he had a wife and children back in
England to whom he must return. He was detained when the ship that
had brought him departed, and was constantly importuned to change
his mind and stay; he was even taken to a "grate" in the wall surrounding the harem where he was allowed to watch thirty of "the Grande
Sinyors' Concobines" at play, with the implication that he might
choose his consorts from among these "verrie prettie" women. He
wrote that he had dined in the seraglio almost every day for a month,
"which no Christian ever did in there memorie that went away a
Christian." Ultimately he seized the opportunity of leaving on another
English ship. On the return voyage his party spent time in Ottoman-
controlled Greece, where they believed they were in danger from
Turkish soldiers. They were saved because their interpreter contrived
to protect them; he was an Englishman, "his name Finche. He was also
in religion a perfit Turke, but he was our trustie frende."[29]

Many other accounts spoke of English captives who had accepted
Islam. John Rawlins, the master of an English ship captured in 1621
near Gibraltar, was bought by two "English Turkes": Henry Chandler,
who had taken the name "Rammetham Rise" (*reis* meant "captain"),

and John Goodale. These two had acquired a ship, the *Exchange,* for which they wanted an entirely English crew, "and for their Gunners, English and Dutch renegadoes." Among the English "renegadoes" on board were gunner Richard Clarke, "called in Turkish Iafar"; gunner's mate George Cooke, or "Ramedan"; carpenter William Winter, "Mustapha"; and John Browne, known as "Memme." Rawlins said they had been "seduced with the hope of riches, honour, preferment, and such like devillish baits, to catch the soules of mortall men, and entangle frailty in the tarriers of horrible abuses, and imposturing deceit."[30]

The potential riches were real. John Ward, who had started life as "a poore English sailer," threw in his lot with the North African corsairs and came to "live like a Bashaw in Barbary." In 1609 King James issued a proclamation against trading with pirates that repeatedly singled out the "great and enormious spoyles and Piracies" committed by "Captain John Ward" as a particular example of the crimes of these "lewd and ill-disposed persons," but English travelers who visited Ward in his Tunis home were bowled over by the opulence in which he lived.[31]

Not only did they condemn people who became pirates, but also some leaders had deep misgivings about all of England's dealings with the Ottoman Empire and Morocco. The parliament of 1614 saw a heated debate over the wisdom of exporting armaments and iron. One member argued that even supplies supposedly bound for Virginia offered cover to carry the cargoes "from thence into Spain and other parts." Another, John Prowse, argued that the West Country he represented was endangered by English ordnance ending up in Muslim hands, his constituents' "children taken, kept for buggery and made Turks." According to a second account of Prowse's speech, he claimed that the country had been brought "into their [the Muslims'] great slavery, and not now able to pass anywhere we are so beaten with our own weapons."[32]

But many others were deeply fascinated by the Ottoman Empire, including several who would later go to America. William Strachey, who would become secretary in Virginia in 1609, went to Istanbul in 1607, the year of Jamestown's founding, as secretary to Sir Thomas Glover, the envoy of the Levant Company and the king. Because of a falling out with Glover, his stay in Turkey lasted only a few months, and he soon signed on for Virginia.[33] George Sandys, who would later spend four years in Jamestown as the colony's treasurer, traveled extensively in the eastern Mediterranean in the early seventeenth century. Sandys, born in 1578, was the youngest son of the archbishop of York; his elder brother Sir Edwin would eventually head the Virginia Company. George Sandys had the education of a gentleman: St. Mary's Hall and later Corpus Christi College, Oxford, which he entered at age eleven after the death of his father, then the Middle Temple of the Inns of Court, to which he followed other family members as an eighteen-year-old to attain the legal knowledge considered necessary to gentry life. George married Elizabeth Norton, to whom he had been betrothed when he was six and she was four; the betrothal secured property arrangements made by the two fathers. The marriage probably took place at about the time Sandys went to the Middle Temple. It was an unhappy union, filled with "discontent and dislike." In 1609 Elizabeth filed suit alleging that her husband had deserted her three years before, leaving her without money on which to live and depriving her of the properties left her by her father. George countersued. The marriage was never formally dissolved, but the couple lived apart for the rest of their lives.[34]

Sandys may have been fleeing his unhappy situation when he set out on his Eastern expedition in May 1610 as a man of thirty-two. On his title page he identified himself as "George Sandes Poet & Traveller." His travels took him first to France and then to Venice, where the East began. He embarked by ship for Turkey; in Istanbul he stayed in Ambassador Thomas Glover's house for four months. Glover had lived in Turkey as a boy and knew both the language and customs of the people; he was stationed in the Ottoman capital as envoy for the Levant Company and the king for almost twenty years. From Turkey,

Sandys's party crossed the Mediterranean to Alexandria in Egypt; he then ventured in a camel caravan to Jerusalem. On his return, he traveled extensively through Italy, even, despite being the son of a Church of England archbishop, undertaking a visit to Rome.

Sandys's *Relation of a Journey*, published in 1615, became a huge best-seller and went through several editions over the course of the seventeenth century, demonstrating the great interest in the cultures and history of the East among the western European reading public. In his dedication to Prince Charles, the heir to the English throne, Sandys asserted that his book concerned "the most renowned countries and kingdomes" and the regions "where Arts and Sciences have bene invented, and perfited; where wisedome, vertue, policie, and civility have bene planted, have flourished: and lastly where God himselfe did place his owne Commonwealth, gave lawes and oracles, inspired his Prophets, sent Angels to converse with men; above all, where the Sonne of God descended to become man." He contrasted these countries' former condition, "once so glorious, and famous for their happy estate," with their present situation, saying that they had become "the most deplored spectacles of extreme miserie: the wild beasts of mankind having broken in upon them, and rooted out all civilitie."[35]

As he described sailing through the Adriatic Sea and beyond, Sandys inserted stories and verses from classical antiquity about each place he passed. He also tabulated the commodities produced in each and the income derived from them, as well as how much went to the Ottoman Empire in annual payments from countries on the sea's western shore. He confirmed that in Ottoman-controlled territory, though the land was "defiled with their superstitions," Christians were allowed their own churches and "unreproved exercise of religion" upon payment of an annual tax. But he also recorded less amicable relationships. For instance, his ship passed the island of Marmora in the Hellespont, where "a number of poore Christian slaves do hew stones daily for

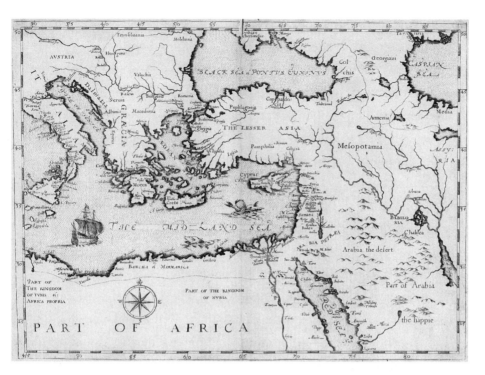

Map of the lands around the eastern Mediterranean from George Sandys, A Relation of a Journey. *By Permission of the Folger Shakespeare Library.*

that magnificent Mosque which is now a building at Istanbul by this Sultan."[36]

As his ship approached the coast of Asia, Sandys insisted on going ashore to view the site of Troy. Even though danger lay in their coming up to the shore, Sandys persuaded the sailors (he was now on a small ship from the Isle of Rhodes) "with much importunitie and promise of reward." Seeing the plain on which Troy had stood "(the theater of those so renowned bickerments)" filled him with many recollections of the great deeds and poets of the past. As he traveled on, he began to encounter new foods; describing kebabs, Sandys wrote that, taking their mutton, the cooks "make no more ado, but slicing it into little gobbets, prick it on a prog of iron, and hang it in a fornace." He had already tasted a "Shurbet" made of honey and water in Chios. And some familiar foods disappeared; the sailors drank up all the wine on board as they neared Istanbul, "it being proclaimed death" to bring alcohol into the Muslim city.[37] The Ottomans had grown lax about consumption of wine before an outbreak of plague in Istanbul and a mutiny in 1601, according to Richard Knolles, and the sultan, Mehmet III, had blamed the troubles on "their excessive drinking of wine, contrarie to the law of their great Prophet." He had ordered everyone who had wine to bring it out "and to stave it, except the embassadours of the Queene of England, the French king, and of the state of Venice: so that (as some report) wine for a space ran down the channels of the streets in Istanbul, as if it had bin water after a great shower of raine."[38]

Sandys presented a long and elaborate description of Istanbul, beginning with the "magnificent Mosques." He described with sadness the remnants of the Orthodox Christian city left from before the Ottoman conquest of 1453. He went on to offer a lengthy discussion of what he called "the Mahometan Religion," beginning with the story of how Mohammed "compiled his damnable doctrine . . . (containing a hodgepodge of sundry religions)." The religion had spread with the conquests achieved by its adherents, so that it had by Sandys's day "wel-nigh over-runne three parts of the earth; of that I meane that hath civill inhabitants." He delineated the beliefs of Islam and compared them with Christianity's tenets, emphasizing that Islam honored Jesus as a great prophet and miracle worker. He devoted several pages to Muslim modes of worship and customs.[39]

The unity of purpose among Muslims impressed Christian observers like Sandys, who reported that he never saw one Muslim strike another. Knolles recorded that "they call themselves *Islami*, that is to say, men of one mind, or at peace among themselves." Sandys praised the Turkish custom of giving alms to the poor, remarking, "In truth, I have seene but few beggars amongst them," and pointed to the endowment of hospitals and mosques by the wealthy. He also noted that the Muslims "extend their charities to Christians and Jewes, as well as to them of their owne religion."[40]

Sandys wrote copiously about Muslim ideas of the afterlife, where the virtuous were to dwell in "magnificent pallaces spread all over with silke carpets" and set in sumptuous gardens "under whose fragrant shades they shall spend the course of their happy time with amarous virgins." The reported centrality of sensuality in Islam was a pivotal flaw on which English writers fixed in their critique of it as a false religion. De-spite the admiration he expressed, Sandys concluded his discussion by declaring that Islam was supported by "tyranny and the sword," and "where it is planted rooting out all vertue, all wisedome and science, and in summe all liberty and civility; and laying the earth so waste, dispeopled and uninhabited; that neither it came from God (save as a scourge by permission) neither can bring them to God that follow it."[41]

One burning question for western Europeans was why the Ottoman sultans were able to extend their power, having become, as Sandys wrote from Istanbul, "Lords of this Imperiall Citie (together with the goodliest portion of the earth)" at a time when many saw Christian Europe as declining.[42] One answer was the unique structure of leader-ship in the bureaucracy and army. The Ottomans took an innovative approach to administration, incorporating into the bureaucracy cap-tives from outside the empire who owed their allegiance directly to the sultan; even those of highest rank were technically slaves of the sultan. Advancement within the imperial structure was possible only for members of this group. Like other writers, Sandys attested that the empire's leadership did not come from "the naturall Turke" but lay "in the hands of [the sultan's] slaves . . . amongst whom there is no nobil-ity of blood, no knowne parentage, kindred, nor hereditary posses-sions: but are as it were of the Sultan's creation, depending upon him onely for their sustenance and preferments." These slaves were cap-tives or "the sonnes of Christians . . . taken in their childhood from their miserable parents." They were circumcised and educated in the Muslim religion, trained in weaponry, "and made patient of hunger and labour, with inured abstinence, and continuall exercise." These men had shaved faces, "the token of servitude," and wore "long coats and copped [peaked] caps, not unlike to our idiots." Some of them rose to positions of great eminence. Others, like Charatza Tragabigzanda's brother, remained military commanders and were situated with their followers on landholdings throughout the empire. These units strengthened the borders and maintained a body of soldiers who were ready for combat wherever they were needed. The military corps included, according to Sandys, "divers Renegados, that have most wickedly quitted their religion and countrey, to fight against both." He concluded, "Thus is the Great Turke served by those whom he may advance without envie, and destroy without danger."[43]

Richard Knolles also pondered how "the mightie Empire of the Turkes . . . is from a small beginning become the greatest terrour of the world." He too pointed to the way the bureaucracy and the army leadership were composed of the empire's most talented men and welded in loyalty to the sultan. The Ottoman sultan rewarded courage and commitment with high office and punished the inadequate regardless of family status; thus was "the way laid open for every common person, be he never so meanely borne, to aspire unto the greatest honours and preferments both of the Court and of the field." The result was "their cheerfull and almost incredible obedience unto their Princes and Sultans." John Rawlins, though he was deeply hostile, echoed this message when he wrote that the men who held him captive had been drawn to convert by "the hope of riches, honour, preferment."[44]

The phenomenon of "taking the turban" was common enough to represent a real challenge to western Europeans, and many speculated on the attractions of Islam or the Muslim world for Christians who came into contact with it. There was no doubt in the minds of Europeans that many conversions were sincere and voluntary, as in the case of Dallam's sympathetic interpreter, who was a "perfit Turke" though English-born. Some argued that Christians did not have a firm enough grasp of the true meaning of their own religion and could therefore be easily led into error. Another principal explanation for the Ottomans' success was their unity in contrast to the division of post-Reformation Christendom. Commentators blamed the split between Protestants and Roman Catholics for weakening Christianity's persuasive power. Knolles proposed that God had allowed Turkish expansion to punish Christians for "the long and declining state of the Christian Commonweale"; it was "the just and secret judgement of the Almightie, who in justice delivereth into the hands of these mercilesse miscreants, nation after nation, and kingdome upon kingdome, as unto the most terrible executioners of his dreadfull wrath, to be punished for their sinnes."[45]

Most adventurers took great risks and hoped for a big strike to make those risks worthwhile. A traveler like George Sandys may have been seeking to demonstrate his competence for office by providing such a detailed and extensive account, and he moved with a degree of ease.[46] But even a man like Thomas Dallam, the organ maker, risked losing his independence of action. For all who crossed cultural boundaries involuntarily, survival rested on their ability to adapt. But their very openness and flexibility carried with it the danger of conversion; a person who could easily play the chameleon might jeopardize the essential core of personality. One wonders how Guillaume Rouffin, who entered America as a French youth and then became an Indian and finally a Spaniard, would have answered later in life if he had been asked his nationality. Finche, the Englishman who was a "perfit Turke" but who nevertheless helped Dallam escape Ottoman control, offers a similar puzzle. Presumably his friendship for Dallam indicates that he retained a sense of common English heritage despite having cast his lot with the Ottoman Muslims. Nationality was most likely not a cate-

gory by which such people would have described themselves. The slippery nature of identity in this period is revealed in their stories. Engagement with the world offered advancement and adventure, but the
price could be very high. Ultimately ties might be cut, becoming a distant memory.

3

Indian Experience of the Atlantic

IN AMERICA as in the Old World, many individuals found themselves in novel situations they had not chosen and in which only their own ingenuity allowed them to survive—and even to thrive. North America's people had had extensive and intimate experience of Europeans long before colonies were thought of, and through this experience they had come to understand much about the different kinds of people across the sea. Indians from a variety of locations had also lived among Europeans for extended periods, and the knowledge brought back by those who returned to their people allowed them to calculate how to deal with Europeans once they made clear their interest in founding permanent bases.

Europeans were fascinated by the question of who the Indians were, and they were committed to the idea that the Americans' ancestors were the first transatlantic migrants. The Indians must have come from some known diaspora in ancient times, as everyone on earth was descended from Noah's family after the great flood described in the Bible. So they wondered how and why the ancestors of these people had come to the Americas. They also were curious about the timing. Indian origins stories that appeared to echo the Old Testament, as well as the reported use of crosses, seemed to indicate that the Americans had been in contact with the Bible's teachings in the very distant past. Some interpreters of American cultures believed they saw evidence that New World peoples had been exposed to the Christian message, possibly even during biblical times.[1]

Although Europeans of this period were not aware of the actual Norse settlement in North America around the year 1000, they had stories of earlier expeditions that might smooth their own paths to a rich relationship with the land and its people. Spanish exploration had been spurred on by hopes of finding the island containing the seven cities of Antilia, supposed to have been founded by seven Portuguese and Spanish bishops who had fled westward with their followers to escape invading Muslims from North Africa early in the eighth century; the islands of the West Indies were called the Antilles because of this association. Early reports of the cities built by pueblo-dwellers in the West fed hopes that the seven cities lay there.[2]

Even vaguer were British claims of early association with North America through the medieval Welsh prince "Madock ap Owen Gwyneth," who, "beinge wearye of the civill warres and domesticall dissentions in his Contrie," was said to have sailed westward in 1170; he returned to Britain, then went back to America with colonists, as proven by "very auncient and auctenticall Chronicles written in the welshe or brittish tongue." The traces of his colonists' presence, it was argued, could be discerned in the survival of Welsh-sounding words such as "penguin" in some Indian languages.[3] The Virginia Company claimed the right to colonize on the basis of Madoc's prior settlement, and the Jamestown colonists actually thought they had found Indians whose language might have derived from Welsh. These were the Monacans, who lived to the west. The colonists were right in thinking that their speech differed significantly from the Algonquian languages spoken nearer the coast; the Monacans were Siouan speakers. Peter Winne, who knew Welsh, attempted to act as interpreter when an exploring party met the Monacans.[4]

Map of the Isle of Utopia, 1518. By permission of the Folger Shakespeare Library.

There were also stories of travel in the opposite direction. Sir Humphrey Gilbert recalled an account in the works of Pliny, the ancient natural historian, saying "that there were certain Indians driven by tempest, upon the coast of Germanie," though Gilbert was determined to demonstrate that they had originated in India and that their voyage proved the existence of a northwest "passage to Cataia," or China.[5]

America quickly became a screen on which the European imagination could project dreams and fantasies. The hero of Sir Thomas More's 1516 book *Utopia*, Raphaell Hythlodaye, was described as a Portuguese scholar who had sailed to America three times with Amerigo Vespucci. At the end of Vespucci's last voyage in 1502, Hythlodaye had not gone back to Europe but stayed behind with five others and traveled widely, becoming fully accepted by the people among whom he lived. Ultimately he came to know the land of Utopia, about which he reported back to Europe in More's story.

Stories of early voyages such as Madoc's or the seven bishops' were incapable of proof, and More's *Utopia* was fiction. But there were many genuine Hythlodayes who helped to shape the experience of Americans and Europeans as each attempted to understand and manipulate the other. As in the Old World, people on all sides of the early relationships in the colonies brought many layers of experience to the encounter. There was no chance of a sudden appearance of bearded Europeans before amazed virginal native populations by the time the English got involved in American ventures. Indians had had almost a century to gather information about the hopes, fears, and weaknesses of these transoceanic newcomers.

Indians living along North America's east coast had seen many ships, beginning with the coastal voyage of Giovanni da Verrazano in 1524, and some inland Americans had gained intimate knowledge of the newcomers and their ways. Panfilo de Narváez had led an ill-fated Spanish expedition to the Gulf Coast of Florida in 1528; although most of the three hundred men perished, some traveled on rafts to Texas. Four survivors—Cabeza de Vaca, Alonso del Castillo, Andrés Dorantes, and Estevanico, an enslaved Arabic-speaking man from Morocco—turned up in Mexico in 1536, having made their way there on foot and with many stories to tell of how they occupied the roles of holy men and healers among the Indian communities through which they had passed. As they traveled, Estevanico became the main spokesman for the group. Another African from the original expedition lived the rest of his life among Indians along the Gulf Coast; Doroteo Teodoro, a Greek Christian, decided to stay there rather than accompany the group trying to reach Mexico, and he "took a black man with him." Both were described as Christians. Cabeza de Vaca's strenuous efforts to get them back were unavailing.[6] So common was the phenomenon of Europeans living among South American Indians that William Strachey mentioned in passing in his account of Virginia that in Peru many of the leaders known as caciques had "naturall Spaniardes, that attend them in their houses." He knew this from a man named "Capt. Ellis . . . who lived amongst them some few yeares."[7]

In 1534, as Jacques Cartier sailed along the coast of Canada's Chaleur Bay, any notion he might have had that his expedition was the first visit of Europeans to this region were dispelled when a large group of Indians "set up a great clamour and made frequent signs to us to come on shore, holding up to us some skins on sticks." Clearly the Indians knew what the Europeans wanted, and that they were willing to offer valuable manufactured items in payment for furs. Other Indians soon appeared, "dancing and showing many signs of joy, and of their desire to be friends, saying to us in their language: *Napou tou daman asurtat,* and other words we did not understand." Cartier felt overwhelmed and, as he and his men were surrounded by Indians in canoes, afraid as well, so he finally shot off "two small cannon" over their heads to force the Indians to back off.[8] In fact, by the 1530s Europeans had been visiting the rich fishing grounds of the Newfoundland Banks for decades; David Beers Quinn even argued that these annual visits may have begun before 1492. Cartier himself was a veteran of voyages to Brazil and to Newfoundland when he attempted his first navigation of the St. Lawrence River.[9]

The expedition led by the Spaniard Hernando de Soto traveled throughout the Southeast and across the Mississippi River beginning in 1539, at a time when colonization was in its early stages and America north of Mexico largely unexplored by Europeans. Yet, shortly after they landed on the Gulf Coast near Tampa Bay, they learned that "a Christian" named Juan Ortiz had been living among neighboring Indians for twelve years. As Ortiz approached with nine Indians, the Spanish were apprehensive because they thought all ten were Indians: "He was naked like them, with a bow and some arrows in his hand, his body decorated like an Indian." The man had mostly forgotten Spanish, but he "remembered how to call to Our Lady, and by this he was recognized to be a Christian." Although they felt "much joy," the reunion ended with a thud: "He told us upon seeing us that there was not a bit of gold in the land."[10]

Half a century later the story of Juan Ortiz was told in great detail in a book written by a man who was himself a product of the kind of interchange set in motion by the arrival of Europeans in America. Garcilaso de la Vega, el Inca, was the son of a Spanish captain and the granddaughter of the Inca emperor Tupac Inca Yupanqui. Garcilaso interviewed surviving members of the De Soto expedition and learned that Ortiz was one of four Spaniards who had been captured by a cacique named Hirrihugua, who led the people of Uçita and whose heart was filled with unquenchable anger because of Spanish atrocities. Three of the four were soon killed, but Ortiz, who was only eighteen, was spared on the entreaty of Hirrihugua's wife and daughters. Those who crossed from one cultural context to another gained and lost from the experience, and they always lived to some extent as outsiders. Some reports said that Ortiz, on joining De Soto's party, could not tolerate clothes and had to learn little by little to wear them again. The "faithful interpreter Juan Ortiz" never made it back to Spanish life; he died as De Soto's expedition moved through Arkansas in the winter of 1641–42.[11]

De Soto's expedition also found Spanish iron axes and rosaries with attached crosses in burials at Cofitachequi in present-day South Carolina, more evidence of an earlier European presence. Lucas Vásquez de Ayllón, with the guidance of an Indian whom the Spanish called Francisco de Chicora, had brought six hundred people, including women and children, to found a colony there in 1526. The De Soto expedition's recorders also believed they had found evidence that other Europeans had lived in Cofitachequi. None of these people ever returned to Spanish life.[12]

De Soto and his men moved on through the large domain of Coosa (Coça) to the west, where three of their party abandoned the Spanish. One was identified as a "Levantine" Christian named Feryada. At another stop a gentleman from Salamanca named Manzano left the march. The third person who slipped away from the main party here was "a very shrewd black man, who was called Joan Vizcaíno." Thus from early in the sixteenth century, Indian peoples in the southeastern interior had prolonged and intimate experience of people originating not just from Europe but from the Ottoman Empire and sub-Saharan Africa as well.[13] While De Soto explored the East, Francisco de Coronado simultaneously led an expedition through America's West, and his party also apparently contained people from Muslim countries as well as Christendom.

French leaders, like the Spanish, considered the Carolina coast a prime place to found colonies; as with later English puritan migrants, French Huguenots hoped to create a Protestant refuge should one be needed.[14] The 1562 colony of Charlesfort in Port Royal Sound had departed after a year, abandoning Guillaume Rouffin, but the French determined to try again. Ironically, their second expedition was traveling north up the Florida coast in 1564 just as the Spanish were carrying their captive Rouffin south on the same route toward Havana. Whereas the 1562 group had consisted of only twenty-six men, this new venture comprised about three hundred men, almost all Protestants, and one woman, who was Laudonnière's servant. This group built Fort Caroline on the Florida coast at the mouth of the St. Johns River in the lands of the Timucuans, with whom the 1562 venture had had a friendly encounter.[15]

The French soon learned of more Europeans who, like Guillaume Rouffin and Juan Ortiz, had spent many years living among the Americans. They ransomed two Spaniards who had been marooned fifteen years earlier; the French were shocked to discover how thoroughly acculturated these men were: "They were naked, wearing their haire long unto their hammes as the Savages use to do, and were Spanyards borne, yet so well accustomed to the fashion of the countrey that at the first sight they found our maner of apparell strange." Laudonnière had his men dress the Spaniards in European clothes and cut their hair. They refused to allow their rescuers to dispose of their hair after it was cut, "but lapped it up in a linnen cloth, saying that they would cary it into their countrey to be a testimony of the misery that they had indured in the Indies."

The two told Laudonnière that they had been in a fleet of three ships, and that most of the people aboard had been saved by an Indian leader whom they called "the king of Calos." Calos was the principal town of the Calusa Indians on Florida's southwest coast. This king, possibly the Calusa leader known to the Spanish as Carlos, was "the goodliest, and the tallest Indian of the country, a mighty man, a warrior, and having many subjects under his obedience." They testified that among the shipwrecked Spanish this king had saved were "many women; among which number there were three or foure women married, remaining there yet, and their children also, with this king of Calos." The French found a small gold piece in one man's hair, and the

**Was der König Utina/wann er in XIIII.
Krieg zeucht/ für Kriegsordnung halt.**

ANN Saturioua/der König/in Krieg zeucht/ so halten seine Kriegsleute keine Ordnung/sondern lauffen hin vnd her/einer vmb den andern/ gantz zersträuwet. Hergegen aber sein Feindt/ Holata Outina (welches ein König vieler Könige heisset/) dessen jetzunder gedacht/ ist viel mechtiger an Volck vnd Reichthumb/ zeucht in guter Schlachtordnung/ vnd stellet sich mitten in Hauffen/ mit rehter Farbe angestrichen. Die Flügel oder Hörner am Heer / sind eytel junge Gesellen/ vnter welchen die Hurtigsten/ so auch roht angestrichen/ Lackeyen vnd Kundtschaffer seyn müssen/ die Feinde zu erkundigen: Dann wie die Spürhunde ein Wilde/ also auch sie die Fußstapffen der Feinde außspähen können. Vnd so baldt sie derselbigen Fußstapffen erkannt/lauffen sie wider hindersich/ dem Heer solchs zuvermelden. Ferner/gleich wie die Vnsern im Kriege Trommeten vnnd Paucken haben/ darmit anzuzeygen/ was man thun soll: Also haben sie jhre Herolden/ welche mit gewissen Geschrey jhnen zuverstehen geben/wann sie stillstehen oder fortrücken/ dem Feinde entgegen ziehen/oder ein ander Kriegsgeschäfft verrichten sollen. Wann die Sonne vnter gangen/ halten sie still/ vnd streiten nicht mehr. So sie jhr Feldtläger schlagen wöllen/ werden sie in gewisse Rotten abgetheilet/ vnd die Dapfferstenvon den andern abgesondert. Wann der König auff dem Feldt/oder im Wälden einen Platz zum Nachtläger erwöhlet/ vnnd nun zu Nacht gessen/ vnnd allein sitzt/ ordnen die / so den Platz abgemessen/ auß den Dapfferstenzehen Rotten ringsweiß vmb den König/ Vber zehen Schritt ohngefehrlich zwentzig Rotten / wider ringsweiß : Aber ober zwentzig Schritt/ werden viertzig Rotten geordnet/ vnd also fortan/nach anzahl vnd menge deß Heers/ pflegen sie die Schritt vnd Rotten jmmer zu mehren.

Wie deß

The Timucuan leader Outina in battle array. Courtesy of the John Carter Brown Library at Brown University.

castaways insisted that the king of Calos had great riches in gold and silver. But they also said that much of it was salvaged from Spanish ships wrecked in the difficult straits; the rest came from trade with other Indians.[16]

Laudonnière's colony endured the classic experiences of early colonization: a breakdown of order and purpose in the men, who found life in America far different from their expectations; the onset of debilitating diseases, which attacked the commander among others; and worsening relations with the Timucuans, who resisted pressure to provide the French with food. In the "exceeding strange famine" the men began to sell everything they had for food. If they objected to high prices, the Indians told them "roughly & churlishly: if thou make so great account of thy marchandise, eat it, and we will eat our fish: then fell they out a laughing and mocked us with open throat." The combination of adverse environmental conditions and pressure to feed so many extra people had pushed the Timucuans beyond their limits.[17]

Laudonnière and his colonists, who had expected to be resupplied by April, were making preparations to abandon the colony when English ships commanded by John Hawkins appeared at the beginning of August 1565. Hawkins was returning to England from his second attempt to carve out an English role in the slave trade between Africa and the Spanish colonies in the Caribbean; his young cousin Francis Drake sailed in this fleet as an ordinary seaman. Hawkins left food with the colonists, who "had made the inhabitants weary of them by their dayly craving of maiz."[18]

Rumors, some containing bits of authentic information, flew between Spain and France and their American outposts about threats posed by the other side's activities. The Spanish king, Philip II, sent ships under the command of Pedro Menéndez de Avilés to find and root out the French presence in lands long claimed by Spain. When the French authorities heard about the Spaniards' preparations, they added soldiers and weapons to the ships they were sending to resupply their colony. Both fleets raced across the Atlantic, arriving simultaneously. Menéndez found the harbor that would become his base on the Florida coast on the feast day of Saint Augustine, August 28, 1565, and the French fleet under Jean Ribault appeared before Fort Caroline on the same day.

Menéndez soon attacked and destroyed Fort Caroline with almost all the people in it. Only the women and children, some men whom Menéndez determined to be Roman Catholics, and four "carpenters and caulkers of whom I had great need" were spared. Ribault had already left Fort Caroline with his ships in pursuit of the Spanish before the attack. Others who escaped the fort and ran to the woods were picked up by French ships. Some colonists, including Laudonnière, made it back to France, but most were pursued and killed over the next weeks. Some were said to have been taken by Indians, and a few were later found living with the Guales. Ribault was among the executed. Menéndez reported to the king that he had "made war with fire and blood" upon those who had "come to these parts to settle and to plant this evil Lutheran sect."[19]

St. Augustine, the first permanent European settlement in North America above the Rio Grande, was the product of these events. The Spanish also founded Santa Elena near the site of the destroyed Fort Caroline. These settlements, along with several other small forts and missions in the interior, ensured that no other Europeans would attempt to plant colonies along this southern coast past which the Spanish treasure fleet sailed on its annual journey from Havana to Seville. Menéndez heard reports that over two hundred Spanish shipwreck survivors were living or had lived as captives with the Calusas, and as he traveled along the coast, he frequently encountered Spaniards who lived as Indians among Indians. His brother-in-law Gonzalo Solís de Merás, who accompanied Menéndez in 1565, wrote a long eyewitness account of their experiences.

One small expedition up the coast encountered a man in a canoe who shouted to them: "Spaniards, Brothers, Christians, be welcome! We have been expecting you for 8 days, for God and Holy Mary told us that you were coming, and the Christian men and women who are here alive, have ordered me to come and await you here with this canoe, to give you a letter which I bring you." When they had brought the man, "who came naked and painted, turned into an Indian," on board, the letter turned out to be a cross, which he had concealed "under the deerskin belt he wore." He pleaded with the Spanish "for the sake of the death that Our Lord had received on that cross in order to save us, not to pass by without entering the harbour, and endeavoring to rescue them from their cacique and take them to a land of Christians." The next day Carlos, the Calusa leader, arrived with three hundred warriors; Menéndez invited him onto his ship for a meal, then held him prisoner until the Spanish captives, "5 women and 3 Christian men," were brought to the harbor. Menéndez gave them shirts and chemises to cover their nakedness; then "from some English woolen cloth he carried with him, he ordered 4 or 5 tailors who came there to make clothes for them." Although the captives "wept for joy," Solís de Merás added that the women "felt great sorrow on account of the children that they were leaving there."

The Christian who had originally approached the fleet continued to function as an intermediary. Through him, Carlos promised that he would soon bring two more men and one woman who were living inland. He then offered to cement their friendship through the marriage of his sister to Menéndez, whom he addressed as his elder brother. When Menéndez went to dine at Carlos's village, he traveled in state, "taking 200 arquebusiers with him and a flag, 2 fifers and drummers, 3 trumpeters, one harp, one violin and one psaltery, and a very small dwarf, a great singer and dancer, whom he brought with him." When he entered the house, Menéndez ordered his men to stay outside with their weapons ready to fire in case of trouble. After much singing and dancing, Menéndez read his address to the cacique's sister, who was "not at all beautiful, although very grave." Though reluctantly, he did go through a ceremony of marriage and spent the night with Doña Antonia, as she was named when baptized before the wedding. When Menéndez departed from the village, Doña Antonia was sent to Cuba with her attendants with the promise that she would soon be brought back to her people. He took only seven Spanish former captives with him, because two women "had already gone back to the Indians, from the longing they had for the children that they were leaving behind."[20]

Guillaume Rouffin apparently became a Roman Catholic, or revealed himself to be one, while in Havana and as Guillermo Rufín became Menéndez's principal interpreter.[21] Menéndez was firmly convinced of Rufín's loyalty and relied heavily on him. Late in 1567 Menéndez sent Juan Pardo on an expedition into the interior for the purpose, among other things, of discovering the route to the silver mines in Zacatecas, Mexico. Rufín, who Menéndez believed understood all the Indian languages in the Southeast, accompanied him. He was constantly by Pardo's side, interpreting his words and relaying the Indians' responses; as they moved farther into the country, translation had to be carried out through a chain of people each of whom knew two languages. If Pardo's men saw any of those who had left De Soto two and a half decades earlier, or their descendants, they were unaware of it.[22]

Hernando de Escalante Fontaneda also worked with Menéndez as a translator. His story, written about 1575 after Escalante was back in Spain, gives a vivid account of the plight of shipwrecked Spaniards among the Florida Indians. He recounted that when he was thirteen his parents sent him and his brother to Spain for their education, but the ship on which they traveled was wrecked on the coast of Florida. He lived with various Indian groups there for the next seventeen years and claimed to understand four of their languages. "No one knows that country so well as I know it," he asserted. He spoke of many more shipwrecks and the people taken in by the Indians: "It was a consolation, though a sad one, for those who were lost after us to find on shore Christian companions who could share their hardships and help them to understand those brutes. Many Spaniards have saved their lives by finding themselves with Christian companions already there."[23]

Escalante Fontaneda described the perilous situation of captives who did not have access to interpreters like him, reporting that "the cacique" asked him one day: "Escalante, tell us the truth, for you well know that I like you much: When we tell these, your companions, to dance and sing, and do other things, why are they so mean and rebellious that they will not? or is it that they do not fear death, or will not yield to a people unlike them in their religion— Answer me; and if you do not know the reason, ask it of those newly seized, who for their own fault are captives now, a people whom once we held to be gods come down from the sky." Escalante Fontaneda, addressing the chief respectfully as "My lord," tried to explain that the newcomers disobeyed because they did not understand what was being said to them. His "lord and master" was skeptical, so they tried an experiment in which the cacique commanded the newcomers to look out for arriving ships. Those so commanded turned to Escalante Fontaneda for translation, and another man, described as a "free negro," laughed and said that Escalante Fontaneda's explanation was correct. The "free negro" may have been the man identified in the records as "Luis, mulatto, interpreter of the land of Carlos."[24] Their master, now convinced, "said to his vassals, that when they should find Christians thus cast away, and seize them, they must require them to do nothing without giving notice, that one might go to them who should understand their language." Escalante Fontaneda also affirmed what the Spanish had learned from other castaways: although the Indians in coastal Florida were rich in gold and silver, it all came from shipwrecks; as a boy going to Spain he had carried "twenty-five thousand dollars in pure gold," and his treasure was the smallest on his ship.

Menéndez continued to encounter Europeans who had long lived among Indians in Florida and Georgia. He later reported that in his first year in Florida, he had "ransomed from among the Indians thirty-two persons, men and women, who had been slaves of the caciques and Indians for fifteen, eighteen and twenty years." Some of these included people of South American and African descent as well as Europeans.[25] He also heard that these captives were the remnant of over 230 Spaniards, many of whom had been sacrificed in ceremonies.

When Menéndez traveled to the territory of the Tocobagas, the people who had captured Juan Ortiz, the cacique sent "a Christian . . . the only one he had," to greet the Spanish, a Portuguese man who had lived with the Tocobagas for six years after surviving a shipwreck. Like Carlos's captives, he said he had had forewarning in a dream that the Spanish were coming for him, and he had been expecting them for eight days. When he returned to Spain in 1567, Menéndez carried with him several Calusa and Tequesta Indians as well as Europeans who had lived among the Florida Indians. Doña Antonia, who felt betrayed, was not among them.[26]

Menéndez devoted much attention to rescuing Spanish captives from Indian life and reacculturating them to European and Christian ways. He clearly felt great sympathy for these involuntary cross-cultural migrants whose very personalities had been reshaped by their experiences. Yet Menéndez left behind some of his own men in many villages as he traveled through Florida. In one place he said he was leaving these men "as hostages and teachers of the Indians."[27]

We can only guess how many Europeans lived out their lives as Indians following events such as these, and how many unrecorded shipwrecks added transatlantic migrants to American populations. Tantalizing hints of other interchanges, temporary or permanent, appear in the fragmentary records. At their request John Hawkins put ashore a hundred of his sailors on the Mexican coast near Tampico in Campeche in 1568 after most of his fleet was destroyed in the disastrous conclusion to his third, and last, slave-trading voyage. Ultimately seventy-seven of them went in a body to Tampico and surrendered. David Ingram, who would later tell his story, and his two companions, who had set out to travel on foot north from that point, were picked up by a French ship and soon found themselves back in England. But twenty of Hawkins's men disappear from the record. Their fate, like that of the thousands shipwrecked or otherwise marooned on American shores, is unrecorded; presumably those who survived melted into Indian life.[28]

One of the most remarkable stories comes from the far north. Martin Frobisher, who had been handed over as a hostage on the African coast two decades earlier, led a 1576 expedition to Baffin Island in the Arctic in search of the eastern end of the northwest passage. Inuit there captured a boat and the five Englishmen in it. Frobisher in turn seized an Inuk in his kayak and took him back to England with him; the captive demonstrated kayak handling before dying soon after their arrival.[29]

These Americans had had previous experience of Europeans as early as 1000, when the Norse, led by Leif Eiriksson, crossed Davis Strait from their settlements in Greenland. Norwegian coins have been found in Indian burials as far afield as the Maine coast, and one saga speaks of two Norse boys being taken as "slaves" by the Americans. Other voyages also touched on these coasts, and sometimes captured people, as a German woodcut of an Inuk mother and child from 1567 demonstrates.[30] Frobisher's men found nails and other items of European manufacture, including "certayne buttons of copper, whiche they [the Inuit] use to weare upon theyr forheads for ornament, as our Ladyes in the Court of England do use great pearle." Even more remarkably, they discovered "a Guinney Beane of redde coloure, the which dothe usually grow in the hote Countreys." From all these discoveries Frobisher's men drew the conclusion that the Inuit either engaged in

John White's painting of the Inuit capture of Frobisher's men.

trade with "other Nations which dwell farre off, or else themselves are greate travellers."[31] They also discovered that the Inuit had sophisticated understanding of the power of writing to carry messages over long distances.

There was widespread interest in Frobisher's ventures. In addition to the Inuk and his kayak, Frobisher had brought back a piece of black rock that assayers deemed very promising evidence of the existence of gold. Walter Ralegh's half-brother, Sir Humphrey Gilbert, had written a manuscript advocating an English search for a passage in the far north in 1566, and this was published in 1576, with the title *A Discourse of a Discoverie for a new Passage to Cataia*, as part of the campaign to promote Frobisher's project. Leading scholars of the day such as Dr. John Dee were involved in the planning, as was Thomas Gresham, who would go on to found a college for "the development of pure and applied scientific studies." Once Frobisher returned with his "ore" and news of a promising strait, backers joined together in an informal company, significantly labeled the Cathay (China) Company, to finance two more voyages in the next two years in search of both ore and the northwest passage. Queen Elizabeth, who was an investor, named the region Meta Incognita, the unknown goal or shore; today it is the self-governing Inuk territory of Nunavut.[32] All hopes were disappointed: the thousands of tons of ore brought back by the second and third voyages ultimately proved valueless, and Frobisher Strait led into a bounded bay.

On their second voyage Frobisher's company discovered in a native tent "a dublet of Canvas made after the Englishe fashion, a shirt, a girdle, three shoes for contrarie feete, and of unequall bignesse, whiche they well conjectured to be the apparell of our five poore countriemen, whiche were intercepted the laste yeare by these Countrie people, aboute fiftye leagues from this place."[33] One party in the southern part of the bay under the command of Gilbert Yorke attempted to seize some Inuit they encountered and were fiercely resisted; the Americans seemed to prefer death to capture. The English named the place "the Bloudy Point" because of "the slaughter there." The men were all killed, but two women and a wounded child remained. One was old and they were afraid she might be a witch, so they let her go. The mother and child were taken.

The English had already seized an Inuk man, so they were pleased to present him with this young woman for his "comforte." George Best described how all the English crowded into the room to witness their first encounter: "Every man with silence desired to beholde the manner of their meeting." At first the two captives "behelde each the other very wistly a good space, withoute speeche or worde uttered, with

Egnock and her baby, painted by John White.

greate change of coloure and countenaunce." The woman turned away "verie suddeynely" and "beganne to sing, as though she minded another matter." But when they were again face to face, the man, "with sterne and stayed countenance, beganne to tell a long solemne tale to the woman, whereunto she gave good hearing, and interrupted him nothing till he had finished, & afterwards, being growen into more familiar acquaytance by speech, were turned togither, so that (I thinke) the one would hardly have lived, without the comfort of the other."[34]

Because the fighting at Bloody Point was so fierce and the Inuit seemed so loath to deal with the English, Frobisher began to fear "that

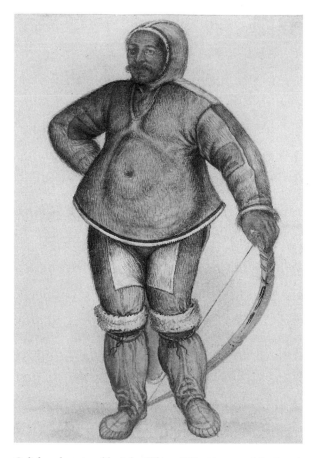

Calichough, painted by John White. ©The Trustees of the British
Museum.

we hadde already hearde the laste newes of our men." But then a large
party of Inuit came to the English camp and demanded the return of
the captured woman and child. Frobisher placed the woman on a high
point of land where she was clearly visible and then took the man with
him to the meeting. When brought before "hys friendes," the captive
wept so copiously that he could not speak for some time. When he recovered he "talked at full" with them and gave his countrymen the
various European goods that the English had given him, "whereby
we noted, that they are verie kynde one to the other, and greately
sorowfull for the losse of their friendes." Frobisher, who knew well

what it was like to be abandoned on a foreign shore, demanded the return of his five men and offered to trade his captives for them, and "also to rewarde them [the Inuit] wyth greate giftes and friendship." The Inuit confirmed that the five were still alive and suggested by sign language that Frobisher should write them a letter, "for they knewe very well the use wee have of writing." They came the next day to get the letter and promised to return in three days. George Best put the text of the letter into his account:

> In the name of God, in whom we al beleve, who I trust hath preserved your bodyes and soules amongst these Infidels, I commend me unto you. I will be glad to seeke by all menes you can devise, for your deliverance, eyther with force, or with any commodities within my Shippes, whiche I will not spare for your sakes, or any thing else I can doe for you. I have aboord, of theyrs, a Man, a Woman, and a Childe, which I am contented to delyver for you, but the man which I carried away from hence the last yeare, is dead in England. Moreover, you may declare unto them, that if they deliver you not, I wyll not leave a manne alive in their Countrey. And thus, if one of you can come to speake with me, they shall have eyther the Man, Woman, or Childe in pawne for you. And thus unto God, whome I trust you do serve, in hast I leave you, and to him we will dayly pray for you. This Tuesdaye morning the seaventh of August.
>
> Yours to the uttermost of my power
> Martin Frobisher
> Postscript. I have sente you by these bearers, Penne, Incke, and Paper, to write backe unto me agayne, if personally you can not come to certifye me of your estate.[35]

While he waited for a reply, Frobisher decided to put his men to work mining the promised ore, leaving the search for the northwest passage for another time. For unknown reasons, the negotiations went no further. They heard nothing from the five men, and their only encounters with Inuit from that time forward were hostile.

Meanwhile, the Inuit captives apparently adjusted to their situation. George Best remarked on how they lived together: "And, for so muche as we could perceive, albeit they lived continually togither, yet did they never use as man and wife, though the woman spared not to do all necessarie things that apperteyned to a good huswife indifferently for them both, as in making cleane their Cabin, and every other thing that apperteyned to his ease." Best also commented on their modesty, reinforcing the point in a marginal note: "The shamefastnesse [modesty] and chastitie of those savage Captives."[36] The adults did not survive long once they were taken to England in 1577. Dr. Edward Dodding in Bristol wrote an account of the final illness and the autopsy he conducted on Calichough, the man. Egnock, the woman, quickly followed him in death. They are both buried in Bristol. The child, Nutaaq, survived longer; he is buried in the same London cemetery as the Inuk man brought in 1576.[37]

Usually we have only the European end of each story; however, the Frobisher voyages lived on in a way unanticipated by the English. The Inuit of Baffin Island retained an exact oral history of these events and of the English who lived among them. Europeans had no clear idea exactly where Frobisher had landed until 1862, when Charles F. Hall spent two years in Frobisher's Bay and heard the story of the five men; ironically, Hall was searching for members of a northwest passage expedition that had disappeared fifteen years earlier. The oral tradition Hall collected remembered that Europeans had come every year for three years, and the oldest inhabitant, a woman named Ookijoxy Ninoo, recounted the number of ships in each expedition. Hall developed a questionnaire to use in interviewing people as he traveled around. The Inuit showed him relics left behind by Frobisher, including a blacksmith's anvil, and described others. They took him to tiny

Kodlunarn (White Man's) Island, where Frobisher had camped and to which the five men had gone when released. There the five used timbers and equipment buried for future use by Frobisher's men to build a boat with a mast in hopes of returning to England, but they died of cold after setting out. Hall saw the foundations and trenches created by Frobisher's men and the remains of the model European stone house he had had built to instruct his hosts. The Inuit also told him of a stone monument erected by the men that they had incorporated into their own cosmology.[38]

In most cases American memories of these encounters were not collected—either at the time or later—as they were in Baffin Bay. Often only hints remain. Arthur Barlowe, one of the commanders of the scouting expedition Ralegh sent as part of the planning for the Roanoke colony in 1584, reported that, although "most" adult coastal Carolina Algonquians had black hair, "yet we sawe children that had very fine aburne, and chestnut colour haire." His native hosts also told him that they had extracted valuable nails and spikes from "some Christian shippe" that had been wrecked on their coast twenty years before with the loss of all aboard.[39]

People from many backgrounds brought their varied experience to North America's southern and eastern coasts. In the general area where Jamestown would be founded, many lost colonists from around the Atlantic rim had already melted into the population. The Roanoke colony, famous for the Lost Colonists who went there in 1587, actually saw several sets of lost or abandoned eastern and western Atlantic people. The first Roanoke settlers, sent in 1585, quickly realized that the Outer Banks are essentially sandbars surrounded by fairly shallow water, and that a true colony would need a better site. A large party of them spent several months near the mouth of Chesapeake Bay, possibly with the Chesapeake Indians on the site of present-day Virginia Beach, and reported back that that region offered a superior location

Roanoke

for English colonization. While they were learning about the bay and its peoples, the region's natives were learning more about Englishmen.

As in Florida, some contacts were not temporary. Sir Francis Drake visited the Roanoke colony in 1586 at the conclusion of a voyage around the Caribbean attacking as many Spanish settlements as he could. One foreign observer in London who admired Drake wrote, "His boldness in large-scale villainy was certainly astonishing." As his fleet moved up North America's east coast, he destroyed the Spanish settlement at St. Augustine; governor Pedro Menéndez Marqués had evacuated most of the people in anticipation of the assault. Some Protestant prisoners who had been held in St. Augustine had been abandoned there, and they joined the English; one approached the English fleet "in a litle boat" and identified himself as a friend by playing "the tune of the Prince of Orenge his song" on a fife, indicating his affiliation with the Dutch Protestants who were resisting Spanish domination in Europe. This fifer told the English that St. Augustine was open to them. Drake's men stripped the town of everything they could carry away, including guns and ordnance, hardware from the doors and windows, and a great chest containing "about five thousand ducats." As one participant wrote, "There was abowte 250 howses in this Towne, but wee left not one of them standinge."[40]

In careering around the West Indies, Drake had collected several hundred men and women, mainly from Cartagena and Santo Domingo. These, who had apparently been promised their freedom, were enslaved Africans, natives of South America, and galley slaves, whose number included some Europeans as well as men identified as Moors. Drake's intention was to leave some of these people in Roanoke to strengthen the settlement, and he had promised to return the Moors and Europeans to their own countries. But when his fleet arrived, Drake found the colony in distress; the men had just attacked the neighboring Roanoke Indians and killed their chief. When a hurricane drove off some of the ships and endangered others, Drake and

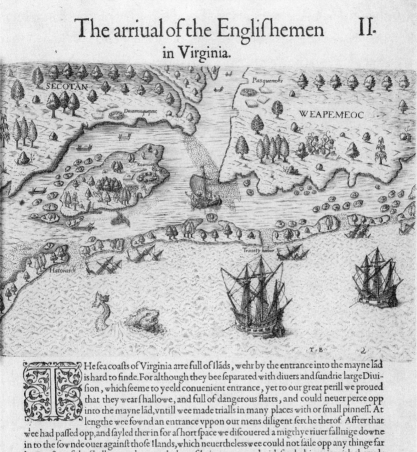

The arriual of the Englifhemen in Virginia. II.

He fea coafts of Virginia arre full of Ilåds, wehr by the entrance into the mayne låd is hard to finde. For although they bee feparated with diuers and fundrie large Diui- fion, which feeme to yeeld conuenient entrance, yet to our great perill we proued that they wear fhallowe, and full of dangerous flatts, and could neuer perce opp into the mayne låd, vntill wee made trialls in many places with or fmall pinneff. At lengthe wee fownd an entrance vppon our mens diligent ferche therof. Affter that wee had paffed opp, and fayled ther in for afhort fpace we difcouered a migthye riuer fallnige downe in to the fownde ouer againft thofe Ilands, which neuertheleff wee could not faile opp any thinge far by Reafon of the fhallewnes, the mouth ther of beinge annoyed with fands driuen in with the tyde therfore faylinge further, wee came vnto a Good bigg yland, the Inhabitante therof as foone as they faw vs began to make a great an horrible crye, as people which meuer befoer had feene men appa- relled like vs, and camme away makinge out crys like wild beafts or men out of their wyts. But been- ge gentlye called backe, wee offred the of our wares, as glaffes, kniues, babies, and other trifles, which wee thougt they deligted in. Soe they ftood ftill, and perceuinge our Good will and courtefie came fawninge vppon vs, and bade us welcome. Then they brougt vs to their village in the iland called, Roanoac, and vnto their Weroans or Prince, which entertained vs with Reafonable curtefie, alt- houg the wear amafed at the firft fight of vs. Suche was our arriuall into the parte of the world, which we call Virginia, the ftature of bodee of wich people, theyr attire, and maneer of lyuinge, their feafts, and banketts, I will particullerlye déclare vnto yow.

Theodor DeBry's engravers added a line of wrecked ships to John White's map of the Carolina Outer Banks, showing how new information was incorporated in representations of America. Courtesy of the John Carter Brown Library at Brown University.

Roanoke's governor Ralph Lane decided to abandon the project and take the settlers home to England. The disposition of the several hundred people brought by Drake was not mentioned; it is presumed that most were left on the Outer Banks of North Carolina. In their haste to depart, the ships also left behind three Englishmen from the colony who were on an errand into the mainland.[41]

Several supply ships had embarked for Roanoke that summer before the colonists arrived back in England with the news of its abandonment. One landed almost immediately after Drake's fleet set sail but apparently departed again without hearing anything of the three men left behind. Then the full supply fleet arrived and spent considerable time looking for the whole group of colonists, who they presumed were still there. Pedro Diaz, a skilled Spanish pilot who had been captured previously and forced to serve the English, later testified that they had found the hanged bodies of an Indian and an Englishman but saw only three people alive, all Indians, whom they attempted to capture. The commander of this fleet, Sir Richard Grenville, decided to leave fifteen or eighteen men (reports vary) at Roanoke with artillery and food sufficient for a year.[42] None of the people from three continents who had been deposited on the Carolina Outer Banks to date—Drake's Africans, Europeans, and South American Indians, as well as the various Englishmen left behind—were ever accounted for. Presumably many lived on for years, and the Americans learned how to deal with transatlantic migrants and absorbed the newcomers' knowledge of the world across the sea.

Spanish authorities, discouraged by long-standing drought conditions, gave up the attempt to maintain a continuing presence at Santa Elena in late summer 1587; when they left the area to consolidate their forces at St. Augustine, they did not know that English colonists had again occupied the site of Roanoke just a few months before.[43] With the backing of a consortium of investors, Sir Walter Ralegh, the venture's main sponsor, had determined to try again, using a new plan of organization that replaced the military outpost model with one of true settlement. His agents collected a group of families who were willing to emigrate with the promise of five hundred acres of their own—a lord's estate—in Ralegh's Virginia. Just over a hundred people embarked in all, including pregnant women. Virginia Dare, the first English child born in America (that we know of), was christened a few weeks after the ships arrived. It is this group—abandoned by the investors first because all English ships were recruited to meet the attack of the Spanish Armada in 1588, and then because of Ralegh's preoccupations at home and in Ireland—that has come down to us as *the* Lost Colonists. But they were only a fraction of the many people from abroad who melted into native populations in eastern North America. We know that they left Roanoke, probably shortly after they were deposited there, and it seems likely from the scanty evidence we have that they may have broken up into smaller groups, with some of them possibly going north to the site on the Chesapeake scouted the previous year. Like Juan Ortiz, they would have become Indians to all outward appearances. We can only imagine what knowledge was shared and how over the long days and nights that followed. Presumably the most successful and long-lived among them ceased to think of themselves as people apart from those they lived with. It does not seem too fanciful to assume that some colonists in Jamestown, founded twenty years after the last Roanoke colony, might have encountered descendants of earlier transatlantic migrants without knowing it.

Eastward Hoe, the comic play written by George Chapman, Ben Jonson, and John Marston in 1605, two years before Jamestown was founded, played with popular memories of Ralegh's Virginia and the possible survival of some of the families who made up the last group of colonists. In this satire on social mobility and the quest for riches, a knight named Sir Petronel Flash marries the daughter of a goldsmith with the intention of absconding to Virginia as soon as he gets control of her money. The ship captain, aptly named Seagull, encourages his company as they prepare to undertake the voyage, crudely employing the sexual imagery of a feminine continent: "Come boys, Virginia longs till we share the rest of her maidenhead." When one of the proposed venturers, Spendall, expresses surprise, saying, "Why, is she inhabited already with any English?" Seagull offers this garbled history lesson: "A whole country of English is there, man, bred of those that were left there in '79 [sic]. They have married with the Indians, and make 'em bring forth as beautiful faces as any we have in England: and therefore the Indians are so in love with 'em that all the treasure they have they lay at their feet." Sir Petronel Flash suggests a ceremonial beginning to the voyage by having the company dine aboard Sir Francis Drake's *Golden Hind* "that hath compassed the world" in hopes that "some good spirits of the waters should haunt the desert ribs of her."[44] Captain George Percy, one of the highest-ranking men in the initial Jamestown group, wrote an account of the colonists' exploration up the James River shortly after their arrival and of the people they met. In a very brief paragraph he mentions that they saw "a Savage Boy about the age of ten yeeres, which had a head of haire of a perfect yellow and a reasonable white skinne, which is a Miracle amongst all Savages." That was all he said; like Arthur Barlowe, he displayed a frustrating lack of curiosity and offered no speculation about whether the boy could have descended from the Roanoke colonists or from some other abandoned group. Neither Percy nor anyone else mentioned this boy again.[45]

The learning process from cross-cultural experience was even more complicated than the stories of the Old World people who lived among the Indians indicate. Transatlantic migration was not all one way. Americans learned about the lands across the ocean from their own people who had traveled the Atlantic eastward. Although many, perhaps most, died away from home, Americans who went or were taken to Europe or Africa sometimes made their way back to bring their new knowledge to their people. The most famous of the Indians in early American history who returned home after living in Europe is Squanto, who joined the Pilgrims after they settled on his people's land in New England in 1620. But Squanto is only one of many whose life stories are known to us.

The practice of taking Americans back to Europe began early. John Cabot brought three men from Newfoundland in the 1490s to present to the court of Henry VII. A man named Robert Fabian recorded his impressions of them upon their arrival and after they had become acclimatized to English life: "These were clothed in beasts skins, and did eate rawe flesh, and spake such speach that no man could understand them, and in their demeanor like to brute beastes, whom the King kept a time after. Of the which upon two yeeres after, I saw two apparelled after the maner of Englishmen in Westminster pallace, which that time I could not discerne from Englishmen, till I was learned what they were, but as for speach, I heard none of them utter one word."[46]

One family's story offers an intriguing glimpse into the surprising mixtures, pursuits, and dangers the Atlantic world presented. Doña Marina, also known as La Malinche, had been given to Mayans by her Aztec family as a child. When she was in her teens she became Hernan Cortés's consort and interpreter in the conquest of Mexico, and in 1522 they had a son, who was named Martín in honor of Cortés's father. Hernan took the boy to Spain when he was six, and Martín spent the rest of his life in Europe except for a disastrous expedition to Mexico in the 1560s with his half-brothers. Legitimized by the pope at Hernan Cortés's request, Don Martín became a soldier, fighting with Spanish forces in Germany, and a knight of the Order of Santiago. The name Santiago Matamoros (Saint James, the Killer of Moors) was traditionally invoked in wars against infidels, whether in America or in Europe. Family lore maintains that Martín Cortés died fighting against the Moors.[47]

In 1508 eight Tupinamba Indians from Brazil were brought to Rouen, where they participated, with many Frenchmen dressed as Indians, in a royal ceremony welcoming Henri II to the city. Then in 1528 Jacques Cartier's wife, Catherine des Granches, stood as godmother to "Catherine de Brézil" at her baptism. Cartier himself took two sons of Donnaconna, the man he identified as the "lord of Canada," in 1534 on his first voyage, promising to bring them back within a few months. On board the ship the French immediately dressed the two, Dom Agaya and Taignoagny, in "shirts and ribbons and in red caps, and put a little brass chain round the neck of each, at which they were greatly pleased." These two returned home next year on Cartier's second voyage, but relationships were rather strained; their people did not recognize them until they spoke in their language. Moreover, having learned the value the French placed on American products, "the two rogues" told their people that they could get much more in the way of trade goods for the things they brought to the French.

On this second voyage, Cartier traveled up the St. Lawrence River as far as Hochelaga, the site of modern Montreal, despite the reluctance of his hosts that he should do so. Donnaconna presented him with three children, a girl of ten or twelve and two younger boys. When Cartier refused the children, thinking they were a bribe to prevent him from carrying out his plans for exploration, he was assured that they were given "out of pure affection and in sign of alliance." Another chief gave him a "little girl" on the river voyage; the older girl, given by Donnaconna, ran away but was brought back.

At the end of their stay, Cartier tricked Donnaconna and his sons into coming aboard the ship, after which he took them captive along with "two other headmen." Donnaconna's people came to the riverbank and cried loudly all night for their chief. Finally, at midday the next day, Cartier brought Donnaconna on deck and showed him to the people, telling them that the chief and the nine other people he held captive would be returned "within ten or twelve moons." For the next several days the people brought presents to the ship for Cartier and for Donnaconna before they departed in May 1536. In fact, none of the ten ever saw Canada again. Cartier's third voyage was delayed for four years, and by 1540 all the captives but one girl were dead. Three had been baptized, including Donnaconna, who, according to the chronicler André Thevet, "died in France a good Christian, speaking French." When he finally returned to Canada, Cartier lied to Agona, the man who had succeeded Donnaconna. He admitted that the former chief was dead "and that his body rested in the earth," but claimed that "the rest stayed there [in France] as great Lordes, and were maried, and would not returne back into their Countrey."[48]

Spanish expeditions occasionally returned Indians who had lived among the Europeans. When Tristán de Luna y Arellano led an ill-fated colonizing expedition northward from the area of Pensacola on the Gulf Coast of Florida through present-day Alabama and into northern Georgia in 1559–1561, his men returned a Coosa woman to her people; she had been taken by De Soto two decades earlier and had lived in Mexico. So her experience was added to what her people had learned from the three men—Ottoman, African, and Spanish—who had deserted De Soto to stay in Coosa.[49]

Several Indians with European experience lived in the coastal area where Jamestown was settled. In 1561, as the Coosa woman was returning to her people, a young teenager named Paquiquineo joined a Spanish party that encountered him in coastal Carolina. Paquiquineo was a high-born Paspahegh man from Chesapeake Bay, and he was treated as an aristocrat by the Spanish among whom he lived in Havana, in Mexico City, and in Spain. At his baptism the viceroy of Mexico bestowed his own name on him, just as Pope Leo had given his name to al-Hasan al-Wazzan, and he became known as Don Luís de Velasco. Pedro Menéndez Marqués sent him with a party of Jesuits to found a mission among his people in the region the Spanish called Bahía de Santa María de Ajacán in 1570; they understood that Ajacán was the Algonquian name for Chesapeake Bay. They located their settlement on the York River. The Jesuits were so certain of their convert that they refused to bring soldiers to protect the mission. But Don Luís/Paquiquineo seemed deeply conflicted about his intended role as soon as they arrived back in his home region. For one thing, devastating drought had sown despair among the Americans, and, as they believed Don Luís/Paquiquineo had returned from the dead to help them, the pull from his relatives was very strong. Moreover, the site the Jesuits had chosen was a day and a half's journey from his home at Paspahegh on the James River, a distance that seemed to force him into a choice rather than allowing him to live in both cultures.

The first few days after the mission's establishment seemed hopeful; Don Luís/Paquiquineo refused political office and told his people that he had come only to lead them spiritually. He also begged the priests to send one of their number to baptize his dying three-year-old brother, which they did.

After just a few days, however, Don Luís/Paquiquineo abandoned the missionaries and returned to his Paspahegh village. Messengers sent to him asking him to return and pleading for food for the mission were rebuffed. Finally, in January 1571, Father Juan Baptista de Segura, the mission's leader, sent three Jesuits to try to persuade him; they were received cordially, but were then followed and killed on their return journey. Soon after, Don Luís/Paquiquineo led the party that attacked the mission and killed all the priests. We know as much as we do because Alonso de Olmos, a boy sent to serve the Jesuits, was spared, and he told the mission's story. There is some indication that Don Luís/Paquiquineo continued to honor the priests although he could not tolerate their efforts to change his people's culture. Father Juan Rogel, a leading Jesuit in Florida, wrote that "Don Luís summoned Alonso and told him to show the Indians how to bury the bodies of the Fathers as was the custom of the Christians. And so they dug a grave in the chapel where Mass had been said and there they are buried."[50]

Alonso lived among Chesapeake Bay Algonquians for almost two years before he was taken back to Spanish life, and his hosts would have learned more about Europeans from him. If Don Luís/Paquiquineo survived, he would have been in his early sixties when Jamestown was founded; the colony site was on Paspahegh land. Whether he lived to survey the arriving ships or not, his account of Europe and Europeans would have been well known among the Americans who greeted the newcomers.

The Roanoke ventures in the 1580s brought several Indians to England and back again. The initial reconnoitering expedition in 1584 brought two men from the Carolina Outer Banks, Manteo and Wanchese. Both spent the year in England and returned with the first colony under Ralph Lane in 1585. Manteo and Thomas Harriot, the Roanoke colony's scientist, worked all through the winter of 1584–85 to learn some of each other's language in preparation for the colony's establishment. Wanchese severed all ties with the English on his return, but Manteo remained with them, returning to England when Drake's fleet took the first colony home, accompanied by another coastal Carolina Algonquian named Towaye. Both came back with the final colony in 1587. On August 13 of that year John White, governor of the colony, recorded the christening of "our Savage Manteo" and named him Lord of Roanoke "in reward of his faithfull service."[51] Manteo's life after the 1587 colony broke up is unrecorded, as are Wanchese's and Towaye's. Yet another man, captured by Richard Grenville when he came to the relief of the earlier colony in 1586, lived out the rest of his life in England in Grenville's household in Bideford. The church register there records his baptism with the name "Raleigh" in March 1588 and his burial in April 1589.[52]

Also in 1588 a Spanish expedition in the northern reaches of Chesapeake Bay took two Indian captives. One, probably captured near the Potomac River, was a "youth of about fifteen years of age." After that they saw no more Indians on the bay's west banks. But on the Eastern Shore, Indians came wading out to their boat, and "the Spaniards seized one of them and sailed away." One of these men died soon after of "grief"; the other was converted to Christianity before dying of smallpox in Santo Domingo.[53] Jamestown colonist Ralph Hamor reported in 1614 that the neighboring Indians hated the Spanish, "whose name is odious amongst them." He said their hatred stemmed from Powhatan's father's having been driven out of the West Indies into the North American mainland, possibly a garbled recollection of Don Luís's story.[54] By the end of the century, that recollection had come to center on Opechancanough, Powhatan's successor. Virginia-born Robert Beverley wrote in his *History and Present State of Virginia* (1705) that the early colonists thought Powhatan and Opechancanough were brothers, "but by the Indians he was not so esteem'd. For they say he was a Prince of a Foreign nation, and came to them a great Way from the South-West: And by their Accounts, we suppose him to have come from the Spanish Indians, some-where near Mexico, or the Mines of St. Barbe."[55]

The voyages we know about are just a fraction of the total; European ships continued to enter Chesapeake Bay during the decades before Jamestown was founded, and their encounters left few or no traces in the records. Historian Alden T. Vaughan estimates that something close to twenty Indians were in England before 1600. One tantalizing document recorded a grant to some "Virginians" in 1603 as a reward for demonstrating canoe handling on the Thames. It is possible that these Indians had been seized by a reconnoitering voyage that year. Shortly after the Jamestown settlers arrived, Captain John Smith was a captive for several weeks of Indians who were tributary to Powhatan, and he was exhibited in a village that had suffered such an atrocity. A European ship had entered the river, and its men had "beene kindly entertained by Powhatan their Emperour." The ship had then moved on to a Rappahannock town where, despite "being received with the like kindnesse," the captain "slue the King" and kidnapped several people. The Indians wanted to know whether Smith was the author of this terrible violation of hospitality, but soon realized that he could not be; the ship's captain had been "a great man" and Smith was simply too short. We know nothing more about the ship's country of origin or the fate of the kidnapped Rappahannocks.[56]

Smith was befriended by a native from the Potomac River named Mosco: "We supposed him some French mans sonne, because he had a thicke blacke bush beard, and the Salvages seldome have any at all." Smith wrote that Mosco considered the English "his Countrymen." Mosco gave invaluable aid in defense of Smith's exploring party. He even decided to change his name to Uttasantasough, which was the name by which the Chesapeake Algonquians called the English.[57] Like Garcilaso the Inca, Mosco may have felt that he belonged fully to no group in the new Chesapeake.

The essential ground of transatlantic ventures in the late sixteenth and early seventeenth centuries was the accumulation of personal experience, intimate knowledge, that individuals brought to the project and that, however invisibly, underlay all relationships. Boundary permeability characterized these early experiences, especially those in which one or a small group of Europeans was absorbed into an Indian community. Some people crossed lines several times, and often at a young age. Many individuals found themselves in ambiguous circumstances that forced them to make choices.

Contemporaries analyzed these choices in terms of clothing; people wore their hearts on their sleeves, and a change of clothing signaled a change of heart. When a Christian converted to Islam, he was said to be "taking the turban," just as Europeans when they encountered Christians who had been living among Indians immediately cut their hair and dressed them in European clothes. Menéndez de Avilés went so far as to bring woolen cloth and tailors with him so that he could have clothes made as he found prospective returnees.[58] But the transition was not always easy. They wanted to save their long hair after it was cut off; or they were uncomfortable wearing European clothes. Some apparently wanted to make a statement by their self-fashioning: Cabeza de Vaca and his companions appeared in church in Mexico City "dressed in skins, just as they had arrived from the land of Florida." English women and men freed from captivity in North Africa put on the clothes they had worn as prisoners when they walked in huge processions meant to bring home to sympathetic audiences the terrible conditions they had suffered.[59] Some part of themselves was embodied in those alien forms, and it was not to be given up by a simple act of divestiture.

4

English Hunger for the New

IN 1608 A MAN named Thomas Trevilian or Trevelyon created an elaborate commonplace book, a volume in which he recorded information and images that were important to him. Many people kept commonplace books at the time, and most consisted of passages they copied out of things they had read which they deemed significant. But Trevilian's book, and another he made in 1616, comprised hundreds of pages of his own renditions of images depicting important people and themes in biblical and world history; medical and scientific lore; proverbs and renditions of the seven deadly sins, seven virtues, and nine muses; and tables for calculating everything from the dates of agricultural fairs all over England to the liturgical calendar. He included several sample alphabets and garden designs, and he often depicted himself as a spectator, especially in biblical scenes.

Nicholas Barker, who edited the 1616 book, argues that Trevilian, who was sixty years old in 1608, designed the books as models for the "newly fashionable art of embroidery"; he characterizes them as giving an "astonishingly large and diverse picture of the mental furniture of England at the turn of the sixteenth century." Trevilian's 1608 commonplace book includes one fascinating table that illustrates how English people viewed the world. Titled "A Table of Rhombe and

Distaunce of some of the most famous Cities of the world. From the Honorable Citie of London," it listed, in descending order of distance, places from "Quinzay" to "Middleborow." ("Quinzay" was the name Marco Polo gave to Hangzhou; it is his version of "Jing-shi," meaning "golden city.") The column of names was followed by columns giving the direction of each on the compass dial, the distance in miles from London, the "tyme of sune rysing before it douth at London" in hours and minutes, and the hours and minutes of the longest day there. "Quinzay" was followed by "Calicut," then "Virginia, Babilon, Jerusalem, Grand Cairo, Alexandria, Moscove, Constantinople," and so on. The distance to Virginia was listed as 3,650 miles west-southwest of London, and the sun was said to rise there five hours and thirty-two minutes before London's sunrise; its longest day was fourteen hours and twenty-eight minutes. Although in a section illustrating the four continents Trevilian depicted Hispaniola, Cuba, and Peru as feather-adorned figures in the style of contemporary maps, Virginia was the only American site he included in his list of the cities of the world, and it thus takes its place in the English mental universe at the time Jamestown was founded.[1]

As Trevilian's work demonstrates, the English public was keenly interested in the world and in understanding how to categorize the knowledge about all the new things, people, and cultures of which specimens and descriptions were now available to them. People who traveled were in a position to perform a service for the nation by keeping their eyes open and bringing back solid observations. Travel, and writing about travel, was not just a matter of randomly visiting foreign places and spinning accounts of them. Properly done, it was a key source of information for the nation, and dozens of books about how to travel, what to look for, and the best way to report one's findings were published during this period.

One such book, Thomas Palmer's *An Essay of the Meanes how to make our Travailes, into forraine Countries, the more profitable and hon-*

Names of the Cities.	Rhombe or poynt of the Compase,	Diftance in miles	Sune rifeth H · M		Longeft day Hour	Minnig
Quinzay.	Eaft.by.South.	5300.	8.-52.	A.	14.-	52.
Calecut.	Sou, Ea, by, Eaft,	4840.	s.-48.	A.	12.-	40.
Virginia,	Weft, Sou, Weft,	3650.	s.-32.	Po.	14.-	28.
Babilon.	Eaft, Sou, Eaft,	2710.	3.-46.	A.	14-	14.
Jerufalem.	Sou, Eeaft, by Eaft,	2320.	3.-6.	A.	14.-	14.
Grand Cair.	Sou, Eaft, by, Eaff	2260.	2.-50.	A.	14.	2.
Alexandria,	Sou, Eaft, by, Eaft	2120.	2.-36.	A.	14.-	6.
Mofcove.	Eaft, by, North,	1620.	2.-58.	A.	14.17.-	8.
Conftantinople	Eaft, Sou, Eaft,	1480.	2.-22.	A.	17.15.-	24.
Athens,	Sou, Eaft, by, Eaft,	1440.	2.-2.	A.	1514.-	52.
Colmogro,	Nor, Eaft, by, Eaft,	1380.	2.-28.	A.	20.-	6.
Marocco,	South, by, Weft,	1290.	0.-24.	Po.	14.-	13.
Rome,	South, Eaft,	896.	1.-6.	A.	15.-	4.
Siuell,	South, Wefterly,	880.	0.-31.	Po.	14.-	40.
Lisbone.	South, South, Weft,	830.	0.-33.	Po.	14.-	44.
Vienn.	Eaft, South, Eaft,	776.	1.-18.	A.	15.-	56.
Venice.	South, Eaft, by, Eaft,	720.	1.-4.	A.	15.-	32.
Prage.	Eaft, by, South,	640	1.-5.	A.	16.-	10
Copenhge.	North, Eaft, by, Eaft,	510.	0.-50.	A.	17.-	22,
Marcellis.	South, Eaft, by, South,	450.	0.-32.	A.	15.-	16.
Geneua,	South, Eaft,	440.	0.-32.	A.	15.-	34.
Burdeaux.	South, Eafterly,	390.	0.-1.	A.	15.-	26,
Rochell.	South, Wefterly,	340.	0.-2.	Po.	15.-	36.
Dublin,	North, Weft, by, North	290.	0.-36.	Po.	16.-	44.
Edenbrough,	North, Nor, Weft,	286.	0.-16.	Po.	16.17.-	22.
Paris	South, Eaft, by, South	240.	0.-14.	A.	16.-	0.
Antwerpe.	Eaft, South, Eaft,	220.	0.-22.	A.	16.-	16.
Middleborow.	Eafte,	142.	0.-24.	A.	16.-	2s.

A Table of the Rhombe and Diftaunce. of fome of the moft famous Cities of the world, from the Honorable Citie of London.

This former Table confifteth. s. Columnes: the firft whereof, conteineth, the names of Cities: the fecond, the rhombe or poynt of the Compaffe they beare, from London: The third, the diftaunce of each of them from the fayd Citie: the fourth the tyme of fune ryfing before it douth at london: the.s. the longeft day in thek plaeces.

Thomas Trevilian's table of "the most famous Cities of the world," and their direction and distance from London. By permission of the Folger Shakespeare Library.

ourable, was published in London in 1606 as the Virginia Company
was planning its initial colony. His long book gave complicated instructions about the kinds of information travelers should gather and
offered elaborate outlines and charts of his argument, presumably as a
model of the orderly presentation the topic called for, and one he
hoped his readers would emulate. He began with the question of what
types of people should be encouraged to travel and its different purposes, and argued that there was already too much disorderly travel.
Much of the book was devoted to ways of judging the strength and determination of any population, for example, "whether the people of a
Nation bee Warlike, or Effeminate," and the attributes of its government, laws, and customs. Further, the traveler was to observe what
commodities each country produced and consumed through trade, and
the natural situation of the land. Sir Francis Bacon made the same
points briefly in his essay "Of Travel." Such knowledge gained by observant and methodical travelers could be of inestimable benefit to
England. Clearly George Sandys had had just such an agenda in mind
in writing about his tour of the Muslim world.[2]

In addition to observant travelers, another important source of
knowledge was "intelligencers," people who collected information and
disseminated it in newsletters to their subscribers, merchants and other
prominent men who needed to know what was going on in order to
plan their own strategies. John Pory earned his living as an intelligencer, and he continued in this role when he went to Virginia as the colony's secretary. Many intelligencers, like Pory, were well versed in several languages, and they translated books written by knowledgeable
foreigners as well as collecting news.

Every literate person wanted to know about the new. The English reading public avidly devoured books on Eastern regions and the
Muslim religion and its attendant culture. Richard Knolles's massive
Generall Historie of the Turkes was reprinted six times in the seventeenth century. George Sandys's *Relation of a Journey* (1615) was a

large, heavily illustrated, expensive book, yet it went through nine editions by 1683. A second edition, indicating that the stock of the first had sold out in just six years, was published in 1621, just before Sandys embarked for Virginia. The owner of one surviving copy of that second edition created an elaborate handwritten index to the book on its last page so that he could go back and find passages on specific topics. Part of Sandys's book was anthologized, along with fragments of others by Sir Francis Bacon and James Howel, in a 1663 book titled *The Vertues of Coffee*.

Scholars eagerly sought opportunities to meet learned Muslims. Ahmad bin Qasim (al-Hajari), who had fled Spain for Morocco, accepted a commission to go to Europe to seek compensation for Muslims (Qasim called them Andalusians) who had been robbed as they were expelled from Spain on the orders of Philip III in 1609. This mission lasted two years, beginning in 1611. Qasim wrote a long account of his travels, which is now lost, although we do have a condensed version of his narrative, *Kitab Nasir al-Din ala al-Qawm al-Kafirin* (The Book of the Protector of Religion against the Unbelievers). This shorter account concentrated on his encounters with Europeans and their conversations or disputations about religion and culture. Qasim, who knew the Bible thoroughly, was repeatedly drawn into discussions of religion. He was invited to a dinner in Paris where all the guests wanted to discuss religious issues with him. His host assured Qasim that he would be served only foods that were lawful for Muslims. But he also demonstrated the limits of his understanding when he introduced Qasim to the guest of honor as "a Turkish man"; Qasim remarked that to the French, the terms "Turk" and "Muslim" were interchangeable. Qasim met several people who were extremely knowledgeable about Islam and about the cultures of North Africa. In Paris he formed a relationship with Thomas Van Erpe, known as Erpenius, the most prominent European Arabist of the time. Erpenius eagerly sought instruction in classical Arabic from Qasim, whose knowledge of the language was superior to that of anyone with whom he had been able to study thus far.[3]

English scholars, like their counterparts throughout western Europe, pursued a lively interest in Arabic and in the manuscripts, including the Koran, written in that language. In the later sixteenth century it became possible to study Arabic at Cambridge University, and a formal professorship in Arabic was created there in 1632 and at Oxford in 1636; Cambridge acquired a manuscript version of the Koran in 1631. Erpenius had begun his study in England before returning to his native Netherlands, where he established the study of Arabic at Leiden University in 1613. Scholars longed to read the texts of the ancient philosophers that had been preserved in Arabic translations far superior to those previously available in Europe. John Selden, among others, amassed collections of books in Arabic for study by himself and others, and Selden sponsored importation of Arabic type so that books containing words in that language could be published in England. A flawed Latin translation of the Koran had existed for some time, and the first English translation, done from a poor-quality French version, was published in early 1649.[4]

English readers were as curious about America as they were about Islam and the East. Early reports sent back lists of words in native languages so that scholars could study them to figure out what Old World diaspora the Indians were descended from. Descriptions of Indian dress, posture, social organization, and religion served the same purpose. The most important and influential English report of America's resources and people came out of the earliest colony, Roanoke, through the partnership of Manteo, the coastal Carolina Algonquian man who twice went to England, the Renaissance scientist Thomas Harriot, and the painter John White.

The team's instructions from Sir Walter Ralegh, the colony's sponsor, can be inferred from those given to Thomas Bavin, a surveyor who

A weroan or great Lorde of Virginia. III.

 He Princes of Virginia are attyred in fuche manner as is expreffed in this figure. They weare the haire of their heades long and bynde opp the ende of thefame in a knot vnder thier eares. Yet they cutt the topp of their heades from the forehead to the nape of the necke in manner of a cokfcombe, ftirkinge a faier lóge pecher of fome berd att the Begininge of the crefte vppun their foreheads, and another fhort one on bothe feides about their eares. They hange at their eares ether thicke pearles, or fomwhat els, as the clawe of fome great birde, as cometh in to their fanfye. Moreouer They ether pownes, or paynt their forehead, cheeks, chynne, bodye, armes, and leggs, yet in another forte then the inhabitantz of Florida. They weare a chaine about their necks of pearles or beades of copper, wich they muche efteeme, and ther of wear they alfo brafelets ohn their armes. Vnder their brefts about their bellyes appeir certayne fpotts, whear they vfe to lett them felues bloode, when they are ficke. They hange before thé the fkinne of fome beafte verye feinelye dreffet in fuche forte, that the tayle hangéth downe behynde. They carye a quiuer made of fmall rufhes holding their bowe readie bent in on hand, and an arrowe in the other, radie to defend themfelues. In this manner they goe to warr, or tho their folemne feafts and banquetts. They take muche pleafure in huntinge of deer wher of theris great ftore in the contrye, for yt is fruitfull, pleafant, and full of Goodly woods. Yt hathe alfo ftore of riuers full of diuers forts of fifhe. When they go to battel they paynt their bodyes in the moft terible manner that thei can deuife.

DeBry engraving from John White's painting of a coastal Carolina Algonquian leader. Courtesy of the John Carter Brown Library at Brown University.

was supposed to accompany an America-bound English voyage in the early 1580s. Although that voyage never took place, the detailed instructions survive. Bavin was to carry an assortment of clocks, compasses, and other measuring instruments along with pen and pencils, paper, ink, and various colors for recording his observations. Not only was he to note the location and qualities of various types of commodities that might prove valuable, but he was also directed to "drawe to lief one of each kinde of thing that is strange to us in England," and make pictures of American natives "in their apparell" and with their weapons. His backers were particularly interested in having him record the time and location of a solar eclipse due to occur in June 1582. They called for elaborate measures to ensure precise timing, which, when combined with measurements taken in England, would allow scientists to calculate the circumference of the earth.[5]

The observations made by Harriot and White with Manteo's assistance produced a remarkable record. Harriot's book, *A Briefe and True Report of the new found land of Virginia*, was published as a small volume in 1588 to encourage investors. Then his book, along with other Roanoke-related documents, was reprinted in 1589 in the first edition of the large collection of firsthand accounts of worldwide travel compiled by Richard Hakluyt and again in the massive second edition of his *Principal Navigations, Voyages, Traffiques, and Discoveries of the English Nation* (1598–1600). Even more dramatically, the Flemish publisher Theodor DeBry procured a set of the watercolors White had painted out of his American experience and had copperplate engravings of them made in his Frankfurt workshop. He printed these together with Harriot's *Briefe and True Report* in the first book of his great multivolume collection of American travels, called the *Grands Voyages*, published in four languages in 1590. Many copies were commissioned by wealthy patrons, for whom the engravings were carefully colored by hand, often with highlights of gold leaf. News of America was precious, and these volumes were rendered even more precious by their embellishment. The engravings were reprinted again and again and came to represent all Indians in the eyes of most Europeans.[6]

As books poured from the presses, ordinary men and women were able to experience the new in a wide variety of ways: in drama, gardens, foods, even new vogues in clothing and hairstyles. Fashionable gardens necessarily contained exotic plants. Prominent and wealthy patrons, seeking to convert their solid but old residences, some built in medieval times, into modern showplaces, sent representatives to find new and glamorous plants abroad. The more unusual they were, the better, and vast sums were spent on such expeditions. Ordinary travelers were also commissioned to bring back specimens. Within a few decades of Columbus's voyages, a Spanish physician named Nicolas Monardes created a garden of American plants in Seville. He commissioned mariners to bring back seeds, slips, and plants. His efforts expanded the number of species known to Europeans. As a doctor, Monardes experimented with these new plants to discover their medicinal properties, and he published a book providing directions for their use so that all Europe could benefit from them. The colorful flower *Monarda*, commonly known as bee balm, commemorates Monardes's pioneering efforts.

Later in the sixteenth century John Gerard traveled throughout Europe seeking plants for his patron, Queen Elizabeth's chief minister, Lord Burghley. Then in the early seventeenth century a prominent gardener named John Tradescant made numerous trips on an ever-widening circuit. He first went to the Netherlands and then to France, where he conferred with such important counterparts as the king's gardener, Jean Robin. Often he joined diplomatic missions, as when he accompanied the royal envoy Sir Dudley Digges to Muscovy. In other cases he actually went as a soldier on military expeditions, as in a 1627 campaign to aid French Protestants at La Rochelle, in order to get where he needed to go for his plants. He signed on with the English fleet to Algiers "that went against the Pyrates in the yeare 1620" and brought back the fruit known as the "Argier Apricocke." As he rose to become the king's gardener, his gardens became famous for the rare specimens they contained.[7]

American plants began to appear in European gardens very early, although most specimens did not survive. Venturers were eager to comply with calls to be on the lookout for unknown varieties. Those interested in the larger world moved in the same circles. George Sandys and Captain John Smith were Tradescant's friends; Smith remembered the gardener by a gift of books in his will. Tradescant invested in the Virginia Company, particularly in a company-sponsored venture led by another friend, Captain Samuel Argall. Tradescant's son, also named John, went to Virginia at least three times on the king's commission for plant-gathering expeditions. The effect of broad efforts to collect new plants was stupendous. Scholars estimate that the number of plant species known to Europeans rose from around five hundred at the time of Monardes's birth to over twenty thousand at the end of the seventeenth century.[8]

Ordinary Europeans, those not invited to the royal gardens, still had access to these new things in a variety of ways. John Frampton, a merchant involved in trade with Spain, translated Monardes's book and published it as *Joyefull Newes Out of the Newe founde World* in 1577; the title page praised the "singular vertues" of American herbs, "which being well applyed, bring such present remedie for all diseases, as may seeme altogether incredible: notwithstanding by practice found out to be true."[9] Two more editions appeared before the end of the sixteenth century. Gerard published an illustrated book, which came to be known as *Gerard's Herbal*, describing the plants he grew; it was corrected and expanded by Thomas Johnson in the seventeenth century with admiring references to John Tradescant.

Meanwhile another author, John Parkinson, published books celebrating, among other attributes, the sheer beauty of the flowers then present in England, thus adding to the more practical emphasis of earlier books; Parkinson's herbal was excerpted in *The Vertues of Coffee*. Parkinson frequently referred to his "very loving good friend" John Tradescant and his immense efforts. In his description of plums, he wrote that "the choysest for goodnesse, and rarest for knowledge, are to be had of my very good friend Master John Tradescante, who hath wonderfully laboured to obtaine all the rarest fruits hee can heare off in any place of Christendome, Turky, yea or the whole world." Parkinson also featured "the soon-fading Spider-wort of Virginia, or Tradescant his Spider-wort" (*Tradescantia*), for which "the Christian world is indebted unto that painfull industrious Searcher, and lover of all natures varieties, John Tradescant . . . who first received it of a friend, that brought it out of Virginia, thinking it to bee the Silke Grasse that groweth there." That friend may have been George Sandys; we know Sandys collected plants for Tradescant. For his part, Tradescant treated Parkinson's book as his principal catalogue for the next few years and used the blank pages bound in at the end to record each new plant as it came into his garden.[10] Tradescant published his own plant list in 1634 with the title *Catalogus Plantarum in Horto Johannis Tradescanti nascentium*.

Another way that Europeans consumed the new was through early museums, called cabinets of curiosities. These brought together exotic items from across the world, and people came to marvel. The Tradescants, who collected all kinds of things as well as plants, opened a museum, called The Ark, in their London home in 1631. In 1656 the younger John Tradescant greatly expanded his father's description of their plant collection with a catalogue of The Ark in his *Musaeum Tradescantium: or, a Collection of Rarities, preserved at South-Lambeth neer London*. Their collection, part of which can still be seen at the Ashmolean Museum in Oxford, contained, among many other items, a whole decorated deerskin that tradition says had belonged to

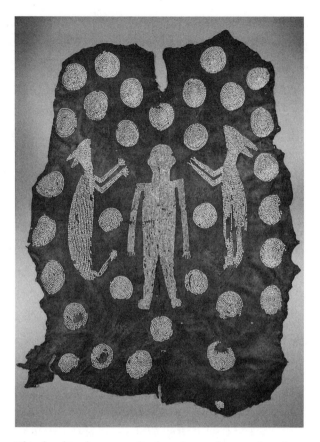

This deerskin, known as Powhatan's mantle, may have been a map, with the circles of shells representing polities within Powhatan's domain. Ashmolean Museum, Oxford.

Powhatan. The Ark was considered a great educational site. Peter Mundy, an enthusiastic traveler, recorded spending an entire day there seeing

> beasts, fowle, fishes, serpents, wormes (reall, although dead and dryed), pretious stones and other Armes, Coines, shells, fethers, etts. of sundrey Nations, Countries, forme, Coullours; also diverse Curiosities in Carvinge, paintinge, etts., as 80 faces carved on a Cherry stone, Pictures to bee seene by a Celinder which other-

wise appear like confused blotts, Medalls of Sondrey sorts, etts. Moreover, a little garden with divers outlandish herbes and flowers, whereof some that I had not seen elswhere but in India, being supplyed by Noblemen, Gentlemen, Sea Commaunders, etts.

He thought one could see "more Curiosities" in one day in The Ark than if "hee spent all his life in Travell." A few days later Mundy went to see a unicorn's horn at the Tower of London.[11]

Many English cabinets of curiosities contained American items, and these were displayed mixed with things from all over including, in one case, a mummified child and an American canoe in a cabinet belonging to Sir Walter Cope. These sights were enormously popular. Shakespeare's *Tempest* satirized the curiosities craze when his character Trinculo speculated about the possibility of making a fortune by bringing home rarities, saying of the English public, "When they will not give a doit to a lame beggar, they will lay out ten to see a dead Indian."[12]

Just as they were eager to see items brought from afar, contemporaries were fascinated by stories of their compatriots who were caught in the great dramas being played out in the regions where different cultures clashed and meshed. Most of the people who faced cross-cultural challenges are lost to us, but some emerged as famous figures in their own times. The English public avidly consumed their published stories, and the London theaters presented numerous plays reenacting their exploits. Drake, Hawkins, and Ralegh were celebrated in later centuries as writers sought the origins of the British Empire, but at the time it was the adventures of ordinary men and women raised to greatness by their own heroic feats that thrilled audiences. Through them, English men and women who never ventured abroad experienced the wider world. Central to this exciting literature was the risk and allure of conversion to alien religions and cultures; all engagement abroad presented such dangers, and the English knew that those who were flexible enough to cope might also be especially vulnerable.

Sir Thomas Stukeley became the hero of many plays and ballads; by his death Stukeley achieved the stature that had escaped him in life, and his story became the subject of romance, despite the massive distrust he had inspired in official circles. Before the sixteenth century was out, there were two popular plays about his life and death. One, probably by George Peele, was *The Battle of Alcazar, fought in Barbarie, betweene Sebastian king of Portugall, and Abdelmelec king of Marocco. With the death of Captaine Stukeley. As it was sundrie times plaid by the Lord high Admirall his servants* (1594). The other was by an unknown author; *The Famous Historye of the life and death of Captaine Thomas Stukeley. With his marriage to Alderman Curteis Daughter, and valiant ending of his life at the Battaile of Alcazar* was registered with the Stationers' Company in London in 1600 and printed in 1605. Stukeley's life was also the subject of popular ballads, and some of these were anthologized in the seventeenth century.

These plays were prototypes of a genre that became very popular at the end of the sixteenth century: dramas in which men rose above their circumstances by uncommon exploits abroad. As Thomas Churchyard, poet and chronicler of the many overseas campaigns in which he fought over thirty years, wrote in his *A pleasant Discourse of Court and Wars*:

> But such that seekes, for fame in foren place,
> Forsakes great ease, & welth where they were bred,
> Are speshall men, and do deserve more grace,
> Than all the rest, what ever may be sed.
> Leaves wife and friends, to try the tumbling seas,
> Makes open sale, of life and all they have,

Are men that may, both prince and country pleas,
Who shall of right, be honord to their grave.

Churchyard contrasted men who sought wealth and fame in overseas exploits with those who "spend their time in vaine" attempting to win favor at court. Ralegh, who was "among the worthiest sort," successfully combined the life of the courtier with that of the man of action; but most, like Stukeley, foundered in the attempt to gain the monarch's attention:

The court is but a pleasant cage
For birds to plume their feather in,
A joy to youth, a paine to age
Where many lose, and few do win.

Churchyard put his finger on an essential element of the path to true renown: publication. Of Ralegh he wrote, "Who reads his booke, and waies what he hath don, / Shall sound his fame, as far as shines the sun."[13]

Captain John Smith's story seemed tailor-made for the themes of these fashionable dramas.[14] He was born into an ordinary family and given the most common of names, and yet, through a series of incredible adventures, he succeeded in raising himself to gentle status and command of the colony in Virginia. Moreover, as he wrote in dedicating his 1624 *Generall Historie of Virginia, New-England and the Summer Isles* to Frances Howard, duchess of Richmond and Lennox, "heretofore honorable and vertuous Ladies . . . have offred me rescue and protection in my greatest dangers: even in forraine parts, I have felt reliefe from that sex."[15] There is documentary evidence of a 1623 play, *The Hungarian Lion*, that may have been based on Smith's adventures, but neither the text nor any record of performances survives.

Captain John Smith. Courtesy of the John Carter Brown Library at Brown University.

After his American years were over, Smith lived mainly in London and wrote about the theory and practice of colonization. He always emphasized the importance of experience for those who wanted to succeed in overseas exploits. High-born men might or might not be able to cope in novel situations, but only those who had known foreign cultures and circumstances could truly lead. Despite his own exploits "in some parts of Africa, and America, as in the most partes of Europe and Asia by land or sea," even he had "againe to learne his Lecture by experience" in Jamestown. In his *Generall Historie* he recommended New England as a good place for "men that have great spirits and small meanes."[16]

Smith knew that his story, embedded within the great saga of England's early colonial ventures, was his only capital. By the time he wrote his autobiography, *The True Travels, Adventures, and Observations of Captaine John Smith*, these dramas in which men of ordinary birth assumed extraordinary proportions through their exploits in exotic lands were a subject of consuming interest in the London literary world, and Smith clearly fashioned his own story to fit those categories. Cross-cultural adventures, with their attendant danger of the taint of apostasy, sent a frisson of horror and fascination through theater audiences. Women featured in these plays as the agents of men's salvation or damnation. Smith had already told the story of his captivity by "the great emperor Powhatan" in Virginia and his rescue by Pocahontas in his principal work, *The Generall Historie*, six years before he wrote of his earlier adventures in eastern Europe. By the time the *Generall Historie* was published, Pocahontas had come to England as the Christian Lady Rebecca Rolfe, mother of baby Thomas Rolfe, and her visit had caused a sensation. In his *True Travels*, Smith told the story of his earlier captivity and rescue by Charatza Tragabigzanda, casting himself as one who had fiercely resisted conversion into an Ottoman subject. Smith saw the dramatic possibilities in his own story and presented those remembered events from decades earlier in a form that would draw the attention of the world he then inhabited.

Dramas on these themes abounded in London. Ben Jonson's 1609 play *Epicene, or the Silent Woman* conflated the potential stages of action in referring to impoverished knights who sought to "repair" themselves "by Istanbul, Ireland, or Virginia."[17] Some plays, such as *The famous historye of the life and death of Captaine Thomas Stukeley* or Richard Daborne's *Christian Turn'd Turke: or, The Tragicall Lives and Deaths of the Two Famous Pyrates, Ward and Dansiker* (1612), took off from the published life stories of real people who became renegades and in some cases turned their coats more than once. John Ward, who was English, and Simon Dansiker, a Fleming, were the subject of two books, both published in 1609. Daborne, in turning Ward's story into drama, condemned the English renegade as an apostate. The dramatic high point of the play was his circumcision, as required by his new Muslim faith. In the play, the character Ward killed himself in remorse amid the wreck of his fortunes, but as Captain John Smith pointed out, Ward the man actually lived in considerable opulence in Tunis.[18]

The theme of circumcision, or even castration, featured prominently in these dramas. Philip Massinger's very popular play *The Renegado, or The Gentleman of Venice* (1624), though set in Tunis, portrayed a man who, like Smith, was the captive of an Ottoman woman. *The Renegado*'s Donusa, a Turkish princess, owned an English slave named Carazie who had been castrated so that as a eunuch he could enter the princess's living quarters. Carazie, punning on the English unit of weight, the stone (fourteen pounds), and the vernacular for testicles, told his mistress that he "was made lighter by two stone weight, at least, to be fit to serve you!"[19]

In many plays, as in Smith's story, the central character resisted the lure of Islam and the riches of the East. The Moluccas, a chain of islands in Indonesia, were the scene of John Fletcher's play *The Island Princess*, written in 1620–21. Its hero was Armusia, a Portuguese ven-

turer who mightily resisted forced conversion to Islam, which was required if he was to marry the princess, Quisara. Armusia's steadfastness
was so impressive that Quisara chose to convert to Christianity—as
did Donusa in *The Renegado*.[20] In Thomas Heywood's *The Fair Maid of
the West, or A Girl Worth Gold*, Part I (1602), the cross-dressed hero-
ine, Bess Bridges, embarked on a privateer to avenge the death of her
lover, who she believed had been killed by the Spanish. The ship,
whose sides were blackened with pitch, was called *The Negro*. Bess and
her lover were reunited at the Moroccan court, where she had won the
sultan's admiration without surrendering either her virginity or her religious identity.[21]

Africa south of the Mediterranean rim was another exotic region that
the English consumed emblematically. John Hawkins, whose early
foray into the slave trade was so disastrous, nonetheless became associated with it in the popular mind After his second slaving voyage to the
coast of Africa, Queen Elizabeth granted him a coat of arms; its design
featured a bound slave, "a demye moore in his proper coolor bounde in
a corde as captyve" with gold bands on his arms and gold earrings.
Similarly, the queen gave Sir Francis Drake a sumptuous locket with
her portrait in miniature on one side and on the reverse a cameo
showing an African head in classical profile superimposed on a European head. Whereas the Hawkins arms depict an African enslaved,
David Shields argues that the Drake jewel actually celebrated the alliance Drake had forged with African-born Cimarrons who had liber-
ated themselves from Spanish control in Panama. Drake, who had
been in the Caribbean with Hawkins as a young man in the 1560s,
commanded his own fleet in 1576; Cimarron aid allowed him to capture an immense Spanish treasure.[22]

When James I, the first of the Stuart monarchs, ascended the throne
at Elizabeth's death in 1603, his triumphal entry into London through
a series of specially constructed arches was replete with representations

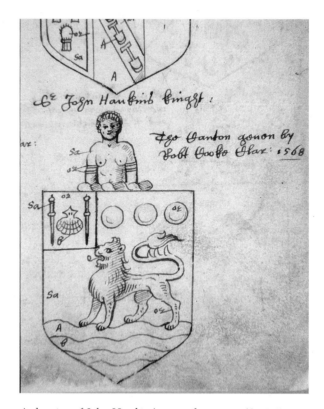

A drawing of John Hawkins's coat of arms, 1568. College of Arms MS Miscellaneous Grants 1, f.148.

of the world's people. The Stuarts loved court masques, lavish private productions in which the queen and courtiers, male and female, often took part. In 1605 Ben Jonson and Inigo Jones inaugurated their stormy partnership with a stunningly staged production, *The Masque of Blackness*. This spectacle brought the staid Tudor-era masques to a new level. For their roles as "noble Moors," Queen Anne and her ladies donned blackface, apparently the first instance of this practice. The prologue, citing "Leo the African," depicted the ladies as daughters of "a river in Æthiopia, famous by the name of Niger," and Niger as the son of Oceanus. They were presented inside a "great concave shell like mother of pearl." Jonson's text describes Niger's offspring as "his beauteous race," and goes on:

Who, though but black in face,
Yet are they bright,
And full of life and light,
To prove that beauty best
Which not only the color but the feature
Assures unto the creature.

Although they were renowned for their beauty, Niger's daughters had become depressed on learning that "some few poor brainsick men, styled poets here with you," praised pale beauty above all. As they had been burned black by the sun, they were advised by the moon, whose name, according to Jonson, was Æthiopia, to seek a temperate climate where their skin would become fair. Albion, or Britannia, was the land where the beneficial light of the virtuous king's presence could "blanch an Æthiop." John Pory, the future Virginia colony secretary whose recently published translation of Leo Africanus's *Geographical Historie of Africa* was cited in the prologue, was present at court for this production. *The Masque of Beauty* returned to the theme in 1608. Soon feathered crowns, recognizable as emblematic of America, began to appear in court masques.[23]

Theater was not only a way to understand the exotic but also a vehicle for representing Englishness abroad. English and French merchants gave great banquets "to the sound of music from violins and other instruments," according to one report, which argued that it was this lavish entertainment that won the newcomers a share in the coastal African commerce. The Venetian envoy in Istanbul disgustedly described early English envoys entering the city on Good Friday in 1583 "accompanied by a continual music of trumpets and drums" and reported that the Muslims "abhorred" such disrespect to Christianity.[24]

Sir William Keeling kept a journal, now lost, of the East India voyage he commanded in 1607. His ship, the *Red Dragon*, had to land on the Sierra Leone coast when his crew became disabled by scurvy. The

Design by Inigo Jones for the costume and makeup to be worn by Queen Anne and her ladies when they appeared as daughters of Niger. Devonshire Collection, Chatsworth. Reproduced by permission of the Duke of Devonshire and the Trustees of the Chatsworth Settlement. Photograph: Photographic Survey, Courtauld Institute of Art.

fragments of Keeling's journal that were published at the time contain a most intriguing—and frustratingly spare—anecdote. He and his officers encountered several African leaders with extensive experience of Europeans and were able to form valuable relationships with them. Late in their stay they invited four African dignitaries on board their ship, and "we gave the tragedy of Hamlet; and in the afternoon we went all together ashore, to see if we could shoot an elephant." That is all the diary has to say about the performance. We can only speculate about how the drama was presented or what the guests thought of it.[25]

Both English consumers at home and those who ventured abroad tended to think of the new in familiar categories. Just as items from around the world could be exhibited together in cabinets of curiosities as long as they were made from similar materials, many seemed to assume that the best way to think of the new was through comparison and conflation. In the midst of their improvisation, European migrants in America constantly evoked their experience, personal or vicarious, of Old World others as they tried to make sense of their transatlantic experiences. Pedro de Castañeda, who wrote the account of Coronado's expedition through the American Southwest in 1540, told how an advance party had come upon "an Indian slave, a native of the farthest interior of the land extending from there to Florida, which is the region discovered by Don Fernando de Soto." This man, whom the Spanish recruited as a guide, they called "the Turk because he looked like one." He told them of great stores of gold, though ultimately they came to believe that he had deliberately misdirected them and "was the cause of all the misfortunes that ensued." Suspicions were first raised when the soldier who guarded him "swore under oath that he had seen the Turk talk to the devil in an olla [pitcher] filled with water." He also said that the Turk had knowledge of Spanish activities that he could have gained only by supernatural means. As they moved on to the plains, they encountered Americans who lived in tents. One girl they saw was "as white as if she were from Castile, except that her chin was painted like that of a Barbary Moorish woman." In writing to the king, Coronado testified that the Plains Indians of Quivira were very tall; in fact he had had several measured and found them "ten spans tall." He wrote that the women of Quivira "are comely, with faces more like Moorish than Indian women."[26]

Everything from daily lifeways to religious beliefs was up for comparison in English sources. Writing about Virginia, William Strachey likened Indian deerskin leggings to "the fashion of the Turkes or Irish Trouses." Captain John Smith was reminded of his Mediterranean experience and his impression of the Moroccan sultan Mulai Ahmad, when he encountered the Chesapeake emperor Powhatan "proudly lying uppon a Bedstead" with "such a grave and Majesticall countenance, as drave me into admiration to see such state in a naked Salvage." He also wrote that "if any great commander arrive at the habitation of a Werowance [chief], they spread a mat as the Turkes do a carpet for him to sit upon. Upon an other right opposite they sit themselves. Then doe all with a tunable voice of showting bid him welcome." Roger Williams, who mastered the Narragansett language in early New England, compared a native American idea of paradise to his notion of the Muslim model, "where they have hopes (as the Turkes have) of carnall Joyes."[27] This transatlantic association lived on. In the early eighteenth century a Mohegan sachem died while on an embassy to England; his name was Mahomet.[28]

As the English consumed exotic worlds just for the sheer joy and interest of seeing their products and hearing of foreign adventures, the huge outpouring of publications about America served a very practical purpose. These books glorified English exploits, but they also were meant to encourage investment in American ventures. Their authors had to convince hardheaded businessmen that America offered prospects as good as those to the east and south of England. And they had to persuade investors that they knew what they were talking about, that they had adhered to the principles set forth in manuals such as Thomas Palmer's about how to make travel and writing about travel "profitable and honourable" to the nation. In the process, men who lacked the credentials of a classical education argued for a very different type of credential: the direct experience of the eyewitness. And in maintaining that only eyewitness testimony should be respected, they created a new standard of evidence.

Early reports reflected shared assumptions about how the natural world functioned. As they looked at the American environment, English observers drew on their understanding of the relationship between any group of people and the land on which they lived. All early reports described beautiful and fruitful American landscapes, implying that the New World would be a good place for English colonists. But contemporaries would also have read these descriptions as evidence of the Indians' accomplishments and their high level of development. The condition of the environment was a principal indicator of the qualities of the people who lived in it. The reverse was also true: the level of human development was the best indicator of the goodness of the land. The environment represented pure potential, which must be developed by human activity—tending, pruning, and weeding. Species would degenerate if not carefully and constantly tended, so if a landscape was described as poor and devoid of good fruits and other plants, it meant that the people living in it did not—or were not able to—play their proper role. And the healthfulness of the landscape could be judged by the nature of the people on it. Early modern Europeans, steeped in the doctrine that the body's four humors reflected and interacted with the four basic elements in nature, believed in a very close correspondence between any environment and the people who lived in it. So the Virginia Company's initial "Instructions given by way of advice," after directing the colonists to look for a deep river flowing northwest toward the Pacific for their secure fort site, warned against settling in a "low and moist place," and told the colony's leaders to

"Judge of the Good Air by the People for Some part of that Coast where the Lands are Low have their people blear Eyed and with Swollen bellies and Legs but if the Naturals be Strong and Clean made it is a true sign of a wholesome Soil."[29]

Familiar words often had unfamiliar connotations in these early texts. "Natural" was such a word. It could refer to an indigenous person, one who was "natural" to a specific place, as in the Virginia Company's instructions. But in England a person seen as lacking normal intelligence was called a "natural." When they thought about landscapes, early modern people's scale of values reversed ours. We think of wild nature, untouched by human intervention, as the most beautiful, and some early modern people agreed. The great essayist Montaigne, for example, wrote, "It is not sensible that artifice should be reverenced more than Nature, our great and powerful Mother." But for the English involved in developing links with America, natural meant undeveloped, and implied a kind of deficiency. "Artificial," on the other hand, was a word of high praise, implying that humans had fulfilled their God-given role and had brought the land to its fullest potential through the application of art and intelligence.[30] All those plants and artifacts prospectors sought were the products of Indian development.

Edward Hayes wrote that English merchants who came to Newfoundland every year for the fishing proudly showed him and Sir Humphrey Gilbert "a place they called the Garden," where they liked to stroll on a Sunday morning. But Gilbert and his lieutenants were unimpressed: "Nothing appeared more then Nature it selfe without art." Hayes did admit that although nature "confusedly hath brought foorth roses abundantly, wilde," they were "odoriferous, and to sense very comfortable." Bermuda, which was uninhabited when a Virginia-bound English ship was forced onto it by a hurricane, was similarly promising, even if undeveloped. Sylvester Jourdain wrote that although the reef-ringed islands had been considered "the most dangerous, in-fortunate, and most forlorn place of the world," in reality they were "the richest, healthfullest, and pleasing land . . . and merely natural."[31]

God had so ordered the world that nature offered opportunities, but human beings had to work hard to realize the promise they recognized in the land. As the future Newfoundland leader John Guy wrote, God "hath ordeyned that the earth of it selfe should not be fruitfull without the sweate of mans browes." And he went on to point out that "Adam havinge the whole earth to make choise of, could not find any place fruitfull without his labour and travell [travail, pains]." William Strachey argued that even the Garden of Eden required improvement: "Adam himself might not live in Paradise without dressing the garden."[32]

Captain John Smith offered this explanation of the perceived barrenness of New England in comparison to other lands: "They are beautified by the long labour and diligence of industrious people and Art. This is onely as God made it when he created the world." A decade later, Robert Gordon of Lochinvar echoed Smith's words in arguing that Cape Breton was as fertile as any land in the same latitude: "Onlie this advantage I find in nature, that they [other lands] have above this: they are bewtified by the long labour & diligence of industrious people & airt: & this is only as God made it when he created the world, uncultured, planted, & manured by men of industry, judgment & experience."[33] America as a virgin land, redolent of promise and ready to blossom with the infusion of European technology, was a powerful image in promotional writing encouraging the English to embark on a whole range of novel enterprises as the sixteenth century gave way to the seventeenth.

But was it all really true? Gordon's copying of Smith's description and applying it to a very different region brings up a central question for contemporaries as well as for modern readers: What sources were actually trustworthy? Indeed, were there any accounts that should be taken as accurate and knowledgeable representations of American realities? All early accounts were written for a purpose, and most had the goal of provoking interest in the particular region the writer was promoting and explaining away failures. Sometimes promoters tried to manipulate the flow of information, as when the Virginia Company instructed Jamestown's leaders to forbid colonists to "write any Letter of any thing that may Discourage others."[34] As Gordon's lifting of Smith's text shows, people with an interest in America avidly read the work of their predecessors, and often applied tests to them. Thomas Dermer, writing to Samuel Purchas from New England in 1619, for example, said that he found "that former relations were true."[35]

Almost every book about American experience began with a heartfelt statement of its truthfulness and of the depth of experience on which it was based, and the titles often contained the word "true." William Wood, offering the "first fruites of my farre-fetcht experience" in New England, railed against English people who were so cynical that they believed nothing they had not seen with their own eyes. Some were so simpleminded, he wrote, that they even asked if the sun shines in America. These cynics said of travelers, "They may lye by authority, because none can controule them."[36] This was the mentality that vexed everyone who wrote about America, and this is why authors stressed their personal experience. Especially in cases where information from America contradicted the wisdom of the ancients that was taught in the universities, those who had been to America argued that experience trumped academic knowledge. They could begin with the fact that the ancients had had no knowledge of the two vast continents across the ocean.

Travelers to America who wrote about their exploits all made the same claim: eyewitness authority supersedes all other kinds of knowledge. Samuel Purchas, the English compiler of voyage chronicles, wrote that despite his admiration for the ancient writers, experience from America required a new attitude toward them: "Herein we bid you fare-well."[37] Jacques Cartier, a very early venturer in Canada who made his first voyage in 1534, confronted the picture of the world that had come down from "wise philosophers of ancient times," who had concluded on the basis of "some natural reasonings" that the earth was divided into five zones, of which three—the tropics, the Arctic, and the Antarctic—were deemed uninhabitable. As Cartier pointed out, they had arrived at these conclusions "without adventuring or risking their lives in the dangers they would have incurred had they tried to test their statements by actual experience." To those who still cited the received wisdom, he wrote, "I shall simply reply that the prince of those philosophers left among his writings a brief maxim of great import, to the effect that 'Experience is the master of all things.'" Cartier here referred to the opening passages of Aristotle's *Metaphysics,* where the philosopher replied to those who placed art above mere experience by asserting that "science and art come to men through experience."[38]

For his part, far from misleading readers by overpraising the land, Cartier found the coast of Labrador repellent, an opinion he put in a biblical frame: "If the soil were as good as the harbours, it would be a blessing; but the land should not be called the New Land, being composed of stones and horrible rugged rocks . . . In fine, I am rather inclined to believe this is the land God gave to Cain."[39] Cartier was referring to God's punishment of Cain for killing his brother Abel: "Now therefore thou art cursed from the earth, which hathe opened her mouth to receive thy brothers blood from thine hand. When thou shalt til the grounde, it shal not henceforthe yelde unto thee her strength: a vagabonde and a rennegate shalt thou be in the earth." Having received this sentence, "Kain went out from the presence of the Lord and dwelt in the land of Nod towarde the Eastside of Eden."[40]

Thomas Harriot was one of the few who combined real experience with a university education. The governor under whom he served, Ralph Lane, endorsed Harriot as "a man no lesse for his honesty then learning commendable," and wrote that his book "may very well passe with the credit of trueth even amongst the most true relations of this age."[41] Harriot's *Briefe and True Report of the new found land of Virginia* was remarkable for the restraint of its claims about the resources of coastal Carolina.

Many with less education stressed the authority of experience alone. Captain John Smith carefully delineated the places he had personally visited from those about which he had learned from the Indians when he published his Chesapeake map in 1612. Like Harriot, he was careful not to promise too much in the way of rich commodities. But he ended the book that accompanied his map with a heartfelt denunciation of those who slandered Virginia, some of whom had even been in the colony. He argued that they were "men of tender educations and small experience" who stayed in the fort and never "did any thing but devoure the fruits of other mens labours." Because they "found not English cities, nor such faire houses, nor at their owne wishes any of their accustomed dainties, with fether beds and downe pillows . . . the Country was to them a miserie, a ruine, a death, a hell." He compared them to the locusts that plagued Egypt in biblical times. In everything he wrote he hammered again and again on the damage done by ill-informed slanderers who were trying to cover up their own inadequacy and reiterated his claim that experience was the only true source of knowledge. In his final book, *Advertisements For the unexperienced Planters of New-England, or any-where* (1631), he complained again about "curious spectators" who made it their business to censure others and underestimate difficulties, and reiterated his insistence on eyewitness authority: "You may easily know them by their absolutenesse in opinions, holding experience but the mother of fooles, which indeed is the very ground of reason."

The appeal to experience as the only foundation of knowledge became commonplace. William Wood ridiculed those who wrote voluminously about America "(though they have travailed no further than the smoake of their owne native chimnies)." Smith compared himself to Julius Caesar, who led armies in great campaigns and then wrote the stories of those campaigns, saying, "I am no Compiler by hearsay, but have beene a reall Actor." In several places in the *Generall Historie*, and in the conclusion of the *Advertisements*, he asserted the authority of both experience and authorship with the emphatic statement: "John Smith writ this with his owne hand."[42]

Ancient writers like the natural historian Pliny wrote of oddities such as people who had no heads but rather had eyes in their chests, and some continued to believe that such marvels might exist. Sir Walter Ralegh, who visited Guiana in 1595, collected reports of people who had "their eyes in their shoulder, and their mouths in the middle of their breasts, & that a long train of haire groweth backward betwen their shoulders." Although he was aware that such reports might be "a meere fable," he pointed to other apparently bizarre stories that had proved to be true. For example, he had seen oysters growing on trees in Guiana just as Pliny had described.[43]

Shakespeare's play *The Tempest*, first performed in 1611, played on the theme of travelers' tales and the credit due them. In the play, inspired by the wreck of a Virginia-bound ship on Bermuda, his castaways aver, on the basis of what they have seen in their island refuge, that "travelers ne'er did lie" and that people whose heads were "in their breasts" probably did exist. But such dialogue would have rebounded in the audience's minds, as the courtiers were responding to an illusory scene engineered by the spirit Ariel at the command of the sorcerer Prospero.[44] Shakespeare thus played with the Virginia Company's attempt to demystify Bermuda, which had been known as an enchanted Isle of Devils. The company wrote that the fairies and devils were actually friendly birds and animals.[45]

Some writers tried to explain how fabulous stories had gotten started. John Tradescant kept a journal of his voyage accompanying a royal

Samuel de Champlain, who traveled extensively in America, drew this fanciful picture of a dragon around 1600. The accompanying text indicated that the question of their existence there was still open. Courtesy of the John Carter Brown Library at Brown University.

embassy to Muscovy. He believed that he had stumbled on the true explanation for ancient legends of a race of people who lacked heads and had eyes in their chests. When he encountered Siberian Samoyed people, who wore parkas with hoods attached to their coats, Tradescant was sure that it must have been "that people whom the fixtion is fayned of that should have no heads, for they have short necks and commonly wear ther clothes over head and shoulders."[46]

One man, Anthony Parkhurst, took a playful approach to his American stories. As an old friend of Richard Hakluyt, he included some "merie tales" in a letter from Newfoundland written in 1578. He told Hakluyt that he had entertained his friends by pretending to "conjure" squids that, he said, came onto the shore at the sound of his voice. As he admitted, "the vertue of the wordes bee small, but the nature of the fish great and strange." In another entertainment he piled up codfish on the shore and commanded his mastiff to tend the pile as they wriggled away, telling the dog, "Goe fetch me this rebellious fish that obeyeth not this Gentleman that commeth from Kent and Christendome." His friends at first considered his stories "notorious lies, but they laugh and are merie when they heare the meanes howe each tale is true." Parkhurst, who accompanied John Hawkins on his second slave-trading voyage from the west coast of Africa to the Caribbean and Florida in 1565, prompted Hakluyt to recall a time when one of these stories had fooled him: "I told you once I doe remember how in my travell into Affrica and America, I found trees that bare Oisters, which was strange to you, till I tolde you that their boughes hung in the water, on which both Oisters and Muskles did sticke fast, as their propertie is to stakes and timber."[47]

All novel claims, whether truthful or not, left travel writers open to ridicule and doubt. For example, in his youth Joseph Hall, later bishop of Exeter and of Norwich and author of important works on religious meditation, wrote a Latin satire, *Mundus alter et idem,* on the vices of his time disguised as one of the popular collections of travel accounts.

Hall first intended the work for circulation in manuscript among a small circle of his fellow academics at Cambridge. He wrote it in the 1590s, a period when many felt that the country was experiencing divine punishment for its diversion from the path of virtue by the quest for novelty, and it was published in Latin in 1605. A particular target of his satire was Richard Hakluyt's very influential collection *The Principall Navigations, Voiages, Traffiques, and Discoveries of the English Nation*. To Hall's chagrin, a man named John Healey published his own unauthorized English "translation" of the *Mundus alter et idem* in 1609, when Jamestown was in its infancy. Healey's work was actually a substantially new version of the work in much racier and more freewheeling language; he called it *The Discovery of a new world, or A Description of the South Indies. Hetherto unknowne.*

Healey's version of Hall's book told the story of a traveler, Mercurius Britannicus, who set out in a ship called *The Fancie*, or *Phantasia* in Latin, and visited an assortment of countries in the great Terra Australis Incognita with names like Tenter-belly, Fooliana, Moronia, and Theevingen. Among the places visited by the mythical traveler was a female-dominated country called Womandecoia or Shee-landt, whose principal city was Gossipingoa; in this Hall's readers would have recognized Wingandacoia, which Ralegh originally thought was the native name for Roanoke. Hall's traveler also visited a land called "Gynia Nova, which some with a wrong pronunciation call Guinea, but which I call Viraginia," or land of viragoes.[48]

Such broad humor was probably easier to deal with than more subtle slanders, and Healey himself cast his lot with Virginia by emigrating the next year. The more serious point that promoters, especially those with American experience, sought to make was that doubt cripples initiative. Their message was that England had a chance to make its place in America, and the doubts sown by slanderers held the nation back from engaging in exploits that could lead to riches and greatness.

Smith complained that colonization had been supported "in such a pe-
nurious and miserable manner, as if I had gone a begging to build an
Universitie," and he went on to quote (not quite accurately) verses
that the poet George Chapman had contributed to a book written by
Ralegh's lieutenant, Lawrence Keymis. Chapman's verses read:

> *O Incredulitie, the wit of Fooles,*
> *That slovenly will spit on all thinges faire,*
> *The Cowards castle and the Sluggards cradle*
> *How easie t'is to be an Infidell?*[49]

Ralegh strongly seconded Chapman's sentiments in his own book,
pointing out that Spain had not been deterred by naysayers, and now
its "Indian Golde" made that nation wealthy and powerful.[50] While
fools were paralyzed by doubts, other countries were reaping the rewards of American enterprises. Some things had gone wrong, but the
parts of America open to English ventures were extremely promising;
the failures were the fault of human error and weakness. Further hesi-
tation now would be a disastrous mistake: this was the strong message
conveyed by the early colonization literature.

While a broad English audience streamed into theaters, gardens,
and early museums to satisfy their curiosity, and the literate consumed
stories of adventures in foreign cultures, authors, translators, and editors pursued an agenda, often at the behest of highly placed government officials, of encouraging more solid and lasting engagement with
the world. The underlying moral was always that great riches and
power awaited those who dared greatly. This lesson applied to individuals, those ordinary men and women who journeyed into new worlds
and won position through their own exploits, as well as to nations.
Not only could the rank and file rise to greatness, but also England itself could become a powerful nation as Spain had if only its people and

its economic and political leaders rose to the challenge. Engagement with America would be different from the Eastern trades, where the English sought to break into established patterns. America required different modes and novel organization. The question was whether the English would be able to solve the riddle of how to operate there.

5

Grasping America's Contours

OVER THE COURSE of the sixteenth century Europe's attention was increasingly reoriented toward the Atlantic. Peter Heylyn, writing in the middle of the seventeenth century, remarked on how people in former times had feared the great western ocean and had "wondred at [it] on the shore side." The seas known to the Old World were, he said, "but as Ponds or Gullets" in comparison.[1] The great body of water that had for so long functioned as a barrier had now been turned into a vast highway. And England, no longer an insignificant little country clinging to the edge of Europe, could claim a significant role on that thoroughfare.

But Europeans were slow to agree on how to think about the oceans and the lands beyond. The names and categories for seas and lands that we take for granted, even see as simple representations of a preexisting physical reality, were not obvious to early modern Europeans as they looked westward across the ocean. Columbus's title, Admiral of the Ocean Sea, assumed that there was just one ocean that flowed around the then-known world.

In many ways this makes more sense than our later notion of bounded oceans. Modern scientific thinking argues for an integrated global weather and water system. But as Europeans began to travel the world and to understand that previously unknown continents lay between their countries and East Asia, they started to divide up the seas in their minds into bounded spaces. Early maps showed the Atlantic split north to south into several seas, not bearing the simple label "Atlantic Ocean" as modern maps do. These divisions became more, not less, numerous as European involvement in and knowledge of global endeavors grew. For example, a map published in an English book in 1578 applied three divisions to what we call the Atlantic, labeling the ocean between Europe and North America the "Oceanus Occidentalis," and that between the Caribbean and northern Africa the "Mare Atlanticus," while the label "Oceanus Australis" spanned the southern Atlantic and the Indian Ocean, construing those two seas as a single ocean system. The Flemish geographer Abraham Ortelius, who published the first modern atlas in 1570, labeled the Atlantic between Europe and America the "Mar del Nort" and the ocean's southern part the "Ethiopian Ocean," a name that was used until the nineteenth century. John Pory's 1600 translation of Leo Africanus's history of Africa, for example, placed the "Oceanus Atlanticus" across from the entrance to the Mediterranean and the "Mare del Nort" opposite Guinea. Below the equator, the sea on Pory's map was named "Oceanus Aethiopicus."[2]

Occasionally writers reversed the direction of gaze. The poet John Donne referred to England as the "Suburbs of the old world." Peter Heylyn also emphasized Britain's position between the old and new worlds, calling the British Isles "the last Western Diocese." In 1617 Fynes Moryson published his massive compilation of observations taken from his travels throughout Europe and the lands bordering the Mediterranean Sea during the 1590s, and from his two terms of administrative service in Ireland. He began his discussion "Of the Provinces of Ireland" calling it "This famous Iland in the Virginian Sea" just as Heylyn wrote that America was separated from Europe and Africa by the "Atlanticke Ocean, and the Verginian Seas."[3]

If conceptualizing the seas was difficult, claiming and naming the land was contentious. Thomas Gage, a Dominican friar who lived in Spanish America for twelve years before coming home to England as a convert to Protestantism, ridiculed the idea that the Spanish had any valid claim to America by right of discovery. If "the sailing of a Spanish Ship upon the coast of India, should intitle the King of Spain to that Countrey," then "the sayling of an Indian or English Ship upon the coast of Spain, should intitile either the Indians or English unto the Dominion thereof."[4] The power to apply a name and make it stick implied ownership and control. The Spanish named most of the east coast of North America "La Florida," and the English originally applied the name "Virginia" to the entire coast from Newfoundland south. In the early days, New England was called the "North Part of Virginia."

Sir Walter Ralegh, in his *History of the World,* written after the failure of his Roanoke colonies, told the story of how the name Virginia came into being. The reconnaissance voyage to the Carolina coast sent in 1584 to seek out a good location for a settlement returned with a very enthusiastic report about Roanoke. On the basis of this report, early maps appeared with the name "Wingandacoia" or "Wingan de Coy" across the American Southeast. Later the colonists discovered that the whole thing was an embarrassing mistake. When the English pointed to the mainland and asked its name, their Indian hosts had replied "Wingandacon," but what they were actually saying, according to Ralegh, was, "You weare good clothes, or gay clothes." Wingandacon may actually have been the name of the fir trees that grew where the English pointed. Although he claimed that the name "Peru" stemmed from a similar episode of miscommunication, Ralegh moved quickly to recover from the embarrassment of his very public error. Queen Elizabeth showed her favor to the enterprise by knighting Ralegh, and she graciously agreed that English territory in America could be named Virginia in her honor.[5]

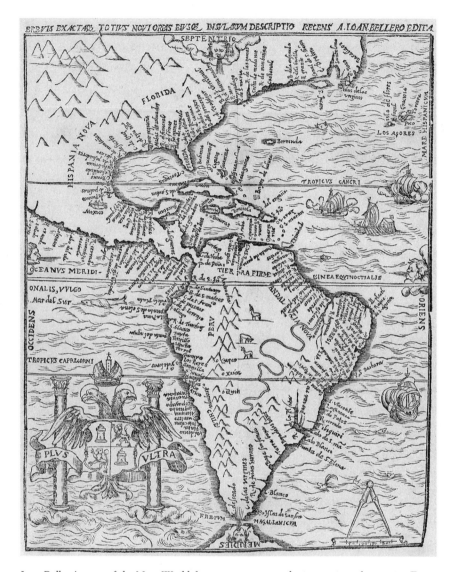

*Jean Bellere's map of the New World from 1554 conveys the impression of extensive Euro-
pean possession at that early date by the multitude of names inscribed on it. This was published in Pedro de Cieza de León, Parte Primera de la Crónica del Perú.* Courtesy of the
John Carter Brown Library at Brown University.

Assigning names to recently "discovered" lands for European consumption was tremendously important. This did not necessarily mean
changing preexisting labels; often venturers tried to preserve what
they thought were native names, as the examples of Peru and Wingandacoia demonstrate. But even where they thought they were using
native terms, those names were written on maps using the linguis-
tic conventions of the Europeans creating the record. The Indians'
name for the river in Maine, for example, was variously written "Qui-
nebiqui" or "Kennebeck." The first might seem to indicate French
rights in that region, while the second would fortify English claims.
Early Spanish maps showed the continent of South America with
newly applied names jutting into the sea all around the landmass like
fine hairs. And English writers trying to awaken an interest in colonization among their compatriots argued, as did Edward Hayes in 1583,
that the French were "imposing" names on features all along the
northern coast of North America in defiance of English claims deriv-
ing from the early exploring voyage of John Cabot.[6] Captain John
Smith also complained that "French men" had tried to establish the
name "Cannada," another supposedly indigenous name, in the region
he called New England.[7]

Peter Heylyn, well after England had planted several permanent
American colonies, demonstrated that names were still fluid when he
wrote that America is naturally divided into "two great Peninsulas,"
the northern called "Mexicana" and the southern one "Peruana."
Mexicana, according to him, contained, running from north to south,
the provinces of "Estotiland, Nova Francia, Virginia, California, Florida,
Nova Gallicia, and Guatimala." Although Estotiland, which included
Newfoundland, still lay mostly "hidden in a Northern Mist . . . some
English Names have been imposed of late." Earlier names given by
English ventures had been overturned by "Normans, Portugals, and
Britons of France."[8]

The name Virginia was redolent of the promise of great potential, the untapped resources of the virgin land which would be brought to fruitfulness by the infusion of European technology. Samuel Purchas, who succeeded Richard Hakluyt as a compiler of accounts of voyages and promoter of America, portrayed North America as a feminine land awaiting the proper lover. That part of America reserved for the English, "whose Virgin Soile not yet polluted with Spaniards lust, by our late Virgin-Mother, was justly called Virginia." He pictured the English colonists as "Wooers and Suters" who had braved the "angrie Ocean . . . to make thee of a ruder Virgin, not a wanton Minion; but, an honest and Christian Wife." By the time Purchas wrote this in 1614, the difficulties and deaths in Jamestown were well known; but he pictured those problems as "Virginian modestie, and after the use of Virgins, shee would say nay at first, holding that love surest in continuance, which is hardest in obtayning."[9]

The physical reality of America was difficult to grasp, and early planning by Europeans for a relationship with America was shot through with misconceptions. Both lack of precise information and faulty reasoning from principles that proved not to be applicable contributed to massive misunderstanding. European leaders made strenuous efforts to collect true and exact information. In the 1570s Philip II of Spain sent out a series of massive questionnaires to his administrators in America in hopes of accumulating complete, accurate knowledge of his overseas territories.[10] And the 1582 instructions to the surveyor Thomas Bavin conveyed English aspirations for clarity.

Precise knowledge, however, was far in the future. Even the basic problem of figuring out the size of the American continents baffled the newcomers almost throughout the entire colonial period; Europeans consistently underestimated North America's east-to-west extent. Part of the problem was technical. Sixteenth-century mariners were able to calculate latitude with almost modern accuracy, but ability to determine longitude, which required accurate timekeeping at sea, did not come until the eighteenth century. The two continents are not lined up on a north-south axis—Denver is due north of Easter Island, for example—so that voyages around South America's southern tip and up the Pacific coast could only guess how far west they had gone.[11]

The simultaneous continent-spanning expeditions of Francisco Vásquez de Coronado from the southwest and Hernando de Soto from the southeast in the early 1540s did not establish the true extent of North America, even though we know that members of both were at one point camped within a few hundred miles of each other west of the Mississippi River. Only one person "bridged the gap between the two parties," and that was unwittingly and unwillingly: a Plains Indian woman escaped captivity in Coronado's force only to be seized by one of De Soto's men as she fled. Pedro de Castañeda, who recorded Coronado's expedition, later learned that this "painted Indian woman" had mentioned traveling nine days after her escape from Coronado's company. From this and other information, Spaniards concluded that the continent was much narrower than it is in fact. Cabeza de Vaca estimated the distance he and his companions had traveled from their shipwreck on the Gulf of Mexico to the Gulf of California on their trek a decade earlier as "two hundred leagues," or about six hundred miles. Both the De Soto and Coronado expeditions, like Cabeza de Vaca's, followed circuitous routes, so the Spanish had no clear idea how far the two expeditions had traveled east to west.[12]

The other reason for underestimating North America's width lay in wishful thinking. Early planning still hoped for an easy route through to the riches of Asia, and the assumption that the continent was only half as wide as it actually is made that seem much more likely. For example, the Virginia Company's "Instructions given by way of advice . . . for the Intended Voyage to Virginia," sent with the first expedition to Jamestown in 1607, included specific directions on how to choose a site. Roanoke had experienced disaster when the ship carrying the first planters' supplies ran aground in the shallow waters surrounding the Carolina Outer Banks. Therefore the first point the Virginia Company made was that the colonists should seek out the entrance to "Some navigable River making Choise of Such a one as runneth furthest into the Land." If they found several suitable deep rivers flowing into Chesapeake Bay, and if one of those had two branches, they should choose "that which bendeth most towards the Northwest for that way shall You soonest find the Other Sea." So from the very beginning the messages were mixed: the men were to create a strong fort in a secure location, but this effort was in some ways ancillary to the main goal of finding a route to the Pacific Ocean, which they called the South Sea. And early reports based on hopeful conversations with local Indians indicated good prospects for this quest. Captain John Smith believed he had learned from discussions with Indians that "the most mortall enimies" of Powhatan's people lived near the source of the Potomac River "upon a great salt water, which by all likelyhood is either some part of Cannada, some great lake, or some inlet of some sea that falleth into the South sea." But these hopes were soon dashed by Powhatan himself when he told Smith, "But for any salt water beyond the mountaines, the relations you have had from my people are false." Powhatan reinforced his statement by drawing maps of the entire region on the ground.[13] Nonetheless, Alexander Whitaker, minister at Henrico near the falls of the James, wrote in 1612 that the South Sea was six days' journey in the direction of the setting sun.[14]

Existence of a navigable water route through the continent was an article of faith that no amount of experience could kill. No one believed that God would have revealed the existence of these two continents previously almost unknown to Europeans only to have them act as barriers to the newcomers' ambitions. God must have created a passage through, and it was up to Europeans to find it. This idea was amazingly persistent; Sebastian Cabot sailed all along the Atlantic coast in 1508 looking for the passage's entrance, and belief in it was not fully abandoned until after the transcontinental journey of Lewis and Clark in the early nineteenth century. Even then, hopes remained that a navigable passage might yet be discovered in the far north.[15]

Many early maps showed an arm of the Pacific Ocean, known as the Strait of Anian, jutting into the continent from the northwest almost to the east coast; most often it was thought to be in about 60° of latitude. Castañeda, transmitting impressions gained by De Soto's expedition, referred to "the arm of the sea that enters this coast inland toward the north," which he thought could be crossed only in large ships. As he tried to describe the best route to the interior, he lamented his lack of "knowledge of cosmography or geometry to make clear what I want to say." Early writers also hoped that the east-west extent of the Pacific might be relatively small, or that the Americas and Asia might nearly meet at some point—as they in fact do across the Bering Strait. Reporting that the Pueblo Indians created and revered crosses, Castañeda wrote, "In my opinion they have gained, in some way or other, some light of the cross of Christ our Redeemer. This may have come by way of India, whence these natives came."[16] A century later Peter Heylyn wrote of the Strait of Anian "lying between Tartarie and America" which Tatars and other northern nations "are thought to have passed over, and to populate that Countrey." And in 1672 John Lederer mentioned a great arm of what he called the "Indian Ocean" stretching from California to the Appalachians.[17]

The Strait of Anian appeared on Gerard Mercator's landmark world map in 1565; this map was very influential because of the projection, the mode of representing a sphere on a flat surface, that Mercator invented. In his three voyages between 1576 and 1578, Martin Frobisher tried to find the eastern entrance of the strait in the region of Baffin Bay. Sir Francis Drake's circumnavigation of the globe began with a venture into the Pacific Ocean and up the coast in 1579 to try to find the western end of the passage "on the backe side of America." In this attempt he was following the route of several previous Spanish voyages. Drake came back with a negative report on the passage, but belief in it was unshaken. The Spanish were keenly interested in these English activities. Part of what we know about Drake's movements comes from Spanish authorities' later interrogation of a Portuguese pilot, Nuño da Silva, captured by Drake to help him in navigating these unfamiliar waters. And the Spanish ambassador in London seems to have succeeded in planting a spy among the company on Frobisher's third voyage, as a letter in code in the Spanish archives contains a highly accurate report on efforts to assay ore on Baffin Island.[18]

The Spanish were as convinced as the English that the North American continent was both much narrower than it actually is and that some kind of easy passage through it must exist. Pedro Menéndez de Avilés, who was responsible for Florida, wrote to the Spanish king Philip II in 1565 warning about the ease with which enemies of Spain could cross the continent. He quoted Don Luís de Velasco (Paquiquineo), the Paspahegh man who lived among the Spanish, as saying that the mountains were eighty leagues inland from Chesapeake Bay and that there were two arms of the sea, one of which "goes in the direction of China, and comes out in the Southern Sea, and this is absolutely certain, although nobody has ever gone this way to the Southern Sea." Menéndez sent Juan Pardo on two westward expeditions in the 1560s to find the overland route to the silver mines of Zacatecas which had recently been developed in northern Mexico.[19] French Protestant settlers on the coast of Carolina in 1562 also believed that they would have relatively easy access to the riches of the fabled city of Cíbola, toward "the Sea called the South Sea." The Indians they interrogated "shewed us by signes . . . that they might goe thither with their Boates (by rivers) in twentie dayes."[20]

Among the hundred sailors John Hawkins left on the coast of the Gulf of Mexico near Tampico in 1568 after his fleet was almost destroyed in a fight with Spanish ships were three who claimed to have made their way from there on foot all the way to Acadia on the east coast, where they were picked up by a French ship in 1569. David Ingram, one of the three, told his story to Richard Hakluyt, who published it in his compilation *The Principall Navigations, Voiages, Traffiques, and Discoveries of the English Nation.* Ingram concluded his description of America, which even his contemporaries ultimately came to see as riddled with fantasy, by claiming that he had seen "the maine sea" to the north and that Indians there could draw pictures of ships with sails, "which thing especially proveth the passage of the Northwest." Before his account was called into question, his testimony was sought even by the highest authorities in England.[21]

Spanish authorities on both sides of the Atlantic watched the plans for settling an English fort at Jamestown with growing alarm. Whereas the Roanoke colony of the 1580s had been situated in what the English thought was a good position from which to attack the Spanish treasure fleet on its homeward journey to Seville, Spanish authorities feared that Jamestown, on a deep river flowing into the interior, posed a direct threat to Mexico. In 1609 Francisco Fernandez de Ecija reported that the English planned to travel westward across the continent from Jamestown "until they shall come to Nueva Mexico, Nueva Galicia, and Vizcaya, and Çacatecas," then on "to the other sea at the west, since from that part of Florida great rivers go up into the land and from the other sea also it is known that others go up, not smaller, and that there is little distance from one set of rivers to the other."[22]

The next year Francis Magnel, an Irishman who had been in Jamestown during its first year, turned up in Spain with vastly exaggerated stories of what the English were accomplishing in their settlement on the James. He praised their good relationships with Powhatan, the "Emperor of Virginia," and testified that the Americans knew of three easy routes to the Pacific and had offered to take the English settlers there. The Indians "assure them that on the other side of Virginia by the South Sea there is a land where the natives wear long silk robes and red buskins," the stereotypical Chinese garb, and these people had "a great deal of gold." As proof of his story, Magnel said, the Indians near Jamestown had shown the English knives and other things that they had acquired from ships that had been to that western land. From Jamestown the settlers planned to build forts a day's journey apart on the best river leading to the Pacific so that they could control the route. Their goal was to "make themselves lords of the South Sea, so as to have their share of the riches of the Indies, and to be in the way of the traffic of the King of Spain, and to seek other new worlds for themselves."[23]

Belief that contact between the east and west of the continent should be easy was widespread and persistent. In 1636 a report by Alonso Botello y Serrano and Pedro Porter y Casanate called for a Spanish investigation to clarify the facts: "We find no uniform course, no certain distance, no true latitude, sounding to undeceive, nor perspective to enlighten." They argued that forces from Chesapeake Bay (which they called Jacal) were "advancing . . . day by day."[24]

In 1634 Samuel de Champlain sent Jean Nicolet, who had lived a decade or more among Algonquian-speaking Indians in Canada, particularly the Nipissings, and who now served as interpreter, to traverse the Sault Ste. Marie and investigate stories of traders who sounded as if they might be from East Asia, and who would therefore know the water route across North America. Although of the Great Lakes only Lake Huron was well known to the French at this time, they had high hopes that other large bodies of water they had heard about might be, or might lead to, the South Sea. As Nicolet and his Algonquian companions approached the Winnebagos, whom the French hopefully called the People of the Sea, they were delighted to receive a very warm welcome. Nicolet, embodying French hopes of Asian trade, "wore a grand robe of China damask, all strewn with flowers and birds of many colours." He was much more awe-inspiring to the Indians, however, as "a man who carried thunder in both hands,—for thus they called the two pistols that he held," at the sight of which all the women and children fled.[25]

Then in June 1640 an Englishman came into the French Canadian settlements who said he had been searching

> for some route through these countries to the sea of the North . . . This good man related some wonderful things to us about new Mexico. "I have learned," said he, "that one can sail to that country through seas that are North of it. For two years I have ranged the whole Southern coast, from Virginia to Quinebiqui [Kennebeck], seeking to find some great river or great lake that might lead me to peoples who had some knowledge of this sea which is to the North of Mexico. Not having found any, I came to this country to enter the Saguené, and penetrate, if I could, with the Savages of the country, to the North sea."

The Jesuit Paul LeJeune, who recorded the man's story, was skeptical: "This poor man would have lost fifty lives, if he had had so many, before reaching this North sea by the way he described; and, if he had found this sea, he would have discovered nothing new, nor found any passage to new Mexico. One need not be a great Geographer to recognize this fact. But I will say, in passing, that it is highly probable one can descend through the second great lake of the Hurons, and through the tribes that we have named, into this sea that he was seeking."[26]

Many continued to hold to the notion of a narrow North America well into the colonial period. In 1647 a Vatican official suggested to the French Capuchin friar Pacifique de Provins that he should move inland from Acadia on North America's northeast coast; one benefit would be that he might then be able to communicate with the Recollet priests of New Mexico.[27] Virginia Company leader John Ferrar developed a map showing the Pacific just beyond the Appalachian mountain range; the map was published in 1651 in the third edition

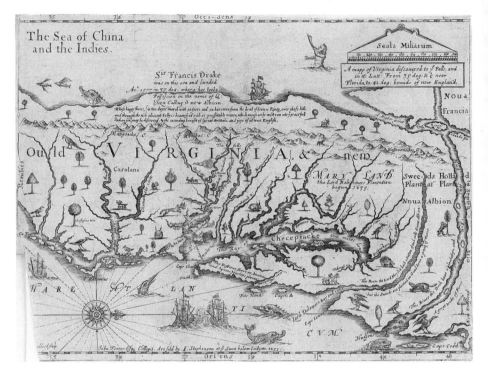

This engraved map showing California and the Pacific just west of the Appalachian Mountains was published in London in 1651. The original drawing was by Virginia Company leader John Farrer. Courtesy of the John Carter Brown Library at Brown University.

of Edward Williams's *Virgo Triumphans: Or, Virginia Richly and Truly Valued*, decorated with a medallion of Sir Francis Drake on the west coast. As late as 1709 John Lawson recorded estimates that a five-day journey would take one to the South Sea.[28]

As they struggled to conceptualize the North American landmass, Europeans found the climate as baffling as the land—and their thinking on it was as subject to wishful misconstruction. Early moderns assumed that the world, as made by God, must be symmetrical. Therefore, not only must climates in any given latitude around the world be the same, but also areas the same distance above and below the equator would have the same resources. Reasoning from natural symmetry led early mapmakers to depict a great southern landmass, Terra Australis Incognita, which they assumed must exist to balance northern lands even though Australia had not yet been discovered. The assumption of a symmetrical earth also led to the conclusion that lands midway between the equator and the pole would have the most moderate climates. The Virginia Company attested in 1620 that Virginia's location "neere the midst of the world, betweene the extreamities of heate and cold," meant that the land was "capable (being assisted with skill and industry) of the richest commodities of most parts of the Earth." At the same time Captain John Smith wrote that New England lay in "the very meane betwixt the North Pole and the Line [equator]."[29]

Hot regions were expected to pose particular problems for English migrants, whose humors were thought to be calibrated for their own moderate climate. Although the warm Chesapeake region was expected to produce lush commodities when cultivated, English migrants would pay a price in risking their health. The "bloody fluxe" and other diseases that attacked early settlers in Jamestown, seen as evidence of violent humoral adjustment, confirmed for many the dangers involved in leaving England for southern regions in America.[30]

Despite these fears, backers favored southern locations because they believed that essential commodities England was not able to produce could come from there. The Virginia Company affirmed in its 1609 instructions to Governor Sir Thomas Gates that the sun is "under god the first cause both of health and Riches." Although the Mediterranean may have had a reputation for unruliness in both its weather and its people, settling in comparable areas in America would enrich the nation and free Britain of dependence on actual or potential enemies for necessary products. Because the Carolina Outer Banks lay in "the selfe same climate" as Persia, Thomas Harriot reasoned, settlers there would be able to produce all of the Persian luxury goods; he proposed experimenting with a kind of silk grass he found growing at Roanoke as the first test case.[31] *Tradescantia*, the plant that George Sandys collected for his friend John Tradescant, was thought to be the same silk grass that Harriot had found.

American realities were quite different from what their inherited ideas led Europeans to expect. As they moved from theory to the level of experience, they had great difficulty interpreting the American climate, because it was both hotter and colder than experience of the maritime climates of western Europe had led them to expect. Deviation from anticipated norms required explanation. Simply put, they had to figure out what was wrong, what caused such extremes, and their explanations reveal their assumptions about the operation of the natural world.[32]

On one topic European writers were glad to disprove inherited theories. The ancient philosophers had argued that the earth was not habitable in the "frozen zone" of the far north or around the equator, the so-called "burning zone." Now that Europeans had traveled extensively, and even lived, in equatorial and northern regions, experience proved that those parts had always been inhabited, and this information led to the spinning of a whole range of theories as to why those climates were not intolerable. As early as 1578 George Best drew on his own travels and the writings of others to explain why the ancients were wrong and wrote an extended analysis of his findings as *Experiences and Reasons of the Sphere, to Prove All Partes of the Worlde Habitable*.[33]

The initial impulse of all migrants was to deny, experience notwithstanding, that America's climate differed from that of comparable latitudes in Europe. Pierre Biard, who was in the first Jesuit mission to Acadia, modern Nova Scotia, put the problem succinctly: "There ought to be in that region the same sort of Climate in every respect as that of our France, from the fact, as we pointed out, of its similar situation, and this is actually the case." In his *Relation of New France, of its Lands, Nature of the Country, and of its Inhabitants*, written after his forced return to Europe, he wrote of New France as "a twin land with ours, subject to the same influences, lying in the same latitude, and having the same climate."[34]

Europeans were not particularly puzzled by the warmth of summers in eastern North America because that was expected in relatively low latitudes, and they knew that even Newfoundland is south of London. They were extremely disconcerted, however, by the cold winters, which were much more extreme than in familiar places at home far to the north. What they were experiencing was the difference between a maritime climate, seen in countries lying to the east of great oceans, and the continental regime that prevails in lands to their west. The global atmosphere moves from west to east, so the different climates are determined largely by whether a region's weather approaches over land or sea. Great landmasses absorb heat quickly and give it up equally fast, but large bodies of water are slow both to absorb and to release heat generated by the sun. Thus maritime climates are characterized by a relatively narrow range between the highest and lowest annual temperatures, whereas continental weather swings widely between very high temperatures in summer and very low in winter. The Gulf Stream also plays a role in producing western Europe's moderate winter temperatures.

Contemporaries did not recognize the role of the west-to-east movement of the prevailing winds in producing characteristic climates; instead they pinned their explanations on the sun's apparent movement from east to west and its propensity to draw up moisture from large bodies of water on earth. Samuel Purchas wrote that the West Indies were less hot and dry in summer than expected: "For never is it moister in those parts between the Tropikes, then when the Sunne is neerest, then causing terrible stormes and showers every day: as if having drunken too much in his long and hot jorney over the Ocean, he did there vomit it up againe." Drawing extensively on the Spanish author José de Acosta, Purchas offered other reasons why the American tropics were less hot than anticipated. Not only did the "exhalations and vapours" of the many lakes and rivers cool the land, but also "Our Heaven hath more Starres, and greater, as Acosta by his owne sight hath observed, challenging those Authors, which have written other-wise, of fabling."[35] Edward Hayes, who traveled to Newfoundland with Gilbert in the early 1580s, offered a similar set of explanations for the region's relative cold despite its location in the same latitudes as "Anjou, [and] Poictou in France." He argued that the sun, in ap-proaching from the east over the ocean, drew up moisture, "which doth qualifie and infeeble greatly the Sunnes reverberation upon this countrey."[36]

As they struggled to understand why America's climate deviated from what their European experience and education had led them to expect, European venturers moved from denial to attempts at explana-tion. Pierre Biard, in the same book in which he had stated firmly that Acadia's climate was the same as that of France, struggled to connect his own observations with what theory told him and wrote of his ef-forts to determine the truth: "Nevertheless, whatever the Astrologers may say, it must be confessed that that country (generally speaking, and as it is at present) is colder than our France, and that they differ greatly from each other in regard to weather and seasons. The causes thereof not being in the sky, we must seek them upon the earth. I shall show accurately some experiments I made."[37] Biard argued that it was the dense forests and plentiful lakes and rivers that kept the region cold.

Peter Heylyn argued conversely that England was less cold in win-ter than its northern location might indicate "because the air of the Kingdom being gross, cannot so soon penetrate as the thin air of France and Spain." So rarely did the sun shine in winter that the Spanish ambassador was said to have told English courtiers as he returned to Spain "to present his humble service to the King their Master, and to the blessed Sun of Heaven when they chanced to see him." Heylyn, presaging modern understanding, also thought that the approach of the winds over water moderated winter's cold in England.[38]

Whatever the causes, early modern people firmly believed that human activity would meliorate America's climate; western Europe's moderation, they argued, was a product of centuries of cultivating the land and cutting down the dense forests. They did not understand that global weather systems produced local phenomena and thought that local changes would produce new microclimates. French venturers believed that Canada's climate would become more like that of France once the woods were cut down and the land was opened to cultivation and the sun's rays. But they also thought that some danger would attach to this process. Biard quoted Champlain on the theory that the vapors people inhaled from newly opened ground produced dangerous diseases.[39] English promoters also argued that opening the land through deforestation and cultivation would necessarily moderate the weather, as would moving away from the coasts into the interior. Anthony Parkhurst scorned the "foolish Mariners" who claimed that Newfoundland was naturally cold, reasoning instead that the cold "commeth from accidental meanes," from the "Isles of Ice" that came from farther north "and not by the situation of the countrey, or nature of the Climate." He predicted that as people moved into the interior, especially to the south, "they shall finde it hotter then in England."[40]

We understand much more now about both the underlying climates and the specific hardships that Americans as well as Europeans faced in the period when English people first attempted colonization. Most important, we know that the sixteenth and seventeenth centuries were a period of unprecedented environmental stress. Much of the Northern Hemisphere experienced cold in this period so severe that many historical climatologists call it the Little Ice Age.[41]

Tracking the fluctuations of the earth's climate before the modern era is a difficult endeavor. Thermometers were not invented until the later seventeenth century, and they remained an expensive rarity for a long time. Moreover, there was no consensus on how they should be used to get reliable findings; early observers like John Locke took their readings indoors.[42] Truly consistent records exist only from the later nineteenth century to the present. But historians and climatologists believe that they can track climate farther back, and they have brought great ingenuity to the task.

The first attempts to understand conditions in the early modern period relied on what scientists call proxy data, records that draw on human interaction with the environment. Clearly sixteenth- and seventeenth-century people had to be keen observers of their environment; their ability to control or regulate it was extremely limited, and their vulnerability to adverse conditions was extreme. Thus people everywhere kept weather diaries, or noted the weather in their diaries, correspondence, and records, and local lore commented on glacial advance or retreat. Tax records and other government documents can chronicle changes in agricultural productivity. Painters conveyed information on environmental conditions by showing snow-covered landscapes, people skating on frozen rivers, or landmarks engulfed by intermountain glaciers.[43] Much of Europe depended on the Atlantic cod fisheries for protein; because codfish thrive at sea temperatures between 4° and 7°C but cannot tolerate water below 2°C, reports of lean years in the cod fisheries may indicate colder periods. Annually recorded events such as the declaration of the vintage in French wine country or the level of the Nile River at flood stage constitute immensely valuable, because consistent, series that tell a great deal about both temperatures and rainfall.[44]

Early modern people also read the weather for signs of God's judgment on their activities. Times of adversity, particularly extreme drought conditions, often brought people to fast and pray together in the hope that mending their relationship to God would mend the weather. Ministers' calls for such dedicated worship and the sermons they preached at these services offer a dramatic record both of hard climatological times and of people's vulnerability to them.

All these kinds of sources, while very suggestive, are difficult to interpret. For example, glaciers in the European Alps and the Canadian Rockies advanced during the sixteenth and seventeenth centuries, as the moraines they left behind clearly indicate. But is glacial advance a function of cooler summers, in which the ice fails to melt, rather than very cold winters? Growing ice fields indicate significantly increased snowfall in upper latitudes, which might mean that winter temperatures were actually elevated in the tropics, where the moisture that later falls as snow enters the atmosphere. Great ice sheets and snowfields in northern latitudes are both produced by and become causes of further cooling. Global weather is an integrated system; component parts operate locally but also interact with other systems. Thus local data from one region must be interpreted with care; drawing inferences about climate in general is risky.[45]

Diaries, letters, and sermons present even more difficulties of interpretation. Naturally, most offer evidence of the unusual and the extreme. Two weeks or a month of very great cold may elicit much comment from sufferers but tell us little about the whole winter of even that year, much less about the climate of an entire period. Drought is most often recorded during the season when newly planted crops are most vulnerable; dryness at other times may not occasion much comment. Thus, except for the rare individual who recorded the weather every day, written sources give us tantalizing evidence that must be interpreted with discretion.[46]

Doubts remain among some climatologists about assertions of a period of colder weather so sustained and widespread as to merit the name Little Ice Age, and various beginning and ending dates have been suggested. Some historians, drawing on European data, assert that the continent began to descend into a colder temperature regime in the middle of the fifteenth century and did not emerge fully until late in the nineteenth. Others argue for a tighter time frame, focusing principally on the period from the middle of the sixteenth century to the middle of the eighteenth; some opt for an even more circumscribed periodization. Setting the beginning and end of the Little Ice Age is difficult because even a generally colder period will be interrupted by warmer decades. Thus part of the problem is determining the underlying pattern and separating out the noise.

More recently climatologists have added scientific evidence to the literary sources in finely calibrated computer readings of ice and lakebed cores, tree-ring records, glacial moraines, and experience locked in coral deposits. These sources offer what the literary do not. They are consistent over long periods of time, and they are not captive to the subjective responses of those living through a particular weather regime. They do require interpretation, however. When used in conjunction with human records from the period, as historical climatologists now do, they can offer a far more complete portrait of past climate than either kind of source alone. Even scientists who see the Little Ice Age label as exaggerating the dimensions of the weather regime agree that the seventeenth century was one of the coldest in the last millennium.[47]

Accounting for such a significant downturn is also difficult.[48] One line of thought is that minor variation in the sun's output of energy might contribute to such a change. Some historical climatologists link colder temperatures to the marked decrease in recorded sunspot activity between 1400 and 1510, known as the Spörer Minimum, and between 1645 and 1720, the Maunder Minimum. Changes in the earth's attitude, that is, its tilt on its axis, and in its orbit around the sun may also contribute. Other scientists posit that changes in ocean currents are the underlying cause of the cycle, and some scholars have pointed to variations in the earth's magnetic field. Particularly bad runs of years or decades are attributed to causes such as volcanic eruptions. The seventeenth century was punctuated by major volcanic eruptions, beginning with Huanyaputina near Arequipa in southern Peru in 1600 and Mount Vesuvius in 1631, and the dust veils created by them could account for significant cooling. Particularly effective eruptions at low latitudes occurred in 1641, 1673, and 1693.[49]

Very recent research has added another variable in global weather change that may explain particularly harsh episodes. El Niño, the periodic appearance of warm water on the surface of the Pacific Ocean off the coast of Peru, is connected with large-scale weather anomalies all over the world. The timing, duration, and intensity of El Niño's appearance varies, and therefore its interconnections with weather systems in other parts of the world also vary. These periodic effects were first documented in the early years of the seventeenth century.[50] Climatologists, and the public generally, have become interested in these occurrences in recent decades, particularly after the 1982–83 El Niño, the most severe of the twentieth century. The more severe or prolonged the El Niño, the more far-flung the effects throughout the world (called teleconnections by climatologists).[51] Little Ice Age cold may also have been accompanied by "occasional peculiarly intense windstorms," including the great storm that swept away the Spanish Armada.[52]

Data compiled from a variety of types of sources demonstrate that Europe experienced significantly colder weather throughout much of the sixteenth century, with a crushing downturn in the last decade and a half. The century was studded with landmark bad years, such as 1540, which was both cold and dry in central Europe; all over Germany drought was so severe that people crossed even the Rhine and Main rivers on foot. The winter of 1573 was so cold that Lake Thun in Switzerland, a very deep lake, froze over completely; this happened again in the very severe period of the 1690s but has never occurred in modern times. The extreme decade and a half at century's end was ushered in by the severe winter of 1587, which saw snow in the Swiss plateau in every month but August. Throughout the 1590s the weather was abnormally wet, accompanied by dangerous flooding in some cases.[53] Repeated crop failures in Norway during the seventeenth century led to famine, and northern farmland yielded to encroaching ice, a process that intensified in the eighteenth century. Glaciers in the Alps also grew precipitously in the later sixteenth and seventeenth centuries, leading to the abandonment of entire villages.[54] There were repeated instances of high mortality in Scotland in the late sixteenth and early seventeenth centuries attributed principally to subsistence crises when abnormal weather contributed to crop failure; some compared it to David's famine in the Bible.[55]

Cold conditions prevailed in eastern and central North America as well in the sixteenth and seventeenth centuries, and glaciers advanced in the Northwest beginning in the sixteenth century.[56] The 1590s and 1690s were clearly among the coldest decades on record. Changes in concentrations of pollen in layers from across North America show that the mix of plant species altered during these centuries.[57]

There was apparently a strong El Niño appearance in 1607–8, when Quebec, Santa Fé, Jamestown, and the short-lived Sagadahoc colony in Maine were founded.[58] Everyone knew that the winter of 1607–8 was one of the worst ever experienced. Sagadahoc failed completely after a winter "fit to freeze the heart of a plantation," and extreme cold was felt as far south as Chesapeake Bay. Francis Perkins wrote from Jamestown, that "the cold was so intense that one night the river at our fort froze almost all the way across, although at that point it is as wide again as the one at London." Captain John Smith reported violent winds and storms as well as extreme cold. William Strachey acknowledged that the Virginia winter was "so extreame unseasonable and frostie" that movement was impeded, but pointed out that "the extraordinary Frost was felt in most parts of Europe" as well.[59]

This was one of those severe winters in which the Thames froze completely. Following "bitter weather" in December, John Chamberlain wrote in January that the river was "quite frozen over and the

archbishop came from Lambeth on Twelfth-day over the ice to court."
The unusual conditions inspired not only regular foot traffic on the
river and "many fantastical experiments" but also, Chamberlain reported, one "honest woman (they say) that had a great longing to have
her husband to get her with child upon the Thames." And "The Late
Great Frost" was commemorated in a ballad registered with the Statio-
ner's Company on March 7, 1608.[60] In America, Indian oral tradition
remembered this landmark winter more than a hundred years later.
The next winter also saw extreme cold.[61]

French voyages to Nova Scotia and the St. Lawrence in the early
seventeenth century reported dramatic evidence of frigid temperatures. The ships carrying Jesuits to Acadia in 1611 encountered Samuel de Champlain in late April,

> who was making his way through the icebergs to Kebec. These
> masses of ice were enormous, for the sea was in some places cov-
> ered with them as far as the eye could reach. And, to cross them,
> they had to be broken with bars and pointed irons inserted in
> the escobilles or beak of the ship; it was fresh-water ice, and had
> drifted down more than a hundred leagues to the deep and open sea
> through the great St. Lawrence river. In some places there appeared
> vast and lofty pieces of floating and wavering ice, thirty and forty
> fathoms out of the water, as big and broad as if several castles were
> joined together, or, as you might say, as if the Church of notre
> Dame de Paris, with part of its Island, houses, and palaces should go
> floating out upon the water.

Father Pierre Biard and his fellow priests "lost nearly all sensation from
numbness and exposure" at sea.[62]

Colder temperatures were compounded by unprecedented drought
throughout North America in the period of contact and first settle-

ment. Descriptions of extreme dryness and crop failure abound in the written record, and these are now corroborated by computer readings of the record of past conditions embedded in trees, ice, and lakebeds. Drought conditions in the sixteenth century across the American West, the Southeast to the Mississippi River, and the Great Lakes region were the most severe of the last five hundred years—far exceeding the Dustbowl climate of the 1930s, the worst arid period of the twentieth century. Moreover, these conditions persisted throughout much of the century.

In the New Mexico territory many Spanish accounts reported widespread abandonment of pueblos, resulting in the consolidation of the population in larger pueblos, and distress among the Indians there. In the Southwest and northern Mexico the sixteenth-century drought may have been the worst in two thousand years. Unusually dry conditions obtained in the Southwest and the northern Rocky Mountains from the middle of the sixteenth through the seventeenth and into the eighteenth centuries. A wave of abandonments had occurred in the fifty years preceding Spanish settlement of the area.[63]

Tree-ring analysis, conducted on living thousand-year-old baldcypress trees, has recently added to our understanding from literary sources of the specific hardships experienced in southeastern North America in the period when Europeans first attempted colonization. Unprecedented drought conditions prevailed when the Roanoke and Jamestown colonies were founded. Archaeological work on the Florida coast has uncovered evidence of changes in seasonal settlement patterns in response to the effects of drought combined with the demands of transatlantic migrants for food.[64]

The written record abounds with reports of devastating drought that conditioned encounters between Europeans and Indians. When, in the spring of 1566, the chief of the Guale Indians on the coast of Georgia complained to the Spanish commander in Florida, Pedro Menéndez de Avilés, that it had not rained for eight or nine months,

Menéndez replied that the drought was God's punishment. The Guale chief said that he was already a Christian and had made peace with his enemies, the Orista Indians, "in order not to anger God," so Menéndez should ask God to give him rain for his fields. Menéndez replied that God was angry because Guale had not done fully what he was ordered to do and therefore "He would not give the cacique water." Then, "the cacique turned away very sadly and went to his house: the youths who had been left to teach the natives the doctrine, hearing of this, went to the cacique with the interpreter and told him not to be sad; that they would supplicate God that it might rain." Menéndez was furious when he heard this and ordered the boys whipped; he thought they had taken this initiative in order to get presents from the chief. The cacique intervened "very sadly" and asked that their punishment be remitted; "he said he was content that it should rain when God willed." The chief then demonstrated his adherence to Christianity by kneeling before the cross and kissing it and said through Menéndez's interpreter, "Behold, how I am a true Christian." The result was dramatic. "This occurred at about 2 o'clock in the afternoon: not half an hour had gone by when there came thunder and lightning, and it began to rain very hard, and a bolt struck and splintered into many pieces a tree near the village: all the Indian men and women ran to it to take the broken branches and bring them to their houses, to keep them." The rain fell widely and lasted for twenty-four hours; as a result the Indians implored Menéndez to leave Christians with them.[65]

When the Spanish Jesuits, accompanied by Paquiquineo, whom they knew as Don Luís, came to inaugurate their mission on Chesapeake Bay in 1570, they "found the land of Don Luís in quite another condition than expected, not because he was at fault in his description of it, but because Our Lord has chastised it with six years of famine and death, which has brought it about that there is much less population than usual." The people had no maize, nor could they gather any of the fruit or roots that usually sustained them, "save for a small amount obtained with great labor from the soil, which is very parched." The winters were marked by "great snows" that impeded efforts to hunt. Some Paspaheghs had left, and the remaining ones stayed because they "wish to die where their fathers have died." So desperate was their situation that they believed Paquiquineo had returned from the dead to help them.[66]

Fifteen years later Thomas Harriot recorded conversations with Roanoke Indians similar to that between Menéndez and the Guale chief: "On a time also when their corne began to wither by reason of a drougth which happened extraordinarily, fearing that it had come to passe by reason that in some thing they had displeased us, many would come to us & desire us to pray to our God of England, that he would preserve their corne, promising that when it was ripe we also should be partakers of the fruite."[67] Although these colonists returned to England in 1586, the second Roanoke colony planted the following year found evidence of continued drought. John White reported the poignant meeting between the new colonists and the friendly Croatoans. Although their posture was guarded at first, the Indians eventually responded and "came unto us, embracing and entertaining us friendly, desiring us not to gather or spill any of their corne, for that they had but little."[68] At the same time, the Spanish began to consolidate and reduce their colonies, abandoning Santa Elena after two decades. The next year, 1588, Pedro Menéndez Marqués wrote to the Spanish king of the hardships St. Augustine and the missions in Florida faced: "There has been a very long drought the present year in this part of the world, particularly so in Florida, where not a grain of maize could be planted; and we were in very great distress."[69] Marooned in America, the second Roanoke colony, the Lost Colony, faced terrible drought conditions. The years 1587–1589, when these planters were struggling to get established without help from England, were the region's driest three years in the last eight hundred.[70] There are also indications that the 1590s were bad in America as in Europe.

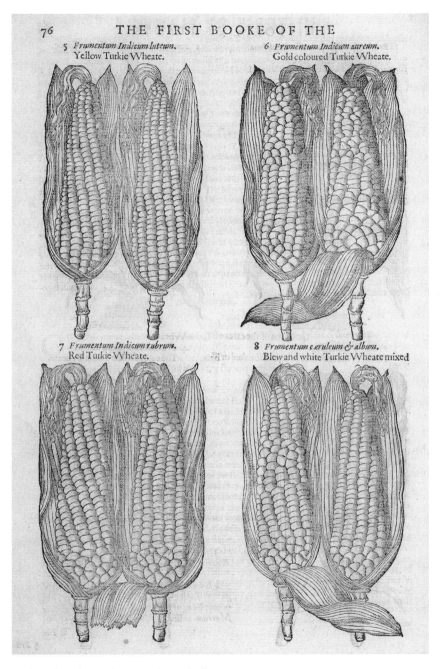

Turkie wheat from John Gerard's Herball, *1597*. This item is reproduced by permission of The Huntington Library, San Marino, California.

Migrants in England's early American colonies were famously dependent on their Indian neighbors for the food to keep them alive, and the resistance of those native people to colonists' demands is equally well known. In the mid-1580s in Roanoke and in Jamestown twenty years later, leaders reacted with alarm to rumors that the Americans planned to make war on them by withdrawing from contact. Governor Ralph Lane of Roanoke wrote that had Wingina, the Roanoke chief, done that, "there had bene no possibilitie in common reason, (but by the immediate hande of God) that we could have bene preserved from starving out of hand. For at that time wee had no weares for fishe, neither could our men skill of the making of them, neither had wee one grayne of corne for seede to put into the ground."[71]

The Jamestown colonists pressed the Pamunkeys and their clients in Chesapeake Bay similarly hard. Captain John Smith and other Jamestown leaders believed that Powhatan, that "subtell owlde foxe," was manipulating the corn supply in order to control the relationship.[72] What the colonists of both Roanoke and Jamestown only dimly recognized was that the region along the east coast was experiencing previously unknown levels of environmental hardship when the settlements were founded. The perceived clever bargaining of native leaders was underlain by a harsh reality.

Environmental stress raised in some Indians a poignant theme of loss and alienation from their own deities. Henry Spelman, an English boy in Jamestown who lived among Virginia Algonquians for extended periods, wrote of how the Indians appealed to their deities "if at any time they want Rayne or have to much," and many wrote of the Indians' distress and confusion when their appeals went unanswered. Captain John Smith, for example, wrote of Chawopo, the "honest, proper, good promis-keeping king" of the Quiyoughcohannocks in Virginia, that "though to his false Gods he was yet very zealous, yet he would confesse, our God as much exceeded his, as our guns did his bowe and arrowes, often sending our President [Smith] manie presents to praie to his God for raine, or his corne would perish, for his Gods were angrie."[73] The year before Jamestown's founding, 1606, was the beginning of the driest seven-year period in the last 770 years in the Chesapeake. No wonder the Indians thought that their "Gods were angrie."[74]

It was the Christian God's willingness to deploy his powers for the colonists that made Christianity so impressive. God thus honored his promise given in Jeremiah 33:3, "Call unto me, and I wil answer thee, and shewe thee great & mightie things, which thou knowest not."[75] The Indians' God, as native priests described him to European observers, was not so reliably amenable.

Early English observers had some comprehension of the Indians' situation in the Chesapeake. Powhatan repeatedly told John Smith the truth—that corn was in short supply—when he resisted demands for food, "valuing a basket of corne more pretious then a basket of copper, saying he could eate his corne, but not his copper." Smith reported that he had seen impressive stores of food during his captivity in the early months of Jamestown, but he also realized that crops were adversely affected by the extreme weather regime. While forcing the Chickahominies to provide corn to feed his men, Smith acknowledged that the Indians' harvest had been "that year bad," and he added that the Chickahominies "complained extreamly of their owne wants." When Smith repeatedly enforced his demands for loads of corn, he as often noted that the Indians "wanted themselves," and he frankly admitted that "the Spanyard never more greedily desired gold then he victuall." If food was as important as gold to the English, for the Algonquians of the bay, "their victuall is their chiefest riches." Readers in England, having lived through harsh conditions themselves, would have understood about bad harvests, but it is hard for us to judge whether they would have seen simple savagery or the effect of extreme environmental conditions in Smith's claim that for three quarters of the year the Chesapeake Algonquians lived "from hand to mouth."[76]

Some researchers believe that extreme drought conditions, especially when interspersed with rare wet years, may have created conditions that spread disease and intensified its impact on American Indian populations at the time when the European colonies were settled. Viruses carried by rodents or other fauna whose habits were disrupted by adverse environmental conditions spread through American populations.[77]

What did this all mean? Exaggerated weather phenomena always carried significance, and they affected everyone; they had to be read for God's message in them. As the Reverend Nicholas Bownde preached in England, only "Atheists" spoke of extreme weather in "a meere worldly manner"; the godly searched each episode for its providential meaning.[78] Reformation leader John Calvin, in his commentary on Genesis, wrote that "the intemperature of the aire, yce, thunder, unseasonable raines, drouthe, hailes, and what soever is extraordinarie in the world, are the fruites of sinne."A marginal note reinforced the point: "Wether untemperate and such like are the fruites of sin."[79] Ignoring God's message would only bring greater disaster.

Richard Beacon, who had been in Ireland from the mid-1580s to the early 1590s, wrote a book about the general problem of creating plantations and governing with discretion. He used examples from Roman times to assert that "signes" of coming calamities should be read in the dearth and earthquakes afflicting England and Ireland in the 1590s and argued for the necessity of reform.[80]

The year of Jamestown's founding, 1607, saw the culmination of a series of catastrophes in Britain that were collectively seen as "tokens" of God's "heavy wrath extended toward us." In a pamphlet titled *Gods Warning to his people of England*, William Jones called his readers to remember "the late grievous and most lamentable Plague of Pestilence, wherein the wrath of God tooke from us so many thousandes of our friendes, kindred, and acquaintance." He also pointed to "the late Papisticall Conspiracie of Traytors, that with powder practised the subversion of this beautifull kingdome"—the Gunpowder Plot, which aimed to blow up the parliament in November 1605 at a time when King James I, his queen, and his eldest son, Prince Henry, would have been present. Then, less than three weeks after the Jamestown-bound ships set sail, huge waves comparable to "the greatest mountains in the world" inundated the west country of England and South Wales drowning thousands—some still in their beds. The "mercyless Waters" came on so fast that even birds were scarcely able to fly up in time to escape their "furie." So destructive were "these outragious Waters" that "many men that were rich in the morning when they rose out of their beds, were made poore before noone the same day: such are the Judgements of the Almightie God."[81]

The year 1607 was also marked by a comet, a sure sign of a message from God, whose appearance coincided with the departure of the first Jamestown-bound fleet. George Percy, whose brother was known as the "Wizard Earl" for his scientific experiments, recorded that as the ships were finally under way after being held on the coast of England for several weeks by "greate stormes," the company "saw a blazing Starre, and presently a storme." The 1607 comet struck fear into Indians in northern Mexico, where native priests at Laguna brought the people together for ceremonies to "favorably dispose the comet." They held a massive sacrifice, burning many possessions that "would rise up as smoke to the comet. As a result, the comet would have some food during those days and would therefore do them no harm." Despite their efforts, the comet's appearance coincided with the outbreak of a devastating epidemic.[82]

Christians associated comets and other extraordinary phenomena with epidemics. Thomas Harriot, deeply troubled by the diseases that had struck so many coastal Carolina Algonquians while he was there with the first Roanoke colony in 1585–86, wrote that some of the English had pointed to a comet that had appeared just a few days before "the said sicknesse" broke out, and they also thought that a solar eclipse the previous year might have played a role. In the 1680s Increase Mather in New England published *Kometographia. Or a Discourse Concerning Comets*, in which he wrote about both the 1585 and 1607 comets and the troubles that followed them all over the world.[83]

Christians studied signs and portents for their providential meaning, but they knew that God sent them to recall the people to their true path, and they could always ask for divine protection. The Reverend Patrick Copland began the sermon he preached before the Virginia Company in London with verses from Psalm 107: "They that goe downe to the Sea in Ships . . . they see the worke of the Lord, and his wonders in the deepe." The Psalm described how God raised storms at sea in which the sailors were powerless; "all their cunning is gone." But when they put their trust in God, he calmed the storm and brought them into port.[84]

The first Virginia fleet experienced exactly the kind of providential intercession promised by the Psalm. Having endured "unprosperous windes" that kept them on English shores for six weeks after their intended embarkation date, the men then encountered problems in the western Atlantic. As the ships coasted along the Virginia shore, the mariners were unable to find the entrance to Chesapeake Bay, and some began to mutter about giving up and returning to England. At that point they experienced the direct intervention of God, who, "forcing them by an extreame storme to hull all night, did drive them by his providence to their desired Port, beyond all their expectations, for never any of them had seene that coast."[85]

Some colonists feared that Christians were not the only ones with the ability to influence the natural world. Many suspected that Indian religious leaders were able to manipulate weather to their own advantage, forming a mirror image to Christians' prayers for rain. For their part, the Indians quickly came to understand the Europeans' unique vulnerability to certain kinds of weather. In 1566 Pedro Menéndez de Avilés wrote a long report to King Philip II from the recently founded colony of Florida telling of his accomplishments and his plans for further exploration and conquest. Although he had been triumphant over his success in bringing the Guale leader to a public demonstration of his Christian faith and the rain it brought, he acknowledged his men's vulnerability. He urgently asked for crossbows for his soldiers, who were equipped only with arquebuses, or muskets. Sixteenth-century muskets required the user to apply a lighted match, a smoldering length of rope, to the powder in the pan in order to ignite the powder in the barrel and shoot the ball. As Menéndez pointed out, they made poor weapons in wet weather, and the Indians understood this: "Without crossbows, the arquebuses are wasted weapons, because these savages are so skilled, so confident in their quickness and force that they did not lose their confidence, attacking us when it rained, and when we could not take advantage of the arquebuses. And we cannot defend ourselves against the Indians, nor make war upon them, without crossbows, for every day they kill Christians without our being able to kill an Indian, unless we have crossbows."[86] Unfortunately for the Europeans, to be used effectively, bows, unlike muskets, required skill gained only from long training.

Reports from Jamestown also recorded Indian attempts to manipulate the weather, sometimes with the goal of making the colonists' muskets inoperable. William Strachey described what he called "Botanomantia," rites and sacrifices priests conducted at the water's edge when storms made the seas rough. Their goal was "to pacefy that god, whome they thinck to be very angry in those stormes."[87] The Reverend Alexander Whitaker wrote about a Virginia expedition traveling to attack the Nansemond Indians that saw a "mad crewe dauncinge like Anticks, or our Morris dancers," on the riverbank, led by a priest who "tossed smoke and flame out of a thinge like a censer." Machumps, an Indian who was traveling with the English, predicted that "there would be very much raine presently." But although there was "exceeding thunder and lighteninge," the rain when it came was far off and "not so much there as made theire powder dancke." George Percy wrote about the same episode, describing the priests' "exorcismes, conjuracyons and charmes, throweinge fyer upp into the skyes, runneinge up and downe with rattles and makeinge many dyabolicall gestures with many nigramantcke spelles and incantacions, imageninge thereby to cawse raine to fall from the clowdes to extinguishe and putt outt our mens matches, and to wett and spoyle their powder."

European colonists wrote triumphantly of instances where the pow-wows' efforts failed, precisely because they took those powers very seriously; they were often constrained to include episodes where the priests' success rivaled that of the Christians. In his formal description of Virginia, Whitaker called the Indian priests "a generation of vipers even of Sathans owne brood," but he did not doubt that they used their powers for their people's good: "If they would have raine, or have lost any thing, they have their recourse to him, who conjureth for them, *and many times prevaileth*.[88] Even after a century of experience, such thinking still resonated. Cotton Mather recorded the effect of early failures in New England: colonial backers "began to suspect that the Indian Sorcerers had laid the place under some Fascination; and that the English could not prosper upon such Enchanted Ground."[89]

The American environment was deeply puzzling to English people used to Britain's maritime climate with its relatively small range of temperatures. Violent hurricanes, earthquakes, and other phenomena provoked comparisons to regions renowned for their outlandish weather. The suspicion that America's native people might have spiritual resources for controlling the weather and harming English interests, intensified colonists' misgivings about settling in southern re-

The Coniuerer. XI.

Hey haue comonlye coniurers or iuglers which vſe ſtrange geſtures, and often cō-
trarie to nature in their enchantments: For they be verye familiar with deuils, of
whome they enquier what their enemys doe, or other ſuche thinges. They ſhaue
all their heads ſauinge their creſte which they weare as other doe, and faſten a ſmall
black birde aboue one of their ears as a badge of their office. They weare nothinge
but a skinne which hangeth downe from their gyrdle, and couereth their priuityes. They weare a
bagg by their ſide as is expreſſed in the figure. The Inhabitants giue great credit vnto their ſpeeche, which oftentymes they finde
to bee true.

B 3

*Engraving of an Indian powwow, a religious practitioner called The Flyer, from a painting by
John White.* Courtesy of the John Carter Brown Library at Brown University.

gions, especially as they feared the effects of hot climates on British
bodies whose humors were adjusted to a more temperate regime.

The key to health and economic success lay in the combination of
latent fruitfulness in the land and human labor enhanced by technology. Western Europe had a moderate, healthy climate and relatively
productive land, according to this thinking, because of the work of

countless generations. As Europeans emigrated to America and applied their systems consistently, bringing the landscape to mature per-
fection, then the climate would moderate, the violent storms of imma-
ture nature would be tamed, and the best crops would grow. America
would cease to be an enchanted land, and the benevolent God would
reign over it.

6

A Welter of Colonial Projects

THE FIRST DECADE of the seventeenth century saw a great rush of new projects set out by English merchants and courtiers, and they began to achieve the success denied to earlier ventures. When the Scottish king James Stuart, son of the executed Mary Queen of Scots, succeeded Queen Elizabeth as James I in 1603, he quickly reversed the decades-old hostility between England and Spain. With the signing of the Anglo-Spanish peace in 1604, the privateering war that had fueled and shaped English relationships with America was suddenly over. Now promoters had to think in very different terms if England was to have a continuing American presence. The accumulated technical knowledge and capital accrued in the war would allow backers to sustain more expensive and expansive commitments. But in the atmosphere of peace, other parts of the world also beckoned to merchants.

The East India Company, founded as the century opened, initiated a series of voyages around Africa. The company established its first Indian Ocean base at Surat in 1608 and began challenging the Portuguese monopoly. African trade also opened. Merchant John Davies established regular commerce in redwood with Sierra Leone about 1607 and had placed a permanent factor there by 1611 in the first English station on the African coast. And there were intimations of even richer trades: Captain William Keeling's East India–bound fleet which put in to the Sierra Leone estuary in 1607 procured thousands of lemons to treat the seamen's scurvy but also many gold rings and "elephants' teeth" during several weeks on the African coast. And in 1607 the Ottoman Empire sent its first official ambassador, Mustapha, to England.[1] The kinds of trading stations or "factories" that English merchants and other foreigners created in the Ottoman Empire, communities in which merchants' representatives often lived for years, were the ideal model for the American trades. But all these other opportunities represented alternative investment possibilities with which Virginia would have to compete for resources.

Even among American projects, Jamestown's founding in 1607 did not stand out at the time as a singularly important event. In fact, the little fleet of three ships set out amidst a flurry of activity in those years, and American ventures were scattered widely across the North American and West Indian coastlines. Several of Jamestown's leaders had first considered other American venues. George Percy, a principal figure in the first group of colonists, was in the West Indies in 1602. Captain John Smith wrote in his autobiography that he had actually signed on to go in 1605 to a colony founded by Captain Charles Leigh on "the River Weapoco" in Guiana, "but hee dyed, and there lyes buried, and the supply miscarrying, the rest escaped as they could." English attempts to found West Indian colonies on St. Lucia in 1604 and Grenada in 1609 also failed. So, even for central actors in Jamestown, that colony was just one possible choice among many.[2]

Charles Leigh was a puritan and sympathetic to those whose antipathy to the Church of England led them to cut themselves off completely and form independent congregations; most puritans in this period were able to find ways to satisfy their consciences without taking such a drastic step. In 1597 Leigh had led a colony that included a large number of such separatists in an effort to create a refuge on the Magdalen Islands in the Gulf of St. Lawrence. The attempt failed when the advance party met resistance from Basque fishermen in the region, and those separatists returned to join others already in the tolerant Netherlands.[3] In 1607 the separatist puritans who have become known to us as the Pilgrims tried to leave England for the Netherlands; they were finally allowed to emigrate the next year. Ultimately they left their Dutch refuge and settled Plymouth in Massachusetts Bay, the first successful American separatist colony.

Charles Leigh tried again. In attempting to found a colony in Guiana, Leigh built on Sir Walter Ralegh's exploring voyage there in 1595, two years before the Magdalen Islands project. Ralegh was drawn to the region contemporaries called Guiana, which then included all of the Orinoco Basin and the northern Amazon, by persistent rumors of the rich kingdom of El Dorado in its interior. He had gathered reports from many sources, including the high-ranking Spanish colonial official Don Pedro Sarmiento de Gamboa, who was brought to England as a prisoner by one of Ralegh's privateering ships. Sarmiento genuinely believed in El Dorado's existence, and the idea that there might be a second Peru in South America seemed promising.

Ralegh's expedition did not find El Dorado, although he continued to believe in rich sources of gold in the interior, where the Spanish had not yet spread their control. He also proudly claimed that the Indians had welcomed him as a potential liberator from the harsh Spanish presence. To cement the relationship he left two Englishmen, young Hugh Goodwin to learn the language and a literate man named Francis Sparrey (Ralegh called him "Sparrow"), with Topiawari, the "chief lord of Arromaia." In return Topiawari's son Cayoworaco agreed to go to England with Ralegh; two others, Leonard Ragapo and Harry, also accompanied the returning ships. In all, Ralegh and the captains of the various reconnoitering voyages he sent to Guiana may have brought as many as ten Indians to England. Ralegh later wrote that he would have called in at Roanoke on the return voyage to try to lo-

Ralegh conversing with Topiawari in Guiana. Courtesy of the John Carter Brown Library at Brown University.

cate his abandoned colonists of the previous decade "if extremity of weather had not forst me from the said coast."[4]

Francis Sparrey finally made it back to England in 1602; he had been "taken by the Spaniards and sent prisoner into Spaine, and after long captivitie got into England by great sute." During his captivity he had converted to Roman Catholicism. Hugh Goodwin was killed in Guiana. All three Indian men apparently returned to Guiana, and Cayoworaco did become lord of Arromaia; while in England they had been part of Ralegh's household. Voyages in 1597 and 1604 are known to have carried Indian men home; they may also have traveled westward on any of countless other ships. Robert Harcourt, a Roman Catholic Englishman who founded another small colony on the Guiana coast in 1609, reported that he had met and talked with Leonard. Harcourt's colony gave up and returned home in 1613.[5]

When he referred to Charles Leigh's ill-fated Guiana colony, to which he had been slated to go, Captain John Smith mentioned attempts to resupply the colony "miscarrying." In 1607, just after Smith embarked with the first Jamestown colonists, one of the survivors of the 1605 supply voyage, John Nicholl, published an account with the chilling title *An houre glasse of Indian newes. Or A true and tragicall discourse, shewing the most lamentable miseries, and distressed calamities indured by 67 Englishmen, which were sent for a supply to the planting in Guiana in the yeare. 1605 Who not finding the saide place, were for want of victuall, left a shore in Saint Lucia, an island of caniballs, or men-eaters in the West-Indyes, vnder the conduct of Captain Sen-Iohns, of all which said number, onely a 11. are supposed to be still liuing, whereof 4. are lately returnd into England.*[6]

Ralegh had warned in the mid-1590s that French venturers had plans to found a settlement in the Guiana region, and many English, French, and Dutch voyages did converge on Guiana in these years, often with crews drawn from several nations. Competition between potential colonizers added urgency to all these efforts. Between the two English colonial attempts in Guiana of 1604 and 1609, a more ambitious French venture tried to settle on the "River Weapoco" in 1607. English outposts along the Amazon were evicted by the Portuguese in these years.[7] All American ventures carried a threat of danger, and all were based on wishful thinking. Guiana drew attention in particular because the potential rewards were seen as so exceptional.

Although the south seemed promising, European attention also focused on the northern coastline. Very large numbers of ships went to Newfoundland and northern New England every year for the fishing, and informal camps had been created by the fishermen. In 1602 an expedition led by Bartholomew Gosnold explored the coast of New England, the "North part of Virginia," in expectation of finding a good site for a trading station; as with Ralegh in Guiana, the reports of Gosnold's voyage stressed the excellent relationships they had formed with powerful Indian groups. Other voyages exploring the New England coast followed in 1603 and 1605. The latter venture, a major effort designed in part to locate a good site for a religious refuge, was sponsored by several Roman Catholic gentlemen. Sir Thomas Arundell considered including Irish and English Catholics who had served with Spanish forces in the proposed Maine colony, but Spanish and Jesuit resistance killed the plan.[8]

The various English expeditions culminated in a true settlement attempt. In 1606 two Virginia Companies were chartered in England: the London Virginia Company sponsored the Jamestown colony, and the Western Merchants' Virginia Company, headquartered in Plymouth, founded the colony of Sagadahoc on the Kennebec River in Maine. Bartholomew Gosnold became a prime mover of the Jamestown project, and Gabriel Archer, who had accompanied Gosnold's New England expedition, was in the first Chesapeake-bound group in 1607.

The Plymouth Virginia Company moved first, and their venture's experience showed once again the extreme difficulty such projects faced. In 1606 the company sent two ships to their intended site in New England; both carried Indian men who had been brought to

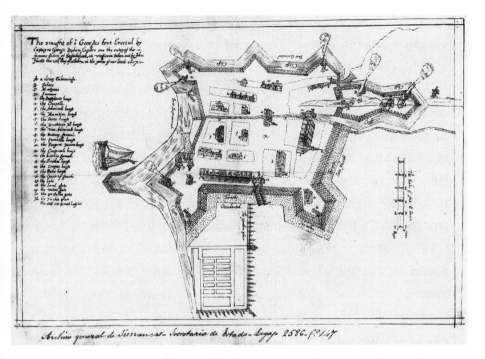

St. Georges Fort at Sagadahoc drawn by John Hunt in October 1607. The Spanish ambassador obtained the original and sent it to Philip III of Spain; it is now in the Spanish archives, Simancas. This version is a nineteenth-century tracing. Collections of Maine Historical Society.

England by previous voyages. The first ship, commanded by Henry Challons, followed the route common at the time down the coast of Africa to catch the trade winds across to the Caribbean, where the men could refresh their supplies before sailing northward. Virginia-bound ships followed this route, which always entailed some danger. Challons's ship was captured by a Spanish fleet, and the crew was carried into Spain. Mannedo and Assacomoit, two Abenaki men brought to England from the Maine coast the previous year, were among the captives. Challons, Assacomoit, and many of the crew were back in England from their Spanish captivity by 1608; Mannedo died in Spain. A second 1606 voyage under Thomas Hanham and Martin Pring brought a third Indian man, a sachem named Nahanada, back to

Maine. This voyage did achieve its destination but, not finding the Challons group, eventually returned to England, leaving Nahanada with his people.[9]

Both Virginia Companies founded plantations in 1607. The Maine colony was able to build on relationships and knowledge created by the voyages of preceding years. Not only did Nahanada remain interested in the settlement's welfare, but the 1607 ships also brought back another man taken to England in 1605, Skidwarres, who settled nearby. Yet despite its apparent advantages, Sagadahoc lasted only a few months. One unanticipated hardship was the extremely harsh winter of 1607-8. Jamestown hung on through its difficult early years, but Sagadahoc folded, and some blamed "the bitterness of that great Frost 1607." All colonial efforts were tenuous in the extreme, and most could not sustain the delicate balance of support such ventures required. Although reverses among sponsors in England were also responsible for Sagadahoc's demise, Captain John Smith later argued that its failure contributed to New England's reputation as a "cold, barren, mountainous rocky Desart."[10]

European interest in the north did not end with Sagadahoc. Everyone knew that 1607-8 had been an anomalous year all around the Atlantic, and backers assumed that normal conditions would be more favorable. And as in the West Indies, English promoters understood that they were always racing against the competition. French adventurers planted a colony at Port Royal in Acadia, modern Nova Scotia, in 1605 and an associated Jesuit mission in Maine, and Champlain inaugurated the little colony of Quebec in 1608. Quebec, like Jamestown, survived to become a permanent settlement where so many others failed.

English venturers continued to look north. The year 1607 saw Englishman Henry Hudson's setting out in an English voyage to discover the northwest passage to the Pacific. Although the ships reached an unprecedentedly high latitude, ice prevented them from completing their mission. Then in 1609 Hudson found employment with the Dutch and, drawing on information from Smith, explored the coast-line south of the St. Lawrence, discovering the Hudson River in the process. The great river had been noted by Verrazano early in the six-teenth century, but its mouth was unknown to contemporary mariners when Hudson successfully sailed up it. In 1610, back in English em-ploy, he attempted to find the straits Frobisher had described. This voyage discovered the bay which would be named for him. Hudson himself never made it back to England; his men mutinied and, having left Hudson and his supporters to die, returned with the claim that they had indeed discovered the northwest passage.[11]

The Bristol merchant John Guy sailed to Newfoundland in 1608 and on the basis of his survey the Newfoundland Company sent out a colony with Guy as governor two years later. This settlement at Cu-pid's Cove on the Avalon Peninsula was to be built on fishing, a proven commodity that already brought profits of £100,000 a year to England. The little colony went through many permutations and divi-sions, but Newfoundland colonization survived. By the 1620s new pro-moters had been attracted to the region, and some began to recruit mi-grants, most actively in Scotland and Ireland; St. John's emerged as the principal plantation.[12]

All these British overseas ventures shared several characteristics, the principal one being their funding. All were created by joint-stock companies, the new corporate form that brought investors together to finance projects that were too large for an individual or a simple partnership. Many such companies were limited to a small group of backers, but some sought large-scale investment. Shakespeare's Globe Theatre was created by a joint-stock company, as were Jamestown and Massachusetts Bay. The crown's role lay in encouraging subjects to undertake important projects by granting patents, monopoly rights over certain regions or commodities, and by maneuvers such as free-ing Ralph Lane of his responsibilities in Ireland so he could go to

Roanoke. Although the monarch sometimes contributed a ship to a colonial project and therefore was personally an adventurer, as investors were called, no government funds went directly into founding colonies.

Joint-stock companies were not like modern corporations with continuing capital funds; usually they operated as umbrella organizations that allowed members to subscribe to more limited joint-stocks under the company's aegis. Each voyage, for example, would be financed by a separate joint-stock agreement among some Virginia Company members, and that arrangement would be ended when the ships returned. After the first decade, the company also decided to allow investors to join together in small companies to finance and control individual plantations in Virginia.

Jamestown was just one American site among many and, especially in its very rocky first years, there was no reasonable expectation that it would survive to be the foundation of the first transatlantic British Empire. But this colony did stand out from its contemporaries in one very significant way: the London Virginia Company eventually attracted a huge number of investors by making the cost of one share of company stock relatively low. This scale of involvement proved to be crucial, especially once it became clear that the trading station model would not work in America and that only permanent migration by large numbers across the Atlantic would suffice to make colonies succeed—a very expensive proposition.

As the Virginia Company sought backers and government favor, many other possible ventures competed for attention, including a renewed Guiana project proposed by Sir Walter Ralegh. Ralegh, who had figured so heavily in colonization projects during Elizabeth's reign, found himself in a dramatically changed situation soon after James I came to the throne in 1603. The childless Elizabeth had deliberately stifled any planning for the transfer of the crown after her death, which ended the Tudor line of monarchs. Many courtiers had been secretly in touch with James VI of Scotland, who was deemed to have the best claim to the throne, laying the groundwork both for his succession and for their own position in the new government. Ralegh had not been among them and was treated coldly when the Scottish king became England's monarch. Ralegh was soon caught up in accusations over rumored plots to cooperate with Spain in overturning the English government and was convicted of treason before the year was out. The evidence suggests that he, like so many others, had at least considered supplying information to foreign governments in exchange for a pension.[13] He spent almost all of the rest of his life in the Tower of London. In his imprisonment Ralegh pursued various scientific projects with the aid of Thomas Harriot, and wrote his famous *History of the World*. But he continued to hope that a truly great success in a Guiana voyage would win him the king's friendship and his own freedom. Thus in the summer of 1607 he campaigned to enlist support at the highest levels of government for an expedition to find the gold mines he felt certain were there. Although the Privy Council, after serious discussion of the plan, declined to sponsor it, Ralegh sent a ship in 1608 to refresh his contacts in the region.[14]

Ralegh's 1607 scheme harked back to older models: ventures funded and directed by a small group of wealthy and highly placed supporters. The contemporary Virginia Company of London instead opted to widen its base of support, and this proved to be the model that would succeed in the infancy of colonization. According to Captain John Smith, Bartholomew Gosnold, fresh from his 1602 voyage to New England, was "one of the first movers of this plantation" in Jamestown. He tried for several years to win support for the project and succeeded in attracting "some Gentlemen," including Smith, to agree to go to the colony. Still, even after several years, "nothing could be effected, till by their great charge and industrie, it came to be apprehended by certaine of the Nobilitie, Gentry, and Marchants."[15] It is hard to see why all this attention came to center on Chesapeake Bay; none of the ventures of the preceding decade had focused on that region. But the exploring party sent up to the great bay from the Roanoke colony two decades earlier had returned with enthusiastic reports about its potential both for trade and for possible settlement. In fact, the last group at Roanoke, the Lost Colonists of 1587, had expected to found their plantation on one of the rivers feeding into Chesapeake Bay. Perhaps they or their descendants were still there. That would be an enormous boon to any novice group.

As the many ventures that failed or gave up indicate, picking a good location for a colony was only the tiniest of first steps. Creating a functioning settlement was a far more difficult, and crucial, matter, and the English were keenly aware that the practical mechanics of colonization were uncharted territory for them. Such enterprises were so expensive to build and maintain that the window within which backers worked was extremely limited.

In fact, the English had had a good deal of experience close to home with colonization, and they had very clear ideas of how it should work. But this experience had also taught them how difficult it was to put their ideas into operation. The British Isles were the scene of England's first imperial ventures. Bringing Scotland and Ireland within the scope of English control and reforming their cultures and language to fit English models of civility were construed as essential to the nation's security. The island to the west was closely linked to Scotland by migration and by the Gaelic language, and both fiercely maintained their separateness from the political and cultural regime centered in London. English imperialism in Ireland, and sometimes in the Scottish borders district and highlands, relied first of all on military campaigns to put down rebels. Following military action, the ideal model called for bureaucratizing local government—often employing demobilized English soldiers and commanders as officials. The final step that would bring everything to a successful conclusion in planners' eyes was removal of Irish populations from the rebels' forfeited lands, followed by colonization—sending over British families who would teach civility by example. Policy makers drew on classical and biblical models in arguing for this approach. As in American promotional tracts, some argued that only through Roman imperialism had the English been brought from the most vicious savagery to the blessings of Christianity and civility. Ralegh, who had colonizing interests in Ireland and in America, was one of many who began to use the word "plantation" for both the repeopling of the world after Noah's flood and contemporary projects for planting Europeans among others as a way of spreading civility.[16]

Ireland presented particularly difficult challenges. Its proximity to England and its adherence to Roman Catholicism after England had officially converted to Protestantism combined to make English leaders fear that the island could be a staging ground for a hostile invasion. Thus their firm goal was to make Ireland, as historian Nicholas Canny has written, British.

As they looked at Ireland, English leaders saw a horrifying scene of primitive barbarism. Difference was construed as defect, and the problem was seen as nothing less than raising the Irish to civility. Ireland was controlled by powerful clan leaders, many of whom were descended from previous English migrations meant to curb Irish independence. The challenge of powerful nobles with their own armies of retainers and their swaggering manner beset English administration in Scotland and the north of England as well. In Ireland, however, the problem seemed to be powerfully reinforced by the social and economic organization of life. English leaders looked down on the Irish practice of "booleying," moving cattle from low-lying pastures to high for the summer months; especially when combined with a relative lack of large towns, this looked suspiciously like nomadism to English eyes. It all seemed very tribal, and commentators constantly referred to the Irish as savage, barbarous, and primitive, living more like animals than people. Although England had nominally ruled Ireland for hundreds of years, only the Pale—Dublin and its surroundings—saw a really strong English presence in the late sixteenth century.[17]

It was in the Elizabethan period that English policy makers, especially fearing the kind of assistance Irish Roman Catholics might give to an invading Spanish army, began to try to bring the island under closer political control and to make it conform culturally to evolving English norms. A series of rebellions, led by Shane O'Neill in the 1560s and Gerald Fitzgerald, earl of Desmond, at the end of the 1570s, showed how volatile the situation was. Sir Humphrey Gilbert, Walter Ralegh's much-admired older half-brother, took up a command in Ireland fighting to put down O'Neill's rebellion. He sought to instill maximum fear into the population; as historian David Quinn observes, "His method of waging war was to devastate the country, killing every living creature encountered by his troops."[18]

The Desmond rebellion ended with the English capture of the fort at Smerwick in 1580. The garrison consisted of about four hundred Spanish and Italian volunteers, whose presence confirmed English leaders' worst fears about the dangers of allowing Ireland to remain Roman Catholic, and about two hundred Irish women and children. Every one of them was executed at the direction of the commander, Lord Grey of Wilton. One of Grey's lieutenants, who actually supervised the day-long slaughter, was the young Walter Ralegh.

In the latter years of the sixteenth century analysts tried to determine what had gone wrong with previous English policies toward Ireland and figure out how to create lasting change that would sustain English control. Planners' attention centered on Munster in the southern part of Ireland, and they envisioned a grand colonization scheme that called for nothing less than creation of an idealized version of English society. Promoters who would go on to American ventures, such as Sir Humphrey Gilbert, who served as military governor of Munster, and Richard Grenville, asked to be granted Irish plantations. As Edmund Spenser wrote, the region had been devastated by "these late warres of Mounster," and the population was much reduced and living in "such wretchednesse, as that any stony heart would have rued the same." The people came creeping out of woods, "for their legges could not beare them; they looked like anatomies of death."[19]

The land seized from rebels was carved up into "seignories" of four thousand to twelve thousand acres. Landlords agreed to import sufficient English families into this depopulated country to work the land—ninety-one families for twelve thousand acres. The seignories were to be divided among the families in a complicated system of ownership for some and tenancy for most. Landlords were responsible for supplying the families on their land with everything necessary to begin farming, and for importing skilled workers for the model village each of the twenty-five seignories was to contain.

Ralegh, now Sir Walter, was the most favored of landlords, with three and a half estates in the counties of Cork and Waterford. He and other large holders had British soldiers stationed on their estates to help defend them against both foreign and domestic attack. Ralegh worked hard to populate his holdings in Ireland with English families. Ironically, his dedication to fulfilling the terms of his Irish estates contributed to diminishing his commitment to the families he had planted at Roanoke in 1587; while he was sending large numbers of tenants to Munster, he made only minimal efforts to locate and support his abandoned colonists in America.

The Munster plantation scheme had some real success in that several thousand settlers were transported there. But it proved impossible to control tenants once they were in Ireland. Even if their way had been paid by the landlord, they would seek out the best terms, sometimes from Irish landholders, rather than stay on the land for which they had been intended. Then 1594 saw the beginning of the Nine Years' War in Ireland, in which the Munster plantations were devastated by forces led by Hugh O'Neill, earl of Tyrone, aided by discontented and dispossessed Irish within Munster. England fielded a very large and expensive army, which experienced much disease and discontent and from which there were many desertions. Although Tyrone surrendered in 1603, many planters had already gone home. The lesson the English drew was that the Irish were irredeemably savage. They should have paid more attention to the other lesson this experience afforded: that it was extremely difficult to motivate and control colonists as well as colonized populations.

There was always a great deal of overlap between American and Irish projects; the same people were sponsors of both kinds of enterprises. As investors came together to form the Virginia Company in 1606, they were all conscious of the record and problems of plantations in Ireland, as well as of the abandonment and loss of Ralegh's Roanoke colonists in the 1580s. And yet failure could always be explained away: the colonists had been of the wrong sort and government of them had been lax; or the knowledge and will necessary to develop resources had been lacking.

Beginning in the latter years of the sixteenth century, many with long experience of Ireland analyzed that country's relationship with England and recommended policies for its rectification. Although they contained many specific diagnoses of Irish conditions, these analyses formulated general principles of the theory and practice of colonization. The analyses of mistakes and problems in Ireland resonated through American experience in Jamestown.

All those who recommended policies for Ireland stood to gain if their suggestions were implemented. The English poet Edmund Spenser, best known as author of the *Faerie Queen*, was an official of the English administration in Ireland, initially as the secretary to Lord Grey of Wilton, from 1580. He may have been present at the Smerwick slaughter, and, despite Grey's recall by a horrified English government, he vigorously defended "that good lord Grey" against charges that he had led English forces into barbarism. Like many people who rose to prominence in overseas exploits, Spenser was from a family of modest means; service in Ireland was a way to make a place in the world, and he was rewarded with a large landholding in the Munster plantation. Office and land made him a gentleman.

Not all commentary was unrelievedly negative, nor was all blame placed on the Irish. Sir Philip Sidney, writing in the early 1580s, enunciated a theme that was taken up by his friend and fellow poet Spenser in arguing that the Irish, like all supposedly primitive peoples, were deeply immersed in poetry as a mode of expression. Sidney had traveled widely in Europe as a young man, and he took a keen interest in American projects. He became involved in the defense of the Protestant Netherlands, and died in 1586 from wounds he received in the battle of Zutphen. According to his biographer and friend Fulke Greville, after the battle, though he was bleeding profusely, he refused the water that was offered to him because a common soldier nearby needed it more than he did. In his *Apologie for Poetrie*, written in the early 1580s, Sidney lumped together the principal others with whom the English then dealt:

> In Turkey, besides their law-giving divines, they have no other writers but poets. In our neighbour countrey Ireland, where truely learning goeth very bare, yet are their Poets held in a devout reverence. Even among the most barbarous and simple Indians where no writing is, yet have they their Poets, who make and sing songs, which they call areytos, both of their ancestors' deeds and praises of their gods . . . In Wales, the true remnant of the ancient Britons, as there are good authorities to show the long time they had poets, which they called bards.

In his description of America's poetry, Sidney demonstrated that he had read deeply in transatlantic reports; his knowledge of *areytos* on

Hispaniola came from Richard Eden's 1555 translation of Peter Martyr's *De Orbe Novo* of 1530. Martyr's book was a massive collection of Spanish reports from America; on the title page of his translation, Eden wrote that in it "the diligent reader may not only consyder what commoditie may hereby chaunce to the hole christian world in tyme to come, but also learne many secreates touchynge the lande, the sea, and the starres, very necessarie to be knowne to al such as shal attempte any navigations, or otherwise have delite to beholde the strange and woonderfull woorkes of God and nature." Sidney's quoting Spanish sources through Eden shows how involved English intellectual and political leaders were with American interests even before England actively pursued colonization. In his *Apologie for Poetrie* Sidney argued for employing the formidable persuasive power of poetry in approaching the peoples Europeans wished to confront.[20]

Sidney's *Apologie for Poetrie* was published in 1595, at a time when several books recommending policies for Ireland appeared. Like Spenser, Richard Beacon was involved as an English official in opening lands in Munster confiscated from the earl of Desmond and his followers in the mid-1580s to settlement by English colonists. He acquired lands in Cork and Waterford and became a settler himself in 1589, but was ousted by infighting between factions by 1591. He wrote *Solon His Follie, or a Politique Discourse touching the Reformation of common-weales conquered, declined or corrupted* in 1594 and offered it as a contribution to the debate about how colonies should be governed and how alien populations should be assimilated. He argued for reform in English government and society to aid efforts to create change in Ireland.[21]

Soon after the outbreak of the Nine Years' War in 1594 Spenser wrote a long treatise, cast as a dialogue between two fictional characters, Irenius, a person with long experience of Ireland, and Eudoxus, an Englishman. In it Spenser both analyzed what had gone wrong and laid out a plan for a civil future for Ireland. The manuscript of his *View of the Present State of Ireland* circulated widely among policy makers, even though it was not published until 1633. Delayed publication does not indicate that the document was not considered valuable or was censored; the most influential documents were often reserved for private circulation, and it is known that Spenser's *View* was read by people in authority in England, as is indicated by the survival of several manuscript versions.

Spenser began by describing Ireland as a sick society and posing the question why. It is "a most beautifull and sweet countrey as any is under heaven," but many attributed its state to "the fatall destiny of that land." The central issue for Spenser, as for all people in colonial situations, was how to bring about social and cultural change, although Spenser and his contemporaries would have phrased it differently. Their statement of the problem was how to make the Irish civil, "to settle a sound and perfect rule of government." The one thing everyone knew was that it would be extremely difficult. They had before them the example of the Old English, some of whom had come to Ireland ostensibly on a civilizing mission as early as the twelfth century; instead of raising the natives to a higher level, their descendants were depicted by Spenser as having wholly degenerated into Irish habits. In the dialogue Eudoxus naively assumes that when the Old English came, "most of the old bad Irish customes were abolished, and more civill fashions brought in their stead." Irenius quickly sets him straight, saying that "the cheifest abuses which are now in that realme, are growne from the English, and some of them are now much more lawlesse and licentious then the very wilde Irish." When Eudoxus expresses his amazement that "men should so much degenerate from their first natures, as to grow wilde," Irenius responds: "So much can liberty and ill examples doe." Only those living within the Pale were still recognizably English, according to Irenius.

The problem, then, was that relying on people with the set of ingrained customs that the English called civility was not enough in colonial circumstances; human nature was naturally prone to degenerate in situations where society's controls were inadequate. As Spenser wrote, even in his own more enlightened time men who had "beene brought up at home under a straight rule of duty and obedience, being alwayes restrayned by sharpe penalities from lewde behaviour, so soone as they come thither, where they see lawes more slackely tended, and the hard restraint which they were used unto now slacked, they grow more loose and carelesse of their duty" because "it is the nature of all men to love liberty." Good laws made good people, but it was foolish to rely on people's virtue to make a good society.[22]

English planners believed it was necessary to change everything about Irish life. Religion, of course, was crucial, and policy aimed to start with educating the children, especially the children of elite families, to make them see the light of the reformed religion. But everything needed to be transformed—inheritance practices, the language they spoke, their mode of farming, the houses they lived in, and even the clothes they wore.

Some hoped that changing the laws, especially the laws of inheritance, would change the people for the better. But Spenser argued that more thoroughgoing change was necessary, because Irish loyalties and habits could subvert the rule of law. He believed that the custom of booleying demonstrated Irish descent from the ancient Scythians, and that it opened the way to thieving and allowed outlaws to hide among the people. Habits were crucial in sustaining Ireland's perceived incivility, and this was true of both senses of the word: customs and clothing. Clothes were of tremendous importance, because one's whole identity was bound up in the self-presentation of dress. The Scots and Irish—and soon the American Indians—could not be civil unless they dressed in English clothes, like civilized people, and cut their long hair. Spenser, like all English commentators, argued that wearing Irish clothing had been primarily responsible for the degeneration of the Old English. Irish "Mantles, and long glibbes, which is a thicke curled bush of haire hanging downe over their eyes, and monstrously disguising them, . . . are both very bad and hurtfull." As Irenius goes on to explain, the long mantle worn by both men and women in Ireland was just too useful, "for it is a fit house for an out-law, a meet bed for a rebel, and an apt cloke for a theife." Wherever and in whatever conditions the Irish found themselves, the mantle served for cover and protection. And the long thick bangs falling over their foreheads, the glibbe, both disguised their identity and was so thick as to be able to ward off sword blows, or so it was claimed.[23]

All these ideas stemmed from a widely shared understanding of human psychology. The psychological lore of the time had little place for a superego, an internal governor; without external control, human nature inevitably degenerated. Rather than seeing human beings as possessing an inborn and fundamental character, Europeans in this period believed that people's nature was shaped by the environment in which they lived and by the way they chose to present themselves to the world. Self-presentation was not external or accidental but essential. Even in England the government attempted to regulate dress through sumptuary laws that spelled out in intricate detail exactly what kinds of fabrics and embellishments people of each social class, occupation, and gender could wear.[24]

Dress was of crucial importance to character, but language was the key to consciousness. As Irenius said of the Old English, who drank in Gaelic with their nurse's milk, "the speach being Irish, the heart must needes bee Irish: for out of the abundance of the heart, the tongue speaketh." And it was an article of faith that reformation of customs and self-presentation must precede attempts to change religious beliefs. Christians firmly believed that in approaching those whose culture they saw as inferior, the natives must first be lured by the "book of the world." When they had come to value the goods and comfort that came with civility, then they could be introduced to the book of the spirit. Recurring to the image of Ireland as an ailing society, Irenius asked rhetorically, "For if you should know a wicked person dangerously sicke, having now both soule and body greatly diseased, yet both recoverable, would you not thinke it evill advertizement to bring the preacher before the phisitian?"[25]

Office in Ireland was a good opportunity for men of humbler birth, who went over as captains or administrators, often after other military service, and found places for themselves there. Like Captain Ralph Lane, several other returnees from Roanoke were placed in Ireland. Thomas Harriot held an estate that was part of the former Augustinian abbey of Molanna on an island in the Blackwater River and spent some time there after his American sojourn. His partner John White also came to live in Ireland.

White had returned to Roanoke as governor of the second colony in 1587. His settlers urged him to go home with the ships that had brought them, to make sure that they remained high on Ralegh's list of concerns and to help speed the sending of supplies and additional set- tlers. Ireland, and the conflict between Protestant England and Roman Catholic Spain in which it figured, became interposed between good intentions in England and the colonists' plight in America as rumors of the great Spanish Armada in 1588 came to the ears of the English government and all ships capable of meeting the enemy were com- mandeered for the nation's defense, as were the supplies stockpiled for the little settlement's needs. White searched frantically for a way to get back to his people, and managed to find a small ship that was al- lowed to embark, but his efforts to reach American shores were frus- trated by the ship's crew and their desire to go privateering once they entered open waters. He did not reach Roanoke again until a brief visit in 1590, and by that time the planters had dispersed.

White himself then went to live in Ireland at Newtown, modern Ballynoe, in County Cork near Harriot's Molana Abbey; Richard Bea- con was also a near neighbor. White and Harriot collaborated on surveying and mapping Ralegh's Irish estates as they had done in America.

Harriot returned to England in the late 1590s and continued to work with Ralegh. But White wrote a sad last letter to Richard Hakluyt in 1593 from Newtown going over again the "evils & unfortunate events" that had led to the colony's abandonment. Finally, he said he would "leave off from prosecuting that whereunto I would to God my wealth were answerable to my will." As for the Lost Colonists, including his daughter and granddaughter Virginia Dare, he committed "the reliefe of my discomfortable company the planters in Virginia, to the merciful help of the Almighty, whom I most humbly beseech to helpe & comfort them, according to his most holy will & their good desire."[26] In a world dominated by the many projects of great men, he had done what he could and it was not enough. White disappears from the record at this point; presumably he, like governor Ralph Lane under whom he had served, died in Ireland.[27] Edmund Spenser was forced out of Ireland in 1598, and he and his family lived henceforth in poverty in London.[28]

Within the government's highest circle of advisers, two British concerns loomed as the seventeenth century began. One was a real fear that Ireland might become formally a client of Spain, given that country's willingness to support Irish resistance to English control. The other centered on the approaching end of Queen Elizabeth's life and the expectation that James VI of Scotland would succeed her. James was a committed Protestant, but the Scots had maintained close ties with Irish leaders who had defied the English government, and James had also kept up a relationship with the Spanish government. A last effort by a combined Spanish and Irish army met a disastrous end at Kinsale in 1602; and the Nine Years' War was settled in negotiations with Tyrone just as the queen was dying but before news of her death early in 1603 reached the Irish leader. Tyrone was soon in London for a meeting with the new king, now James I of England, and was granted a royal pardon. Shortly thereafter, James's government negotiated peace with Spain. As the new regime embarked on an official policy of friendliness toward Spain, it reversed the Elizabethan attempts to find common ground with Muslim governments in the Mediterranean.

Attention now turned again to Ireland and creation of a new relationship. Sir John Davies, Ireland's attorney general, traveled through the counties of Monaghan, Fermanagh, and Cavan, the "most unsettled and unreformed parts of that province," in 1606, the year when the Virginia colony was planned and organized. On behalf of the English government he inquired into forms of landholding and the state of religion and rashly dismissed any danger from the defeated leaders: "Assuredly these Irish Lords appear to us like glow worms, which afar off seem to be all fire; but, being taken up in a man's hands, are but silly worms." He wrote that a few days before his party had arrived, Hugh Maguire, lord of Fermanagh, "gave out a false alarm . . . that himself with the Earl of Tirconnel were going into Spain, a common and poor Irish policy practised in this realm, ever since the conquest, to amuse the state with rumours, that are utterly false, which notwithstanding, in former times, hath prevailed to do hurt in this kingdom, according to the observation and saying of the old Cardinal of Loraine, 'that a lie, believed but for an hour, doth many times produce effects of seven years continuance.'"

Davies presented colonization as a way of liberating the poor downtrodden Irish from the "absurd and unreasonable" demands of corrupt elites, and offering the consolation and uplift of true religion. The only way this could be done, he argued, was by bringing in civil colonists from England and Scotland, the same policy that had already failed in Munster. So pressing was the need that it must be carried out even at the price of removing native tenants from their lands. Ironically, he pointed to the example of Spain and its removal of the "Moors out of

Grenada into Barbary" as a precedent. He portrayed King James as a loving father rather than a monarch and wrote that "his Majesty doth in this imitate the skilful husbandman, who doth remove his fruit trees not with a purpose to extirpate and destroy them, but that they may bring better and sweeter fruit after the transplantation."[29]

Davies and those policy makers in London who listened to him guessed wrong on the intentions of the Irish lords. In September 1607 the great earls of Tyrone and Tyrconnell suddenly left Ireland with many of their followers for Roman Catholic Europe. No one knew whether they would one day return with Spanish support; but, as it turned out, their exile was permanent. Tyrone himself spent the rest of his life in Rome. Other Irish who had served in the armies also sought their fortunes in Europe, especially in Spain and Portugal. Their lands were seized, and soon a major program of colonization by English and Scots sought to change Ireland forever.[30]

Ulster, in the northern part of the island, was colonized in line with Davies's recommendations in the first decade of the seventeenth century just as the Virginia experiment was getting under way. Sir Francis Bacon urged King James to focus primarily on the Ulster plantation initiative in Ireland—"not a flash but a solid and settled pursuit." Bacon remarked that the American project for Virginia resembled the medieval chivalric romance "Amadis de Gaul" more than Julius Caesar's *Commentaries* on the wars in Gaul; *Don Quixote* by Miguel de Cervantes had satirized Amadis and the whole chivalric tradition the previous year. At the same time, Bacon argued for new approaches, saying that the Munster experiment "hath given more light by the errors thereof, what to avoid, than by the direction of the same, what to follow." Commentators drew lessons from the failed Munster experiment, arguing that the key to success was sending enough of the right kind of people under the leadership of high-ranking men.[31] In Ulster colonization the English government tried to involve a large number of people from different backgrounds, including some Irish, as landlords in a complicated system of landholdings. The merchant companies of London were given responsibility for colonizing the county of Londonderry. Some estates were set aside to endow schools and churches; Trinity College was created out of one such endowment. Huge numbers sailed west to Ireland from Britain—as many as 100,000 people by 1641, including 30,000 Scots to Ulster and 70,000 Welsh and English to Ulster and other parts of Ireland. These numbers far outstripped the contemporaneous migration to America, even during the period American historians have labeled the Great Migration of the 1630s.

All colonization projects everywhere were sold on the promise that they would be self-supporting, and Ulster, like Munster, was no exception. The plan for Ulster stipulated that rents from the forfeited lands of rebels would be the first source of support, and that once commercial agriculture and other enterprises were thriving, the plantations would provide revenue both for royal coffers and for investors. These expectations were not on the whole met, and most investors eventually pulled out. Scots found Ulster far more attractive than did many English migrants, and their presence had a powerful effect in shaping the region.[32]

So, by the early seventeenth century, there was widespread agreement on colonization, the transplantation of already civil populations into uncivil regions, as a method for making those regions civil by English lights and able to be incorporated into the larger polity. The notion that planting a tightly controlled colony of people forced to be virtuous by continuous oversight was the only way both to transfer a social order and to transform a native population was firmly established by experience of Irish colonization. But although this mode was an agreed article of faith, it had never actually been done successfully, and controlling the supposedly civil seemed often to loom as large as transforming the uncivil. Failure of the paradigm only reinforced it, and English planners persevered with this model in Ireland and would soon employ it in America. What they gleaned from their experience in Ireland was that control was supremely important; colonists were to be motivated by force at first with incentives to follow. What was not clear as the seventeenth century opened and the Tudor age drew to a close was the place of North America in the spectrum of English concerns.

Jamestown's Uncertain Beginnings

THE GREAT HISTORIAN William Camden was one of very few who were prepared to enunciate the most fundamental truth about colonization: plantations required massive investment over a long period of time before they could begin to make a return on investment; and it was extremely difficult to motivate transplanted people to work hard for the benefit of investors. In his *History of the Most Renowned and Victorious Princess Elizabeth Late Queen of England,* which he began writing in 1608, he recorded the aspirations of Sir Humphrey Gilbert. After his blood-stained service in Ireland, Gilbert had led an English force sent to aid the Protestant Dutch fighting the Spanish in the Netherlands. Then Queen Elizabeth granted him a patent for American colonization. He embarked on a voyage intending to found a colony somewhere on America's northeast coast in 1583 and died in the attempt. Camden wrote in his entry for 1583, "Near the same time was swallowed by the Ocean sir Humphrey Gilbert Knight, a quick and lively-spirited man . . . [H]e suffered so much by Shipwrecks and want of necessary Provision, that he was constrained to give over his Enterprise, learning too late himself, and teaching others, that it is a difficulter thing to carry over Colonies into remote Countries upon private mens Purses, than he and others in an erroneous Credulity had perswaded themselves, to their own Cost and Detriment."[1]

Eastward Hoe, written by George Chapman, Ben Jonson, and John Marston in 1605, the year before the Virginia Company was chartered and began collecting colonists, satirized promoters who argued that colonization was easy and riches from it assured. The play centers on Sir Petronel Flash's plan to abscond with the fortune he obtained through an opportune marriage by going to America in a voyage with the disreputable Captain Seagull. In addition to assuring the proposed venturers he was collecting for Virginia that the Roanoke colonists were still alive and well, Seagull sought to stir up enthusiasm by describing a land of both comfort and great riches. Comically echoing Sir Thomas More's description of Utopia, he exclaimed: "I tell thee, gold is more plentiful there than copper is with us: and for as much red copper as I can bring, I'll have thrice the weight in gold. Why, man, all their dripping pans and their chamber pots are pure gold; and all the chains with which they chain up their streets are massy gold; all the prisoners they take are fettered in gold: and for rubies and diamonds, they go forth on holidays and gather 'em by the sea-shore, to hang on their children's coats, and stick in their caps as commonly as our children wear saffron gilt brooches, and groats with holes in 'em." Not only was Virginia pleasant and temperate and full of all kinds of meats—even the wild boar and venison that were reserved for the few in England—but also, according to Seagull, one could live there free of "serjeants, or courtiers, or lawyers, or intelligencers [informers]." Everyone could find advancement there "and never be a slave." Seagull knew that a ship that sailed down the coast to Africa could catch the trade winds west to America, but in the play his ship got no farther than the Isle of Dogs in London's dockland.[2]

Seagull's claims were outlandish, and everyone knew that hard work and investment were required to create a settlement. But without the hope of riches or access to the eastern trades, it is doubtful that colonies would have been undertaken in this period. The Virginia Company's "Instructions given by way of advice" to Jamestown's founding party directed the settlement's leaders to send men up their river as soon as they arrived "to try if they Can find any mineral." The instructions also called for determining the source of the river; if it originated in a lake, "the passage to the Other Sea will be the more easy."[3] In short, investors looked for either a rich commodity that colonists could extract or, even better, gain in trade with the Americans, or a passage through to the rich eastern trades.

Hopes for some kind of commodity that would be valuable enough to repay the costs of sending out colonies and provide a return on investment were not necessarily venal or ridiculous. Chapman, Jonson, and Marston's mention of red copper indicated some knowledge of earlier reports that Indians had ornaments of very red copper; others had mentioned pearls. Precious minerals were not the only possible resource; as English leaders renewed their interest in an American base in the first decade of the seventeenth century, French mariners were participating in a very successful and lucrative trade in furs at the mouth of the St. Lawrence River. And English merchant companies were moving into rich trades in commodities produced in other parts of the world. It did not seem unrealistic to hope that Americans living in the Chesapeake region might already have some kinds of goods that would be valuable to Europeans, and that they might be willing, even eager, to trade them for European products.

North America thus was seen in the hopeful context of all the other trade relationships English merchants were constructing at this time. In fact, as Robert Brenner demonstrates, the English economy was being transformed by the growth of the import trade in the later sixteenth and early seventeenth centuries. Tentative beginnings were consolidated in the new century as the peace treaty with Spain closed some kinds of enterprises to English trade and made others more possible.[4]

As they approached American projects, Europeans were often much more pragmatic than their rhetoric leads us to expect. Despite the ferocity of their language and the picture of absolute and unbridgeable divisions that their statements portray, in reality people crossed lines all the time. For one thing, business had to be carried on and goods exchanged. English merchants customarily traded with Roman Catholic and Muslim countries; English representatives resided in those countries, and these trades continued even in wartime. Gordon of Lochinvar, asking rhetorically whether it was unlawful to trade with the Americans, pointed out in his answer that "all Christendome" had "commerce with Turkes, and miscreants." He cited American ventures as an alternative to "spoyle, pyracie, or other villanie as to serve the Portugale, Spaniard, Dutch, French, or Turk (as to the great hurte of Europe too manie doe) rather than our GOD, our King, our Countrie, and our selves."[5]

Nor was it completely farfetched to think that American Indians might willingly participate in such trade. In fact, the possibility of trading in furs was originally proposed to French fishermen by Americans, and the acquisition of furs from throughout the great Canadian interior was organized entirely by native-run networks. Only the final exchange on the coast involved Europeans. American Indians gladly received manufactured goods which they did not produce themselves in exchange for their furs. Beaver pelts were highly valued in Europe because of the beautiful lustrous felt that was made from their downy hair, so American furs underpinned the vogue for large felt hats. Best of all was the fact that the fur trade worked most efficiently with a very small and mostly temporary cadre of European migrants who did not threaten the Indians' land base. Thus the French avoided the enormous expense of maintaining large colonies.

It was highly possible that Indians could supply products that would prove valuable for European uses, as with furs and felt, that the Indians had not anticipated. Precious metals were always the preferred items, but dyes, medicines, and spices would also have been excellent commodities. Tobacco, the product that ultimately made Virginia profitable, was a perfect example of what backers were looking for. Unfortunately, though, it was not acquired in trade with Indians but had to be produced by labor imported from across the ocean. It took a decade for American experience to persuade the Virginia Company to accept the unwelcome news that investment sufficient to sustain a large and permanent body of colonists, even a full re-creation of English society abroad, was necessary. In short, the Irish model, not that developed in the Eastern trades, applied in English America.

Sir Francis Bacon believed that England's interests were best served by focusing on Ireland rather than on new and untried projects abroad. But he did suggest emulating one innovation in the Virginia Company's patent: having an appointed "council of plantation" in London as well as in Ireland to keep close contact between Irish affairs and the government.[6] Bacon's perception was acute. The London seat of the Virginia Company was a major factor in the colony's ability to survive. Many of the original company sponsors were in parliament or had the ear of leading government officials and were thus able to focus attention on the project. Where many attempted settlements had foundered when their resupply "miscarried" or failed altogether, the Virginia Company's fleet under Captain Christopher Newport made record times both in sailing to and from the colony and in lessening turnaround requirements in London. So the faltering colony did not have to endure the long, sometimes unceasing, periods of uncertainty and waiting that had ended the existence of other ventures.

As promoters gathered men and supplies for the first voyage, the London Virginia Company's council drew up "Instructions given by way of advice" to guide the venture. The first point enjoined careful selection of a settlement site: find the deepest and longest river flowing from the interior, and do not be too hasty in unloading all your gear. The best place would be upriver—away from surprise attacks by Spanish enemies, but still reachable by English supply ships. Reminding the colonists of Spanish strikes that had eliminated the French colony on the southern coast in the sixteenth century, the London council recommended an outpost with ten men and a very fast boat at the river's mouth to warn Jamestown when threatening vessels appeared.

Getting the relationship with the Indians right at the outset figured heavily in the council's thinking, and the instructions assumed that friction was inevitable. Jamestown, unlike its contemporary Sagadahoc, was not able to build on preexisting good relationships with native people, nor did the initial colonists carry Indians with them from England.[7] Choice of a healthy settlement site rested on examining those who lived there. If the people were strong and healthy, then the land would be good. But the company's main concern was the colony's safety: "You must in no Case Suffer any of the natural people of the Country to inhabit between You and the Sea Coast." This was, of course, impossible; the small group of English venturers was in no position to dictate where Indians lived. But the reasoning behind this instruction was startling. The Virginia Company stated baldly that the colonists could not "Carry Your Selves so towards them but they will grow Discontented with Your habitation and be ready to Guide and assist any Nation that Shall Come to invade You." The council also suggested that the men try to get Indian corn and other foods in trade, "and this you must Do before that they perceive you mean to plant among them." The migrants were cautioned not to choose a heavily wooded area; not only would it be slow and troublesome work to open it up for cultivation, but woods also would offer cover for enemies. Clearly, despite their further instruction to take utmost care not to offend neighboring Indians, the Virginia Company knew at the colony's inception that the settlers' presence would be troublesome.

Colonists were warned never to allow themselves to become vulnerable. As they moved around the country, they would necessarily rely on American guides, but they should never allow them to carry the muskets. And they must take care to ensure that the guides did not abandon them in remote places; the council suggested noting locations using a compass as they traveled, but acknowledged that without Indian help, explorers "Shall hardly Ever find a Passage back." Knowing the unreliability of the matchlock muskets the colonists employed, and the inexperience of many in the first company, the council suggested that the Indians should be allowed to see only the very best marksmen shoot, "for if they See your Learners miss what they aim at they will think the Weapon not so terrible and thereby will be bould to Assaillt You." The council in London was remarkably realistic about future conditions within the colony, saying that the leaders should make sure that the Indians did not know when colonists died or became sick. If English vulnerability were revealed, then the Indians, they argued, would certainly attack.

The council was as pessimistic about colonists' behavior as about relations with the Indians. One small ship would be left in the colony, and its sails and anchors were to be stowed ashore when not in use, lest "Some ill Disposed Persons Slip away with her." The English mariners must be prevented from conducting private trading to the detriment of the long-range relationship with the Indians. No colonist would be allowed to return to England without permission from the colony's government, and all letters home were to be censored to make sure that they contained nothing "that may Discourage others."

The instructions outlined a plan of action for the settlement's beginning. The colonists were to be divided into three teams: one would build the settlement, the second would prepare ground and plant crops, and the third would go exploring for mineral resources and to see whether the river promised access to other waterways that might lead through the continent to the East. The carpenters were told to construct public buildings such as the storehouse first and only then to move on to homes. The council cautioned against helter-skelter siting of buildings, and directed that streets be laid out in a grid surrounding a market square, "Seeing order is at the same price with Confusion."[8]

These "Instructions given by way of advice," with their tone of grim realism, reflected study of previous colonial attempts and the pitfalls they had encountered; some backers had been involved in other ventures. Hopes for converting Indians and forming a harmonious relationship with them would come in the future, even in the midst of hostile and tense times; for now the Virginia Company focused on getting the colony established in a good location and without advertising its vulnerability.

The fleet, commanded by Captain Christopher Newport, arrived in Virginia after a stop in the West Indies at the end of April 1607. The 108 colonists, whose ages ranged from fifty-seven to nine, selected their site up the James River on land belonging to the Paspaheghs, Paquiquineo/Don Luís de Velasco's people, and began to build their settlement in mid-May. They paid close attention to parts of their instructions: George Percy wrote that their ships were "moored to the Trees in six fathom water," so clearly they were on a deep river.[9] And Captain John Smith asserted that their chosen site was "a verie fit place for the erecting of a great cittie."[10] Other requirements were less easy to gauge, and Jamestown was to prove an unhealthy location.

Trouble arose almost immediately. The royally appointed Virginia Council in London had tried an innovative approach to governing the colony. In previous colonies such as Roanoke the sponsors had appointed the governor and council, and those were known to the settlers before they embarked. In this case the London council appointed the council for Virginia but did not make its choices known. Instead the settlers were given a sealed box containing the councilors' names; once they had reached America and opened the box, then the named councilors would elect their president, who would act as governor. Until the new government was known and sworn in, Newport, the Virginia Company admiral, would have supreme command. It was an interesting plan that might have helped to build solidarity, but it did not work out as hoped. Six men were named to the council that would govern once Newport had departed: veteran explorer Bartholomew Gosnold; Captain John Ratcliffe (whose family name was actually Sicklemore); Edward Maria Wingfield, who was elected the first president; Captain John Martin; Captain George Kendall; and Captain John Smith.

Of all the councilors, Smith was the only one who did not come from a well-connected background, and he had already adopted something of an oppositional stance on the voyage over. He was in detention accused of mutiny when the settlers learned that he was actually on the council. On the intervention of the Reverend Robert Hunt, the council reluctantly freed Smith and accepted him among them. Gabriel Archer wrote darkly (and mysteriously) of "a murmur and grudg against certayne preposterous proceedinges and inconvenyent Courses" on the council. For his part, Smith never concealed his contempt for the ineptitude and selfishness of those who were selected for leadership because of their birth and connections rather than, as he was, for his skill and knowledge.[11]

The councilors prepared a preliminary report to go with Newport as he returned to England in late June. They praised the land and the river on which they had settled and predicted all kinds of valuable commodities to come in the future; meanwhile they sent "a taste of Clapboord"—not the kind of rich product the investors hoped for. They testified that they had already built fortifications and some houses, and had planted "good store of wheate." The report ended with a strong appeal for support; unless the Virginia Company supplied their needs, the councilors wrote, with the greatest grief "wee shall against our willes, not will that which we moste willinglie would." Though hidden in convoluted language, the threat of giving up and coming home was clear. The six councilors signed off as "Your poore Friends."[12]

Everything hung by a thread, and all planning assumed that every contingency would go well. Human beings were the most contingent factor of all. Wingfield proved to be a particularly inept and ineffectual governor; he was deposed in September after just a few months in office and left the colony the next spring. By the end of August many colonists, including Bartholomew Gosnold and George Kendall, two of the councilors who had signed the June letter, were dead.[13]

The loss of Gosnold was particularly hard, and he was buried with full honors. Once he was gone, the council was rent by dissension centering on the enigmatic figure of George Kendall. Kendall, like Sir Thomas Stukeley, played such an intricate set of roles that they cannot today be fully untangled. He was, like so many others, from a well-connected family but had few assets other than his wits and an education as "Her Majesty's scholar in Westminster School." He had served in the armies in the Netherlands for seven years and then in 1600 apparently offered to spy on Roman Catholic renegade Englishmen in Europe for Robert Cecil, the queen's principal secretary. He made it clear to Cecil, who accepted his offer, that he would need regular compensation. Kendall's inclusion as a member of the council in Virginia befitted a man of his rank. But in the turmoil of that early period, when accusations flew among the leaders in Jamestown, Kendall was tried and convicted of mutiny. He was sentenced to death and shot. English sources from the colony offer only the most cryptic descriptions of his supposed crime. George Percy said that "hainous matters" were proved against him, and Edward Maria Wingfield, who was president of the council at the time, simply recorded his sentence.[14] Francis Magnel, an Irish sailor who was in Jamestown during its first year, gave a deposition in Madrid in 1610 in which he claimed that the English had executed the "Catholic English Captain called Captain Tindol, because they knew that he wanted to come to Spain to reveal to His

Majesty what goes on in that land." Philip L. Barbour, who has pieced together Kendall's story, concluded that he had played a double game all along, working simultaneously for the English and the Spanish.[15]

Whatever the causes of dissension among the settlers, everyone knew that Virginia's Indians held the key to the colony's initial success or failure. And whereas the colonists were largely inexperienced and often inept, Indian people around Chesapeake Bay had had long experience of Europeans and knew much about them. Gabriel Archer, a veteran of other voyages, sent back an initial report making clear both the sophisticated approach of the Indians to the colonists and the colonists' perplexity. Many details were confirmed in Captain John Smith's first letter a few months later, even though the two men had become enemies in the colony.

Following company instructions, Newport did indeed set out to explore almost immediately after the colonists' arrival. As soon as they embarked, his party began to encounter Americans whose knowledge and self-possession were evident in the way they approached the English. Archer wrote that among the first Indians they saw was one who offered to draw them a map of the river. Given paper and pen, he proceeded to lay out the river's entire course and informed them of the falls beyond which their boats could not go. Each werowance, or chief, they encountered came to them in state, managing the beginnings of the relationship. George Percy, the son and brother of earls of Northumberland and therefore a man well acquainted with aristocratic display, described these episodes of self-presentation vividly. At Rappahanna, the werowance "met them, playing on a flute of a reed, with a crowne of Deeres haire coloured red, fashioned like a Rose, with a chaine of Beads about his necke, and Bracelets of Pearle hanging at his eares, in each eare a birds claw." Percy judged him a man "of a modest-proud behaviour." At Paspahegh the "King" appeared before the English "painted all black, with hornes on his head like a Divell." They also met a female ruler, the "Queene of Apametica," who wore a

"Coronet beset with many white bones" and elaborate earrings and necklace. Archer wrote that when they first encountered Powhatan, the assembled Indians all stood up and greeted him with a shout, but the English explorers "saluted [him] with silence sitting still on our mattes." The newcomers understood perfectly well the significance of a shouted acknowledgment; they "gave a greate showte" when Christopher Newport set up a cross and claimed the land for King James. When next they came into Powhatan's presence, their guide "made signe to us we must make a shoute, which we Dyd."[16]

The English moved among the Indians in a state of perplexity. Although they were impressed by what they saw and gratified by indications of friendship, they also constantly saw signs of potential hostility, and they were keenly aware of their own vulnerability. Navirans, brother-in-law of the Arrohattoc werowance, offered to be their guide, and they valued the assistance of this "kynde Consort" highly. When he asked to sleep in their boat with them, they agreed. But then Navirans suddenly told them that he was going to return to Arrohattoc, and they immediately feared some danger. They quickly returned to Jamestown to find that the settlement had been attacked, possibly by the Paspaheghs on whose land the colony had intruded.

What is remarkable about this story is the sequel, which demonstrated the unpreparedness, even the fecklessness, of the English. Archer and Smith both wrote that *after* the attack the men set about building a palisade around the little plantation. Moreover, the men had been at a disadvantage when assaulted because their muskets had not yet been unpacked. Had the ships not fired their ordnance, the colony would have been overwhelmed. As sniper attacks continued over the next several days, the colonists were imprisoned in their settlement. Clearly they had obeyed the company's orders to make searching for some precious commodity or a passage through to the Pacific the top priority—even at the risk of their own safety. Finally, Navirans and another man came to the fort unarmed and offered to help the English make peace with those who resented their presence. Also, noting that the snipers hid in the tall grass outside the walls, Navirans "counselled us to Cutt Downe the long weedes rounde about our Forte." One might have expected the English to have thought of that themselves. Navirans came to them on June 14, 1607; on June 22 Newport sailed away carrying Archer's report and the council's letter, and the colonists were on their own. According to Smith, within ten days sickness was so widespread than only ten men were still able to walk or stand.[17]

Left on their own, the colonists faced immense continuing and inter-locking problems. First, they had to figure out their relationship with the Indian polities on which they had intruded. Most important, this meant attempting to understand the connections among the peoples and rulers they encountered, and the Indians who undertook to be their guides invested a great deal of effort in imparting such informa-tion. In the course of the first year the English came to understand that Powhatan was the overlord of thirty chiefdoms or more around Chesa-peake Bay, and they took to calling him an emperor. Emperor was a technical term designating a king who ruled over other kings, and they took great care to use it accurately. Smith presented the distillation of his understanding of Chesapeake Algonquian polities in this para-graph:

> Although the countrie people be very barbarous, yet have they amongst them such governement, as that their Magistrats for good commanding, and their people for du subjection, and obeying, excell many places that would be counted very civill. The forme of their Common wealth is a monarchicall governement, one as Emperour ruleth over many kings or governours. Their chiefe ruler is called Powhatan, and taketh his name of the principall place of dwelling called Powhatan. But his proper name is Wahunsonacock. Some

countries he hath which have been his ancestors, and came unto him by inheritance. . . . All the rest of his Territories expressed in the Map, they report have beene his severall conquests.[18]

All the English who wrote about their experiences testified that Powhatan, and most of the men and women, called werowances, who ruled under him, were extremely impressive. William Strachey wrote of Powhatan's "Majestie . . . which oftentimes strykes awe and sufficient wonder in our people." He was convinced that this American ruler had "an infused kynd of divinenes."[19]

The English also very clearly understood that their relationship with these Indian polities would always be contentious and that they could never relax their guard. As the Virginia Company had warned in its first instructions, the Americans might tolerate the English presence because of the manufactured products they brought for trade, but they would always seek to manage that relationship. There was no room for romanticism on either side.

Access to food was the key complication as English and Indians maneuvered to control the terms on which they would deal with each other. The colonists had been left with insufficient food to get them through the coming winter, and they had not been able to plant anything like what they would need; their long delay on the coast of England had depleted their supplies and brought them to Virginia in late spring, where they needed to clear land before planting. In the severe drought conditions, the Indians already felt a strain on their food stores without the pressure to keep more than a hundred extra people alive. Moreover, both Indians and English were soon to face one of the harshest winters of the cold seventeenth century. In one poignant passage Smith, triumphant over having obtained a great deal of corn, noted the women and children at "Youghtanund and Mattapamient, where the people imparted that little they had," weeping as his barge pulled away with the food they had planned on for the coming winter.

This portrait of Powhatan sitting in state appeared on John Smith's map of Virginia. Courtesy of the John Carter Brown Library at Brown University.

He said that one would have "beene too cruell to have beene a Christian, that would not have beene satisfied and moved with compassion." The women had grown that corn, so it was their property that was being traded away. Smith, apparently concerned that his English readers might think he was not strong enough, explained, "Men may thinke it strange there should be such a stirre for a little corne, but had it beene gold with more ease wee might have got it; and had it wanted, the whole Colony had starved."[20]

As Smith took charge of the exploration of Chesapeake Bay and of the relentless quest for food, his policy was to trust no one. He admired Powhatan and Opechancanough, who would succeed him, and many of the other werowances he encountered, but he admired them in part because he could not trust them. He saw their alternating friendliness and hostility as evidence of policy and as part of their toughness. Smith and Percy, who also ventured out from Jamestown, used adjectives like "subtle" and "politic" to describe these leaders. Although they would have preferred simply to have overawed Virginia's Indians (as they sometimes claimed they had done), they could not help but be struck by the determination and intelligence of the leaders they faced—and by the way these chiefs were able to throw the English off-balance. Smith argued that his experience in the Ottoman Empire had helped him in approaching Powhatan. But he also admitted the colonists' vulnerability: "Had the Salvages not fed us, we directly had starved." Despite leaders' claims of their constant vigilance, recent archaeological work at the fort site has confirmed Francis Magnel's testimony that Jamestown was visited by Indians bringing goods to trade for English products at "the market which the English hold at their fort daily."[21]

The second massive and continuing problem, and one that Smith considered far more difficult, was controlling the English back at the fort. The settlement's pathetic first president, Edward Maria Wingfield, had been deposed, but relations did not improve under the new presi-

Engraving of the Carolina Algonquian town of Secota by John White resembling a European country village surrounded by neat fields of growing crops. Courtesy of the John Carter Brown Library at Brown University.

dent/governor, John Ratcliffe (or Sicklemore). Smith, who later referred to Ratcliffe as "a poore counterfeited Imposture," continued to be an outsider on the council, and his fellow councilors repeatedly accused him of crimes.[22] For his part, Smith considered them foolish and inept and argued that he alone actually got things done, especially as he was the one who went out and traded with the neighboring Indians for food. A colonist named Richard Perkins, who arrived in early January 1608 in the first ships sent to resupply the colony, wrote home to an unknown patron asking for assistance in being appointed to the council in Virginia. His (somewhat sinister) reason was that office would not only be "an honour to me, but also . . . enable me the better to pay my debts." Besides, he argued, many councilors "understand affairs of state no better than I do." He looked forward to a day when the council would be so "competent and intelligent . . . that I should not deserve to appear among them."[23] Smith would finally become president, almost by default as the last of the able-bodied councilors, in September 1608.

Poor leadership was intertwined as a problem with the progressive weakening of the men. Many colonists died, as George Percy put it, of "cruell diseases . . . and by warres," but most of "meere famine" and terrible living conditions that reduced the men to "most feeble wretches." The site was the cause of many of the problems, especially as the settlers drank river water that, in the extraordinary drought conditions, "was at a floud verie salt, at a low tide full of slime and filth, which was the destruction of many of our men." Never were "Englishmen left in a forreigne Countrey in such miserie as wee were in this new discovered Virginia."[24] In all, of the 105 men and boys left by the departing Newport in June 1607, only thirty-eight were still alive six months later when he returned with the first supply. By that time, according to John Smith, the colonists were sunk in "mallice, grudging and muttering," and completely dependent on the Indians for food: "At this time were most of our chiefest men either sicke or discontented, the rest being in such dispaire, as they would rather starve and rot with idlenes, then be perswaded to do anything for their owne reliefe without constraint."[25]

Jamestown's leadership faced the classic colonial conundrum in this period: How do you motivate men to work when they are far away from the constraints of home and without any certain rewards to come from that work? The leaders always wanted to blame the men, arguing that only the dregs of English society had been sent and they were unequal to the task. As Smith put it vividly in his last book, "Much they blamed us for not converting the Salvages, when those they sent us were little better if not worse."[26]

As Powhatan and his werowances increasingly realized that Jamestown was intended to be the foundation of a permanent, and growing, English presence, they sought to deal with that presence by keeping the colonists off-balance, but also by incorporating the newcomers into their own structures. Smith was captured on an exploring voyage early in the colony's existence; after several days of ceremonies, he was brought into Powhatan's presence. Smith was sure his life was near its end as he was placed on the ground with his head on a rock. As Powhatan's men stood around him with clubs, Pocahontas, "the kings dearest daughter . . . got his head in her armes, and laid her owne upon his to save him from death." Smith believed that Pocahontas had risked her own life to save his, but modern scholars argue that she was playing a role in a scripted ceremony through which Smith experienced a symbolic death that ended in his being adopted into Powhatan's family. Two days later Powhatan told Smith that "now they were friends," and if Smith would bring him two cannon and a grindstone from Jamestown, he would give Smith a territory to govern and "for ever esteeme him as his sonne Nantaquoud."[27]

If Powhatan believed that incorporating Smith as a werowance under him was the best way to deal with the English, his reasoning was matched by the Virginia Company's plans. Just as the final Roanoke

King Powhatan comands C. Smith to be flayne, his daughter Pokahontas beggs his life his thankfullnes̃ and how he ſubiected 39 of their kings. reade ÿ hiſtory.

printed by Iames Reeve

Pocahontas saves Smith's life. Courtesy of the John Carter Brown Library at Brown University.

colonists had been directed to make Manteo lord of Roanoke under the English, the Virginia Company decided that Powhatan should be crowned as a vassal of King James. The company sent a red coat and a crown and ordered the colonists to invite Powhatan to Jamestown for the ceremony; they also included an English bedstead and a ewer and basin in the package. Powhatan clearly understood the meaning of the English invitation, and "this subtile Savage" replied to Smith: "If your King have sent me Presents, I also am a King, and this is my land: eight dayes I will stay to receive them. Your Father is to come to me, not I to him, nor yet to your Fort, neither will I bite at such a bait." So the English brought the presents to Powhatan. Even then, "a foule trouble there was to make him kneele to receive his Crowne." Explanations did not persuade him, so "at last by leaning hard on his shoulders, he a little stooped, and three having the crowne in their hands put it on his head." However much the Virginia Company might later claim that Powhatan had accepted the crown "with a full acknowledgment of dutie and submission," those who were present knew better.[28] They later learned that Powhatan kept the bedstead and crown in the royal mortuary, a sacred space, and wore the crown when he formally thanked his people for coming to plant corn for him.[29]

Both Indians and English in these tense relationships manipulated the language of friendship while also maintaining the underlying threat of conflict. No colonist stepped outside of Jamestown without fear that he might be picked off, as many were, and Smith and other colonial leaders often struck out violently when they felt threatened. But because the English were so dependent on his people for food, Powhatan pointed out that he had a weapon more powerful than the English guns: he could simply move away from contact with the colonists and deprive them of sustenance.

Smith recorded an extended exchange with Powhatan that he labeled "Powhatans discourse of peace and warre." Powhatan warned Smith that his people believed the English sought to "destroy my Country," and that they were afraid to trade for that reason. He went on: "What will it availe you to take that by force you may quickly have by love, or to destroy them that provide you food. What can you get by warre, when we can hide our provisions and fly to the woods? whereby you must famish by wronging us your friends."[30]

In the midst of growing tensions both within the fort and between the English and the Indians, there were some people who were able to continue the pre-settlement pattern of crossing boundaries with a degree of ease. Newport's ships sailed away, leaving 105 men and boys in

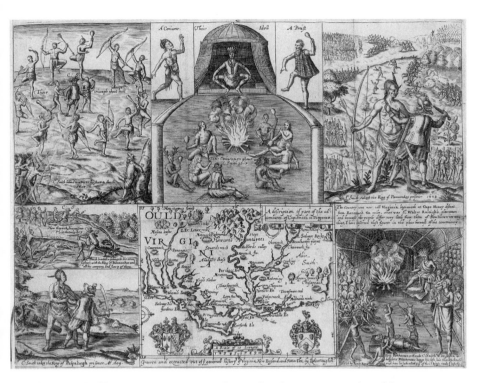

This map of Old Virginia, meaning Roanoke, employed many images adapted from engravings of John White's map of the Carolina Outer Banks and his paintings of Indian life. The cartouches around the edges show John Smith's exploits in Virginia. It was published in Smith's Generall Historie *in 1624.* Courtesy of the John Carter Brown Library at Brown University.

Virginia. The men often presented problems, but the boys turned out to be especially useful, particularly in uncertain times. American and English leaders apparently shared a fundamental psychological assumption that youngsters were both more receptive to new languages and able to move freely across cultural and political boundaries that adults crossed only with difficulty. So young teenagers occupied an essential role in establishing the lines along which early relationships were constructed.

Such roles were planned for the boys who accompanied the initial colonists. Smith told Powhatan that Christopher Newport intended to give Powhatan his own son when he came on his first official embassy.

Actually Newport handed over "a Boy of thirteen yeares old, called Thomas Salvage," but because the Indians believed that Savage was the admiral's son, they called him Thomas Newport.[31] Smith also casually mentioned that he had left "Samuell Collier his page to learne the language" at Warraskoyack.[32] Henry Spelman was another such boy whose name and story have come down to us. Like many people who went to America, he was from a distinguished but not wealthy family; his mother was a widow, and he was the eldest of eight children when he was sent across the Atlantic in 1609 at the age of fourteen. He had been in America for a month when Smith handed him over to Parahunt, werowance of a village near the falls of the James who the colonists believed was Powhatan's son. Spelman's role was to help settle a peace between Parahunt and a small English settlement planted there, but he believed that he had actually been sold for the village site.

Indian leaders usually offered one of their own men in exchange for the boys the English left. Powhatan's "trusty servant" Namontack accompanied Newport to Jamestown after the gift of Thomas Savage. Namontack went to England on Newport's ships and returned with him on the next supply; thenceforth he acted as interpreter of English language and habits for Powhatan. Such Indian visitors caused a sensation in England; Namontack's presence was sufficiently well known that a character in Ben Jonson's 1609 play *Epicene, or The Silent Woman* claimed to have made a sketch of him during his stay in London.[33] Other native people, notably two Paspaheghan men named Kemps and Tassore, and Machumps, Powhatan's brother-in-law, were brought to Jamestown as captives; Machumps and another captive, Kainta, traveled to England. All these men functioned as intermediaries.[34]

The key actor on the American side was Pocahontas, who was a girl of ten or eleven when Jamestown was founded; she consistently acted as emissary for her father, Powhatan. In the early years she was in

A cheife Herowans wyfe of Pomeoc.
and her daughter of the age of. 8. or.
.10. yeares.

John White's painting of a coastal Carolina mother and daughter shows a girl eight to ten years old. This is as close as we can come to a picture of Pocahontas when the first colonists arrived in Jamestown. ©The Trustees of the British Museum. All rights reserved.

Jamestown frequently; colonists remembered her teaching the English boys to turn cartwheels. She would "gett the boyes forth with her into the markett place and make them wheele, falling on their handes turning their heeles upwardes, whome she would follow, and wheele so her self."[35] Smith's writing is peppered with moments when Pocahontas came to Jamestown carrying Powhatan's messages and food for the men. He wrote that she "for feature, countenance, and proportion, much exceedeth any of the rest of his people, but for wit, and spirit, the only Nonpariel of his Country." He credited her with repairing breaches when tensions flared, and on one occasion she came in "the darke night . . . through the irksome woods" to warn him that Powhatan was plotting to kill the colonists. She refused the presents Smith offered her; with "teares running downe her cheekes, shee said shee durst not be seene to have any: for if Powhatan should know it, she were but dead." When the adult Pocahontas, now Lady Rebecca Rolfe, was in London, Smith wrote a letter to Queen Anne in which he summed up her contribution: "During the time of two or three yeeres, she next under God, was still the instrument to preserve the Colonie from death, famine and utter confusion."[36]

The English boys did learn Indian languages and much more besides about the cultures and expectations of Indian people. Like Guillaume Rouffin they also became to some extent independent operators, who moved easily back and forth between English and Indians—and who could make distinctions between various Indian as well as European polities. Their lives became entwined with those of the Indians among whom they had lived, and they were often viewed with corresponding suspicion by the English who relied on their interpretation skills.

Early reports described the Indians as loving parents, and the leaders to whom English boys were given extended parental care to them. For example, as tensions increased between the colonists and his subjects, Powhatan angrily sent Thomas Savage back to Jamestown. But almost as soon as he had arrived in the fort, Pocahontas came with a message from Powhatan asking for the boy, "which he loved exceedingly," to come back.[37] After Smith left the colony, open guerrilla warfare broke out and Savage returned to Jamestown. When the war ended with the marriage of Pocahontas and John Rolfe in 1614, he accompanied an embassy to Powhatan. When Powhatan saw the youth, he ignored Ralph Hamor, the official ambassador, and spoke to Thomas Savage in loving terms: "My childe you are welcome, you have bin a straunger to me these foure yeeres."[38]

Henry Spelman stayed for a time with Parahunt, and he wrote that the werowance established bonds of love with him: "He made very much of me givinge me such thinges as he had to winn me to live with him." Both Parahunt and Powhatan employed Spelman as an emissary to carry messages to Jamestown, and Spelman willingly went on expeditions back to the Indians when food was scarce in the fort. Events made clear the bonds of affection that tied these young boundary-crossers. In 1609, after Smith had left the colony, Captain John Ratcliffe, now using his family name of Sicklemore, set out on an expedition in search of corn. He and his "carelesse" men were attacked and all were killed except for two: one, Jeffrey Shortridge, escaped on his own, while "Pokahontas the Kings daughter saved a boy called Henry Spilman, that lived many yeeres after, by her meanes, amongst the Patawomekes" on the Potomac River in the village of the werowance Iopassus. Once, in Iopassus's absence, Spelman had an argument with two of the chief's wives that ended in an exchange of blows. When the chief returned, Spelman hid in a nearby house. During the night Iopassus sent his young baby to Spelman because only he could quiet the frightened child. The next day Iopassus came to him, "telling me he loved me, and none should hurt me."[39]

Ironically, it was Iopassus who, under considerable pressure from the English, helped Captain Samuel Argall capture Pocahontas in April 1613. Powhatan had sent her to live on the Potomac away from the English. Argall, getting wind of her location when he was on a corn-

Pocahontas being lured on board Argall's ship by Iopassus and his wife. Courtesy of the John Carter Brown Library at Brown University.

trading expedition, resolved "to possesse my selfe of her by any stratagem that I could use, for the ransoming of so many Englishmen, as were prisoners with Powhatan." He casually mentioned that he had left five hostages, including two boys, on his previous visit "as a pledge of our love and truce," and one of these hostages, Ensign Swift, was instrumental in Pocahontas's capture. Argall told Iopassus that his people would henceforth be treated as enemies if he did not "betray Pocahontas into my hands." The werowance in turn consulted the Patowomeck king and his council, who agreed to cooperate. Pocahontas was tricked into going aboard Argall's ship and taken back to Jamestown.[40] The initial goal of exchanging Pocahontas for colonists held by the Indians was quickly transformed into the project of making her the first convert in Virginia. She died in 1617 in her twenty-first year as she and her husband, John Rolfe, prepared to return to Virginia at the end of their tremendously successful London visit.

Pocahontas and the English boys helped keep the lines of communication open and, despite all its problems, the colony held on. But survival was never going to be enough. The third great problem the colonists faced was that they had to find some product of value to make investment in the project worthwhile. The Roanoke colonists had been cut loose, and their successors in Jamestown never doubted that the same could happen to them through the vagaries of ocean travel or changes in European politics. The initial instructions telling the colonists to make exploration, both for the passage to the Pacific and for precious commodities, their top priority were in deadly earnest; and the men knew it. Ralph Lane, governor of the first Roanoke colony, had been quite clear on the apparent value of North America's east coast two decades earlier: "The discovery of a good mine, by the goodnesse of God, or a passage to the Southsea, or someway to it, and nothing els can bring this country in request to be inhabited by our nation."[41] "Nothing else" meant that however much people might think a colony in America would be a good thing, without some products of value or a way through the continent to the proven riches of the East, it would not happen.

All English people involved in this enterprise on both sides of the Atlantic knew that it was exactly that—an enterprise. Investors had made the project possible, as was the case in all overseas ventures, and further investment was required to keep it going. Thus much attention was diverted from building essential infrastructure to the continuing effort to find those indispensable "marchantable commodities." So the first group of new colonists sent with the resupply included essential skilled workers such as tailors, a blacksmith, a cooper, a surgeon, and a gunsmith, but also two apothecaries, a jeweler, two refiners, two goldsmiths, a perfumer, and a tobacco pipe maker. When Newport re-

turned with the second supply in September 1608 just as Smith was as-
suming the presidency, he brought a letter from the Virginia Company
harshly criticizing the colonists and with renewed instructions not to
return without a lump of gold, definite discovery of the passage to the
South Sea, or one of the lost Roanoke colonists, who presumably
could lead the present group to mines or other valuable resources. The
result, according to Smith, was that the colonists became "slaves" to
the aspiration for gold; "there was no talke, no hope, no worke, but dig
gold, wash gold, refine gold, load gold, such a brute [noise] of gold, as
one mad fellow desired to bee buried in the sandes, least they should
by their art make gold of his bones." He wrote that "never any thing
did more torment him, then to see all necessarie businesse neglected,
to fraught such a drunken ship with so much gilded durt."[42]

In order to further the quest for precious commodities, the company
sent experts from other parts of Europe. Just as the colonists resented
their dependence on their Indian neighbors, Smith also hated these
essential foreigners and considered them utterly untrustworthy. Promoters of English development were keenly aware that their country
lagged behind much of Europe in technology. Eastern European metal-
lurgists were imported to bring English mining and industry up to continental standards. And in America, where backers expected to grow
and process crops suited to far hotter environments than in England,
French vignerons and silk workers as well as mineral experts would
soon be seen as necessary. One metals expert who had come to rejuve-
nate the English copper industry in the sixteenth century was a Jew
from Prague named Joachim Ganz, and Ganz went to Roanoke at
Ralegh's urging to work with the copper everyone hoped would be
found in America; he appeared in the list of colonists as "Dougham
Gannes." Modern archaeological work has uncovered his forge at Roanoke and the remains of copper from which he had begun to extract silver.[43] Sixteenth-century expeditions to the far north led by Sir
Humphrey Gilbert and by Martin Frobisher also carried continental

mineralogists from Saxony. Although these men were essential, colonial leaders hated their dependence on them and never trusted them. Jonas Schutz, Frobisher's Saxon mineralogist, was blamed for the false ore that expedition brought back. And Joachim Ganz, once back in England, was brought to court accused of denying Christ's divinity.[44]

Eight continental European experts, listed as Poles and Germans, were sent to Jamestown in the second supply in 1608. Their skills involved glassmaking and preparing potash and pitch and tar; the remains of their glassworks have been found at Jamestown as well as quantities of broken glass the company sent over to help with getting the glassmaking started. Four of the Germans, whom Smith condemned as "those damned Dutch-men," particularly aroused his ire. To please Powhatan, he had sent three of them, Adam, Francis, and Samuel, and two English colonists to build a European-style house for him. Smith became convinced that these men had begun to identify with Powhatan's Pamunkeys rather than with their fellow Europeans at Jamestown, and had conspired to betray the colony. Francis actually made a trip back to the settlement inflammatorily dressed as an Indian. Smith blamed them when European weapons seemed to flow out of the fort into Indian hands, and accused a fourth man named William Volday, "a Switzer by birth," of helping the conspiracy from within the settlement.[45]

Everyone in Jamestown knew how uncertain things were. They were keenly aware of all the contemporaneous or near-contemporaneous failed ventures, and knew that investors would eventually withdraw support unless they could demonstrate a degree of success in achieving the company's goals—or offer some other kind of achievement that investors would see as comparably important. But because success seemed so remote and chancy, every person in the colony was also to some extent an independent operator looking out for his own position. The goal of submerging individual desires in common work for the general welfare had never been realistic, and even though leaders blamed the rank-and-file colonists for the failure to achieve it, they also recognized the absurdity of the planners' expectations. To the extent that migrants had backgrounds and skills that made them valuable to the colony, they were also people who would make sure of their own interests first as far as they possibly could.

The remarkable thing about Jamestown is that the investors and the colonists did not simply walk away from the project. The Plymouth Virginia Company colony in Maine had already been abandoned by this time, as so many others were. Whereas earlier ventures, like Sagadahoc, had been conceived in England's West Country, where engagement in maritime enterprises was a long tradition, the London location of the Virginia Company, and its access to both government and merchant circles, was crucial to the investors' willingness to rethink their venture and forge ahead in the face of massive disappointment. Despite a record of unremitting problems, and even in the absence of any concrete hope for future success, the backers determined not to give up.

8

The Project Revised

THE JAMESTOWN COLONISTS were "loose, leaud, licentious, riotous, and disordered," according to the reports that piled up during the early months. The migrants' "idleness and bestial slouth" had brought everything to a low point, and the investors in London found themselves stymied by the dismal, even alarming, news they received with each ship's return. They were incredulous that the men should be so weak and ineffectual, so unwilling to do the simple things that would have made the settlement healthy and safe, and so obtuse about the search for precious commodities. And the leadership, the people of quality who were supposed to set the example, seemed worse than the rank and file. The Virginia Company took stock as the colony moved through its second year and began to make plans to rectify its problems.[1]

For their part, the colonists were incredulous that the company supported them so inadequately and understood so little the huge obstacles they faced. The investors' grandiose expectations for exploration and development of crops and other kinds of commodities, and their assumption that the men could simply overawe the Indians and force them to do their will, utterly devalued the colonists' efforts. As Captain John Smith wrote at the end of his life, the company thought "an

Egge-shell . . . had beene sufficient against such enemies." The company did send more settlers, but without the supplies necessary to keep them, and with too few of the kinds of skilled workers an infant plantation needed. Dealing with the weaklings, the men of "tender education and small experience" who were downcast when they discovered that Virginia offered none of "their accustomed dainties," only made every problem worse.[2]

Smith had written a long letter to a patron describing the colony's beginning, and it arrived in England with the resupply ships early in 1608. He was chagrined to learn that his communication had been published in a mangled form by the same John Healey who would "translate" and publish Joseph Hall's *Mundus alter et idem* as *The Discovery of a new world* the next year. *A True Relation of such occurrences and accidents of noate, as hath hapned in Virginia, since the first planting of that Collony* was the first Jamestown news to appear in print, and it was frank about the problems of that initial year. In his preface to the *True Relation* Healey admitted that the colony had experienced hard times but encouraged new migrants and investors, "the worst being already past." The first colonists had "endured the heate of the day," and new venturers "may at ease labour for their profit, in the most sweete, coole, and temperate shade."[3]

But letters and reports of returnees continued to tell a disturbing story. Although the settlers found it hard to believe, the company leaders were reading their letters and were aware of their complaints. They finally interviewed Thomas Harriot to learn from his firsthand experience. This was the point at which attempts in many other locations were given up, but the council in London decided to try again. In 1609 the Virginia Company really began to innovate. On the basis of what they had learned, and their revised plans, the investors applied to King James for a new patent. The 1609 charter enlarged the boundaries of the colony to include all of Chesapeake Bay and much of

Carolina and restructured the company itself, broadening its membership by offering stock for sale at the price of £12 10s per share. Though still a large sum of money, this was a price that many more could afford, and company membership went from the typical small number of wealthy and well-connected men to include hundreds of people across the country. Every investor was promised land in Virginia and a monetary return when the stock was divided in 1616. The company also won the right of self-government; in place of the royally appointed council, investors now elected the council and its head, whose title was treasurer.

Virginia became a truly national venture with this new patent. The 1609 charter listed 650 investors by name and fifty London companies or guilds as corporate subscribers. The first council included such figures as Sir Francis Bacon, Shakespeare's patron the earl of Southampton, Sir Edwin Sandys (elder brother of George Sandys), Sir Thomas Roe, and Sir Dudley Digges; the great merchant Sir Thomas Smith was elected treasurer. Six hundred English agreed to go to the revitalized colony; most of those became "adventurers in person" (as opposed to investors, who adventured "in purse"), and received the same guarantee of land in 1616. A smaller number bargained for a company salary, which would be their total reward.[4]

The new charter was accompanied by a huge campaign to drum up interest in Jamestown, including a publication program that sought to make the colony a national priority. Not only did this level of membership make much more money available for company activities, but it also meant that huge numbers of people now had an interest in following Jamestown's progress. From this point forward, Virginia occupied a special place in England's consciousness of the larger world. Intelligencer John Chamberlain wrote to Dudley Carleton in February 1609: "Newes here is none at all but that John Dun [presumably the poet John Donne] seekes to be preferred to be secretarie of Virginia." In the event, the company appointed another man; when he was accidentally drowned in Virginia, William Strachey became the colony's secretary.[5]

As the reorganized company prepared to send out its largest fleet thus far, the adventurers commissioned a series of sermons by interested preachers and published them to help focus the nation's attention on the colony. These sermons and tracts cited biblical examples, particularly that of the Israelites approaching the land of Canaan and the doubts and fears that assailed some. They argued that God had waited to reveal the Indians' existence so that true reformed Christianity could be preached to them. To allow the colony to fail would be to abandon a sacred commission. These tracts urged potential investors and colonists to emulate the active faith of Caleb and Joshua rather than the timid naysayers. William Symonds, after listing the great events of the Old Testament, preached that "these things were done in a corner, in comparison of that which is in hand, and remaineth to be accomplished at the last judgement."[6]

The sermons largely eschewed the emphasis on worldly success that characterized other tracts sponsored by the Virginia Company. While not denying that Virginia was a good land that would be fruitful, they castigated the impiety of potential investors who hung back or even reneged for fear of losing their investment. Daniel Price, for example, pictured London as the filthy and profane center of pride and "the disease of the fashions" in which men built their fortunes on "the ruines of broken poore Citizens." Those who spent their time wrangling in the law courts were nothing less than persecutors of Christ. Price compared the avaricious rich to the most savage cannibals: "The bread thou eatest is the flesh of man, the wine thou drinkest is the bloud of man." Symonds preached that those who refused to contribute to Virginia were "Sowes that still wallow in the mire of their own pleasure and profit." Because they were not true Christians, they had no care to convert others. These preachers insisted that the English live up to their responsibility to "those scattered Gentiles, our kinsmen and younger brethren (as I may say) the sundrie nations of America."[7]

One of the most powerful voices sounding this note was that of Alexander Whitaker, the young puritan minister at the new settlement of Henrico near the falls of the James River. He was the son of a very prominent man, the Regius Professor of Divinity at Cambridge University. As his English editor Reverend William Crashaw pointed out, Whitaker went to Virginia out of conviction rather than necessity. He sent home an extended meditation on the biblical text "Cast thy bread upon the waters: for after many daies thou shalt finde it," arguing that wealthy men must understand that riches are only lent by God for God's purposes. Those who hoarded their wealth, or, worse, spent their money on "hawks, hounds, whores, and the like" instead of helping the needy in England and the poor Indians in America, "must give a straite account . . . at the day of judgement." But those who bestowed their wealth in good works would receive a reward in time, and the most important reward of all would be spiritual. Expectation of quick returns had distorted the whole Virginia project. Whitaker argued that some Virginia Company investors were "miserable covetous men, sold over to Usurie, Extortion and Oppression" and they had sent over the most unsuitable men, the kind of people "God hateth even from his very soule."

Whitaker argued that the Indians were ripe for conversion; in fact, they resembled his English forebears before they had heard the Gospel. They were descended from Adam, and "they have reasonable soules and intellectual faculties as well as wee," and were therefore ready to be persuaded. Whitaker's greatest triumph was winning Pocahontas for Christianity, and, with the contributions of pious English, he hoped she would be the first of many. Even after the three years he had signed up for were over, he wrote that he was determined to stay. Whitaker never returned to England; he drowned crossing a creek in 1617.[8]

With the new charter in hand, the Virginia Company reconfigured its colonial project in 1609. After hearing and reading all the reports, company members decided that their original plan had had three principal defects. The first was what they called the "equality of Governors," that is, diffusing authority in a council that elected its own head. They concluded that this design had inevitably led to factions and ineffectual government—as John Rolfe later wrote, all the councilors wanted to be "Keisars, none inferior to other"—and so they decided to send "one able and absolute Governor." Although the new governor, Sir Thomas Gates, would have a council, councilors' role was only advisory, and his instructions stipulated that he could ignore them at will. Those instructions also authorized the governor to institute martial law and not to worry too much about "the nicenes and letter of the law" in dealing with rebellious colonists.[9]

As they analyzed what had gone wrong in Virginia, the company also responded to the extraordinary health problems plaguing the men. Letters from leading colonists such as Peter Winne had convinced them that most of the strange lethargy and sickness was a direct result of Jamestown's "unwholesome" site in "the marish of Virginia." England had its unhealthy fen country; William Strachey pointed out that newcomers to the town of Plumstead in Kent routinely fell sick, just as new colonists were stricken in Jamestown, but no one therefore condemned the whole county of Kent. Even in England, foreign experts from the Netherlands were imported to create the great engineering works to drain the fens and free England's marsh regions from the "corrupt" water that made them unhealthy. So Jamestown's alarming record of disease and death was simply the result of an unfortunate choice of location. Gates's instructions directed the colonists to build three new settlements farther inland on dry, high, healthy ground and said that Jamestown should be kept only as a depot. And as in the original instructions, the company reminded the colonists that it was as easy to plot the streets and houses in "order as confusion" and that straight intersecting streets converging on a central marketplace would help in their defense when they were attacked.[10]

An unprecedentedly large fleet of five ships commanded by Sir George Somers set out with the colonists and Governor Gates in June 1609. This fleet was to pioneer the route chosen in response to the third major problem the company had diagnosed: the "*length* and *danger* of the passage*." The customary route to North America at that time involved sailing down the coast of Europe and Africa to the latitude of the trade winds, which would carry the ships across to the West Indies, where they could reprovision before taking the northward current to their destination. This new fleet was to sail more directly across the Atlantic, shortening the trip from months to weeks. Thus the colonists would arrive in better health and the food supplies sent by the company would be preserved.

The more northerly route would eventually become standard, but this first experiment went horribly wrong, as the fleet was scattered in an enormous storm that lasted for forty-eight hours. One survivor called it "an Egyptian night of three daies perpetuall horror." William Strachey, reporting that "winds and seas were as mad as fury and rage could make them," also reached for his experience in the East. He compared the tempest to storms he had encountered "upon the coast of Barbary and Algiers, in the Levant, and once, more distressful, in the Adriatic gulf."[11] Four of the ships eventually limped into Chesapeake Bay, but the flagship with Somers and Gates and the charter aboard was wrecked on Bermuda. Bermuda had no human inhabitants, and had been avoided by European mariners as the "Isle of Devils" because of the dangerous submerged reefs that ring it, but it was populated by huge numbers of hogs, descendants of a breeding pair left by some unknown predecessor ship.

Now English venturers in both Bermuda and Jamestown faced a novel problem: return to the philosophical state of nature. The stragglers arriving in Virginia included Governor John Smith's antagonists from the first year: Captains Gabriel Archer, John Ratcliffe (Smith could not resist adding "whose right name was Sickelmore," and John Martin. They informed Smith that he had been replaced as governor, but they had no patent to show him. He and his supporters contended that the old system was in place until the new charter arrived, while the newcomers (and his enemies within the colony) insisted that Smith could no longer govern. As Smith described the situation, "Those lewd Captaines . . . would rule all or ruine all." George Percy, one of Smith's critics, turned the blame around, saying, "Smithe wolde rule all and ingrose all authorety into his owne hands." So, the Virginia Company wrote, "every thing returning from civill Propryety, to Naturall, and Primary Community . . . no man would acknowledge a superior: nor could from this headlesse and unbrideled multitude, bee any thing expected, but disorder and ryott."[12]

The shipwrecked in Bermuda had both charter and governor, but neither was legal for that location. A man named Stephen Hopkins, a puritan belonging to the extreme group that had separated itself from the Church of England, argued, drawing on his impressive knowledge of the Bible, that "authority ceased when the wreck was committed." As in the state of nature, he maintained, each person's responsibility was to provide for self and family, and the castaways should establish their own agreements to achieve that end. Like many others, he did not want to leave Bermuda for the rigors of life in Virginia when the ship the refugees were building should be ready. Hopkins was charged with mutiny but apologized and was pardoned. A decade later he was among the band of his fellow separatist puritans known in American history as the Pilgrims when they landed on Cape Cod. As they had a patent for a plantation in Virginia, they also faced a situation in which there was no legal government for their location, and the fifty or so puritans were only half the company. Their English backers had insisted that they take along another fifty skilled workers, whom they called "strangers." As the strangers began to utter "discontented and muti-nous speeches" and pointed to the dissolution of legal authority, the male colonists drew up an "association and agreement," the Mayflower Compact, by which all adult men (except servants, who were not free agents) agreed to be governed. Stephen Hopkins was among the signers.[13]

Shakespeare's play *The Tempest*, first performed in 1611, conjured with all these themes of wreck and redemption. It began with a great storm, and Shakespeare's language paralleled the descriptions in the vivid reports published by those who had experienced the momen-tous 1609 hurricane. *The Tempest* also engaged the idea of an is-land shipwreck that resulted in a return to the state of nature, as his characters played out their aspirations and shortcomings in this world turned upside down. Gonzalo, the benevolent old counselor, en-visioned a truly utopian society without property, laws, or even learn-ing. But others of the shipwrecked men tried to make themselves into lords, even contemplating murder and treason in order to achieve their goals.

The Tempest played with the way the English conflated the many others with whom they dealt. Caliban, the island's native, was the son of a woman who came from Algiers. Prospero, the deposed duke of Mi-lan, had landed on the island with his daughter, Miranda, twelve years before the shipwreck with which the play opens. Shakespeare placed a critique of colonialism in Caliban's mouth, as he castigated Prospero for having taken the island from him and made him his slave. Like the Chesapeake Algonquians, Caliban eventually vowed no longer to pro-vide food for Prospero, and referred to the intricate and irreplaceable native-built weirs on which the colonists depended: "No more dams I'll make for fish."[14] On this island, as in John Smith's Virginia, the truly noble engaged in unaccustomed hard labor to prove their virtue, as Ferdinand stacked and carried wood to prove his worthiness to marry Miranda. And, as in Jamestown, some among the rank and file demonstrated their unworthiness by their fecklessness—even in trying to realize their greedy plans.

Before Shakespeare's play was presented, the Virginia Company published two declarations to reassure their investors that the venture was still on track. One was published early in 1610 and told the story of the storm and the arrival of the stragglers in a desperate Jamestown; backers in London did not then know that Somers and Gates and the flagship had survived and would eventually make it to the Chesapeake. The *True and Sincere declaration of the purpose and end of the Plantation begun in Virginia* analyzed the problems and solutions and outlined their actions to rectify the situation. The company castigated those who sensed disaster: "Who can avoid the hand of God, or dispute with him? Is hee fitt to under-take any great action, whose courage is shaken and dissolved with one storme?" As Jamestown's present problems stemmed from eminently fixable circumstances and would dissolve when the new government was in place, there was no need for discouragement. In comparison to its promise, the Virginia project's difficulties were "smoake and ayre." And Captain Samuel Argall had successfully inaugurated the new shorter direct route—he claimed the crossing could be done in seven weeks. Moreover, Jamestown's leaders believed they had sure intelligence of the Roanoke colonists "(yet alive) within fifty mile of our fort." These, with their experience of twenty years' residence, "can open the wombe and bowells of this country" to the Jamestown residents.[15]

Making the venture a national mission with a strong London base meant that the project could continue when so many others had been given up. In spring 1610 the company sent a new governor, Thomas West, Lord de la Warr, with a fresh supply of 150 men. Lord de la Warr, as the company pointed out, was not only a peer but also a man "whose Honour nor Fortune needs not any desperate medecine." Portraying him as a man of substance, not someone who was fleeing creditors or other problems, speaks volumes about the kind of gossip that must have been circulating in London about the general run of recruits.[16]

Meanwhile Somers, Gates, Newport, and the others shipwrecked in Bermuda had managed to construct two new small ships, named the *Patience* and the *Deliverance,* out of Bermuda cedar and the remains of the wrecked *Sea Adventure*. During their sojourn in Bermuda, two children had been born, both christened with the name of the island. Little Bermuda Rolfe, John Rolfe's daughter, died and was buried there; her mother, Rolfe's first wife, whose name is not known, died shortly after they arrived in Virginia. The latecomers finally entered the James River in May 1610, almost a year after their intended arrival date.

Instead of a flourishing settlement, they found a scene of despair at Jamestown with only a small fraction of the colonists still living. Things had gone terribly wrong over that winter, which became known as the "starving time." The struggle between Captain John Smith and his rivals had ended after five weeks when Smith was seriously injured; his powder bag exploded in his lap while he was traveling in a small boat, and his burns incapacitated him. Although he would spend the rest of his life writing about the theory and practice of American enterprises, his association with Virginia ended in October 1609 when he returned to England. Smith thus missed the winter of horror; he and his partisans insisted that if he had stayed and continued his "he who does not work, does not eat" policy, it would never have happened.

If we had the testimony of Powhatan and his people, the problems would appear as they truly were—larger and more fundamental than Jamestown's situation or one governor's policies. Continuing drought conditions combined with hard winters meant that pressure on food supplies and native polities was increasing while the colonists' willingness and ability to feed themselves seemed to decline.

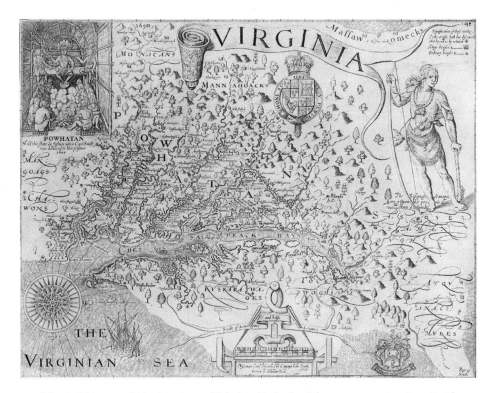

John Smith's map of Virginia first published in his book of the same name in 1612. Smith marked the extent of his own exploration with a series of small crosses. Knowledge of the waterways and lands beyond came from his conversations with Indians. Courtesy of the John Carter Brown Library at Brown University.

We do not hear natives speaking in their own voices, but even in the English sources and with insights gained from archaeology, we can extrapolate something of their viewpoint and the hardships they endured. Early in 1609, as the ships carrying the new colonists straggled in, Powhatan made good on his threat to move away from ready contact with the Jamestown settlers. As the Virginia Company's *True and Sincere Declaration* said, the Indians "withdrew from all commerce and trafficke with them, cunningly making a war upon them, which they felt not, who durst no other-way appeare an enemye."[17] By August when Gabriel Archer's ship arrived, many of the men had been dispersed out of the fort to try to live off the land. Archer wrote that "the people of the Country" were not "able to relieve them if they would."[18]

English behavior became increasingly aggressive and erratic in a situation in which the Indians, as virtually the sole source of food, held the power. George Percy wrote of an expedition to Nansemond, downriver from Jamestown. When the party learned that their messengers to the Nansemond chief had been "sacrifysed, and thatt their braynes weare cutt and skraped outt of their heades with mussell shelles," they exacted extreme retribution: "We beate the salvages outt of the island, burned their howses, ransaked their temples, tooke downe the corpes of their deade kings from of their toambes, and caryed away their pearles, copper and braceletts wherewith they doe decore their kings funeralles." On the verge of a winter of extreme cold and want, such actions could only make their problems worse.

Soon other English were cut down, and a party that had been sent upriver to the falls was found dead. Percy wrote that the men were discovered "slayne with their mowthes stopped full of Breade beinge donn as it seamethe in Contempte and skorne thatt others mighte expecte the Lyke when they shold come to seeke for breade and reliefe amongste them." This gesture of "contempte and skorne" reminded Percy of an episode he had read about in which a Spanish general named Baldivia had been captured and forced to drink molten gold in Chile; his captors had taunted him, "Now glutt they selfe with gowlde." Percy remarked that Baldivia had sought gold with the same intensity with which the English sought food. Percy reported that many colonists ran away "unto the salvages, whome we never heard of after."[19]

When Governor Gates and Admiral Somers finally arrived from Bermuda in May 1610, they were astonished to find "all things so contrary to our expectations, so full of misery and misgovernment." The men were reduced to eating "vermin," and there were even rumors of cannibalism in the fort. One man, "beinge pinched with extreme famin . . . did come openly into the markett place, blaspheameinge, exclameinge, and cryeinge outt thatt there was noe god, alledgeinge thatt if there were a god he wolde nott suffer his creatures whome he had made and framed to indure those miseries, and to perishe for wante of foode and sustenance."[20]

And the wellborn were no better than the rank and file. Francis West, Lord de la Warr's brother, abandoned the colony, taking a load of corn he and his men had gathered. Rather than bringing the food to Jamestown to relieve the sufferings of the starving time, at the urging of his men he sailed for England "and lefte us in thatt extreme misery and wantte." Not only had these men done terrible wrong to the Indians from whom they took corn, thus creating greater animosity, but they also slandered Virginia back in England.[21]

Meanwhile, the colonists were tearing boards off abandoned houses and ripping up the palisades for firewood rather than go "into the woods a stone's cast off." Such behavior was not as bizarre as it sounds in the prevailing guerrilla warfare conditions: "It is true the Indian killed as fast without, if our men stirred but beyond the bounds of the blockhouse, as famine and pestilence did within." From inside the fort, the men knew that the "watching, subtile, and offended Indian" waited for them to die.[22]

The new arrivals from Bermuda had not brought extra food from their well-supplied islands, and the Indians had none to spare—even if they could be made to hand it over—as it was their planting time. Moreover, the colony lacked the equipment for effective fishing. So, after much consultation, Gates decided to abandon the settlement and take the whole company home. Jamestown had arrived at the same impasse as the first Roanoke colony, having alienated the Indians on whom the settlers relied for food and instruction without having gained the mastery—over themselves, the environment, or the Indians—they believed they needed to survive. Only with difficulty did the leaders prevent the disgruntled survivors from burning what was left of "James Cittie" to the ground.

As the ships made their way down the James on June 7, 1610, they encountered a longboat coming up from the river's mouth. In the kind of dramatic coincidence we associate with novelists' imaginations, the departing English learned that Lord de la Warr's fleet, with four hundred men and supplies for a whole year, had entered the James the day before and would soon be in Jamestown. The colony was saved. The government was formally handed over to de la Warr, and he installed his own council with all pomp and formality.[23]

What they all learned from their experience confirmed the fundamental psychological understanding already applied in English ventures in Ireland: human nature, at least in the common sort of people, is wholly malleable, lacking any internal governor. Without rigid external control, all human beings degenerate into the kind of shapeless, aimless mass seen in Jamestown at the end of the starving winter. William Strachey, the colony secretary, who described the chaos he and the other Bermudians found on their arrival, asserted firmly that even the best counties of England could be brought to the same state without good government. In other words, instead of hoping for virtuous people to create a proper society, planners needed to create structures that would force colonists, even the "excrements" in Virginia, into virtue. William Bullock later outlined this theory succinctly: "Good Laws duly executed, will make good men." Now that Virginia was to be governed by a peer of the realm with virtually absolute powers, proper development could occur.[24]

Near the end of 1610 the Virginia Company published its second statement on the situation in the colony. The *True and Sincere Declaration,* published as the year began, had assumed that the flagship of the 1609 fleet and the leaders it carried had all perished in the hurricane; it therefore made the best of what was left. In November the company published A *True Declaration of the Estate of the Colonie in Virginia, with a confutation of such scandalous reports as have tended to the disgrace of so worthy an enterprise*, announcing the deliverance of the flagship and the salvation of Virginia. It began: "There is a great distance, betwixt the vulgar opinion of men, and the judicious apprehension of wise men." The "compiler" vowed to include only the words of men who had taken leading parts in the action, and, banishing "Blacke envie, and pale feare," to draw on the experience of historical movements of people, both ancient and modern, to prove that colonization was "Lawfull, Possible, Profitable." Some people in England were arguing that such expansion was unethical, and it was in great part to answer those "slie whisperers" that the Virginia Company sponsored this long tract. The company confronted detractors who argued that the transatlantic passage was too dangerous, the country barren, and the climate unwholesome, beginning with the "tragicall Comaedie" of the shipwreck of the 1609 fleet. Once again the Virginia Company announced that all difficulties were over and, citing the prevailing view of human nature and many examples from ancient history, blamed the storm that "seperated the head from the bodie, all the vitall powers of regiment being exiled with Sir Thomas Gates," thus opening Virginia to "the tempest of dissention." Nothing less than divine intervention in the arrival of the Bermuda group and then of Lord de la Warr had saved the colony. If God favored the venture, mere humans could not doubt; to withdraw support now would show the English to be "too effeminate in our longings, and too impatient of delaies." Virginia could supply all the products England lacked and now was forced to buy from potential enemies.[25]

As the second decade of the century opened, plans were laid for keeping Jamestown as a port while creating new settlements on higher and healthier sites both up and down river. Recent experience had reinforced the conviction among leaders on both sides of the Atlantic that strict and unquestioned government was required. Lord de la

Warr set these initiatives in motion, but, overcome by disease, he soon left the colony, leaving George Percy in charge. Percy, who acted as governor until the arrival of Sir Thomas Dale, departed in the spring of 1612.

In January of 1611 the Virginia Company issued a one-page broadside calling for recruits, saying that a new effort was in train "and for that it is not intended any more to burden the action with vagrant and unnecessarie persons: this is to give notice to so many honest and industrious men, as Carpenters, Smiths, Coopers, fishermen, Tanners, Shoomakers, Shipwrights, Brickmen, Gardeners, husbandmen, and labouring men of all sorts, that if they repair to the house of Sir Thomas Smith in Philpot Lane, before the end of this present moneth of Januarie," they "shall be entertained for the Voyage, upon such termes as their qualitie and fitnesse shall deserve."[26]

Sir Thomas Gates and Sir Thomas Dale had been comrades in arms in the Netherlands, and they made a team in Jamestown that really enacted the new policies. Both had been sent back to England by Lord de la Warr to gather supplies and colonists; they returned in 1611 with Dale as marshal and lieutenant governor under Governor Gates. Their administration imposed the martial law they knew from their service in Europe as suitable for such people as the colonists had proven themselves to be. Martial law was a volatile issue, and the government's occasional attempts to employ it in England, and to billet soldiers on subjects, were seen as intolerable. Thus it is a measure of how dramatically Jamestown's problems threatened the entire project that the company was happy not only to impose martial law there but also to publish the law code in England so all potential investors knew what kind of order had been established. The martial law code envisioned a regimented society in which all people would wake up and go to work together at the beat of a drum, and every other activity was to be similarly synchronized. The most extreme punishments were set down for any dereliction of duty.

This new regime might create an orderly society, but it would not be traditional English order. Dale arrived in May 1611 and immediately wrote to the Virginia Company about the state of the colony and the orders he had given to get the settlers working effectively. When Gates came in August to take command, Dale was ready with recommendations, which he sent home in a letter to the earl of Salisbury. He described the sites he had picked out for new settlements. Now that all colonists were going to be forced into virtue, Dale suggested that the Virginia Company, rather than trying to find worthy people, except for a few specialists such as surgeons, should send men he could coerce effectively to build a truly functioning economy. Whereas the company had announced that it would no longer accept "vagrant . . . persons," Dale actually suggested that the investors contract with the king to ship out all men who were condemned to death for crimes in England for the next three years, remarking, "Thus doth the Spaniard people his Indes." Although he admitted that the present colonists had good reason to be discontented, he argued that they had degenerated so completely that condemned criminals would be preferable to the "diseased and crased bodies" now in Virginia. If the company could contrive to ship two thousand men in two lots and make sure that they came with full provisions for six months, he could guarantee that the colony would never again have to ask for support from home. He would build five strong forts from which, within two years, the colonists would be able to feed themselves as well as to explore the country. Moreover, he promised that he would be able to "overmaster the subtle, mischievous Great Powhatan" and force him either to leave the country or accept English control.[27]

Some colonists were horrified by the new regime. Percy, who had been supplanted as governor by Dale and then by the full governor, Sir Thomas Gates, in 1611, wrote of the extreme exemplary punishments Dale had imposed when he was in command at Fort Henrico upriver near the falls of the James:

Sir Thomas Dale haveinge allmoste finished the foarte and settled a plantacyon in thatt parte, dyvers of his men beinge idell and nott willeinge to take paynes did runne away unto the Indyans, many of them beinge taken ageine Sir Thomas in a moste severe mannor cawsed to be executed. Some he apointed to be hanged, some burned, some to be broken upon wheles, others to be staked, and some to be shott to deathe, all theis extreme and crewell tortures he used and inflicted upon them to terrefy the reste for attempteinge the lyke. And some which robbed the store he cawsed them to be bownd faste unto trees and so sterved them to deathe.

So widespread was hunger and privation that the Indian intermediary Kemps, still living in Jamestown, died of the nutritional deficiency disease scurvy in 1611.[28]

Ralph Hamor, who was among those shipwrecked in Bermuda and who arrived in Jamestown with Governor Gates, argued that only strict enforcement of the laws could have saved the colony. So "Sir Thomas Dale hath not bin tyranous, nor severe at all." To those who alleged that "the manner of their death . . . hath bin cruell, unusuall and barbarous," he acknowledged that the punishments "have bin more severe then usuall in England," but suggested that critics look at what was done in "France, and other Countries for lesse offences." Terror was the only way to control the kind of people with whom Dale had to deal; "the feare of a cruell, painefull and unusuall death, more restrains them then death it selfe." Samuel Argall returned to Virginia in the summer of 1612 and a year later he wrote that on his arrival, "by the discreet and provident government of Sir Thomas Gates, and great paines and hazard of Sir Thomas Dale, I found both the Countrey and people in farre better estate."[29]

The Virginia Company applied for a third charter to allow for incorporation of Bermuda in its patent. This 1612 charter also granted the company the right to institute a lottery in England to contribute to the support of the project. Robert Johnson published an authorized pamphlet titled *The New Life of Virginea* urging readers to gamble in the lottery as a patriotic gesture. While acknowledging that lotteries "bee no usuall course in England," he pointed out that they were used in other countries "for the publike service of most commendable actions." For less literate potential customers, the company sponsored ballads promoting the lottery to be sung to the tune of "Lusty Gallant."[30] Although it was not immediately successful, the lottery eventually became a major source of income for the Virginia Company. A printed broadside ad for the lottery in 1615 featured large portraits of two Virginia Indian men, identified as Eiakintomino and Matahan, who were probably among a small but steady flow of Indians who were being sent to England for education. Their presence was taken to signify progress toward success and was exploited by the company. At least one of the portraits was similar to a painting by a visiting Dutch artist, who noted on the picture that Eiakintomino could be seen in St. James's Park in London.[31]

Despite all these promising efforts, negative reports continued to flow from Virginia even in the midst of the strict new regime. The indefatigable news disseminator John Chamberlain wrote in the summer of 1612 that the Spanish ambassador, Don Pedro de Zúñiga, was expected to renew complaints about the English plantation in the lands claimed by Spain; but Chamberlain predicted, on the basis of reports from recently arrived ships, that if the Spanish simply waited, the colony "will fall to the ground of yt self, by the extreem beastly ydlenes of our nation." His informants told him that both Gates and Dale were "quite out of hart." One of the recently arrived ships was a renegade; ten men had been sent out to fish but had absconded home to England with their catch. As in the earlier desertion by Captain Francis West and his company, they not only abandoned their comrades but also spread "yll reports" about the colony, which harmed the project's interests more than "the Lottery or any other art" could help it.[32]

Virginia Company Lottery broadside. The Society of Antiquaries of London.

Back in England, company members were beginning to default. At the very end of 1612 and into 1613 the Virginia Company initiated a series of suits in the Court of Chancery against investors who were refusing to pay in sums that the company alleged they owed and that were required to keep the joint enterprise going. In response to the first of the suits, Sir Thomas Mildmay testified that whereas great profit had been promised when he joined the company, now he and other investors were told that no income would accrue for twenty years or more. He commented darkly that he knew shipments were coming from Virginia and wondered if the revenues were going to company insiders. Noting that they had still received nothing from Virginia but "fayre tales and hopes," John Chamberlain, who was himself a Virginia Company investor, wrote that adventurers being hauled into court had been falsely told they would not have to make further payments until profits began to come in.[33]

Spain consistently tried to gather information about what was really happening in Jamestown. Although Spain and England had established peace in 1604, the Spanish authorities fumed over Jamestown's encroachment on land they considered to be within their claims. They sent some ships to see what the English were up to and how far they had succeeded in establishing a flourishing colony. They also tried to glean as much information as they could. Each successive Spanish ambassador in London sent home rumors and reports and an occasional map or sketch he had obtained from contacts in the Virginia Company or other sources. Some documents, including the earliest map of the James River drawn by a colonist, now exist only in the Spanish archives, the English copies having been diverted or lost. The early 1608 letter from Francis Perkins to his English patron is in the Spanish archives; presumably his requests for office in Virginia went unfulfilled because his friend never received it. Occasionally Spanish leaders had the opportunity to interrogate someone who had been in "Villa Jacobo."[34]

But information gained in these ways was always frustratingly and tantalizingly vague and offered wildly conflicting pictures. Some informants insisted that the English had discovered precious metals and were on their way to finding riches and the passage to the South Sea. Others said the settlers lived in extreme poverty in a fort so poorly constructed that it could easily be pushed over. But the Spanish had their own problems in Europe and in South America to worry about, and they could never decide whom to believe. Loyalties and identities were so slippery that no one could be trusted completely.

Irishman Francis Magnel presented just the kind of problem that confounded the Spanish. In 1610 he turned up in Spain trying to capitalize on his having been in Jamestown in 1607 with stories about the riches of the Chesapeake region and the rival English presence there. Magnel described the situation of Jamestown and its fortifications, including the best way to approach it. He claimed that even in its first year the colony had produced valuable dyes, drugs and medicines, and furs. Magnel claimed that the colonists had made wine as good as Spanish Alicante wines from the native grapes; he knew because he had "tried one or two." Not only were samples of ores bearing gold, silver, and copper taken back to England in 1608, but "there are many large pearls in that land, and a great quantity of coral, and in the mountains they find stones very much like diamonds." Magnel praised the Chesapeake Algonquians, especially the "Emperor of Virginia," Powhatan, and said they came to trade in the daily market in Jamestown and were very receptive to Christian teaching. The English, he reported, had indoctrinated their American neighbors with the idea that the Spanish are "very cruel and wicked." The English were so eager to keep "the secrets of that land," especially from the Spanish, that all colonists' letters were opened and read by the governor. The Spanish did not offer Magnel a place in their service as he had hoped, but they did send a reconnoitering voyage to try to verify his stories.[35]

In 1611 the Spanish reconnaissance entered Chesapeake Bay ostensibly looking for a lost vessel; three men from the ship, including the leader, Don Diego de Molina, went ashore to the English fort at Point Comfort near the bay's entrance and an English pilot, John Clark, boarded their ship to help guide it. After some discussion, the three men from the Spanish ship were seized, and their ship sailed away with John Clark. Diego de Molina was able to send letters home from Jamestown; some were open and were conveyed to the Spanish ambassador by Virginia Company officials in London, but at least one was smuggled out sewn into the shoe sole of an unidentified "gentleman of Venice." Clark was interrogated in Havana and later in Spain. Both Diego de Molina and John Clark were eventually repatriated, but only after half a decade in captivity. Each had shaped the information he gave in order to heighten the chance that the Spanish would be more interested in Jamestown in ways that would help him. Clark continued to be active in Atlantic voyages, and served as pilot and master's mate on the *Mayflower* when it carried the first colonists to Plymouth in 1620.

There was a more problematic person among the three men from the Spanish ship, a man known to the Spanish as Francisco Lembri and as Francis Limbreck or Lymbry to the English. During his interrogation Clark said he had recognized Limbreck as an English renegade who had entered the Spanish service, and the Spanish were disturbed by this news. Diego de Molina insisted that Lembri was really Spanish, but the authorities in Havana now worried that he had been an English spy all along. For their part, the English in Jamestown saw him as a traitor; in the words of Captain George Percy, he was "our hispanyolated Inglisheman Limbrecke." Samuel Purchas later revealed that this "English . . . Judas" had actually guided Spanish ships in the great armada of 1588.[36]

Jamestown was crowded with captive outsiders during these years. In April of 1613 Captain Samuel Argall captured Pocahontas, and thus "Powhatans delight and darling" joined Diego de Molina and Francis Limbreck in captivity in Jamestown.[37] Others unwillingly joined the varied population there. Argall, fresh from having seized Pocahontas, commanded a party in July 1613 with a commission to prevent French settlement on lands to the north within the patent of the Virginia Company. Although Nova Scotia may have been his target, Argall was confounded by dense fog and instead found the small Jesuit mission of St. Sauveur on the coast of Maine. In what the French saw as "a piece of outrageous rascality," he challenged the settlement's legality and declared the French pirates. In fact, they were within the Virginia Company's patent. Driven by English "inborn love of robbery," Argall attacked: "The English ship came on swifter than an arrow, driven by a propitious wind, all screened in pavesade [canvas] of red, the banners of England flying, and three trumpets and two drums making a horrible din." Some of the French were given a small ship in which to try to return to France after the English seized their own ship. But Argall took two Jesuits, Pierre Biard and Jacques Quentin, in his ships as they sailed to "their principal settlement, which they call Jeutom [Jamestown]." The "ferocious Englishman" Sir Thomas Gates, then governor in Virginia, determined on "severe punishment" for the priests. But Argall, who had promised them safe travel, protected them. Playing on the association of "Argall" with "argali," wild ram, the priests reported that he acted "boldly and vehemently, as was fitting his name and race."

Governor Gates then directed Argall to return to Acadia with the priests and eradicate the remaining French presence at Port Royal on Nova Scotia; after this renewed attack the ships again headed south. Biard wrote that he and Father Quentin expected to be executed upon their second arrival in Virginia, but "divine Providence frustrated all the efforts of the English sailors to land. A violent storm cast them upon the Azores islands, which belong to Portugal." Further storms forced the ship on which Biard and Quentin traveled toward Wales, where they were freed in gratitude for their silence during the enforced visit to the Roman Catholic Azores. According to the Jesuits, the ship's master, a man named Turnell, recognized God's message in the storm that drove them across the Atlantic and "frankly acknowledged that the power of the Deity, which avenges injury done to the innocent, was deservedly hostile to him and his upon that voyage."[38] Recent archaeology at Jamestown has uncovered crucifixes, rosaries, and religious medallions, which could have been brought by any of the captives, though they could also have belonged to English Roman Catholics within the fort.[39]

The settlements always included many non-British Europeans, largely because they needed the skills of continental specialists such as the German and Polish glassmakers and mineralogists who had so vexed Captain John Smith. The Swiss William Volday, whom Smith accused of conspiracy against the colony, had "made a shift to get for England" and convinced the company that he had found very rich mines, so he was sent back with Governor de la Warr in 1610. According to Smith, Volday was found to be "a meere Imposter" and "dyed most miserably" back in Virginia. But faith in his discoveries and in the other continental experts lived on; Dale wrote in outlining his plans on arrival in May 1611 that he intended to launch a search for the mines described by "Faldoe the Helvetian." And the picture of orderly and purposeful labor presented by the Virginia Company in its pamphlet announcing the miraculous recovery of those shipwrecked on Bermuda and the providential arrival of Governor de la Warr included "the French preparing to plant the Vines."[40]

Another colonist, John Martin, was identified in the Virginia correspondence as "the Persian," although he apparently was from Armenia. He came to Virginia in the train of Captain Samuel Argall, and was described in a lawsuit in 1621 as wholly dependent on Argall and ignorant of the Lord's Prayer. Nonetheless, Governor George Yeardley made him a freeman in Virginia. Martin petitioned the Virginia Company in person in 1622 asking to be exempt from the double customs payments that were levied on his tobacco because he was "a Stranger." The company, respectfully calling him Mr. Martin, decided to enfranchise him, using powers bestowed in their charter, thus giving him the same status as English-born colonists, "which may happily encourage other Strangers to the like resolucion to goe over thither." Patrick Copland recorded that Martin had lived in Virginia for six or seven years by 1622 and was wholly committed to return "there to live and die . . . I have travailed (said he) by Land over eighteene severall kingdomes; and yet all of them in my minde, come farre short of Virginia, both for temperature of ayre, and fertilitie of the soyle."[41]

John Martin came to America in the mid-1610s and found a home there, but at the same time other "strangers" apparently preferred death to life in Jamestown. The Spanish ambassador, Diego Sarmiento de Acuña, conde de Gondomar, wrote to Philip III of two "Moorish thieves" who were offered the chance to escape their sentence of hanging if they would go to Virginia. They replied "at once, decidedly and with one accord, that they would much rather die on the gallows here, and quickly, than to die slowly so many deaths as was the case in Virginia."[42]

In 1614 Sir Thomas Dale, left in charge in Virginia by the departure of Governor Gates, wrote a long letter to a friend describing his and the colony's situation. He lamented the recent death of James I's eldest son, Prince Henry, for whom Henrico had been named. Many had placed their hopes in this intelligent youth who would have become king: "He was the great Captaine of our Israell, the hope to have builded up this heavenly new Jerusalem." Now investors were losing interest, and Dale feared that the entire project had fallen "into his grave." He believed that Virginia "stands in desperate hazard."

And yet he had good news to report as well. As the plan to exchange Pocahontas for English held by the Indians had been transformed into a project of incorporating her into English life, her presence in Jamestown had been the occasion for a peace with Powhatan and all the client chiefdoms under him. According to Dale, "Powhatans daughter I caused to be carefuly instructed in Christian Religion, who after shee had made some good progresse therein, renounced publickly her countrey Idolatry, openly confessed her Christian faith, was, as she desired, baptised, and is since married to an English Gentleman of good understanding." He specified that Powhatan, though he did not attend, blessed her marriage to John Rolfe and sent her uncle to give her away. He reckoned that "the gayning of this one soule" made his "time, toile, and present stay well spent." His letter was published in a volume that included one from Reverend Alexander Whitaker, who instructed Pocahontas in the Christian faith, and a long detailed letter Rolfe wrote explaining his motives in seeking to marry her.

Dale's other success was an alliance with the "stout and warlike" Chickahominies, who had remained independent of Powhatan. He wrote that he intended to stay on in Virginia at least through the har-

Negotiating the alliance with the Chickahominies. Courtesy of the John Carter Brown Library at Brown University.

vest and strongly implied that no one else could have accomplished all he had done. Were he to leave and the colony to fail in consequence, it would be "to the scorne of our Nation, and to give cause of laughter to the Papists that desire our ruine."[43]

Dale was to see two more harvests before his final departure in the spring of 1616. He wrote to a supporter that he left Virginia "in great prosperytye and pease [peace], contrarye to manye mens Exspectatyon," but that it was "the hardest taske that ever I undertooke."[44] The *Treasurer,* the ship on which he traveled back to England, carried a panoply of Jamestown's varied residents. Diego de Molina sailed on this ship, ending his long captivity, and his companion Francis Limbreck also embarked on it, although Limbreck was never to arrive. Whereas Diego de Molina was freed and allowed to return to Spain, Limbreck was hanged from the yardarm as soon as the ship came within sight of the English coast.

Pocahontas, now Lady Rebecca Rolfe, her husband John, and their infant son Thomas also traveled on the *Treasurer,* and Pocahontas was accompanied by a considerable train. Her brother-in-law Uttamattomakin, a principal priest and very prominent man, sailed with her, as did several women who attended her. Pocahontas and her party caused a sensation in England. John Chamberlain included it in the news he gathered: "Sir Thomas Dale is arrived from Virginia and brought with him some ten or twelve old and younge of that countrie, among whom the most remarquable person is Poca-huntas (daughter of Powatan a kinge or cacique of that countrie) married to one Rolfe an English man."[45]

Pocahontas's portrait was taken from life and rushed into print to satisfy the public's curiosity. It differed from all previous representations of visiting Indians in that she was painted as an Englishwoman rather than in a stereotypically Indian pose and outfit. The name Pocahontas did not appear on the engraving, which identified her as the daughter of the powerful emperor of Virginia and gave her name

Pocahontas in London. Courtesy of the John Carter Brown Library at Brown University.

as Matoaka or Rebecca. In 1617 Purchas recorded Uttamatomakin's statement that Pocahontas was only a nickname, and that her true name, Matoaka, had been concealed from the English "in a superstitious feare of hurte by the English if her name were knowne." So in applying the name Matoaka, the engraver showed how current he was. Most, however, continued to use the name by which she had become famous. Ben Jonson's play *The Staple of Newes* cited John Smith, "the historian," for its description of "the blessed Pocahontas . . . and great king's daughter of Virginia."[46]

In the same kind of gathering as Ahmad bin Qasim had met in Paris and the Netherlands, the prominent physician and classical scholar Theodore Goulston hosted several meetings with Uttamatomakin, who was also known as Tomocomo, where interested friends could learn about American religious beliefs at first hand. Henry Spelman acted as interpreter, and Uttamatomakin not only answered questions but also sang and danced "his diabolicall measures." The Reverend Samuel Purchas recorded what Uttamatomakin told them about the nature of God and the afterlife, and about the special roles of priests; he said that on occasion priests had the ability to summon the deity Okeeus to appear among them in secret conclaves. He discouraged his Christian interlocutors from trying to convert him—Purchas wrote that he was "very zealous in his superstition, and will heare no persuasions to the truth"—and suggested that the missions should focus on the children.[47]

Pocahontas was treated as visiting royalty; she and Uttamatomakin were received at court and saw a masque created by the partnership of Ben Jonson and Inigo Jones, *The Vision of Delight,* performed on Twelfth Night. As in earlier masques, Queen Anne herself danced in this production.[48] For his part, Uttamatomakin was not impressed with James I and later had to be persuaded by Captain John Smith that the person he met really was the king about whom he had heard so much. Pocahontas also met with Smith and expressed her happiness at finding him alive; leaders in the colony had told the Indians that he was dead.

The Virginia Company saw Pocahontas's conversion, marriage, and motherhood as the opening they needed to begin a true religious mission to her people. They voted to give the Rolfes the large sum of £100 with which to initiate a Christian education program that would bring the Chesapeake Algonquians to "embraceing of true religion." But as the ship on which she was to sail home waited on the coast, Pocahontas grew increasingly sick and died. She was just twenty. Now another grave consumed the hopes invested in the Virginia project.[49]

John Rolfe returned to Virginia alone. His young son Thomas was left at Plymouth in the charge of Sir Lewis Stukeley, of the same family as the renegade Sir Thomas who had died four decades earlier at the battle of Alcazarquivir. Rolfe wrote to Virginia Company leader Sir Edwin Sandys shortly after his arrival and explained that Thomas had been sick, and friends, especially Captain Argall, had convinced him that the boy could not survive the journey. Stukeley would look after him until Rolfe's brother could take him. Rolfe wrote that the Indians "much lamented" Pocahontas's death and longed to have her son with them, but were glad that he survived. Rolfe reassured Sandys about the colony—everyone was working well and crops were in the ground in June. The Indians, he reported, were "very loving." Moreover, he attested that the mission had not ended with Pocahontas's life, because the Indians were "willing to parte with their childeren" for education with the English. He offered to perform any commission he might be given to further that aim and hoped that Sandys would favor his son, "the lyving ashes of his deceased Mother." Thomas would not return to Virginia for almost two decades; he came home at almost the same age his mother had been when she died.[50]

Several of Pocahontas's party remained in England. One, named Abraham, died shortly after their arrival. Another man lived with George Thorpe, a member of parliament who would eventually go to Virginia to further the mission effort. This man was literate in English by early 1619, when Thorpe mentioned a document "written by the virginian boy of mee." He was baptized and, like Don Luís, was given his sponsor's name. His burial at St. Martin's in the Fields in London occurred just two weeks after his baptism in 1619.[51]

Pocahontas's female attendants also stayed on. In 1620 two women identified as the daughters of Virginia "Viceroyes" were sent to Bermuda to be married; each woman had two boys to attend her, and they were well provided for as befitted people of high status. One died en route; the other was married to a Bermuda settler, "as fitt and agreeable an husband as the place would afford," in a lavish wedding in the governor's house.[52]

Many of those originally involved in the Jamestown project ended their association with it in the mid-1610s. From 1616 Powhatan moved away from contact with the English, reportedly somewhere to the south, and his brothers Opitchapam and Opechancanough increasingly took power around the Chesapeake. Powhatan was old and may have been ailing; he died in 1618.[53] Gates and Dale were now finished with Virginia. Both had asked for and received extended leaves from military duty in the Netherlands from the Dutch States General in order to go there and the records indicate that they had been in the Dutch service the entire time they were in Virginia. Dale's leave, requested by Prince Henry, was initially to extend for three years from 1611. Then in 1614 King James personally intervened to ask the States General to extend his leave for another two or three years, arguing that his presence was essential to the maintenance of Virginia. When Gates returned, the Dutch government gave him a "present" of all the money he would have been paid had he remained in its service, indicating, according to the ambassador, Sir Dudley Carleton, "that his duties were agreeable to you." Carleton asked that Dale be given a similar gratuity. Dale's petition, mentioning that he had accumulated a great deal of debt, pointed out that one of his goals in trying to get Virginia on a sound footing was "to establish a firm market there for the benefit and increase of trade," and presumably that trade would be good for the Dutch as well as the English. Maps in their archives demonstrate that the Dutch had detailed knowledge of the plantations along the James and about the river's navigation from the first decade of the colony's existence. After long discussion during which they considered giving Dale only half his pay for the seven years he was in America, the States General did decide to give him the full amount, but specified that this should not be considered a precedent for others.

Gates's employment from this time forward is uncertain, but Dale took command of an East India Company fleet and attacked Dutch shipping in Indonesia. He died there in 1619. Christopher Newport entered the service of the East India Company in 1612 and died in Bantam, also in Indonesia, in 1617. For his part, Samuel Argall tried for command of an East India Company ship in 1614 but was unsuccessful.[54]

Interest in possible rich ventures in Guiana continued high. George Percy wanted to go to the Amazon in 1615 with a "Captain Bud" who had maintained trading bases along the river since 1612. Percy asked his brother, the earl of Northumberland, for an advance on his allowance to pay his debts and for his place on the voyage, "otherwise I shall not be able to keepe my selfe oute of trouble." Percy, who may have suffered from epilepsy, argued that "my fitts here in England are more often, more longe, & more greevous, then I have felt them in other partes neere the lyne [equator]." His letter showed that experience had not affected the expectations for colonization, as he claimed that the Indians on the Amazon were pleased with the colonists' presence and provided for all their needs. Northumberland was at this time imprisoned in the Tower of London, where he and Ralegh were friends and colleagues in scientific experimentation.[55]

Ralegh himself finally achieved the release from the Tower for which he had lobbied so long and made preparations for his second voyage to Guiana. Restoration of his high place would follow if he could find El Dorado, and his fleet sailed in 1617. The expedition was a disaster. Ralegh's second in command, Lawrence Keymis, and Ralegh's son Walter, called Wat, led a party exploring the Orinoco. They clashed with Spanish forces at the town of San Thomé; both Wat and the Spanish governor were killed. The fighting violated the promise Ralegh had made to the king that there would be no violence against the Spanish. Ralegh, in his mid-sixties and suffering from fever, had remained behind in Cayenne, where he again met and talked with

Harry, the Guiana native who had lived in his English household after the 1595 voyage; he also searched for Leonard. Further explorations produced no evidence of gold, and the exploring party returned to Cayenne to tell of the scope of their failure. Ralegh wrote to his wife from the island of St. Kitts telling her of Wat's death: "I was loath to write, because I knew not how to Comforte you: and, God knows, I never knewe what sorrow meant till now." Many of his men and ships deserted him, and Ralegh sailed back to England in his one remaining vessel. When he arrived he was placed under arrest by his cousin Sir Lewis Stukeley, the same man with whom John Rolfe had left young Thomas the previous year. John Chamberlain wrote that Stukeley "is now most commonly knowne by the name of Sir Judas Stukeley." After an investigation, Ralegh's 1603 death sentence was carried out in 1618. Thomas Harriot's notes of his final speech on the scaffold are among Harriot's papers in the British Library. According to John Pory, "Every man that sawe Sir Walter Ralegh dye sayd it was impossible for any man to shewe more Decorum, courage, or piety; and that his death will doe more hurte to the factions that sought it, then ever his life could have done."[56]

John Smith made a reconnaissance voyage to the north part of Virginia in 1614. He brought an Indian man home to Cape Cod from England; Smith identified him as Tantum, and some have speculated that he might have been the Squanto (or Squantum) who lived with the later Pilgrim colony. We do know that Squanto was soon to be captured by Captain Robert Hunt, who had sailed in consortship with Smith's ship but who had gone off on his own once they were in New England waters. Hunt sold Squanto in Spain, along with around twenty of his compatriots, but he made it to England and thence back to New England in 1619. Smith met and conversed with Nahanada, the Abenaki leader brought back to Maine by the reconnoitering voyage for Sagadahoc in 1606. Smith, writing his name as Dohannida, identified him as "one of their greatest Lords; who had lived long in

England," and asserted that Dohannida would support future English colonists and traders. He believed that the region had an undeserved reputation as inhospitable after the rapid failure of the Sagadahoc colony in 1607–8 and argued that English people could live healthful and productive lives in that environment.[57]

Even the Virginia Company's attention was largely diverted elsewhere. Under its 1612 charter the company had begun the colonization of Bermuda by creating a subsidiary joint-stock company that sent over the first settlers under the governorship of Richard Moore. At their landing Moore, recognizing the difficulties of inaugurating a settlement, called his people together to form a compact by which they agreed to abide. Moore's three-year term as governor was stormy, but this colony, though strictly limited in its available land, outstripped Virginia in the drive to produce profits and create a functioning plantation. Chamberlain wrote in 1613 that the colonists had sent home a rich cargo of ambergris, and that they "begin to nestle and plant there very handsomely." In 1615 a distinct Bermuda or Somers Islands Company was granted a royal charter and the venture became separate from Virginia, although membership in the two companies overlapped. Population grew in the healthful islands, and the younger colony was soon more populous in English migrants than Virginia was; in 1616 John Rolfe reported that Virginia's six plantations numbered 351 people; In the same year Bermuda's population was reported to be 600.[58]

Despite all the bad news, not everyone was prepared to give up on Virginia. In 1614 the Reverend Samuel Purchas argued that the testing period was now really over: "Almightie God that had thus farre tried the patience of the English, would not *suffer them to bee tempted above that they were able*."[59] Still, it remained to be seen what the test and its results actually were. Leaders had demonstrated that a colony under a regime that attempted to regiment every aspect of life could manage to hang on in America; but hanging on was not enough. The breakthrough would require some product that would lure investors and motivate colonists sufficiently that they would become self-supporting. With the passage of time it was increasingly clear that whatever commodities the country might offer would be produced by English labor, not acquired through trade with the Indians. This meant that the entire conception of the colony needed to be rethought in the direction of large-scale migration rather than maintenance of a small military unit. Until that breakthrough came, martial law was as much a confession of failure as a mark of success.

James Cittie in Virginia

IN THE MIDDLE of the 1610s many actors who had been involved in the early years of Jamestown turned their attention elsewhere or left the scene completely in death, and matters looked bleak in the colony as it seemed capable of surviving only through the imposition of the most grim martial law. No passage through the continent had been discovered. More important, the land seemed to be incapable of producing the valuable products or materials to support English industries that investors had hoped for. As John Chamberlain wrote in 1616 reporting on the arrival of Pocahontas: "I heare not of any other riches or matter of worth, but only some quantitie of sassafras, tobacco, pitch, and clap-board, things of no great value unles there were more plentie and neerer hand."[1]

But although it was not then apparent, Virginia was on the road to success by this time. Some English had cast their lot wholeheartedly with Virginia, and through their efforts the disdained tobacco would become the colony's gold. The native Virginia tobacco was deemed too harsh for the European market, but John Rolfe had begun experimenting with other strains. The peace that attended his marriage to Pocahontas and the end of the severe drought that had overshadowed Jamestown's first six years contributed to his success. Silvester

278

Tabacco. 15

re[pe]ct in which their worth may
inter e[t] them.

And thus farre for drinking of
Tabacco, which is more vulgarly
receiued with vs now than euer,
and although it [eem]s that the Indians

Illustration of pipe-smoking man from Anthony Chute's book Tabacco published in 1595.
This item is reproduced by permission of The Huntington Library, San Marino, California.

Jourdain, the first to publish an account of the 1609 shipwreck on Bermuda, wrote that they had found "very good tobacco" in the islands, and it may have been seed from there that Rolfe introduced in the Chesapeake. In his own description of the six plantations in 1616, Rolfe recorded that the majority were farming tobacco in most places; in Jamestown itself, thirty-two of the fifty inhabitants were so engaged. He also argued that everyone who planted tobacco was required to plant food crops as well. His claim of widespread involvement in agriculture is substantiated by the archaeological record established by the team headed by William Kelso, which is excavating the original fort site and its immediate environs. They uncovered only two hoes in the pre-1610 context, but have found a large number of hoes in the next layer. As Ralph Hamor wrote, "No country under the Sunne, may, or doth affoord more pleasant, sweet, and strong Tobacco, then I have tasted there, even of mine owne planting." Previous problems had stemmed from their inability to cure and pack it properly; but now knowledgeable people were instructing them and he expected the colony to produce a crop of such quality "that even England shall acknowledge the goodnesse thereof."[2]

Even Sir Thomas Dale, who enforced the martial law regime that assumed only force could make people virtuous, understood, however dimly, that getting people working for themselves would actually lead to success. He reported in 1613 that he had set the colonists to work planting corn and recommended dividing up the company's stock of pigs among the planters, with the stipulation that piglets born of company pigs would be theirs to keep so they could use the offspring for food. He also urged the company to understand the problems involved in trying to inaugurate the English agricultural regime and asserted that if farmers in England had to do all the hard labor without draft animals, the complaints would be as loud there as in America.[3]

By the time Rolfe returned from his trip to England with Pocahontas in 1617, the initiative of allowing people to farm for themselves

Anthony Chute's drawing of a tobacco plant. This item is re-produced by permission of The Huntington Library, San Marino, California.

gave all appearances of working well. He wrote that even though colonists had "scarce ragges to cover their naked bodye," they all "cheerefully labor about their grounds, their harts and hands not ceasing from worke." This confirmed his portrait of the previous year of "every man sitting under his figtree in safety, gathering and reaping the fruites of their labors with much joy and comfort." While he was in England, Rolfe described the various categories of occupation, with the duties of each. The laborers included "Artyficers," such as smiths, carpenters, tailors, shoemakers, and tanners, and these also tended food crops for themselves. For their part, the farmers were required to contribute part of their harvest to the colony's general stores, and all tobacco planters had to plant corn as well. Recent archaeological discoveries have given substance to colonists' claims that they really were involved in productive labor within the fort. Most striking is the evidence of settlers' industriousness in blacksmithing and in making iron, fishnets, and bricks; they even apparently worked to produce glass for shipment back to England. The men were creating copperwork designed with specific native requirements in mind from the beginning and Jamestown-made copper items have been recovered from Indian community sites.[4]

So there were people still committed to the Virginia project and, although the road ahead was not smooth, the foundations of success had been laid. No one would have accepted at this date that tobacco monoculture would be the way to the future. Colonists continued to experiment with various kinds of fibers from which a silk-like textile might be made and had hopes of true silk production. The vines of Virginia might yet produce good wine, and minerals might still be found.

Agriculture, whether tobacco monoculture or diversified crops, involved a tremendous shift in thinking about America's role. Rather than exchanging European manufactured goods for Indian-produced items of value as merchants involved in the Africa, Levant, and East India trades did, the new model required transplanting populations across the Atlantic to create or grow the commodities that would repay investors and bolster the English economy. Many of the greatest merchants preferred engagement in the already established trades as it became clear that American profits would come only after large-scale investment and support of both production and marketing.[5] And the old dreams died hard; at the time when the Virginia Company was coming to this realization, Ralegh secured support for his final attempt to find the fabulous mines of El Dorado in Guiana, a prime example of the enduring unfulfilled hope.

The transition to the more open society that would foster development was fraught with problems on the ground. Samuel Argall returned to Virginia as governor on the same ship as John Rolfe in 1617. Lord de la Warr, who had been sickly when he was in Virginia earlier, was sent out to resume the governorship but died on the voyage over in 1618; therefore Argall served for two years. His term was so filled with conflict that the company prosecuted him. He was acquitted, but his association with Virginia was finished just at the time the colony really began to thrive. Argall's tenure marked the shift from the older military model, and much of the conflict reflected differing visions of the plantation's future.

John Smith had written that the site of Jamestown was "a verie fit place for the erecting of a great cittie."[6] Even though farming on scattered plantations was to be the venture's future, it mattered a great deal that colonies be centered on a city. Sir Dudley Carleton thought the name Jamestown was not "gracefull" and mentioned an unnamed Dutchman quoted by John Pory who employed a variant, saying he wrote from the newly founded "towne in Verginia, Jacobopolis." But they had to be called cities; when Sir Walter Ralegh formed a small company to back his last attempt to settle a Roanoke colony, it was named the Corporation for the City of Ralegh in Virginia.[7]

Cities meant orderly life; they signified civility. So from the beginning the Virginia Company had urged its representatives to make sure that the settlers' houses were constructed around a market square in neat rows. Hamor's report of Virginia in 1614 included a description of each of the settlements. Jamestown, he wrote, "is reduced into a hansome forme, and hath in it two faire rowes of howses, all of framed Timber, two stories, and an upper Garret, or Corne loft high." Henrico was even more impressive in his sketch; it had three rows of streets and "a hansome church" in which Alexander Whitaker preached.[8] Early reporters were pleased to find that the Indians they encountered lived in settled towns because that implied much about the environment's suitability for their endeavors. So crucial were cities that the later designers of Maryland's capital, St. Mary's City, even though they knew the colony's economy would be tobacco-based, laid out their city on an elaborate baroque plan of squares and vistas anchored by the principal buildings.[9]

The Virginia Company itself was transformed as the conception of how to create a profitable colony was changing. In 1619 the company's longtime leader, the great merchant Sir Thomas Smith, who also headed the East India and Somers Islands companies, was replaced by Sir Edwin Sandys, elder brother of George Sandys and a leading member of parliament.[10] Sandys and his supporters believed that critical mass was essential to the venture's success, and they set about sending over thousands of migrants in the next few years. They also intensified the trend that was already in progress by formally transferring greater control over economic and political life to the colonists themselves. In order to attract people who would emigrate with the expectation of spending the rest of their lives in America, the company offered land to all comers. Those who had been in the colony for some years were to receive one hundred acres each. From then on, in an initiative that came to be known as the headright system, everyone who paid his or her own or someone else's passage over would receive fifty acres per head. In the beginning, those who came at someone else's expense also received fifty acres when their terms of servitude were up. Land of their own in something close to absolute ownership was a goal that England's poor and many of the middling could never hope to achieve at home. The island's eastern end was divided up into twelve-acre homesteads for the "Ancient Planters," those who had arrived before 1616. Archaeologists have discovered that many of these plots were developed as artisanal workshops from the earliest days, reinforcing the argument that Jamestown was a port and fledgling manufacturing

PARS DECIMA AMERICÆ.
XI.
Equeftris ordinis viri , quibus exercitiis fefe in Virginia
oblectare poffint.

Queſtris ordinis viri variis exercitiis ludicris animum poſſunt recreare. In dies enim datur occaſio loca incognita, ſilvaſque remotas venatus, piſcatus atque aucupii gratia adeundi; ubi diverſi generis fera variique fructus non ſi-ne voluptate ſeſe offerunt. Videas in amœnis portubus, ſex ſeptem aut octo accipitres ex alto præcipites ferri, ac duas circiter horas piſcium capitibus advolutos, ſuum inde pabulum quærere. Alibi videbis illos reliquas aves perſequi, adunco roſtro contundere, atque in terram proſternere: quæ res lepidum intuentibus præbet ſpectaculum. Ipſi verò accipi-tres, utut feri ſint, facili negotio cicurari poſſunt.

d

Capita-

This engraving from 1618 shows Virginia as a settled place with plentiful game for hunting. Courtesy of the John Carter Brown Library at Brown University.

center. Other plots promise to reveal unique frontier architectural forms. Closer to the fort on the island's west end, the New Towne site for more recent arrivals was laid out around 1621, and it also provides evidence of artisanal and trade activity.

What made the new plan work was the institution of indentured servitude. It was common for young English men and women to leave their family home at around the age of fourteen; this is one reason why it was not shocking to contemporaries that boys such as Henry Spelman and Thomas Savage were on the Jamestown-bound ships. A tiny minority received some form of higher education, and the few acquired apprenticeships, which had to be paid for. Most went into servitude, which was itself a form of education and a transitional phase in which many young men and women spent about ten years until they were ready to set up a home and family of their own. Servitude in England was based on annual contracts. The great autumn agricultural fairs were also hiring markets where masters and servants signed contracts for the next year. Thus, servants were actually free for one day a year, and both servants and masters were bound by the contracts they signed. Justices of the peace would enforce the contracts if a suit were brought, but the greatest control over the behavior of both sides lay in reputation. A master who was too harsh, or a servant who was negligent, would have trouble negotiating a contract at the next fair, where gossip was sure to be exchanged.

 Temporary servitude became the basis of the system through which the American colonies were largely populated, but it was transformed in the process. Now the servant got the benefit—the £5 cost of passage over—before the period of servitude began, and then had to work seven years to repay the master. In later years, as the Virginia economy became more productive and an individual's work was therefore more valuable, seven years was steadily reduced down to four. But the degree of leverage that servants in England had over the conditions of servitude was gone in Virginia, as they had signed a binding contract for the whole term. Moreover, most had little or no control over the choice of master. It is unclear how many received land at the end of their terms, but some who began as servants certainly became landowners and even officeholders, and servants clearly expected that they would be able to obtain land.

The new system came to Virginia in the instructions sent with the man who replaced Samuel Argall as governor, Sir George Yeardley, and they were known as the "greate charter." Not only were colonists promised control over their own land that they worked for themselves, but they were also promised a general assembly in which matters of local concern, especially levies of labor and food for the common needs of the plantation, would be decided by elected representatives of each settlement. The first meeting of the Virginia Assembly was in 1619.

The new company leadership also paid attention to another fundamental requirement: the need for family structures to give meaning to landownership and to create a society of permanent migrants. In his 1616 description of Virginia John Rolfe had written that there were sixty-five women and children in the colony.[11] Now company members returned again and again to the necessity of sending over "Maides young and uncorrupt to make wifes to the Inhabitants and by that meanes to make the men there more setled & lesse moveable." Otherwise, they believed, the migrants would go back to England as soon as they had made some money, which would ultimately destroy the whole project. "By long experience," they wrote, "we have found that the Minds of our people in Virginia are much dejected, and their hearts enflamed with a desire to return for England only through the wants of the comforts without which God saw that Man could not live contentedly, no not in Paradise." The company repeatedly took steps to send out groups of young women in the period 1619 to 1621. Both at the time and since, many have maligned those recruits and charged that the company swept up women of the streets to found families across the ocean. But recently rediscovered documents have demonstrated the genuine care company members took in recruiting suitable women. They collected certificates from the women's ministers and kept track of the particular skills each possessed. Many of the "Maides" were actually brought to the port of embarkation by their parents, who thereby certified their approval.[12]

Africans begin to appear in the records in this period. John Rolfe famously wrote in a 1619 letter to Sir Edwin Sandys of the arrival of a Dutch ship that had established a consortship agreement with an English vessel, the *Treasurer,* in which Samuel Argall held a part interest. The Dutch came into the James River looking for the *Treasurer,* and the English authorities at Jamestown traded food supplies for the ship's cargo of "20. and odd Negroes." Recent research has established that these Africans came directly from São Paulo de Loanda, the Portuguese capital in Angola.[13] They were probably not the first Africans in Virginia; early in 1620 thirty-two Africans, seventeen women and fifteen men, were recorded in a census of the Virginia plantations. That same census records that the total population of the plantations had climbed to 982.[14] Slavery as it was later defined did not yet exist in the Chesapeake, and some of these Africans lived to achieve their freedom, but they served much longer terms than English servants.[15]

New kinds of English men began to look across the Atlantic to repair their fortunes. In 1619 George Sandys tried for the governorship of Bermuda as his brother became head of the Virginia Company; this attempt was unsuccessful, but he would go to Virginia two years later. News gatherer and translator John Pory did go in 1619, accompanying Governor Yeardley, his cousin by marriage. This assignment was timely because, as John Chamberlain wrote, Paul Pindar, the ambassador to Istanbul whom Pory had served as secretary, was recalled in 1616. In December 1618 Chamberlain reported that the "greatest newes" he had was that Pory "is in the way of high preferment, for yesterday he was chosen Secretarie of Virginia for three yeares." Saying that Pory would depart by the end of the week with Yeardley, Chamberlain concluded, "No question but he will become there a sufficient sober man seeing there is no wine in all that climat."[16]

In his capacity as secretary, Pory wrote the official report of the first Virginia Assembly, which met from July 30 to August 4, 1619. Among the topics on which the delegates deliberated were the regulation of tobacco planting in order to guarantee the crop's quality, and the need to plant corn and other food crops as well as tobacco. They passed regulations against idleness, gambling, and excessive drinking (Chamberlain had apparently been misinformed about the absence of alcoholic beverages). They also discussed plans for the mission to the Indians.

On the last day the assembly met as a court to hear charges against Henry Spelman. Another interpreter, Robert Poole, testified that Spelman had derided the governor in front of Opechancanough, who had succeeded Powhatan as paramount chief. Spelman admitted that he had told Opechancanough that a new governor "greatter than this that nowe is in place" would be coming soon. He believed he had information that Sir Robert Rich, a major promoter of colonization, intended to take up command in Virginia. But no one in the colony knew that Rich had become earl of Warwick on his father's death in March of 1619 and now had many other possibilities before him. Poole accused Spelman of conspiring secretly with Opechancanough. The assembly contended that he had endangered the colony by bringing the present government into disrepute with the Indians. Pory reported much heated debate about how to punish Spelman, including possibly imposing the death penalty. In the end, however, they only stripped him of his rank as captain and sentenced him to serve the governor for seven years as interpreter. Clearly his language skills were too valuable to be sacrificed, so the colonists had to rely on him even though they no longer trusted him "as one that had in him more of the Savage then of the Christian." Pory reported that Spelman "muttered" to himself when told of the sentence and showed neither gratitude nor remorse.[17]

Early the next year John Rolfe wrote that the governor had decided Spelman's behavior stemmed from "Childishe ignorance." Moreover, according to Rolfe, colonial leaders had found Poole to be "very dishonest" and feared that he had "even turned heathen." But Pory attested that they did not dare to "call Poole to account" because of the damage he could do to their relationship with Opechancanough.

Jamestown's leaders now saw him as "a publique and as it were a neutral person"—a man not fully belonging to either Indian or English culture.[18] Clearly these men who moved easily between cultures were viewed with suspicion, and their true identity was increasingly suspect. Earlier William Parker, who had been captured and lived among the Indians for three years, had startled a party of visiting Englishmen including Ralph Hamor: he had "growen so like both in complexion and habite to the Indians, that I onely knew him by his tongue to be an Englishman."[19]

A few months after his report of the assembly, Pory seized the chance of sending a letter to John Chamberlain by the Dutch ship that brought the "20. and odd Negroes" to Virginia. Pory had taught Greek at Cambridge University and traveled and lived for extended periods in Europe, and he had always been primarily an intelligencer; like Chamberlain, he was a correspondent who wrote newsletters for subscribers. He told his friend that his first months had been painful: "The solitary uncouthnes of this place, compared with those partes of Christendome or Turky where I had bene; and likewise my being sequestred from all occurrents and passages which are so rife there, did not a little vexe me." In short, he wanted to know the news and he begged for pamphlets and information.

Acknowledging that "all our riches for the present doe consist in Tobacco," Pory estimated how much a person could make on his own or with servants working alongside him, and he went on, "Our principall wealth (I should have said) consisteth in servants." He believed the land gave great promise for diversified agriculture, arguing that when they had the resources to till the land as in England, "we shall produce miracles out of this earth." He especially noted the varieties of grapes growing naturally there—possibly looking forward to Virginia wines. The next year, in the same letter in which he reported his conclusions about Robert Poole, Pory again praised the variety and abundance of grapevines in Virginia and stipulated that Governor

Yeardley wanted the company to send both skilled vignerons and good grape stock; he also recommended where the best vines could be found at home. He wrote so much on this subject, he averred, "not because I thirst after yt; for I thanke god, I drinke water here withas much (yf not more) pleasure and contente, as I dranke wine in those partes."[20]

Looking back we can see 1618 as the beginning of Jamestown's turn toward permanence, but contemporaries had seen many previous declarations that the worst was over and the future looked bright. Moreover other interests elsewhere continued to overshadow Virginia. The Guinea Company was organized in 1618 for trade in "Gynney and Bynney," by which they meant Guinea and Benin, or the entire West African coast from Senegal to Nigeria. English ships continued to concentrate on Senegambia and Sierra Leone where relationships were already established. Although their hopes were for gold, as always, the Sierra Leone trade in dyewood inaugurated in 1607 was more consistent and profitable.[21] In 1619 the Amazon Company was founded to sustain English interests in the wake of Ralegh's disastrous last voyage; the Pilgrims who founded Plymouth actually considered Guiana as a possible destination.[22]

The year 1618 became famous for its four great "Blazing Stars," including the most spectacular comet seen for 150 years. Increase Mather, who, later in the seventeenth century, wrote a scientific tract about comets and their consequences, said the 1618 comets were attended by all kinds of catastrophes, such as drought, an earthquake, and great plagues among the New England Indians and in Cairo. The "great and fatal consequent of this Prodigy" was the outbreak of religious warfare in Europe that would continue intermittently until the Peace of Westphalia in 1648. The Thirty Years' War began in central Europe, where over three hundred principalities and city-states, some Protestant and some Roman Catholic, made up what would become the nation of Germany in the nineteenth century. When Bohemian Protestants rebelled against the Austrian Hapsburg monarchy, the Spanish Hapsburgs came to the aid of their cousins, so the conflict became a European-wide war by 1621, and "Rivers of Blood were poured forth." King James's daughter Elizabeth was married to Frederick, the Elector of the Palatine States, who accepted the crown of Bohemia in 1619. The Protestant leaders of England expected their nation to come to their coreligionists' aid in what they saw as a struggle between good and evil. James, however, resisted the call to involve England in this destructive war, and instead joined France in attempting to negotiate a settlement. Although the country remained at peace, the English cloth trade collapsed because of commercial disruptions.[23]

Conditions at home in the 1620s made emigration more attractive both for those financing it and those seeking new opportunities. Rising population and a stagnant economy meant that real wages were actually dropping. The 1620s were characterized by a series of harvest failures and the resurgence of the bubonic plague; numbers of deaths climbed to crisis levels in 1624.[24] England was seen as overpopulated and America could help solve the nation's social problems. In 1618, at the inception of the new Virginia Company policy, Chamberlain reported from London that "the citie is now shipping thether an hundred younge boyes and girles that lay starving in the streetes, which is one of the best deeds that could be don with so litle charge not rising to above £500." Four years later the Reverend Patrick Copland praised London's leaders for their wisdom in "removing their super-increasing people from the Citty to Virginia" so "that they may ease the Citie of a many that are ready to starve, and do starve dayly in our streetes (to the great griefe of all tender-hearted and mercifull men) for want of foode to put into their mouthes." He compared the mayors to farmers who regulate the number of cattle in their fields to keep the whole herd healthy. Such a policy, he argued, benefited both Virginia and London.[25]

remove starving population from streets of London to Virginia

The disruptions of the Thirty Years' War may also have contributed to English willingness to look Atlantic-ward. Some separatist puritans began to feel that their options were running out in Europe. Many had emigrated to the Netherlands, but now that Protestant country was threatened by the European war, and they were willing to consider the possibility of recreating English society in a completely new setting. As early as 1617 Sir Edwin Sandys initiated a correspondence with many of these separatists, and over the next few years he worked to convince them that Virginia would make a good safe location for them. From Sandys's point of view, such a committed group would not only help populate the colony but also were exactly the kind of dedicated and strong-willed people Virginia needed. Those fifty or so separatists known as the Pilgrims actually sailed in 1620 with a patent for a plantation within the Virginia Company's lands but landed in Cape Cod instead. Hundreds of separatist puritans, however, did migrate from the Netherlands to Virginia beginning in 1618, an exodus that continued through the 1630s.[26]

The puritans joined a substantial migration of people to Virginia in the early 1620s. This period has become notorious because of the high death rate among newcomers. In fact, despite the roughly four thousand people sent over in the late 1610s and early 1620s, the population in 1624 was about what it had been at the beginning of Yeardley's term—just over a thousand. Officials in London had dramatically underestimated the supplies and other support that needed to be sent with such large numbers, and the colonists complained that their resources were overwhelmed. Governor Yeardley wrote to Sandys in June 1620 thanking him for his care of the colony but also saying that among the many problems he faced, "this great nomber of people also ariving Enexpected it hath not a littell pusseled me to provide for the lodging of them, it being a thing of spetiall consequence and nessesity for theire healths." Trying not to offend the Virginia Company leader, Yeardley suggested that Sandys's "zealous desires over hasted you" so that the colony had had no warning that a huge number of settlers would be arriving. Had they known, "I should have bine able to have done much better then now I can." He also mentioned that the new arrivals were poorly supplied with food and clothing, thus creating enormous strains on the struggling colony.[27]

Colonial leaders also pointed out that newcomers were sent at the wrong time of year so that they faced the summer with its complement of diseases, but calls to send them in the fall so they could adjust over the winter went largely unheeded. Yeardley predicted that many of those who had just arrived in June 1620 would soon die; at least a hundred had landed already ailing from the passage over, "some very weake and sick some Crasey and taynted a shore." (In this period "crazy" referred to bodily impairment or infirmity, or to the effects of disease.) Now the heat was striking more of them. In future he hoped the company would "but observe the season." By the same ship Sandys received a letter from John Pory arguing that spring and summer were "both fatall and unproffitable to newe Comers," and that migrants in the last three ships had been sickly on arrival. He wrote that "Wee here are in our opinions absolutely for the leafefall and the winter."[28] The previous year Pory had reported that the summer had been "Torride" and that both colonists and Indians had been "visited with great sicknes & mortality." John Rolfe had also written that the summer of 1619 had been "very contagious for sycknes." Company officers thus got plenty of advice from people in the colony, but it was discounted as the colonists' complaints and suggestions had always been.[29]

In May 1620 the Virginia Company published a broadside designed to deal with reports of widespread mortality in the colony. It spoke of the company's "great griefe" in learning of the deaths of "hundreds, and almost the utter destruction of some particular Plantations," and acknowledged that such catastrophe must be seen as the "chastisement" of God to draw people on both sides of the Atlantic away from sin. The broadside also noted that most deaths had occurred in new foundations that lacked the means to care for the sick, and argued that although the disease had spread to older settlements, people in them had recovered. It went on to detail the various measures that were in hand to make the plantations more settled and able to cope. Later that same year newcomer George Thorpe wrote that he had been quite healthy and he believed that many deaths resulted from despair: "more do die here of the disease of theire minde then of theire body." He argued that potential migrants needed to be given a much more realistic picture of the conditions they would encounter. Still, the onrush of population continued. In 1621 the company sent by its own reckoning close to fifteen hundred new settlers in twenty-one ships.[30]

As the company dispatched ever larger numbers of colonists, investors reiterated and strengthened their interest in two fundamental initiatives: the mission to the Indians and diversification of Virginia's economic base. The plan to bring Christianity to the Chesapeake Algonquians was extremely ambitious. John Rolfe and Pocahontas had accepted the company's commission to inaugurate the campaign to convert her people to Christianity, but her death suspended it. Rolfe had argued strongly for the work. In the conclusion of his 1616 *True Relation,* addressed to King James, he ventured to "crave Your Honorable patience a little longer" as he turned to "a more heavenly meditacion." Rolfe argued that a "good Christian" could not look at the faces of the thousands of "poore, wretched, and misbeleiving people" without "sorrow, pittie, and commyseracion." Not only did the Indians come from the same mold as the English, but they "beare the Image of our heavenly Creator." Nonetheless they were damned purely because they had not had the opportunity to hear the Gospel preached. Christians must act in these circumstances.[31]

[margin handwritten note: more Investors concerned Converting natives to spend money]

The mission began in earnest in May 1620 with the arrival of "that vertuous gentleman" George Thorpe, which, Pory wrote, was greeted "as of an Angell from heaven." No one's presence could "more joy me," because Thorpe "will helpe to beare our burthen."[32] All planning focused on Indian children; they were presumed to be the most receptive to new ways of thinking, and, once converted and educated, they could return to their homes and spread the word. The first step would be for colonists to take children into their homes for basic education. In February 1619 the company proposed to reimburse householders out of an anonymous bequest of £500. Company member Sir John Wolstenholme suggested that some of the children be placed with "John Peirce and his Associates," referring to the Pilgrims, who were then expected to come to Virginia.

In the next step at least some of the students would go on to the college the company planned. The sum of £1,500 had been contributed in churches throughout England in a campaign conducted by the bishops at the command of the king. Other large bequests came in. In a 1620 publication the company reported two anonymous gifts: one of rich communion plate for the college and for a newly founded church in Virginia, and another of "550 pounds in gold, for the bringing up of children of the Infidels" in the Christian religion and "in fit Trades whereby honestly to live." The proposed college was also promised a large bequest of £300 from the will of company official Nicholas Ferrar as soon as ten Indian children were actually enrolled. In the meantime, he had designated £24 for three "discreet and Godly men" who would each promise to take an Indian child into his home for education. Two years later the company announced gifts of books for the college. The company planned to invest the money gifts to create a steady income as modern colleges do. In this case it granted the project ten thousand acres both as a site for the Indian school and to support it, and sent fifty tenants to work on the land. The tenants would keep half of their proceeds, and the other half would go to the school. Thorpe was placed in charge of the project; he was to oversee the tenants' work as well as to inaugurate the mission.[33]

In May 1621, a year after his arrival, Thorpe wrote hopefully of his progress. His plan was one that underlay all American missions: he would first entice Indians through "the booke of the worlde as beinge nearest to theire sence." He had hopeful signs to report: the Indians "begin more and more to affect English fassions." If the company would send over "apparell & househouldestufe" for the Indian kings, he thought that he could "make a good entrance into their affections." Just as "taking the turban" signified a change of heart toward Islam, so Indians could be brought to Christianity more easily if they could be persuaded to adopt European dress and live as Europeans did. But this strategy meant that the company would have to appropriate money to buy the outward trappings of European civility for the Indians. Thorpe's biggest problem was with the other colonists, who, he said, were violently "mispersuaded" that the Indians had done much to injure the English, whereas "if there bee wronge on any side it is on ours who are not soe charitable to them as Christians ought to bee." The settlers gave the Indians nothing but "maledictions and bitter execrations." He also warned his supporters in England that they might hear complaints against him, but these stemmed only from his attempts to curb drunkenness and "somme other sins" among the English. He went on to say, "If I live I doute not but I shall doe it."[34]

Very large plans were laid. There was to be a preparatory college at Henrico and then eventually a university where both Indian and European children would study.[35] A chance meeting also led to plans for a preparatory college for settlers' children to be built at Charles City. The Reverend Patrick Copland, a minister from Aberdeen who served as a shipboard chaplain for the East India Company, learned about the Virginia project from Sir Thomas Dale, who was then in the service of the East India Company. Copland happened to encounter some Virginia-bound ships in African waters in 1621 and learned more about the dearth of schools and churches there. He immediately took up a collection on the ships returning from the East and came up with over

£70 on the spot. Copland had a long-standing interest in missionary activities. He had brought back a boy from Surat in 1614 after his first East India Company voyage, and that boy, named Peter Pope at the suggestion of King James himself, was baptized as "the first fruits of India" in London in a ceremony attended by the eminent people of the city. Copland also arranged for the publication of Pope's Latin writings translated into English. Now he became a major fund-raiser for Virginia and was made a member of the company's inner circle. The Charles City school was to be named the East India School to commemorate the generosity he initiated; other anonymous bequests were received.[36]

Early in 1622 leaders in Virginia believed that the mission was well under way. Paramount chief Opechancanough had promised that some Indians would come and live with the English. Thorpe reported a conversation in which Opechancanough had acknowledged that "theirs was nott the right waye" and that "god loved us better than them." Thorpe believed that Opechancanough himself wanted to be instructed in Christianity. In fact, he was surprised to find real "motiones of religione" in him, and he was pleased to learn that the Indians understood the stars and the constellations as Europeans did. In short, bringing the Indians to European-style civility would not be as difficult as many imagined.[37]

At the same time in England, John Brinsley, a young puritan minister, published A Consolation for our Grammar Schooles to help in the work. On its title page he wrote that the book would serve as a guide for those attempting to found schools, especially for "all those of the inferiour sort, and all ruder countries and places; namely, for Ireland, Wales, Virginia, with the Sommer Ilands." The Virginia Company asked Patrick Copland to peruse the book and report back about its suitability for their purposes. Investors voted to send over very large numbers of Bibles, catechisms, and other religious tracts for the edification of colonists.[38] Thus the Virginia Company planned for a mission and education program on a very grand scale, and people throughout England supported it with their contributions. This initiative set the Jamestown project apart from all other English overseas engagements.

Plans for economic diversification progressed at the same time. In their declaration of 1620 the investors again denounced Virginia's detractors as "corrupt" and "of ill disposed mindes," and reiterated their claim that the country was rich in natural resources and healthy "after men are a little accustomed to it." Not only was the climate temperate, but also the land was fruitful in plants and animals. They avowed that their colony would supply England with all the products it now had to import from places as far-flung as Russia, Scandinavia, and Persia. They appended a list of all the skilled workers they had recently sent and descriptions of the specific products they were prepared to initiate. At the same time they sponsored the publication of a manual, Frenchman John Bonoeil's *Obseruations to be followed, for the making of fit roomes, to keepe silk-wormes in as also, for the best manner of planting of mulbery trees, to feed them. Published by authority for the benefit of the noble plantation in Virginia*, which contained a four-page list of commodities "growing and to be had in Virginia" with the price each would fetch. The company arranged to send hundreds of these books so that every planter would have one.[39]

But, as so often in the past, the reality was very different. The same month that the company published its declaration, June 1620, Governor Yeardley reported that "the Cheife men for the Iron worke being dead at sea and upon their present landing will give a great blow to the stagering of the biwsines." And he added, "Your boatewryght dyed soone after his landing at James Cyty."[40] The government in Virginia also reacted strongly to demands that the colony curtail tobacco production, saying flatly that the life of the plantations depended on it. Early in 1621 the governor and council sent a formal petition "of the distressed Collonye in Virginea" which they asked company leaders to deliver to the king, whose government had begun collecting duties on every pound of Virginia tobacco imported into England. In their petition colonists argued for their right to send their tobacco freely into England and hinted darkly that some company members were seeking to manipulate the trade for their own benefit. Nothing less than the continued existence of Virginia was at stake. If their "ancient liberty" was not restored, then the king should arrange to bring them all home "and not to suffer the Heathen to triumph over us and to saye Where is now their God?" This language, a reference to Psalm 79:10, quoted the prayer that was ordained to be "duly said morning and evening upon the Court of Guard" in Jamestown and appended to William Strachey's edition of the *Lawes Divine, Morall and Martiall* of 1612.[41]

However strident its criticism of the evil weed and of the colony's dependence on it, the company grudgingly accepted the idea that, at least in the short run, that crop was essential to getting the colony established. The investors were deeply gratified when the king prohibited the growing of tobacco in England, opening the way for Virginia tobacco. Despite the colonists' deep suspicions, Sandys and other leaders realized that it would benefit both Virginia and Bermuda immensely if the companies could control marketing of their tobacco. In 1622, after very protracted negotiations, the companies achieved an agreement with the king that limited the importation of Spanish tobacco and gave the companies monopoly control over the sale of tobacco in England. The king was to take a third of all the proceeds from sale of company tobacco.[42]

Nonetheless, tobacco was never supposed to be anything but a temporary solution, and the campaign for diversification continued. In 1621 George Sandys arrived to fill the just created post of treasurer with the new governor, Sir Francis Wyatt, his nephew by marriage. The position had been devised specifically for the purpose of overseeing the development of new commodities. With the initiative represented by the Wyatt-Sandys partnership, the company sent an enormous set of instructions for rectifying all that was wrong in the colony, beginning with idleness, drunkenness, and excess in dress. They specifically directed that no one except families of the leadership "shall weare any gold in ther Clothes or any apparrell of silke" until they were able to produce their own. The company went on to reinforce its commitment to the Christianizing mission. The fourteenth point concerned the command to limit "the excessive planting of tobacco." Each successive point then concerned a different commodity or enterprise and what the investors expected the colonists to do to support it, especially the roles of the various skilled workers—French silk experts, "Dutchmen" to create sawmills, and Italian glassblowers—they were sending over. The principal job of the glassworks, at least in the short run, was to make beads for the Indian trade. Not only were they sending trained men to complement books such as Bonoeil's but they also included silkworm "seed." They warned that the king himself was interested in their progress and all England was watching.[43]

These instructions, written as an entire new administration with renewed commitment was about to embark, suddenly collided with reality. Letters from Virginia written in mid-May arrived on July 24, the day the new instructions were sealed. In them George Thorpe informed the company that the "Silke-worme-seede is all perished att sea." Only a small quantity sent him personally by another ship had survived. He had succeeded in planting ten thousand grapevines on the college lands, and other colonists were planting them as well, but so far the ironworks was in "a poore takinge." At the same time Captain Thomas Nuce wrote very frankly to Sir Edwin Sandys about the practical difficulties of growing sufficient food, much less getting elaborate industries under way. On July 25 company leaders wrote a hasty reply to be included with their formal instructions in which they mainly reiterated what they had said and urged the colonists to work harder to develop valuable commodities. They mentioned their dif-

ficulties in getting backers to invest again in supplies for the colonists, saying that people did not relish the prospect of "being paid in
smoke."[44]

This transatlantic correspondence has the quality of people shout-
ing past each other; it is clear that leaders in Virginia, like leaders in
London, could not understand why their opposite numbers refused
to comprehend simple reality. The Virginia Company could not go
on supporting a losing proposition forever; and colonists clothed in
rags could not produce miracles with inadequate equipment in a frustrating environment. Although the colonists constantly feared they
were being undermined by what Governor Yeardley called "Machevill
villaynes" who spread slanders in England, the root of the problem lay
in wishful thinking. All of the early reports had predicted rich commodities, and the land was certainly capable of producing them, but
everyone underestimated the difficulties of getting operations under
way. All the crops on the company's list were ones with which English
migrants were unfamiliar and they needed to learn how to grow and
process them. Placing all hopes on the individual life expectancy of
foreign experts was very risky. Even tobacco, the product that already
was coming from Virginia, was a difficult crop requiring real expertise
and proper equipment. In 1621 the company complained about the
poor quality of the tobacco they were being sent. But that same summer Thorpe wrote that if the company did not immediately send the
"lynes to sweat our tobacco on" which the colonists had requested previously, it would "undoe us all."[45]

Silk, had such an industry come into being, would have required
even more investment of labor and expertise. Bonoeil's book offered
page after page of advice about how to choose the best among the various species of mulberry trees and how to plant and care for them.
When, after seven or eight years, the tree began producing leaves in
quantity, a thousand pounds of leaves were required to feed an ounce
of silkworms. Bonoeil included elaborate instructions for the kinds of

buildings needed for nurturing the silkworms. Then, if everything went perfectly, that ounce of silkworms would make five or six pounds of silk. So at the very least, silk was a product that required taking the long view. Given that it was so difficult to keep "silkworm seed" alive on a transatlantic voyage, he also included a method he had read about for producing it from scratch that involved placing a calf in a dark enclosed space for twenty days during which it was to be fed only mulberry leaves. At the end of the time, the calf was to be strangled, placed in a tub, and covered with mulberry leaves. Silkworm seeds would eventually emerge from the decaying carcass and fasten onto the leaves, as, he wrote, "bees are made but of the rottennesse of a young Bull or Heifer."[46]

So the expertise on which investors relied could be problematic, and most products would take years to come to fruition. We know that there was a renewal of environmental stress during this crucial period that affected all agricultural endeavors. Drought as extreme as that experienced in 1606–1612 recurred briefly at the beginning of the 1620s, spelling doom for virtually any experiments then.[47]

George Sandys, charged with responsibility for making industrial diversification happen, spent a portion of his time on a literary project that had engaged him before he left England. Sandys had published the first five books of his translation of Ovid's *Metamorphoses* just before his departure in 1621, and the poet Michael Drayton urged him, "Goe on with Ovid, as you have begunne." Drayton wanted to see "what lines Virginia will produce." Sandys testified that translating was the "recreacion of my idle howers." His American experience produced nothing like his detailed and comprehensive account of life in the eastern Mediterranean. A few American references appear in his commentaries on Ovid, but most came from his reading of Spanish authors. Only two began with something like "I have seen. . . ," and these are natural history observations. One concerned "a Beast, which the Indians call a Possoun." Europeans were fascinated by the opossum, the American marsupial, and the way baby possums were able, as they thought, to crawl back into their mother's belly at will. The other was of the frogs in the Virginia summer, "called Pohatans hounds by the English, of their continuall yelping."[48]

Although their efforts may have seemed inadequate to company members in London, colonists' attempts to grow crops made a great difference to relationships along the James. After the peace of 1614, and with the beginnings of tobacco cultivation, they began to take up farmsteads in the prime lands along the river and spreading even to the eastern shore of Chesapeake Bay, disrupting native life at a time when leadership was in flux with the decline of Powhatan. After Powhatan moved away, his relative Itoyatin succeeded him. In reality, Opechancanough was in control of the empire Powhatan had built, and he and his close advisers were increasingly disturbed by what they saw happening around them, particularly after 1618 when large numbers of prospective settlers began to arrive every summer. Not only were the English becoming established on the land that Indians needed for their own subsistence, but efforts at proselytizing, especially when they were aimed primarily at children, were also profoundly troubling. Many young Indians had found employment working on English farms.[49]

Powhatan died in 1618, and in 1621 the period of official mourning ended with a ceremony to bury his bones. Because this occasion brought huge numbers of Indians together, Opechancanough apparently considered coordinating an attack on the English to coincide with it. The colonists would later learn that he had tried unsuccessfully to acquire poison from Eastern Shore allies to spread among the English. The attack did not occur then, because the Accomacks of the Eastern Shore broke with Opechancanough and warned the colonists. Opechancanough then worked to keep the English off guard, especially by his respectful reception of George Thorpe. Thorpe learned that Opechancanough had changed his name to Mangopeesomon, and Itoyatin had become Sasawpen. Colonial leaders apparently failed to read the significance of such a name change, even though the Roanoke colonists had recorded that Wingina, the Roanoke chief, had changed his name to Pemisapan just before a planned attack on the English. And that attack had been timed to coincide with a great memorial gathering to conclude mourning for a Roanoke leader.[50]

In fact Opechancanough and his advisers were laying plans for an offensive designed to remove the English from the Chesapeake, and one enigmatic man played a crucial role in its timing. Nemattanew, whose name the English sometimes wrote as Munetute, was a charismatic war leader. The English first encountered him when he led resistance to Dale's plan to build a settlement at Henrico; George Percy recorded that the colonists called him "Jacke of the feathers, by reason thatt he used to come into the felde all covered over with feathers and swans wings fastened unto his showlders, as thowghe he meante to flye." Dale's men believed that Nemattanew had bewitched them by "sorceries and charmes" as they sat in an Indian house upriver. They heard "hup hup" and "Oho Oho" repeated rhythmically outside. Thinking they were under attack, and unable to recognize one another, they fought among themselves until God lifted the hallucination. Modern research suggests that jimsonweed (Jamestown weed) may have been responsible for the delusion.[51]

In 1619, however, colonial leaders seriously discussed a proposal from Nemattanew that they participate in a joint expedition against a tribe above the falls of the James that had attacked the Powhatans. Nemattanew said that his men would carry the Englishmen's armor and weapons for them and they would be furnished with moccasins for the march. What made the offer attractive was his promise to "share all the booty of male and female children," thus enabling the colonists to get started on the promised mission; they had found they could not get Indians to give up their children "by fayer meanes." Such a shared venture would also help build good feelings with Opechancanough, they believed, but apparently it never took place.[52]

Captain John Smith reported that the Powhatans revered Nemattanew and thought his supernatural powers meant English guns could not hurt him. It is difficult to disentangle the circumstances surrounding his death. The sources say that two young servants believed he had killed their master because Nemattanew had gone off with him and returned alone two days later wearing the man's cap. The servants decided to take him to the governor for examination; when he resisted, they shot him. They claimed that as he was dying, he begged to be buried in an English graveyard so his people would not know he had been killed by a bullet. Opechancanough was described as deeply affected by this loss, though he disavowed any thoughts of revenge. The great attack came shortly thereafter, on March 22, 1622. It is possible that it had already been planned for that date, but the colonists were convinced that Nemattanew's death had precipitated it.[53]

Edward Waterhouse wrote the Virginia Company's official description of the 1622 attack, which was presented as a classic example of savage violence without reason or cause. Waterhouse, who had never been to Virginia, portrayed the colonists as too loving in their attitudes toward the Indians, and lulled into an unwise sense of security. He described how the Indians had unlimited access to English houses and weapons. In fact the attackers had actually been invited in to breakfast in many colonists' homes that fatal morning; at a signal they rose up from the table and, using the colonists' own weapons, struck them down. The attack was planned to sweep all the plantations simultaneously. By the company's count, the Indians killed 347 people, and the true toll was probably higher.

Not only did they cut the English down without sparing even women and children, according to Waterhouse's account, but they then cruelly went on to mutilate some of the bodies. Captain Nathaniel Powell, one of the original planters, was beheaded, and his head was carried off as a trophy. Even more striking was the mutilation visited on the body of George Thorpe, the man who had championed Indian rights in the face of colonists' opposition. He was "too kinde and beneficiall" and had even insisted that the colonists kill their mastiff dogs because the Indians found them too fierce. But Thorpe, with his determination to carry out the plan for conversion of Indian children, represented a greater threat than all the military leaders. As with the Jesuits of the 1570s, that threat had to be eliminated.

One factor complicated Waterhouse's presentation: some plantations, apparently even Jamestown itself, were spared because individual Indians warned them that the attack was coming. Reports are rather confusing, but apparently a convert whose name has come down to us as Chanco or Chauco alerted "one Pace," who had treated him "as a sonne," and Pace then sent messages to other plantations. George Thorpe had also been warned by "his man (who perceived some treachery intended to them by these hell-hounds)," but Thorpe could not believe that the Indians he knew could hurt him and thereby became "a glorious Martyr."[54]

A month after the attack, the Virginia government composed a letter describing the "most lamentable Afflictione" the settlers had endured by "the trecherie of the Indyans." Although the goal of expelling the English entirely had not been met, many of the plantations had been abandoned, and the survivors concentrated in a few locations. The colonists obliquely suggested that company pressure to develop commodities had forced them to neglect their own safety. To say more risked offending the investors on whom they now relied more than ever.[55]

Word of the attack, which arrived in London in the first week of July, spread quickly. Sir Simonds D'Ewes, then a young law student, recorded in his diary for July 7 the "exceeding badd newes" about the damage wrought by the "inhumane wretches" in Virginia. A few days later John Chamberlain wrote contemptuously of the colonists' "su-

28   *Decima tertiæ partis America*

CAPVT NONVM.

De magna clade, quam Angli anno 1622. 22. Martij in virginia acceperunt.

Beo tempore, quo Angli primùm in Virginiam venerūt, multas curas, molestias, labores & pericula exantlarunt. Nam Diabolus per sua organa , nempe sacerdotes , barbaros contra eos incitauit, ita, vt multos, quoties facultas fuit, obtruncarint. Tandem res eò deducta fuit, vt firma pax inter Anglos & barbaros ad aliquot annos contraheretur , & vtrinq; iureiurā-do sanciretur. Rex quoq; Povvhatan promisit, se regi Angliæ subiectum ac tri-butarium fore, pacemq; factam in æs incidi, & tabulam maximæ quercui ad suum palatium affigi curauit: quam pacem vtraq; pars magno cum gaudio amplexa est. Ad eam rem barbaros necessitas impulit, vt se Anglorum ope contra hostes tuerentur. Angli verò eò spe-ctabant, vt per hanc pacem res suas tanto melius in ea regione stabilirent. Hæc pax longo tempo-re inuiolata perstitit , adeò vt Angli passim sine gladiis & scloppetis incederent : & barbari eos crebrò inuisere, cum iis cibum capere, ac familiariter conuersari cæperunt. Vicissim Angli in soli-tudines ad ipsos se contulerunt, & spem conceperunt, fore, vt barbari tanto citiùs ac faciliùs ad Christianam fidem conuerterentur. Nam omnia inter ipsos tranquilla ac pacata erant.

Atq; vt pax hæc tantò firmiùs seruaretur , Angli Povvhatan, cum quo ipsis aliquid negotij erat, mense Martio pacis memoriam refricarunt: quibus ille inter alia respondit, se pacem cū ipsis optima fide culturum, futurumq;, vt cælum potius dissoluatur, quàm illa rumpatur. Sed hæc me-ra suit fraus, simulatio & hypocrisis. Nam barbari clam consilium iniuerant, Anglos omnes truci-dandi. Biduo antequàm hoc facinus exequi decreuerat, quosdam Anglos per periculosas solitudi-nes, incolumes deduxerant, & eos, qui linguæ addiscendæ caussâ aliquandiu apud ipsos comorati fuerant, amicè dimiserant: præterea alios Anglos, qui cum suis nauibus appulerant, benignè exce-

A German engraver's rendition of the 1622 Indian attack on the Virginia settlements. Cour-tesy of the John Carter Brown Library at Brown University.

pine negligence"; he considered the colony's devastation a source of "disgrace and shame." No other country's men, he wrote, would have been surprised in this way. Joseph Mead in Cambridge heard the news at the same time. Company member Christopher Brooke published a long *Poem on the Late Massacre in Virginia*, writing, "Amazement strooke me, horror ceaz'd my powres," when he first heard about the acts of these "men-monsters," "Errors of Nature" who were the "very dregs, garbage, and spawne of Earth." In 1623 a play named *The Plantation in Virginia* was performed, but it was not published, and the text has not survived.[56]

In its reply to the colonists, the company did not bother with any niceties. The first paragraph scathingly placed the blame squarely on the victims:

> to fall by the handes of men so contemptible; to be surprised by treacherie in a time of known danger; to be deafe to so plaine a warning (as we now to late understand) was last year given; to be secure in an occacion of so great suspition and jealousie as was Nenemathanewes death; not to perceive any thing in so opne and generall conspiracie; but to be made in parte instrumentes of contriving it, and almost guilitie of the destruccion by a blindfold and stupid entertaining of it; which the least wisdome or courage suffised to prevent even on the point of execucion . . .

The immediate remedy recommended by the company's leaders was a little less obvious. Arguing that the attack was God's punishment for sins, they commanded the settlers to give up "those two enormous exesses of apparell and drinkeing." Everyone, even those who had only heard the name Virginia, knew of their "infamie . . . to the detestacion of all good mindes, the scorne of others, and our extreame griefe and shame." If they sobered up and sincerely worshipped God, then the plantations would be safe, and they forbade the colonists to abandon any. They also blamed the colonists' fecklessness for King James's change of policy; in March 1621 he had stopped the national lottery which had bolstered the company's income. Now, finally, the king had given the company the control over tobacco imports that it had long sought. The company was sending over hundreds of new settlers but scorned the planters' request for food supplies, saying that they must rely on no one but themselves for sustenance. The company members also reiterated their orders to build "if not hansome Townes, yet compact and orderly villages," and pointed to the wholesome example of the Spanish colonies.

Finally, they turned to the subject of the Indians. The colonists should "roote out from being any longer a people, so cursed a nation." They recommended perpetual war against them, sparing only the young, who could serve on the plantations and who might still be won for civility and Christianity. A very special reward was promised to anyone who captured Opechancanough. As a sign of royal favor, King James had released obsolete weapons from the Tower of London to be sent to Virginia; although they were unusable in Europe, the investors thought they would be "verie usefull" in American combat. Two months later they returned to many of these themes, particularly criticizing the colonists for still needing supplies of food after so many years. They pointed to their own continually growing debt and the lack of good returns from the colony and singled out George Sandys in demanding that they begin to see some revenues immediately. The implicit threat seemed clear.[57]

Member Samuel Wrote, using the company's own records, tabulated changes in the colony's population. He concluded that between 1619 and 1621, 4,270 transatlantic migrants had been sent over. The company reckoned that only 1,240 colonists were alive at the time of the attack, so 3,000 had died in those three years; the attack killed about a third of the remainder. In the latter part of 1622 the investors had sent close to 1,000 new settlers, but they had heard that "by the sword and sicknes there are perished above 500" since the attack, so the population was only around 1,700. George Sandys had informed Wrote about the widespread disease, which so weakened the plantations that the living were scarcely able to bury the dead. Sandys was sure the disease had been brought to the colony in a shipment of "stinking beere" and suggested that the merchant who sent it should be hanged for murder. John Rolfe was among those who died in the general "sicknes."[58]

The company's public face was much less grim. Waterhouse's official account of the attack was blandly titled *A Declaration of the State of the Colony and Affaires in Virginia,* and his dedication to the Virginia Company, while beginning with mention of the "late unhappy accident in Virginia," affirmed the decision to go on "chearfully in this honorable Enterprize" despite the "perfidious treachery of a false-hearted people." In this spirit his book began with a history of the English interest in America going back to the reign of Henry VII and went on to reprint previous company declarations about the richness of the land and the progress already made in industrial and agricultural pursuits.

Before news of the attack arrived in England, the Virginia Company had published two pamphlets containing hopeful updates on the plantation's prospects. On April 18, 1622, Patrick Copland preached a sermon before the Virginia Company, which arranged for its publication along with the writings of Peter Pope, the East Indian convert. This sermon, ironically titled *Virginia's God be Thanked,* exuded a comfortable sense that although the colony had gone through hard times, "all difficulties are swallowed up" in this "Heathen now Christian Kingdome." In a sermon replete with references to the tribulations of the Israelites, he argued that Virginia's difficult early years had been God's punishment for England's sins and neglect of religious duties as well as the colonists' bad behavior. Prayers acknowledging God's mercies were like bonds for repayment of debt that were due at a certain time and place. Failure to pay what was due meant loss of goods. But God had now taken pity and "sayd to the destroying angel, It is sufficient, hold now thy hand." Drawing on his experience in Asia and reports from Virginia, Copland argued that rich commodities would soon be flowing across the Atlantic: "when you advance religion, you advance together with it Your owne profit."[59]

In its second publication of early 1622 the Virginia Company argued that not only had it been assiduous about sending colonists and supplies, including "57 Young maides . . . divers of which were well married before the comming away of the Ships," and several European experts, but the various industrial and agricultural projects were going exceedingly well. Cotton "from the Mogols Countrey" was thriving, and their specialists assured the investors that the land was very well suited for "Vines, Silke, Olives, Rice, &c." John Pory had been busy traveling; he had gone south and confirmed Thomas Harriot's accounts of rich silk grass and other commodities on the Carolina coast. Indians had told the colonists of a nearby copper mine, and at the house of one Indian king they had seen a "China box" acquired in trade with Indians who lived on the other side of the Appalachians, "neare the Sea." These people had gotten it from traders who came in ships "and are called Acanackchina." Descriptions of the traders' clothing made the English pretty sure they were Chinese.[60]

Waterhouse repeated all these claims, implying that the present troubles were at most a temporary setback. In support of the renewed possibility of finding that elusive passage to the Pacific, he appended a treatise by mathematician Henry Briggs suggesting a possible route. Not until page thirteen did Waterhouse actually turn to his description of the attack, and he went on to argue that now the colonists were free to force the Indians to their will, whereas previously their hands had been tied "with gentleness and faire usage." Thus the colony would actually be better off than it had been before. Examples from ancient and modern history reinforced this point, and Spanish courage in the face of adversity called for no less in English colonists.

The tract's final pages reiterated the bequests for religious purposes received over the past several years.[61]

When the governor and council in Virginia responded to the company's criticisms, they did not hold back. Although their answer was couched in respectful language, they said they had hoped investors would not add "sorrow to afflictione," and thought the strictures against excess in apparel must be ironic considering "our povertie and nakedness." They also reminded the investors that it was on their orders that colonists had opened their homes to Indians and lived freely with them, and investors' failure to send proper supplies with new colonists had depleted their stocks of food. The letter's main focus, however, was on all the activities the settlers were pursuing both to punish the Indians and to develop the commodities the investors demanded.[62]

George Sandys wrote more frankly in a private letter to company leaders. He said that "we, whom the hand of heaven hath humbled" were still in perplexity as to the future and he did not want to write to "the generalty" who judged without bothering to find out the truth. Arguing that Virginia's possibilities and problems were still little understood, he hoped his correspondents would not be "offended that I speake the truth." He complained that colonists were still arriving woefully unprepared, and many of the experts and leaders either were incompetent or died shortly after their arrival. Some of the foreigners were malicious as well as inept, especially the Italian glass experts: "A more damned crew hell never vomited." He ridiculed the company's instructions to reoccupy all the plantations and its criticism of the colonists' lack of preparedness, arguing that their weakness stemmed from the investors' neglect.[63]

Governor Wyatt wrote equally frankly to his father about the "Antipathy" between the company's "vast Commands and our grumbling Obedience." He calculated that if the colonists followed all the instructions they had received, each of the plantations would have only half a marksman to defend it. Referring to Virginia Company leader

Nicholas Ferrar he wrote, "I often wish little Mr. Farrar here, that to his zeale he would add knowledge of this Contrey." The adjective "little" said it all.[64]

Richard Frethorne, a young servant who had arrived during the summer of 1622—his ship departed before news of the attack reached England—wrote his mother and father in the spring of 1623 "I your Child am in a most heavie Case." Everyone was sick, and they had no food "but pease, and loblollie (that is water gruell)." Moreover, "wee live in feare of the Enimy every hower." His only hope was that he could be "redeemed out of Egipt." He never made it home. "Richard Frethram" was listed among those who died at Martin's Hundred in the widespread disease between April 1623 and February 1624.[65]

The English in Virginia embarked on guerrilla warfare that would last a decade and was, as Waterhouse predicted, fought in a no-holds-barred manner. In 1623 they invited Indian leaders to a peace parley where they served poisoned wine and then fired on the disabled Indians. They firmly believed that they had killed Opechancanough in this episode, but he lived to lead another attack two decades later. A ballad, "Good Newes from Virginia," was sent home in March 1623 by "a Gentleman in that Country" and published on arrival adorned by an engraving of a fierce-looking Englishman armed with pike and sword standing amidst corpses. Celebrating the war against the Indians and justifying the colonists' tactics, it was designed to be sung to the tune of "All those that be good fellowes."[66]

Other voices and perspectives were not entirely silenced. In November 1622 John Donne preached a sermon before the Virginia Company on Christ's command to his apostles in Acts 1:8 to carry his teachings "unto the uttermost part of the earth." Donne urged the investors not to forget their responsibility to bring the Indians to Christianity. He began by reminding his congregation that the book was called the acts, not the words, of the apostles, and argued that "one Ship that goes, and strengthens that Plantation" did more to vex England's Roman Catholic enemies than "twenty Lectures in matter of Controversie." He concluded with this charge: "Preach to them Doctrinally, preach to them Practically; Enamore them with your Justice, and (as farre as may consist with your security) your Civilitie; but inflame them with your godliness and your Religion."[67]

In 1624 George Wyatt sent a long letter to his son, Governor Sir Francis Wyatt, full of good advice about how to behave as governor and how to conduct this war. Unlike those who wrote immediately after the 1622 attack, he did "not with contempt reccon of them [the Indians] as cowards, as our common opinions esteemes. Neither did this their enterprise or execution, either want politie or corage." So while other homebound advisers assumed that all advantage lay with the colonists if they would only pull themselves together, he recognized the difficulty of fighting this war against a formidable enemy. He also acknowledged a principal weakness of the English: the inaccuracy of their muskets. Nemattanew had been able to convince the Indians that he was invulnerable to English bullets because in fact shooters mostly missed their targets, and "few in proofe were found mortal." He accepted that the English did not and could not immediately have the upper hand, and urged Francis to seek exact intelligence of "your confiners" and their situation. George Wyatt was close to death as he imparted what wisdom he could to his beleaguered son, and he sent this letter as "a token of lastinge love to you."[68]

Samuel Collier, the boy whom John Smith left with the Warraskoyacks, died early in the fighting by the accidental discharge of a gun. Henry Spelman died in 1623; he was apparently killed by Patawomecks, members of the tribe with whom he had lived. A colonist named Peter Arundel wrote about Spelman's death: "Wee our selves have taught them how to bee trecherous by our false dealinge with the poore kinge of Patomeche that had alwayes beene faythfull to the English . . . Spilmans death is a just revenge." But it was "a great loss to us for that Cap. was the best linguist of the Indian Tongue of this Country."[69] Thomas Savage had moved to the Eastern Shore, so Jamestown's leaders were now forced to rely on Robert Poole, the man they considered more "heathen" than English. Chauco, who had given the warning in 1622, also functioned as an intermediary and was apparently trusted by the Powhatans as well as the English. A man named Henry Fleet was taken prisoner in the skirmish in which Spelman died; he was a captive for five years and ultimately became an interpreter and trader.

In the years after 1622 reports came in that several colonists had been taken captive rather than killed in the attack. In 1623 Opechancanough sent a message by Chauco desiring peace and offering to return his captives to make that possible. One, "Mrs Boyse (the Chiefe of the prisoners), was sent home "appareled like one of theire Queenes which they desired wee should take notice of." Interpreter Robert Poole behaved in such a threatening manner, however, that the Indians held the others until they could be reassured by a new messenger that they could plant their corn in peace. In all there were said to be about twenty captives "retayned by Opechanekano in great slavery," and several were redeemed over the next few years. Jane Dickenson, a widow who was forced to work for Dr. John Potts to pay off the price of her ransom, said her "slavery" with him was just as bad as what she had endured with the Indians.[70]

News from Virginia jostled with reports from all over for public attention, and the future of the transatlantic colony was always contingent on events elsewhere. King James appointed a royal commission, including several Virginia Company members, to study the Ulster plantation's progress in 1622, and their report was negative, especially about progress in bringing cultural change to Ireland. The colony, created with great flourish as Jamestown was founded, was deemed to have been a drain on English finances without bringing the promised rewards. Henceforth the government was much less directly involved than previously. Thinking about Ireland, as about Virginia, was placed in an international frame.[71]

Europe was convulsed by the events of the Thirty Years' War, which pitted Protestant against Roman Catholic states between 1618 and 1648. In 1622 King James wrote to the pope asking him to intervene to stop the bloodshed, but his letter went unanswered—except, possibly, in the canonization of Ignatius Loyola, the founder of the militant Society of Jesus, the Jesuits. As Europe descended into general war, James I not only resisted calls to commit English resources to the fight but also believed he had a way to bring about negotiations that would lead to a general peace settlement: marriage between his son, the future king Charles I, and Maria, sister of the Spanish king, Philip IV. Negotiations for the Spanish match, as the English called it, had been dragging on since 1614. As long as the terms of any marriage settlement remained unclear, the Virginia colony's situation would also be uncertain, because the provisions might easily have included an agreement on the part of the English to give up settlements in American lands claimed by Spain. Such imperial trading featured in many treaties throughout the colonial period. A successful conclusion to negotiations for the marriage appeared within reach in 1622, just when Virginia's reputation was at its lowest. Using the names Tom and Jack Smith, Prince Charles and James Villiers, the marquis of Buckingham and James's chief minister, made a dramatic secret trip to Madrid in 1623 to try to break through the interminable delays. But the demands of the two sides were not reconcilable, and Charles and Buckingham returned alone; soon the negotiations collapsed completely. From this point forward, the English government's policy was increasingly hostile to Spain, and conflict intensified when Charles came to the throne in 1625.[72]

Even in the aftermath of the 1622 attack, the Virginia Company, while urging the colonists to wage perpetual war against the Powhatans, feared a Spanish invasion of the James River and sent over plans for new fortifications. In 1625 Gregorio Bolivar, a Franciscan friar with extensive experience in the mission fields of Peru and Mexico, wrote to the newly elected pope Urban VIII urging him to secure the Spanish monarch's cooperation for an invasion of Virginia, "where the Lutheran English have settled and begun to spread their pestilential sect." Writing at the request of the head of the Congregation for the Propagation of the Faith, Bolivar described Virginia's location on the American continent as he understood it and argued that it was best approached overland from Florida. He offered his own services, claiming that the Indians in Virginia were very similar to those he knew in Peru, and implying that he already understood their language. The Spanish crown instead sent a massive fleet in 1624 to recapture Recife in Brazil from the Dutch. Bolivar returned to Peru; he was killed by Indians there in 1631.[73]

Plymouth colony had pioneered New England as an alternate American venue in 1620. In 1622, as he returned to England from his three-year post in Virginia, John Pory visited the Pilgrims and wrote a glowing account of the healthfulness, rich food supplies, and good situation of the northern colony in a letter to the earl of Southampton. He quoted Governor William Bradford as saying that they had lost no colonists that entire year; Bradford apparently neglected to mention that half their number had died during the first year. Pory averred that Plymouth had been welcomed by its Indian neighbors and lived on terms of peace with them, and wished that "our people in the Southern Colony . . . were as free from wickedness and vice as these are in this place!" When he wrote to Governor Wyatt, however, he mentioned hostile relations with Indians to the north of Massachusetts that threatened the fishing industry. For his part, Wyatt complained that some disparaged Virginia in this troubled period, seeking "to raise the Northern colony by the disgrace of ours."[74]

News from the East also competed with Virginia events in the public sphere. John Chamberlain's letter mentioning the 1622 attack was

filled with tidbits of other news, including the arrival of the *Charles,* a
"rich ship" returning from Bantam. New editions of the books on the
Ottoman Empire by Richard Knolles and George Sandys were published in the early 1620s, and two books on the 1622 coup in which
the Ottoman sultan Osman was killed in an assault led by his uncle
Mustapha appeared at the same time as Waterhouse's account of the
Virginia attack. John Rawlins's narrative of his escape from Muslim
slavery also appeared then, telling how he had roused the other English slaves on the ship in which they served under the command of
two "English Turkes" and urged them to rebel. The captain and his
partner, both "English Turkes," and four others accompanied Rawlins
and his associates back to England, as did "all the slaves and Holland-
ers, with other Renegadoes who were willing to be reconciled to their
true Saviour."[75]

But many continued to enter involuntary servitude in Muslim lands.
In 1620 and 1621 the English government sent out a naval expedition,
which included Samuel Argall, against the Algerian pirates; but it accomplished little, and the seizing of captives continued. Those who
sailed on the Virginia-bound ship *Tiger* in August 1621 were among
the fortunate few; although the ship was captured by "Barbary" pirates,
it was ransomed and continued on its way. In 1624 the royal government received a petition from captives whose case was presented to
the public in a ballad, *The Lamentable Cries of at Least 1500 Christians:
Most of Them Being Englishmen (Now Prisoners in Argiers Under the
Turks).* It told of the agonies of those condemned to be galley slaves,
beaten and called "Christian curs" when their spirits sank under the
work, and said that converts, "half-Turks and half-Christians," were
the worst masters. Two years later, when the number of prisoners in
Algiers alone was said to have doubled, the government received another petition, this one from two thousand bereft wives. Like Richard
Frethorne in Virginia, Robert Adams wrote home from Salé on the
Moroccan coast pleading for his father to redeem him from his "most

miserable captivity" under "most cruel tyrants." He complained of hard labor with only bread and water to eat and said that he was beaten daily "to make me either turn Turk or come to my ransom." His sad postscript said that he had already sent three or four letters without any reply. A ship returning from the Pilgrims' colony at Plymouth was seized right in the English Channel in the same year, and the "master and men were made slaves." Not only were all these captives said to suffer unendurable pains, but they also ran the constant risk of conversion to Islam.[76]

Returned captives occasioned both joy and introspection. In a celebrated case a convert was welcomed back into the church in 1627 with two sermons stressing the danger in which the souls of Christian captives lay. One, perhaps with "taking the turban" as the image of conversion in mind, warned that some seemed to consider changes of religion as simple as a change of clothes.[77]

Returnees from American captivity were rarer and less noted. Anne Jackson was twenty years old when she went to Virginia in 1621. When she sailed with her brother John, who had already established himself in the plantation of Martin's Hundred, her father brought her to the ship to show his approval. Martin's Hundred was destroyed in March 1622, and many of its inhabitants killed. But a few years later John Jackson learned that his sister had been taken captive and was alive. In 1625 he and another colonist named Robert Linsey traveled "with certaine Indians unto Pamunky." Jackson testified under oath on his return that Linsey had been "retained" by the Indians and had told Jackson how he wanted his possessions disposed "if he never came home againe." No one explained why Jackson was allowed to return and Linsey was not, nor whether John was looking for Anne. At some point, however, Anne Jackson was brought back; in January 1629 the Virginia General Court decreed that "Anne Jackson which Came from the Indians shall bee sent for England with the first oportunity of Shipping and that her brother John Jackson shall give security for her passage and keepe her safe till shee bee shipped aboard." It seems probable that Anne was returned against her will; after so many years, she, like the female captives who refused Pedro Menéndez de Avilés's offer of repatriation, may have had a family among the Indians. The order that John must "keep her safe" until she was put aboard a ship for England indicated the court's assumption that she would go back to her Indian relatives if she was not watched constantly and removed from the colony.[78]

In the wake of Virginia's massive problems, dissension rent the Virginia Company. The factions have left a copious record; those involved on both sides of the Atlantic were divided over whether the original regime under Sir Thomas Smith's leadership of the company or the revised scheme of Sir Edwin Sandys had been the right one. The royal government was necessarily involved in the ongoing investigations, and ultimately the company was dissolved. Captain Nathaniel Butler, a client of the earl of Warwick who headed one of the factions, visited Virginia in late 1622 and wrote a damning account, "The Unmasked Face of our Colony in Virginia," essentially saying that all the hopeful reports had been nothing but lies. The people lived in misery in inadequate houses situated in swamps, and none of the economic projects still stood, he wrote. Sir Edwin Sandys's opponents petitioned the king to investigate what had gone wrong in the colony, implying that things had been fine until Sandys began to change the company's program in 1618. The Ancient Planters, those who had been in the colony from the early years, wrote scathing statements repeating their insistent argument that the colony had never been properly supported; they painstakingly reviewed the plantation's history from the beginning and wrote in detail about the loathsome food they had been forced to eat: "The happyest day that ever some of them hoped to see, was when the Indyans had killed a mare they wishing whilst she was boyling that Sir Thomas Smith was uppon her backe in the kettle." Some had been overcome by despair and died.

Now they were unanimous in condemning the harsh martial law they had endured.[79]

Virginia Company members were horrified to learn that Sir Edwin Sandys and his deputy John Ferrar had awarded themselves unprecedentedly huge salaries (£500 and £400) for their administration of the tobacco contract. This set in motion an ever more heated discussion that contributed to the company's eventual demise. More and more people came forward to expose the conditions in the colony and accuse the Virginia Company of extreme mismanagement under Sandys's leadership. The Privy Council appointed three commissions to investigate, just as the government had investigated the Ulster colony in 1622. John Pory was entrusted with the task of carrying the Privy Council's orders to Virginia and served on the commission that investigated conditions there in 1624. That commission's report seems to have indicated that the state of the colony was better than expected, but the decision had already been made by the time Pory returned with it in June. The company was formally dissolved in May 1624, and Virginia became the first royal colony. Soon Pory was placed on the newly appointed commission to establish a government for Virginia. In July the Privy Council voted to give him the very large sum of £150 for his service about the king's "special affairs"; the council in Virginia hinted that in exchange for this "Princely reward" he had kept quiet about the favorable report.[80]

Francis Wyatt was retained in office as the first royal governor. George Sandys returned to England in 1625 but continued his association with Virginia, serving as the colony's London agent for a time. Patrick Copland had been appointed rector of the East India College, but he never went to Virginia. Instead he sailed to Bermuda, where he led a puritan congregation. Ultimately he was involved in settlement of the colony of Eleuthera in the Bahamas.

Underneath the flurry of charges and countercharges, and with new kinds of evidence becoming available, one can see signs that normal patterns were increasingly possible as colonists made lives for themselves. Archaeological investigation has demonstrated that the colonists really were engaged in the kinds of diversified production that the company kept calling for, and that this engagement actually intensified after company control ended. As Ralph Hamor had testified, a genuine town was begun to the east of the fort in about 1618; a trained surveyor laid out twelve-acre lots for "James Cittie" in the early 1620s, and settlers were soon moving out beyond the confines of the city to the island's eastern end. Moreover, they had started building in brick. All the leading colonists lived clustered together in the "New Town." Archaeologists have uncovered signs of extensive mercantile activity and have excavated the workshop of gunsmith John Jackson, who took pity on Richard Frethorne in Jamestown. Foundations of shops specializing in pottery making, brewing, and apothecary work have also been unearthed. Governor Wyatt and George Sandys fostered the beginning of some industries; the great period of varied production on the island occurred after 1625 and continued through the 1630s. John Harvey, who arrived in 1623 after three years in Guiana and became governor in 1628, particularly pushed for such development.[81]

Moreover, documentary excavations have discovered records of genuine communities composed of families growing up away from Jamestown—near the mouth of the James River and upriver close to the falls, and on the Eastern Shore, where Thomas Savage had taken up residence and established a family. These communities, like contemporary Plymouth in New England, increasingly resembled English country villages. The census ordered in 1624 as part of the royal investigation revealed that the planters who had been in America the longest were most likely to have families.[82] Although the planned college never materialized, Bernard Symmes, one of the separatist puritans in Virginia, endowed the first free school in English America in 1634.[83]

As we draw conclusions about the nature of Virginia's founding years, Bernard Symmes presents a challenge to received wisdom. It is a shock to learn that that the first English commitment to provide free education was in Virginia. Moreover, the Virginia Company's great planned effort to carry Christianity to the Indians, with contributions from many people on both sides of the Atlantic, was unique. Nothing on that scale was thought of again until the creation of formal organizations such as the Society for the Propagation of the Gospel at the end of the seventeenth century.

Because attention then focused on the revocation of the Virginia Company's charter and charges against the leadership, the first lesson of the great attack of 1622—that Chesapeake Algonquians might welcome an English presence for the "book of the world" but would resist attempts to introduce the "book of the spirit"—was lost, as it had been with the sixteenth-century Jesuit mission and Don Luís/Paquiquineo's rejection of Christianity. Instead colonists drew conclusions about the Indians' fundamental nature and foresaw a future of separation more than convergence.

The colonists' level of engagement in economic pursuits, together with their growing ability to produce a marketable tobacco crop, also led to the 1622 rupture as the Chesapeake Algonquians came to understand how threatening a fully established and expanding English presence would be to their traditional life and its necessary land base. It would have been extremely difficult to predict in 1617 that the colony would grow so dramatically in the coming years. Thus it was not their stupidity and fecklessness but the beginnings of colonists' success that led Opechancanough to try to extirpate them. The 1630s saw a massive English migration into the Chesapeake, overwhelming Indian attempts to control the terms of relationships.

The Chesapeake remained a dangerous place for newcomers, and many died in their first few years, the seasoning period. Those who survived to finish their terms of servitude joined or helped to establish the communities growing up along the James or on the Eastern Shore. Some men who had been able to establish themselves early on added incrementally to their acreage by paying servants' passage over; in

gaining the fifty-acre headright for each servant, they laid the foundation for future large plantations. But in these decades most farms were
a few hundred acres or less. For the fortunate ones who survived the
early years and were able to marry, the opportunity to have a farm of
their own represented realization of an American dream.

It was Captain John Smith who, most prominently among his contemporaries, drew the true lessons of the Jamestown experience. After
he left Virginia he spent the rest of his life, except for a brief trip to
New England in 1614, at home writing about colonization. New England, then called Norembega, had been deemed a hostile environment
after the failure of the Sagadahoc colony in the frozen winter of 1607.
Smith coined the name "New England," one of the great propaganda
strokes in American history, to bolster his contention that the northern environment was healthier for English bodies and more conducive
to English life than the Chesapeake. He wrote several books about his
and others' American experiences and in 1624, as the government was
investigating the Virginia Company, he expanded on all he had written in his great work, *The Generall Historie of Virginia, New-England
and the Summer Isles*. This was the first book that analyzed the whole
record of English colonization in America and drew its lessons; in its
conclusion he lamented his own inability to convince investors of the
right way to proceed. He wrote that American ventures had been "my
children, for they have beene my Wife, my Hawks, Hounds, my Cards,
my Dice, and in totall, my best content."

Smith died at the age of fifty-one in 1631. In his last years he published two smaller books. One was his autobiography, where he told
the story of his early life and Turkish captivity for the first time and
brought the *Generall Historie* up to date. Then in his final year, as the
huge fleet for Massachusetts Bay was gathering, he wrote a more philosophical book, *Advertisements For the unexperienced Planters of New-
England, or any-where*. In this book he reiterated a case he had been
making for some time: that fishing, the economic base on which New

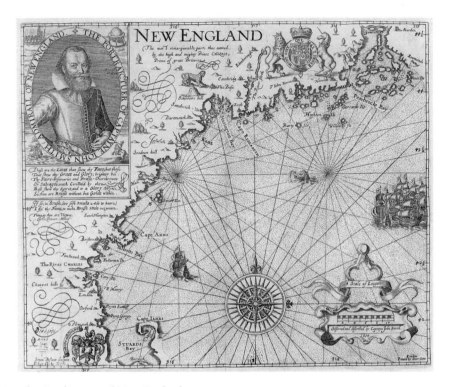

John Smith's map of New England. Courtesy of the John Carter Brown Library at Brown University.

England was to be founded, was far more secure than illusory searches for gold or a passage to Asia—or a nonessential product like tobacco. America needed people who were not afraid to get their hands dirty. "Let not the meanness of the word fish distaste you." He maintained that the sea was as rich as the great silver mine at Potosí, and the fish stocks, unlike mines, were a renewable resource.

Although his book was addressed to Massachusetts Bay's founders—and there is some evidence that they read his books—his plan was drawn from analysis of Virginia's record, especially the revised program after 1618. His central theme, the sum of all experience thus far, was that colonization succeeded only where each family had a stake in the outcome and where merchants rather than aristocrats did the planning. He counseled New England's leaders "not to stand too much upon the letting, setting, or selling those wild Countries, nor impose too much upon the commonalty . . . for present gain." Rather, they should weld colonists to the project by giving each man as much land as he could reasonably manage for "him and his heires for ever."[84]

All colonization projects, whether in Ireland or in America, had grappled with the fundamental question of how policy makers could motivate and control populations of migrants. Virginia's early history, especially as it was formulated out of the complaints and unrealistic claims on all sides, has been deemed a dismal tale of failure. Even the most severe martial law could not force colonists to thrive and lead productive lives. But, as John Smith explained to his readers, the Jamestown experience had produced a fundamental understanding about human psychology. Devolution—transfer of control to America—and fostering initiative on colonists' own account were the answer to all those questions about how to motivate people and create new societies. The key to building English societies abroad, however messy and incomplete, was discovered in Virginia and all successful colonies henceforth followed its model.[85]

Notes

INTRODUCTION

1. Ralph Lane to Sir Philip Sidney, August 12, 1585, in David Beers Quinn, ed., *The Roanoke Voyages, 1584–1590*, 2 vols. (London, 1955), 1:204–206, quote 204; Lane, *An Account of the Particularities of the imployments of the English men left in Virginia* (1586), ibid., 272–273.
2. Alonso Suarez de Toledo to Philip II, July 3, 1586, in David B. Quinn et al., eds., *New American World: A Documentary History of North America to 1612*, 5 vols. (New York, 1979), 5:45.

I. ELIZABETHAN ENGLAND ENGAGES THE WORLD

1. See Charles Webster, *The Great Instauration: Science, Medicine, and Reform, 1626–1660* (London, 1975), chap. 1. The Book of Daniel is quoted from the Geneva Bible.
2. Robert Gordon of Lochinvar, *Encouragements to Under-takers* (Edinburgh, 1625), sig. B3v.
3. On discussion of these topics in Spain, see Anthony Pagden, *Lords of All the World: Ideologies of Empire in Spain, Britain, and France, c. 1500–c. 1800* (New Haven, 1995), chap. 2; Mario Góngora, *Studies in the Colonial History of Spanish America*, trans. Richard Southern (Cambridge, 1975), chap. 6.
4. *The Voyages of Jacques Cartier*, trans. H. P. Biggar, rev. and intro. Ramsay Cook (Toronto, 1993), 36–37.
5. Sabine MacCormack, "Limits of Understanding: Perceptions of Greco-Roman and Amerindian Paganism in Early Modern Europe," in Karen Ordahl Kupperman, ed., *America in European Consciousness, 1493–1750* (Chapel Hill, 1995), 96; Jorge Cañizares-Esguerra, *How to Write the History of the New World: Historiographies, Epistemologies, and Identities in the Eighteenth-Century Atlantic World* (Stanford, 2001), 316.
6. William Strachey, *The Historie of Travell into Virginia Britania* (1612), ed. Louis B. Wright and Virginia Freund (London, 1953), 24.
7. Robert Cushman, *A Sermon Preached in Plimmoth in New-England* (London, 1622), sig. A2v.

8. Robert Johnson, *Nova Brittania* (London, 1609), sig. C2.

9. Edward Hayes, *A report of the voyage and successe thereof, attempted in the yeere of our Lord 1583 by sir Humfrey Gilbert knight*, in David B. Quinn, ed., *The Voyages and Colonising Enterprises of Sir Humphrey Gilbert*, 2 vols. (London, 1940), 2:387–388.

10. Gordon of Lochinvar, *Encouragements to Under-takers*, sig. D3.

11. John Rolfe, *A True Relation of the state of Virginia lefte by Sir Thomas Dale Knight in May last 1616* (Charlottesville, 1951), 14; Sir William Alexander, *An Encouragement to Colonies* (London, 1624), 37.

12. See Daniel T. Reff, *Plagues, Priests, and Demons: Sacred Narratives and the Rise of Christianity in the Old World and the New* (Cambridge, 2005), esp. chaps. 1–2.

13. Robert Poole, *Time's Alteration: Calendar Reform in Early Modern England* (London, 1998), chaps. 1–6. On the changeover in America, see Mark M. Smith, "Culture, Commerce, and Calendar Reform in Colonial America," *William and Mary Quarterly*, 3rd ser., 55 (1998): 557–584.

14. I thank Joseph C. Miller for his image of Europe's relation to the Ottoman Empire.

15. On Süleyman's innovative government, see Metin Kunt and Christine Woodhead, eds., *Süleyman the Magnificent and His Age: The Ottoman Empire in the Early Modern World* (London, 1995).

16. On the extent of the Ottoman Empire in Jamestown's time, see Nabil Matar, *Islam in Britain, 1558–1685* (Cambridge, 1998), 1–2; and Daniel Goffman, *The Ottoman Empire and Early Modern Europe* (Cambridge, 2002). On the changing definitions of what constituted Europe and the Middle East, see Martin W. Lewis and Kären E. Wigen, *The Myth of Continents: A Critique of Metageography* (Berkeley, 1997).

17. D. B. Quinn and Neil M. Cheshire, *The New Found Land of Stephen Parmenius* (Toronto, 1972), 76–77; see also David B. Quinn, "Stephanus Parmenius Budaeus: A Hungarian Pioneer in North America," in *Explorers and Colonies: America, 1500–1625* (London, 1990), 225–238, quote 227.

18. Jean Bodin, *The Six Bookes of a Commonweale*, trans. Richard Knolles (London, 1606), facsimile edn., ed. Kenneth Douglas McRae (Cambridge, Mass., 1962), bk. 4, 537–538. Knolles's translation involved weaving together passages from Bodin's French and Latin versions into a continuous text; ibid., A38. Henry Blount, *A voyage into the Levant. A Breife Relation of a Journey, lately performed by Master H. B. Gentleman, from England by the way of Venice, into Dalmatia, Sclavonia, Bosnah, Hungary, Macedonia, Thessaly, Thrace, Rhodes and Egypt, unto Gran Cairo: With particular observations concerning the moderne condition of the Turkes, and other people under that empire* (London, 1636), 2.

19. "The ambassage of Master Edmund Hogan, one of the sworne Esquires of her Majesties person, from her Highnes, to Mully Abdelmelech Emperour of Maroccus, and King of Fes, and Sus: in the yeere 1577, written by himselfe," in Richard Hakluyt, ed., *The Principall Navigations, Voiages, Traffiques, and Discoveries of the English Nation* (London, 1589), 156–159.

20. Ross E. Dunn, *The Adventures of Ibn Battuta: A Muslim Traveler of the 14th Century* (Berkeley, 1986), 293.

21. Ira Berlin, *Generations of Captivity: A History of African American Slaves* (Cambridge, Mass., 2003), chap. 1; Robin Law and Kristin Mann, "West Africa in the Atlantic Community: The Case of the Slave Coast," *William and Mary*

Quarterly, 3rd ser., 56 (1999): 307–334; George E. Brooks, *Landlords and Strangers: Ecology, Society, and Trade in Western Africa, 1000–1630* (Boulder, 1993), 115–141, 210–223.

22. John Pory, *A Geographical History of Africa* (London, 1600), 1. On the background behind these links, see P. E. H. Hair, "Morocco, the Saharan Coast, and the Neighbouring Atlantic Islands," and "Guinea," in D. B. Quinn, ed., *The Hakluyt Handbook*, 2 vols. (London, 1974), 1:190–196, 197–207.

23. John A. Thornton, *Africa and Africans in the Making of the Atlantic World, 1400–1800*, 2nd ed. (Cambridge, 1998), chap. 2, 116, and chap. 11, and "The African Background to American Colonization," in Stanley L. Engerman and Robert E. Gallman, eds., *The Cambridge Economic History of the United States*, vol. 1, *The Colonial Era* (Cambridge, 1996), 53–94; David Northrup, *Africa's Discovery of Europe, 1450–1850* (New York, 2002), 50–56, 78–106. On the relative value of enslaved Africans and African commodities in this trade, see Ernst van den Boogaart, "The Trade between Western Africa and the Atlantic World, 1600–90: Estimates of Trends in Composition and Value," *Journal of African History* 33 (1992): 369–385, and the reply to van den Boogaart by David Eltis, "The Relative Importance of Slaves and Commodities in the Atlantic Trade of Seventeenth-Century Africa," *Journal of African History* 35 (1994): 237–249.

24. "A voyage made out of England unto Guinea in Affrike, at the charges of certaine Merchants adventurers of the Citie of London, in the yeere of our Lord, 1553," in Hakluyt, *Principall Navigations*, 83–88.

25. "The second voyage to Guinea, set out by Sir George Barne, Sir John Yorke, Thomas Locke, Anthonie Hickman and Edward Castelyn, in the yere 1554," ibid., 89–98, quote 92; James McDermott, *Martin Frobisher: Elizabethan Privateer* (New Haven, 2001), 32–44, 48–51, and "'A right Heroicall heart': Sir Martin Frobisher," in Thomas H. B. Symons, ed., *Meta Incognita: A Discourse of Discovery. Martin Frobisher's Arctic Expeditions, 1576–1578*, 2 vols. (Hull, Quebec, 1999), 1:55–118, Frobisher's deposition reproduced 108, n.18. Strangways's name was sometimes written Stranguishe.

26. For this discussion, see "The second voyage to Guinea," in Hakluyt, *Principall Navigations*, 97; "The first voyage made by M. William Towrson Marchant of London, to the coast of Guinea, with two Shippes, in the yeere 1555," ibid., 98–112, quote 109; "The second voyage made by Maister William Towrson to the coast of Guinea, and the Castle of Mina, in the yeere 1556," ibid., 112–120, quotes 115. On these voyages, see P. E. H. Hair and J. D. Alsop, *English Seamen and Traders in Guinea, 1553–1565: The New Evidence of Their Wills* (Lewiston, N.Y., 1992).

27. Pieter de Marees, *Description and Historical Account of the Gold Kingdom of Guinea* (1602), trans. and ed. Albert van Dantzig and Adam Jones (Oxford, 1987), 63–64, 74, 225.

28. Pory, *Geographical Historie of Africa*, 1; "The second voyage made by Maister William Towrson," 112–120. See W. Walton Claridge, *A History of the Gold Coast and Ashanti*, 2nd ed., 2 vols. (New York, 1964), 1:54–90.

29. Harry Kelsey, *Sir John Hawkins: Queen Elizabeth's Slave Trader* (New Haven, 2003), chaps. 3–4. On all these early voyages, see John W. Blake, *West Africa: Quest for God and Gold, 1454–1578* (London, 1977), esp. chaps. 7–8. This book is an expanded and revised edition of *European Beginnings in West Africa, 1454–1578* (1937).

30. On Morocco during this period, see Jamil M. Abun-Nasr, *A History of the Maghreb* (Cambridge, 1971), 210–220.

31. On the state of the English government's finances, see Pauline Croft, *King James* (Basingstoke and New York, 2003), 71–81.

32. On this privateering war and its effects, see Kenneth R. Andrews, *Elizabethan Privateering: English Privateering during the Spanish War, 1585–1603* (Cambridge, 1964).

33. Anthony Ashley, *The Mariners Mirrour* (n.p., 1588); C. R. Boxer, *The Dutch Seaborne Empire, 1600–1800* (Harmondsworth, 1973), 183–184.

34. For some of the rumors, see Victor von Klarwill, *The Fugger Newsletters*, 2nd ser. (London, 1926).

35. Geoffrey Parker, *The Grand Strategy of Philip II* (New Haven, 1998), 41.

36. Robert Payne, *A Brife description of Ireland: Made in this yeere, 1589* (London, 1590), 5–7, 13–15. See Andrew Hadfield, *Literature, Travel, and Colonial Writing in the English Renaissance, 1545–1625* (Oxford, 1998), 91–98.

37. Robert Brenner, *Merchants and Revolution: Commercial Change, Political Conflict, and London's Overseas Traders, 1550–1653* (Princeton, 1993), 4–23.

38. The charter is printed in Hakluyt, *Principall Navigations*, 234–236.

39. "The Ambassage of Master Henry Roberts . . . from her highnesse to Mully Hamet Emperour of Marocco and the King of Fesse, and Sus, in the yeere 1585," ibid., 237–238; for the decree, see 238; the exchange of letters, 238–239. See J. F. P. Hopkins, trans. and ed., *Letters from Barbary, 1576–1774: Arabic Documents in the Public Record Office* (1982).

40. Pory, *Geographical Historie of Africa*. On al-Hasan al-Wazzan/Leo Africanus, see Natalie Zemon Davis, *Trickster Travels: A Sixteenth-Century Muslim between Worlds* (New York, 2006); and Oumelbanine Zhiri, "Leo Africanus's *Description of Africa*," in Ivo Kamps and Jyotsna G. Singh, eds., *Travel Knowledge: European "Discoveries" in the Early Modern Period* (New York and Houndmills, 2001), 250–266. On the Moroccan embassy, see Bernard Harris, "A Portrait of a Moor," in Catherine M. S. Alexander and Stanley Wells, eds., *Shakespeare and Race* (Cambridge, 2000), 23–36. On the English-Moroccan relationship, see Linda Colley, *Captives: Britain, Empire and the World, 1600–1850* (London, 2002), 122; and Jamil M. Abun-Nasr, *A History of the Maghreb* (Cambridge, 1971), 204–216.

41. Kenneth R. Andrews, *Trade, Plunder and Settlement: Maritime Enterprise and the Genesis of the British Empire* (Cambridge, 1984), chap. 4; Goffman, *Ottoman Empire and Early Modern Europe*, chap. 7, 73.

42. Thomas D. Goodrich, *The Ottoman Turks and the New World: A Study of Tarih-I Hind-I Garbi and Sixteenth-Century Ottoman Americana* (Wiesbaden, 1990). For the future expansion of the Dar ul-Islam (lands under Muslim control) across the Atlantic, see 173, 253.

43. For this correspondence and its context, see S. A. Skilleter, *William Harborne and the Trade with Turkey, 1578–1582: A Documentary Study of the first Anglo-Ottoman Relations* (Oxford, 1977), 35–37, 59, 115, 123–124; for reports by rival Europeans, see 60–64, 78–80, 138, 143, 198–199. On Harborne's appointment as ambassador and his address to Murad III, see Susan Skilliter, "William Harborne, the First English Ambassador, 1583–1588," in *Four Centuries of Turco-British-Relations*, ed. Wm. Hale and Ali Ihsan Bagis (Beverley, North

Humberside, 1984), 10–25, quote 22. On similarities between Protestantism and Islam, see Matar, *Islam in Britain*, chap. 4.

44. Skilleter, *Harborne and the Trade with Turkey*, 22–27, quote 23.

45. Walsingham's letter is reproduced in Conyers Read, *Mr. Secretary Walsingham and the Policy of Queen Elizabeth*, 3 vols. (Cambridge, Mass., 1925), 3:226–228. On the possible alliance, see also Matar, *Islam in Britain*, 122–128.

2. ADVENTURERS, OPPORTUNITIES, AND IMPROVISATION

1. See Joan Thirsk, *Economic Policy and Projects: The Development of a Consumer Society in Early Modern England* (Oxford, 1978); and D. B. Quinn, "Edward Hayes and the Americas," in *England and the Discovery of America* (New York, 1974), 227–245. The quotation is from Geoffrey Parker, *The Grand Strategy of Philip II* (New Haven, 1998), 29; see also 48–55.

2. "A voyage made out of England unto Guinea in Affrike, at the charges of certaine Merchants adventurers of the Citie of London, in the yeere of our Lord, 1553," in Richard Hakluyt, ed., *The Principall Navigations, Voiages, Traffiques, and Discoveries of the English Nation* (London, 1589), 83.

3. For this account, see René de Laudonnière, "The first voyage of Jean Ribault to Florida, 1562," trans. from *L'histoire notable de la Floride* (Paris, 1586) by Richard Hakluyt, who published it as *A notable historie containing foure voyages made by certaine French captaines unto Florida* (London, 1587). Rpt. in David B. Quinn et al., eds., *New American World: A Documentary History of North America to 1612*, 5 vols. (New York, 1979), 2:294–307, quotes 306–307.

4. "Report of Manrique de Rojas," trans. Lucy L. Wenhold, in Charles E. Bennett, *Laudonnière and Fort Caroline* (Gainesville, 1964), 107–124; Rouffin's testimony 116–122.

5. Juan E. Tazon, *The Life and Times of Thomas Stukeley (c. 1525–78)* (Aldershot, 2003), quotes 35, 65–69, 77; J. Leitch Wright, *Anglo-Spanish Rivalry in North America* (Athens, Ga., 1971), 21–23.

6. For this testimony, see Tazon, *Life and Times of Stukeley*, 91.

7. "The voyage of Thomas Stukeley, wrongfully called Marques of Ireland, into Barbary 1578. Written by Johannes Thomas Freigius in *Historia de cæde Sebastiani Regis Lusitaniæ*," in Richard Hakluyt, *The Principal Navigations, Voyages, Traffiques, and Discoveries of the English Nation*, 2nd ed. (London, 1598–1600), bk. 2, pt. 2, 67–68.

8. Ralph Lane to Sir Francis Walsingham, August 12, 1585, in David Beers Quinn, ed., *The Roanoke Voyages, 1584–1590*, 2 vols. (London, 1955), 1:203. For Lane's career in Ireland, see Karen Ordahl Kupperman, "Ralph Lane," in *American National Biography* (Oxford, 2000); Nicholas Canny, *Making Ireland British, 1580–1650* (Oxford, 2001), 77–85.

9. *The True Travels, Adventures, and Observations of Captaine John Smith* is published, with excellent explanatory notes, in *The Complete Works of Captain John Smith*, ed. Philip L. Barbour, 3 vols. (Chapel Hill, 1986), 3:137–244. For Barbour's reconstructions of people and events, see also the introduction to the *True Travels*, 125–136, and to the portion of that book previously published by Samuel Purchas in *Hakluytus Posthumus or Purchas His Pilgrimes* (London, 1625), rpt. in *Works*, 341–363, with Barbour's intro. 328–340.

10. Anne Marbury Hutchinson, born in 1591, was eleven years younger than Smith.

11. Smith, *True Travels*, 155–156.

12. Ibid., 156–159.

13. Ibid., 160–162. "Pyasters" were Spanish pieces of eight, "Chicqueenes" refers to zecchini, Venetian gold coins, and "Sultanies" were Turkish gold pieces.

14. Barbour identifies Olumpagh as the modern town of Lendava (Olimbach in German). He also identifies the source of Smith's stratagem in Peter Whithorne's translation of Machiavelli; see Smith, *Works*, 3:163–164 nn9, 5. Laura Polanyi Striker first identified Smith's account as a valuable source for this period in eastern European history; see her "Captain John Smith's Hungary and Transylvania," in Bradford Smith, *Captain John Smith: His Life and Legend* (Philadelphia, 1953), app. 1; and Laura Polanyi Striker and Bradford Smith, "The Rehabilitation of Captain John Smith," *Journal of Southern History* 28 (1962): 474–481.

15. Smith, *True Travels*, 166. Richard Knolles wrote about these campaigns in *The Generall Historie of the Turkes* (n.p., 1621), 1115–19, 1134–39. On the siege of Szekesfehervar, see Caroline Finkel, *The Administration of Warfare: The Ottoman Military Campaigns in Hungary, 1593–1606* (Vienna, 1988), 18.

16. This description is Barbour's from his intro. to Smith, *Works*, 1:xxx.

17. For this account, see Smith, *True Travels*, 173–175.

18. On the role of Tatars in Ottoman warfare, see Finkel, *Administration of Warfare*, 97–107.

19. On the powers of matriarchs in Ottoman society, see Leslie P. Peirce, *The Imperial Harem: Women and Sovereignty in the Ottoman Empire* (Oxford, 1993).

20. Smith, *True Travels*, 186–189. On the role of the janissaries, see Daniel Goffman, *Ottoman Empire and Early Modern Europe* (Cambridge, 2002), 64–69, 77–83.

21. Smith, *True Travels*, 189–190.

22. Ibid., 194–199. Smith drew on previously published English accounts of this region in his writing. By the time he set down his account, it had been thirty years since he had been there, and he presumably used these sources both to refresh his own memory and to expand the scope of his memoir. See the notes by Barbour.

23. Ibid., 200–202.

24. Ibid., 203–205. Barbour argues that Smith drew on the writing of Samuel Purchas for this account of the Moroccan court.

25. Robert C. Davis, *Christian Slaves, Muslim Masters: White Slavery in the Mediterranean, the Barbary Coast, and Italy, 1500–1800* (New York, 2003), 15, 23 (on numbers), 74–83 (on the "brutal" conditions for galley slaves). See also Linda Colley, *Captives: Britain, Empire, and the World, 1600–1850* (London, 2002), chaps. 2–3; David Delison Hebb, *Piracy and the English Government, 1616–1642* (Aldershot, 1994); and Nabil Matar, "Introduction: England and Mediterranean Captivity, 1577–1704," in Daniel J. Vitkus, ed., *Piracy, Slavery, and Redemption: Barbary Captivity Narratives from Early Modern England* (New York, 2001), 1–53.

26. Knolles, *Generall Historie of the Turkes*, "Preface to the Reader," dated 1610. Knolles died in 1610, so this preface was reprinted in subsequent editions.

27. Patrick Copland, *Virginia's God Be Thanked* (London, 1622), 19–20.

28. Thomas Dallam, "A brefe Relations of my Travell from The Royall Cittie of London towardes The Straites of Mariemediteranum, and what hapened by the waye," in *Early Voyages and Travels in the Levant*, ed. J. Theodore Bent (London, 1893), 1–98, quotes 64, 69–70; Lello's letter to Sir Robert Cecil is xii–xiv, quote xiii.

29. Ibid.,62, 74–75, 84.

30. John Rawlins, *The Famous and Wonderfull Recoverie of a Ship of Bristoll, called the Exchange, from the Turkish Pirates of Argier* (London, 1622), sigs. B3, Ev, E4. On Dallam and Rawlins, see Mary C. Fuller, "English Turks and Resistant Travelers: Conversion to Islam and Homosocial Courtship," in Ivo Kamps and Jyotsna G. Singh, eds., *Travel Knowledge: European "Discoveries" in the Early Modern Period* (New York and Houndmills, 2001), 66–73.

31. *Proclamation against Pirats*, in James F. Larkin and Paul L. Hughes, eds., *Stuart Royal Proclamations*, vol. 1, *Royal Proclamations of King James I, 1603–1625* (Oxford, 1973), 203–206. On Ward's style of life, see Smith, *True Travels*, 239.

32. Maija Jansson, ed., *Proceedings in Parliament, 1614* (Philadelphia, 1988), 200–201, 206–207, 210.

33. S. G. Culliford, *William Strachey, 1572–1621* (Charlottesville, 1965), chaps. 4–5.

34. See James Ellison, *George Sandys: Travel, Colonialism, and Tolerance in the Seventeenth Century* (Cambridge, 2002); and Richard Beale Davis, *George Sandys, Poet-Adventurer* (London and New York, 1955).

35. George Sandys, preface to *A Relation of a Journey begun An: Dom: 1610. Foure Bookes Containing a description of the Turkish Empire, of Ægypt, of the Holy Land, of the Remote parts of Italy, and Ilands adjoyning* (London, 1615).

36. Ibid., 14, 27.

37. Ibid., 19, 21, 12, 27–28.

38. Knolles, *Generall Historie of the Turkes*, 1142.

39. Sandys, *Relation of a Journey*, 31, 34–37, 42–43, 52–35, quotes 31, 53.

40. Ibid., 57–58; Knolles, "Preface to the Reader," in *Generall Historie of the Turkes*.

41. Sandys, *Relation of a Journey*, 58–61, quotes 59, 60–61.

42. Ibid., 42; Christine Woodhead, "'The Present Terrour of the World'? Contemporary Views of the Ottoman Empire c.1600," *History* 72 (1987): 20–37. On Sandys and other travelers, see Daniel J. Vitkus, "Trafficking with the Turk: English Travelers in the Ottoman Empire during the Early Seventeenth Century," in Kamps and Singh, *Travel Knowledge*, 35–52.

43. Sandys, *Relation of a Journey*, 47–51.

44. Knolles, "Preface to the Reader"; Rawlins, *Famous and Wonderfull Recoverie*, sig. Ev.

45. Knolles, "Preface to the Reader." On these issues, see Nabil Matar, *Islam in Britain, 1558–1685* (Cambridge, 1998), chaps. 1–2; and Davis, *Christian Slaves, Muslim Masters*, esp. 42–43. Gary Taylor and Jonathan Bate both assert that Shakespeare probably read Knolles's *Generall Historie* and drew on it in writing *Othello*. See Taylor, "Shakespeare's Mediterranean *Measure for Measure*," in Tom Clayton, Susan Brock, and Vicente Forés, eds., *Shakespeare and the Mediterranean* (Cranbury, N.J., 2004), 245; and Bate, "Shakespeare's Islands," ibid., 296–297.

46. This argument is made in Ellison, *George Sandys*.

3. INDIAN EXPERIENCE OF THE ATLANTIC

1. Sabine MacCormack, "Limits of Understanding: Perceptions of Greco-Roman and Amerindian Paganism in Early Modern Europe," in Karen Ordahl Kupperman, ed., *America in European Consciousness, 1493–1750* (Chapel Hill, 1995), 79–129.

2. David J. Weber, *The Spanish Frontier in North America* (New Haven, 1992), 24, 42; Samuel Eliot Morison, *The European Discovery of America: The Northern Voyages, A.D. 500–1600* (New York, 1971), 97–99.

3. Richard Hakluyt, *A Particuler Discourse concerninge the Greate Necessitie and Manifolde Commodyties that are like to growe to this Realme of Englande by the Westerne Discoveries Lately Attempted, written in the yere 1584*, ed. David B. Quinn and Alison M. Quinn (London, 1993), known as *The Discourse of Western Planting*, Cap. 18, p. 88; M. David Powel, "The voyage of Madoc the sonne of Owen Guyneth Prince of Northwales to the West Indies, in the yeere 1170," in Richard Hakluyt, ed., *The Principall Navigations, Voiages, Traffiques, and Discoveries of the English Nation* (London, 1589), 506–507; George Peckham, *A True Reporte of the Newfound Landes* (1583), in David B. Quinn, ed., *The Voyages and Colonising Enterprises of Sir Humphrey Gilbert*, 2 vols. (London, 1940), 2:459; Edward Hayes, *A report of the voyage and successe thereof, attempted in the yeere of our Lord 1583 by sir Humfrey Gilbert knight*, in Quinn, *Gilbert Voyages*, 2:398.

4. Virginia Company, *True Declaration of the Estate of the Colonie in Virginia*, in David B. Quinn et al., eds., *New American World: A Documentary History of North America to 1612*, 5 vols. (New York, 1979), 5:251; Peter Winne to Sir John Egerton, November 26, 1608, in Philip L. Barbour, ed., *The Jamestown Voyages Under the First Charter, 1606–1609*, 2 vols. (Cambridge, 1969), 1:246.

5. Sir Humphrey Gilbert, *A discourse of a discoverie for a new passage to Cataia* (1576), in Quinn, *Gilbert Voyages*, 1:129–164, quote 148.

6. Álvar Núñez Cabeza de Vaca, *The Narrative of Cabeza de Vaca*, ed. Rolena Adorno and Patrick Charles Pautz (Lincoln, 1999, 2003), 2, 78–79, 153–154.

7. William Strachey, *The Historie of Travell into Virginia Britania*, 1612, ed. Louis B. Wright and Virginia Freund (London, 1953), 92.

8. *The Voyages of Jacques Cartier*, trans. H. P. Biggar, rev. and intro. Ramsay Cook (Toronto, 1993), 20. "Napou tou daman asurtat" has been interpreted as a phrase in Micmac offering friendship.

9. David Beers Quinn, *England and the Discovery of America, 1481–1620* (New York, 1974), chap. 1.

10. Luys Hernández de Biedma, "Relation of the Island of Florida," in *The De Soto Chronicles: The Expedition of Hernando De Soto to North America in 1539–1543*, ed. Lawrence A. Clayton, Vernon James Knight Jr., and Edward C. Moore, 2 vols. (Tuscaloosa, 1993), 1:224; Hernando de Soto to the Justice and Board of Magistrates in Santiago de Cuba, July 9, 1539, ibid., 375–377. For a full discussion of this expedition and the Indian polities among which it traveled, see Charles Hudson, *Knights of Spain, Warriors of the Sun: Hernando de Soto and the South's Ancient Chiefdoms* (Athens, Ga., 1997); see also Daniel K. Richter, *Facing East from Indian Country: A Native History of Early America* (Cambridge, Mass., 2001), 18–26; and Jerald T. Milanich, *Florida's Indians from Ancient Times to the Present* (Gainesville, 1998), 137–148.

11. Garcilaso de la Vega, *La Florida*, in *De Soto Chronicles*, 2:99–120, quotes 101, 108, 112, 114–115, 474. Hirrihugua and his people were Tocobaga Indians; see Ripley P. Bullen, "Tocobaga Indians and the Safety Harbor Culture," in Jerald T. Milanich and Samuel Proctor, eds., *Tachale: Essays on the Indians of Florida and Southeastern Georgia during the Historic Period* (Gainesville, 1978), 50–58.

12. Rodrigo Rangel reported the discovery of Spanish goods in graves. His account was included in *Historia general y natural de las Indias* by Gonzalo Fernández de Oviedo y Valdés; see *De Soto Chronicles*, 1:279. Paul E. Hoffman, *A New Andalucia and a Way to the Orient: The American Southeast during the Sixteenth Century* (Baton Rouge, 1990), pt. 1.

13. Rangel's report in Oviedo's *Historia general y natural de las Indias* is in *De Soto Chronicles*, 1:285.

14. This discussion draws on two works by David B. Quinn, *North America from Earliest Discovery to First Settlements* (New York, 1977), chap. 10, and "The Attempted Colonization of Florida by the French, 1562–1565," in *Explorers and Colonies: America, 1500–1625* (London, 1990), 257–284; John T. McGrath, *The French in Early Florida: In the Eye of the Hurricane* (Gainesville, 2000); and Paul E. Hoffman, *Florida's Frontiers* (Bloomington, 2002), and *A New Andalucia*, pt. 3.

15. See John T. Worth, *Timucuan Chiefdoms of Spanish Florida*, 2 vols. (Gainesville, 1998), 1:19–25.

16. René de Laudonnière, "The second voyage unto Florida, made and written by Captaine Laudonnière, which fortified and inhabited there two Summers and one whole Winter," in Quinn et al., *New American World*, 2:319–353, quotes 339–340. The Calusa leader extended his domain from its core on the southwest coast "throughout south Florida and up the Atlantic coast to the St. Augustine area" in the mid-sixteenth century. See Clifford M. Lewis, "The Calusa," in Milanich and Proctor, *Tachale*, 19–49; and Randolph J. Widmer, "The Structure of Southeastern Chiefdoms," in Charles Hudson and Carmen Chaves Tesser, eds., *The Forgotten Centuries: Indians and Europeans in the American South, 1521–1704* (Athens, Ga., 1994), 125–155, quote 144. In 1763 Ojibwe Indians cut off the hair of a captive, John Rutherford, and "carefully put [it] by"; Gregory Evans Dowd, *War under Heaven: Pontiac, the Indian Nations, and the British Empire* (Baltimore, 2002), 92.

17. Laudonnière, "Second voyage unto Florida," 344–345. On environmental conditions at this time, see David G. Anderson, David W. Stahle, and Malcolm K. Cleaveland, "Paleoclimate and the Potential Food Reserves of Mississippian Societies: A Case Study from the Savannah River Valley," *American Antiquity* 60 (1995): 258–286.

18. John Sparkes, "Report on Florida," in Quinn et al., *New American World*, 2:363–370, quote 366. John Sparkes sailed in Hawkins's fleet. See Harry Kelsey, *Sir John Hawkins: Queen Elizabeth's Slave Trader* (New Haven, 2003).

19. Pedro Menéndez de Avilés to Philip II, October 15, 1565, in Quinn et al., *New American World*, 395–404, quotes 397–398. "Lutheran" was employed as a blanket term for Protestants.

20. For this account, see Gonzalo Solís de Merás, *Memorial of the Adelantado Pedro Menéndez de Avilés*, trans. and ed. Jeannette T. Connor (Gainesville, 1964), 138–152, 173–176, quotes 139–140, 145, 147, 151.

21. Ibid., 167–169, 174.

22. Juan de la Bandera, "Relation," September 1567–March 1568, trans. Paul E. Hoffman, in Charles Hudson, ed., *The Juan Pardo Expeditions: Exploration of the Carolinas and Tennessee, 1566–1568* (Washington, D.C., 1990), 255–296.

23. For this account, see *Memoir of Do. d'Escalante Fontaneda, respecting Florida. Written in Spain, about the year 1575*, ed. David O. True (Coral Gables, 1945), 25–36, quotes 31, 32, 33–34 (rev. ed. of the 1854 trans. by Buckingham Smith); Solís de Merás, *Memorial*, passim. The dates of Escalante's shipwreck and redemption are not clear. Some have argued that he was one of the two Spaniards rescued by Ribault in 1562 and that he had returned to Spain before accompanying Menéndez. Others think he was among those collected by Menéndez after his arrival. See True's introduction to the *Memoir*, 12–13, 19–20.

24. Eugene Lyon, *The Enterprise of Florida: Pedro Menéndez de Avilés and the Spanish Conquest of 1565–1568* (Gainesville, 1983), 149.

25. Pedro Menéndez de Avilés, "Report" (1573), in Jeannette Thurber Connor, trans. and ed., *Colonial Records of Spanish Florida*, 2 vols. (Deland, Fla., 1925–1930), 1:31–35, quote 35; Lyon, *Enterprise of Florida*, 149.

26. Solís de Merás, *Memorial*, 189–194, 205–211, 219–230, 237–238. Another contemporary account is Bartolome Barrientos, *Pedro Menéndez de Avilés: Founder of Florida* (1567), trans. Anthony Kerrigan (Gainesville, 1965). On all the events in Florida, see Andres Gonzalez de Barcia Carballido y Zuñiga, *Chronological History of the Continent of Florida* (1723), trans. Anthony Kerrigan (Gainesville, 1951), Sixth Decade, 44–155; Lyon, *Enterprise of Florida*, 149–182; and Lewis, "The Calusa," 27, 44.

27. Solís de Merás, *Memorial*, 172, 177, 225–226.

28. David Ingram, *The Relation of David Ingram of Barking*, in Hakluyt, *Principall Navigations*, 557–562. On the Hawkins expedition and the background of these events, see Kelsey, *Sir John Hawkins*, 83–93, 112–113. See the discussion of probable amalgamation in Lewis, "The Calusa," 43–47.

29. Quinn, *North America from Earliest Discovery to First Settlements*, 372–373. Inuit is plural; Inuk is singular. On Frobisher's three voyages, see James McDermott, *Martin Frobisher: Elizabethan Privateer* (New Haven, 2001), chaps. 8–12.

30. Kirsten A. Seaver, "How Strange is a Stranger? A Survey of Opportunities for Inuit-European Contact in the Davis Strait before 1576," in Thomas H. B. Symons, ed., *Meta Incognita: A Discourse of Discovery. Martin Frobisher's Arctic Expeditions, 1576–1578*, 2 vols. (Hull, Quebec, 1999), 2:523–552.

31. George Best, *A True Discourse of the late voyages of discoverie, for the finding of a passage to Cathaya, by the Northweast* (London, 1578), rpt. in Vilhjalmur Stefansson, ed., *The Three Voyages of Martin Frobisher*, 2 vols. (London, 1938), 1:86, 126.

32. David B. Quinn, "Frobisher in the Context of Early English Northwest Exploration," in Symons, *Meta Incognita*, 1:7–18; James McDermott, "The Company of Cathay: The Financing and Organization of the Frobisher Voyages," ibid., 147–178; William H. Sherman, "John Dee's Role in Martin Frobisher's Northwest Enterprise," ibid., 284–298.

33. Best, *True Discourse of the late voyages of discoverie*, 65–67.

34. Ibid., 68–69. "Wistly" meant "intently" but also carried overtones of "wistfully."

35. Ibid., 70–72.

36. Ibid., 68–69.

37. Sir James Watt and Ann Savours, "The Captured 'Countrey People': Their Depiction and Medical History," in Symons, *Meta Incognita*, 2:553–562; William W. Fitzhugh and Dosia Laeyendecker, "A Brief Narrative of the Frobisher Voyages," in William W. Fitzhugh and Jacqueline S. Olin, eds., *Archaeology of the Frobisher Voyages* (Washington, D.C., 1993), 11–14. See also William C. Sturtevant and David B. Quinn, "This New Prey: Eskimos in Europe in 1567, 1576, and 1577," in Christian F. Feest, ed., *Indians and Europe: An Interdisciplinary Collection of Essays* (Aachen, 1987), 61–140; and Paul W. DePasquale, "'Worth the Noting': European Ambivalence and Aboriginal Agency in Meta Incognita, 1576–1578," in Jennifer S. H. Brown and Elizabeth Vibert, eds., *Reading beyond Words: Contexts for Native History*, 2nd ed. (Peterborough, Ontario, 2003), 5–38.

38. Charles Francis Hall, *Arctic Researches and Life among the Esquimaux in the Years 1860, 1861 and 1862* (New York, 1865); Susan Rowley, "Frobisher Miksanut: Inuit Accounts of the Frobisher Voyages," in Fitzhugh and Olin, *Archaeology of the Frobisher Voyages*, 27–40; H. G. Jones, "An Early Meeting of Cultures: Inuit and English, 1576–1578," in John Moss, ed., *Echoing Silence: Essays on Artic Narrative* (Ottawa, 1997), 33–41, and "Teaching the Explorers: Some Inuit Contributions to Arctic Discoveries," *Polar Geography* 26 (2002): 4–20; Joyce Chaplin, *Subject Matter: Technology, the Body, and Science on the Anglo-American Frontier, 1500–1676* (Cambridge, Mass., 2001), 57–59; Morison, *European Discovery of America*, 507–510, 516–526.

39. Arthur Barlowe, *The First Voyage Made to the Coastes of America* (1584), in David Beers Quinn, ed., *The Roanoke Voyages, 1584–1590*, 2 vols. (London, 1955), 1:102, 104.

40. Walter Bigges, *A summarie and true discourse of Sir Frances Drakes West Indian Voyage*, 1588, ibid., 296–297; "The *Primrose* Journal of Drake's Voyage," ibid., 305; "A French Account of Drake's Voyage," 1586, ibid., 310. For the foreign observer's report, see Quinn et al., *New American World*, 3:307–310, quote 309.

41. For reports from Santo Domingo, Panama, Cartagena, and Havana of people collected by Drake, see Irene A. Wright, ed. and trans., *Further English Voyages to Spanish America, 1583–1594* (London, 1951), 35, 54, 159, 168, 212. On the decision to abandon Roanoke and the three men, see "*Primrose* Journal," 307–308; and Ralph Lane, *An Account of the Particularities of the imployments of the English men left in Virginia*, 1586, in Quinn, *Roanoke Voyages*, 1:292–293. On Drake's career, see Harry Kelsey, *Sir Francis Drake: The Queen's Pirate* (New Haven, 1998).

42. "The Relation of Pedro Diaz, March 1589," in Quinn, *Roanoke Voyages*, 2:790–791.

43. Hoffman, *Florida's Frontiers*, 76–77. On the drought, see Anderson, Stahle, and Cleaveland, "Paleoclimate and the Potential Food Reserves of Mississippian Societies."

44. George Chapman, Ben Jonson, and John Marston, *Eastward Hoe* (London, 1605), quotes 3.3. "Eastward Ho" and "Westward Ho" were the traditional cries of watermen on the Thames in London. Chapman and Jonson were briefly imprisoned because a line in the play lamenting the spread of Scots over the world was deemed an insult to King James and the Scots who had come south with him when he succeeded Queen Elizabeth.

45. George Percy, *Observations gathered out of a Discourse of the Plantation of the Southerne Colonie in Virginia by the English, 1606*, in Barbour, *Jamestown Voyages*, 1:140.

46. Robert Fabian, "Chronicle," in Hakluyt, *Principall Navigations*, 515.

47. Frances Karttunen, *Between Worlds: Interpreters, Guides, and Survivors* (New Brunswick, N.J., 1994), 4, 305–307; Sandra Messenger Cypess, *La Malinche in Mexican Literature: From History to Myth* (Austin, 1991), 28; Fernando Benítez, *The Century after Cortés*, trans. Joan MacLean (Chicago, 1965), 156, 175–176; James F. Brooks, *Captives and Cousins: Slavery, Kinship, and Community in the Southwest Borderlands* (Chapel Hill, 2002), 25. On "Santiago" as a battle cry, see Weber, *Spanish Frontier in North America*, 15, 20.

48. For this account, see *Voyages of Jacques Cartier*, xi–xii, xxxix, 27, 49–50, 54, 59, 69–72, 83–87, 96–99; and Roger Schlesinger and Arthur P. Stabler, eds., *André Thevet's North America: A Sixteenth-Century View* (Kingston and Montreal, 1986), 9.

49. Marvin T. Smith, *Coosa: The Rise and Fall of a Southeastern Mississippian Chiefdom* (Gainesville, 2000), 34–48; Weber, *Spanish Frontier*, 67–68. Documents from the Luna expedition are collected in Herbert Ingram Priestley, trans. and ed., *The Luna Papers*, 2 vols. (Deland, Fla., 1928). Charles M. Hudson, drawing on a lifetime of research, has imaginatively reconstructed the experience of these men and their reception in Coosa, along with the struggle of the Coosa woman to reintegrate into Coosa life; see Hudson, *Conversations with the High Priest of Coosa* (Chapel Hill, 2003).

50. This account is from "Letter of Luís de Quirós and Juan Baptista de Segura to Juan de Hinistrosa, From Ajacán, September 12, 1570," in Clifford M. Lewis, S. J., and Albert J. Loomie, S. J., *The Spanish Jesuit Mission in Virginia, 1570–1572* (Chapel Hill, 1953), 89–91; "Letter of Juan Rogel to Francis Borgia, From the Bay of the Mother of God, August 28, 1572," ibid., 109–121, quote 120; "Relation of Juan de la Carrerra," 1600, ibid., 131–139; "Relation of Bartolomé Martínez," 1610, ibid., 155–162; "Relation of Luis Gerónimo de Oré," ca. 1615, ibid., 179–185; and Francisco Sacchini, *Borgia: the Third Part of the History of the Society of Jesus*, ca. 1622, bk. 6, ibid., 220–225. Fathers Quiros and Segura were among those killed. On the mission and its context, see Charlotte Gradie, "The Powhatans in the Context of the Spanish Empire" in Helen Rountree, ed., *Powhatan Foreign Relations, 1500–1722* (Charlottesville, 1993), 154–172, and Gradie "Spanish Jesuits in Virginia: The Mission That Failed," *Virginia Magazine of History and Biography*, 96 (1988): 131–156; Hoffman, *Florida's Frontiers*, 42, and *A New Andalucia*, 181–187, 261–266. Carl Bridenbaugh in *Early Americans* (New York, 1981), chap. 1, argued that Don Luís did indeed live to see Jamestown founded and that he was Opechancanough, who led the two great attacks on the colony in 1622 and 1644. But Helen Rountree and E. Randolph Turner III argue that not only was Opechancanough a Paspahegh and therefore not part of Powhatan's family, but also his strategies in dealing with the English were not those of someone with Don Luís's knowledge of Europeans; see Rountree and Turner, *Before and after Jamestown: Virginia's Powhatans and Their Predecessors* (Gainesville, 2002), 51–53.

51. John White, "The Fourth Voyage Made to Virginia" (1587), in Quinn, *Roanoke Voyages*, 2:531.

52. Entries in Bideford Parish Register, ibid., 1:495. See Alden Vaughan, "Ralegh's Indian Interpreters," *William and Mary Quarterly*, 3rd ser., 59 (2002): 341–376.

53. See Lewis and Loomie, *Spanish Jesuit Mission in Virginia*, 56; and "Relation of Luis Gerónimo de Oré," ibid., 185–188.

54. Ralph Hamor, *A True Discourse of the Present Estate of Virginia* (London, 1615), 13.

55. Robert Beverley, *The History and Present State of Virginia* (1705), ed. Louis B. Wright (Chapel Hill, 1947), 61. Beverley's reference to St. Barbe shows how up-to-date he was on his reading. Louis Hennepin, who had traveled with La Salle in the discovery of the Mississippi River, featured the rich mines of St. Barbe "in New Mexico" in the title and dedication of his *New Discovery of a Vast Country in America* (London, 1698), ed. Reuben Gold Thwaites, 2 vols. (Chicago, 1903). The rich silver mines are in present-day San Bartolomé Valley in South Chihuahua, Mexico.

56. *A True Relation of such occurrences and accidents of noate as hath hapned in Virginia*, 1608, in *The Complete Works of Captain John Smith*, ed. Philip L. Barbour, 3 vols. (Chapel Hill, 1986), 1:51. Edward Maria Wingfield, first president of the Virginia council and therefore effectively governor, also wrote about this incident; see Wingfield, "Discourse," 1608, in Barbour, *Jamestown Voyages*, 1:227; David Beers Quinn, "Virginians on the Thames in 1603," in *England and the Discovery of America, 1481–1620* (London, 1974), 419–431; Alden T. Vaughan, "Powhatans Abroad: Virginia Indians in England," in Robert Appelbaum and John Wood Sweet, eds., *Envisioning an English Empire: Jamestown and the Making of the North Atlantic World* (Philadelphia, 2005), 49–51.

57. Captain John Smith, *The Generall Historie of Virginia, New-England and the Summer Isles* (London, 1624), in *Works*, 2:173–178.

58. Robert C. Davis, *Christian Slaves, Muslim Masters: White Slavery in the Mediterranean, the Barbary Coast, and Italy, 1500–1800* (New York, 2003), 105; Nabil Matar, "Introduction: England and Mediterranean Captivity, 1577–1704," in Daniel J. Vitkus, ed., *Piracy, Slavery, and Redemption: Barbary Captivity Narratives from Early Modern England* (New York, 2001), 36–37; Solís de Merás, *Memorial*, 138–152.

59. Adorno and Pautz, intro. to *Narrative of Cabeza de Vaca*, 22; Linda Colley, *Captives: Britain, Empire and the World, 1600–1850* (London, 2002), chap. 3, esp. 79.

4. ENGLISH HUNGER FOR THE NEW

1. Thomas Trevilian, Commonplace Book, 1608, is in the Folger Library, Washington, D.C.; for the table of distances, see fol. 24v. The 1616 book is published as Nicolas Barker, ed., *The Great Book of Thomas Trevilian*, 2 vols. (London, 2000), quotes xv, 15, 81. I thank Zvi Ben-Dor for the interpretation of Quinzay.

2. Thomas Palmer, *An Essay of the Meanes how to make our Travailes, into forraine Countries, the more profitable and honourable* (London, 1606), quote 75; Francis Bacon, "Of Travel," in *The Complete Essays of Francis Bacon*, ed. Henry LeRoy Finch (New York, 1963), 48–50. On guides to travel, see Justin Stagl, *A History of Curiosity: The Theory of Travel, 1550–1800* (Chur, Switzerland, 1995).

3. Ahmad bin Qasim, *Kitab Nasir al-Din ala al-Qawm al-Kafirin*, in Nabil Matar,

ed., *In the Lands of the Christians* (New York and London, 2003), quotes 9, 17–18, 31, 33, 36–38.

4. G. J. Toomer, *Eastern Wisedome and Learning: The Study of Arabic in Seventeenth-Century England* (Oxford, 1996), chaps. 2–4, 200–201; Nabil Matar, *Islam in Britain, 1558–1685* (Cambridge, 1998), chap. 3. The first correct English translation of the Koran was not published until 1734; Toomer, *Eastern Wisedome*, 308.

5. "Instructions to be observed by Thomas Bavin," in David B. Quinn et al., eds., *New American World: A Documentary History of North America to 1612*, 5 vols. (New York, 1979), 3:242–244.

6. The paintings and engravings are reproduced in Paul Hulton and D. B. Quinn, eds., *The American Drawings of John White, 1577–1590* (London and Chapel Hill, 1964). Some of them can be seen online at www.virtualjamestown.org.

7. John Parkinson, *Paradisi in Sole Paradisus Terrestris* (London, 1629), 579.

8. Henry Lowood, "The New World and the European Catalog of Nature," in Karen Ordahl Kupperman, ed., *America in European Consciousness, 1493–1750* (Chapel Hill, 1995), 295–323.

9. John Frampton, *Joyefull Newes Out of the Newe founde World* (London, 1577).

10. Parkinson, *Paradisi*, 152–153, 346, 378, 430, 575. On the Tradescants and their circle, see Penelope Leith-Ross, *The Tradescants: Gardeners to the Rose and Lily Queen* (London, 1984); Mea Allan, *The Tradescants: Their Plants, Gardens, and Museum, 1570–1662* (London, 1964). See also Rebecca Bushnell, *Green Desire: Imagining Early Modern English Gardens* (Ithaca, N.Y., 2003).

11. Peter Mundy, *The Travels of Peter Mundy, in Europe and Asia, 1608–1667*, ed. R. C. Temple, 3 vols. (London, 1919), 3: pt. 1, 1–3.

12. *The Tempest*, 2.2. See Christian Feest, "The Collecting of American Indian Artifacts in Europe, 1493–1750," in Kupperman, *America in European Consciousness*, 324–360; Paula Findlen, *Possessing Nature: Museums, Collecting, and Scientific Culture in Early Modern Italy* (Berkeley, 1994); Oliver Impey and Arthur MacGregor, eds., *The Origins of Museums: The Cabinet of Curiosities in Sixteenth- and Seventeenth-Century Europe* (Oxford, 1985). A doit was worth half a farthing; the term was used to indicate the smallest unit of money.

13. Thomas Churchyard, *A pleasant Discourse of Court and Wars* (London, 1596), sigs. A3v, C3v–C4.

14. Philip L. Barbour, "Captain John Smith and the London Theater," *Virginia Magazine of History and Biography* 83 (1975): 277–279.

15. *The Generall Historie of Virginia, New-England and the Summer Isles* (London, 1624), in *The Complete Works of Captain John Smith*, ed. Philip L. Barbour, 3 vols. (Chapel Hill, 1986), II: 41–42.

16. John Smith, *The Proceedings of the English Colony in Virginia*, 1612, ibid., 1:267–268; Smith, *Generall Historie*, 41, 42. I thank David Shields for the reference to *The Hungarian Lion*.

17. Ben Jonson, *Epicene, or the Silent Woman*, 2.5.12–13.

18. *The True Travels, Adventures, and Observations of Captaine John Smith* (1630), in *Works*, 3:239.

19. Daniel J. Vitkus, ed., *Three Turk Plays from Early Modern England: Selimus, A Christian Turned Turk, and The Renegado* (New York, 2000), quote 256.

20. On all these themes, see Nabil Matar, "The 'Renegade' in English Drama," *Islam in Britain*, 52–63 and passim; Jean E. Howard, "Gender on the Periphery,"

in Tom Clayton, Susan Brock, and Vicente Forés, eds., *Shakespeare and the Mediterranean* (Cranbury, N.J., 2004), 344–362; Richmond Barbour, *Before Orientalism: London's Theatre of the East, 1576–1626* (Cambridge, 2003); Daniel Vitkus, *Turning Turk: English Theater and the Multicultural Mediterranean, 1570–1630* (London, 2003); Charles L. Squier, *John Fletcher* (Boston, 1986), 81–85; A. J. Hoenselaars, *Images of Englishmen and Foreigners in the Drama of Shakespeare and His Contemporaries: A Study of Stage Characters and National Identity in English Renaissance Drama, 1558–1642* (Rutherford, N.J., 1992), 174–178

21. See Jean E. Howard, "An English Lass amid the Moors: Gender, Race, Sexuality, and National Identity in Heywood's *The Fair Maid of the West*," in Margo Hendricks and Patricia Parker, eds., *Women, "Race," and Writing in the Early Modern Period* (London and New York, 1994), 101–117; and Vitkus, *Turning Turk*, 128–143.

22. For John Hawkins's coat of arms, see Harry Kelsey, *Sir John Hawkins: Queen Elizabeth's Slave Trader* (New Haven, 2003), 32–33 and n. 86, 314. On Drake's medal, see David Shields, "The Drake Jewel," *Uncommon Sense* 118 (2004).

23. Ben Jonson, *The Masque of Blackness* (1605) and *The Masque of Beauty* (1608), in *The Complete Masques of Ben Jonson*, ed. Stephen Orgel (New Haven, 1969), 47–74, quotes 49–52, 55–56. On their imagery, composition, and staging, see ibid., 3–7; D. J. Gordon, "The Imagery of Ben Jonson's *The Masque of Blacknesse* and *The Masque of Beautie*," *Journal of the Warburg and Courtauld Institutes* 6 (1943): 122–141; Barbour, *Before Orientalism*, 70–87, 96; and Vitkus, *Turning Turk*, 81.

24. A. A. Almada, *Brief Treatise on the Rivers of Guinea*, trans. and ed. P. E. H. Hair, section reproduced in George E. Brooks, *Landlords and Strangers: Ecology, Society, and Trade in Western Africa, 1000–1630* (Boulder, 1993), 211–212; Susan Skilliter, "William Harborne, the First English Ambassador, 1583–1588," in *Four Centuries of Turco-British-Relations*, ed. William Hale and Ali Ihsan Bagis (Beverley, North Humberside, 1984), 19–20.

25. Keeling's journal is partially reproduced in Ivo Kamps and Jyotsna G. Singh, eds., *Travel Knowledge: European "Discoveries" in the Early Modern Period* (New York and Houndmills, 2001), 211–222, quote 220. For an analysis of this voyage and the context and meaning of *Hamlet*, see Gary Taylor, "*Hamlet* in Africa 1607," ibid., 223–248. For a modern attempt to present *Hamlet* in Africa and its consequences, see Laura Bohannon, "Shakespeare in the Bush," in Alan Terne, ed., *Ants, Indians, and Little Dinosaurs* (New York, 1975), 203–216.

26. Pedro de Castañeda, *Narrative of the expedition to Cíbola undertaken in 1540*, in George P. Hammond and Agapito Rey, eds. and trans., *Narratives of the Coronado Expedition, 1540–1542* (Albuquerque, 1940), 191–283, quotes 219–220, 234–235, 238; Coronado to the king, October 20, 1541, ibid., 180.

27. William Strachey, *The Historie of Travell into Virginia Britania*, 1612, ed. Louis B. Wright and Virginia Freund (London, 1953), 73; John Smith, *A True Relation of such occurrences and accidents of noate as hath hapned in Virginia*, 1608, in *Works*, 1:53; Smith, *A Map of Virginia*, 1612, in *Works*, 1:167; Roger Williams, *A Key into the Language of America* (London, 1643), 130 [misnumbered 122].

28. "Representation of Philip Cortlandt and Daniel Horsmanden to Council of Trade and Plantations," August 10, 1738, *Calendar of State Papers, Colonial Series, America and West Indies, 1574–1739*, consultant editors Karen Ordahl Kupperman, John C. Appleby, and Mandy Banton (London, 2000), CD-ROM.

29. Virginia Company, "Instructions given by way of advice," in Philip L. Barbour, ed., *The Jamestown Voyages Under the First Charter, 1606–1609*, 2 vols. (Cambridge, 1969), 1:52–53.

30. Michel de Montaigne, "On the Cannibals," in *The Essays: A Selection*, ed. M. A. Screech (London, 2004), 83. On definitions, see Penelope Gouk, *Music, Science and Natural Magic in Seventeenth-Century England* (New Haven, 1999), 66–67.

31. Edward Hayes, *A report of the voyage and successe thereof, attempted in the yeere of our Lord 1583 by sir Humfrey Gilbert knight*, in David B. Quinn, ed., *The Voyages and Colonising Enterprises of Sir Humphrey Gilbert*, 2 vols. (London, 1940), 2:402; Silvester Jourdain, *A Discovery of the Bermudas, Otherwise Called the Isle of Devils* (1610), in Louis B. Wright, ed., *A Voyage to Virginia in 1609* (Charlottesville, 1964), 103–116, quote 109.

32. John Guy to Sir Perceval Willoughby, October 6, 1610, in Gillian T. Cell, ed., *Newfoundland Discovered: English Attempts at Colonisation, 1610–1630* (London, 1982), 63; William Strachey, "A True Reportory of the Wreck and Redemption of Sir Thomas Gates, Knight," in Louis B. Wright, ed., *A Voyage to Virginia in 1609* (Charlottesville, 1964), 1–101, quote 96.

33. Captain John Smith, *A Description of New England* (London, 1616), in *Works*, 1:333; Robert Gordon of Lochinvar, *Encouragements to Under-takers* (Edinburgh, 1625), sig. C3v.

34. Virginia Company, "Instructions given by way of advice," 53–54.

35. Thomas Dermer to Samuel Purchas, December 27, 1619, in Purchas, *Hakluytus Posthumus or Purchas His Pilgrimes*, 5 vols. (London, 1625), 4:1778.

36. William Wood, *New Englands Prospect* (London, 1634), sigs. A2,A3, 54.

37. Samuel Purchas, *Purchas His Pilgrimage*, 2nd ed. (London, 1614), 719.

38. *The Voyages of Jacques Cartier*, trans. H. P. Biggar, rev. and intro. Ramsay Cook (Toronto, 1993), 36; Aristotle, *Metaphysics*, bk. 1, in *The Complete Works of Aristotle*, 2 vols., ed. Jonathan Barnes (Princeton, 1984), 2:1552–53. On new ways of thinking, see Barbara J. Shapiro, *A Culture of Fact: England, 1550–1720* (Ithaca, N.Y., 2000).

39. *The Voyages of Jacques Cartier*, trans. H. P. Biggar, rev. and intro. Ramsay Cook (Toronto, 1993), 10.

40. Genesis 4:11–12, 16 in the Geneva Bible.

41. Ralph Lane, dedication to Thomas Harriot, *A Briefe and True Report of the new found land of Virginia* (London, 1588), in *The Roanoke Voyages, 1584–1590*, ed. David Beers Quinn, 2 vols. (London, 1955), 1:319.

42. Smith, *Map of Virginia*, 150–151, 175–177; Smith, *Generall Historie*, 41, 129, 437, 468; Smith, *Advertisements For the unexperienced Planters of New-England, or any-where* (London, 1631), in *Works*, 3:294, 302; Smith, *A Sea Grammar* (London, 1627), in *Works*, 3:47; Wood, *New Englands Prospect*, sigs. A2, A3. Edward Hayes, who wrote the story of Sir Humphrey Gilbert's ill-fated attempt to found a colony in America in the early 1580s, struck the same themes as Smith. He said his words should be believed because "my selfe was an eye witnesse," and he blamed all failures on "ill disposed people" in the company. Hayes, *Report of the voyage*, 389.

43. Sir Walter Ralegh, *The Discoverie of the Large, Rich and Bewtiful Empyre of Guiana, 1596*, ed. Neil L. Whitehead (Norman, Okla., 1997), 131, 179–180.

44. *The Tempest*, 3.3.23–69.

45. Virginia Company, *True Declaration of the Estate of the Colonie in Virginia*, 1610, in Quinn et al., *New American World*, 5:253.

46. Tradescant's journal is reproduced in Leith-Ross, *The Tradescants*, 53–65, quote 57. The journal was discovered and identified in the Bodleian Library at Oxford in 1814 by Joseph von Hamel and published by him in *England and Russia: Comprising the Voyages of John Tradescant the Elder, Sir Hugh Willoughby, Richard Chancellor, Nelson, and others to the White Sea*, trans. John Studdy Leigh (London, 1854).

47. Parkhurst, "Letter to M. Richard Hakluyt," in E. G. R. Taylor, ed., *The Original Writings and Correspondence of the Two Richard Hakluyts*, 2 vols. (London, 1935), 1:130–131.

48. Joseph Hall, *The Discovery of a new world, or A Description of the South Indies. Hetherto unknowne*, trans. John Healey, 1609, ed. Huntington Brown (Cambridge, Mass., 1937), 64–76, 222–223. On Hall's manuscript original and its context, see R. A. McCabe, *Joseph Hall: A Study in Satire and Meditation* (Oxford, 1982), 6–7, 30, 73–109; for a detailed comparison of the Latin manuscript and the published version, see 321–330. On Healey and his career, see Mark Vessey, "The Citie of God (1610) and the London Virginia Company," *Augustinian Studies* 30 (1999): 257–281.

49. Smith, *Generall Historie*, 464; George Chapman, "De Guiana, Carmen Epicum," in Keymis, *A Relation of the second Voyage to Guiana. Perfourmed and written in the year 1596* (London, 1596), sig. A2v. George Chapman was a member of the circle around Ralegh and knew Thomas Harriot; see M. C. Bradbook, *George Chapman* (London, 1977), 10–11.

50. Ralegh, *Discoverie of Guiana*, 127–128, 198.

5. GRASPING AMERICA'S CONTOURS

1. Peter Heylyn, *Cosmographie in Four Bookes. Containing the Chorographie and Historie of the Whole World* (London, 1652), bk. 1, 250.

2. George Best, *A true discourse of the voyages of discoverie* (London, 1578); John Pory, *A Geographical Historie of Africa* (London, 1600). On the naming of oceans, see Martin W. Lewis, "Dividing the Ocean Sea," *Geographical Review* 89 (1999): 188–214.

3. John Donne, *A Sermon Preached to the Honourable Company of the Virginian Plantation*, in *Five Sermons Upon Special Occasions* (London, 1626), 44; Heylyn, *Cosmographie*, bk. 1, 250, and bk. 4, 95; Fynes Moryson, *An Itinerary Containing his Ten Yeeres Travell Through the Twelve Dominions of Germany, Bohmerland, Sweitzerland, Netherland, Denmark, Poland, Italy, Turky, France, England, Scotland, and Ireland*, 1617, 4 vols. (Glasgow, 1907–8), 4:185.

4. Thomas Gage, *The English-American his Travail by Sea and Land: Or, A New Survey of the West-Indias* (London, 1648), sig. A4.

5. All the documents concerning the Roanoke ventures are in David Beers Quinn, ed., *The Roanoke Voyages, 1584–1590*, 2 vols. (London, 1955). On Wingandacon and Queen Elizabeth's agreement that the land should be named after her, see ibid., 1:116–117, 147, 174; 2:853–854. "Wingandacoia" was included in John Healey's version of John Hall's *Discovery of a new World* as "Womandecoia."

6. Edward Hayes, *A report of the voyage and successe thereof, attempted in the yeere of*

our Lord 1583 by sir Humfrey Gilbert knight, in David B. Quinn, ed., *The Voyages and Colonising Enterprises of Sir Humphrey Gilbert*, 2 vols. (London, 1940), 2:385–423, quote 388.

7. *The True Travels, Adventures, and Observations of Captaine John Smith*, 1630, in Philip L. Barbour, ed., *The Complete Works of Captain John Smith*, 3 vols. (Chapel Hill, 1986), 3:221.

8. Heylyn, *Cosmographie*, bk. 4, 101–105.

9. Samuel Purchas, *Purchas His Pilgrimage*, 2nd ed. (London, 1614), bk. 8 chap. 5, 748.

10. Geoffrey Parker, *The Grand Strategy of Philip II* (New Haven, 1998), 63.

11. See Dava Sobel, *Longitude: The True Story of a Lone Genius who Solved the Greatest Scientific Problem of His Time* (New York, 1995). I thank John Logan Allen for the point about Denver and Easter Island.

12. Pedro de Castañeda, *Narrative of the expedition to Cíbola undertaken in 1540*, in George P. Hammond and Agapito Rey, eds. and trans., *Narratives of the Coronado Expedition, 1540–1542* (Albuquerque, 1940), 243; David J. Weber, *The Spanish Frontier in North America* (New Haven, 1992), 42–55, quote 54; Álvar Núñez Cabeza de Vaca, *The Narrative of Cabeza de Vaca*, ed. Rolena Adorno and Patrick Charles Pautz (Lincoln, 1999, 2003), 168.

13. Virginia Company, "Instructions given by way of advice," 1606, in Philip L. Barbour, ed., *The Jamestown Voyages Under the First Charter, 1606–1609*, 2 vols. (Cambridge, 1969), 49–50. For reports of saltwater beyond the mountains, see John Smith, *A Map of Virginia*, 1612, in Barbour, ed., *Works*, 1:165–166, and *A True Relation of such occurrences and accidents of noate as hath hapned in Virginia*, 1608, ibid., 1:55. For Powhatan's refutation, see Smith, *The Proceedings of the English Colony in Virginia*, 1612, ibid., 1:236.

14. Alexander Whitaker, *Good Newes from Virginia* (London, 1613), 38.

15. On the early history of this thinking, see David B. Quinn, "Frobisher in the Context of Early English Northwest Exploration," in Thomas H. B. Symons, ed., *Meta Incognita: A Discourse of Discovery. Martin Frobisher's Arctic Expeditions, 1576–1578*, 2 vols. (Hull, Quebec, 1999), 1:7–18; Richard I. Ruggles, "The Cartographic Lure of the Northwest Passage: Its Real and Imaginary Geography," ibid., 179–256; and David B. Quinn, *North America from Earliest Discovery to First Settlements* (New York, 1977), 369–384.

16. Castañeda, "Narrative of the Expedition to Cíbola," 280–282.

17. Heylyn, *Cosmographie*, bk. 3, 203; John Lederer, *The Discoveries of John Lederer* (London, 1672), 23.

18. For a summary of these voyages, see W. P. Cumming, R. A. Skelton, and D. B. Quinn, eds., *The Discovery of North America* (New York, 1972), 104–114, 130–132. On Frobisher's voyages, see J. McDermott and D. W. Waters, "Cathay and the Way Thither: The Navigation of the Frobisher Voyages," and Bernard Allaire and Donald Hogarth, "Martin Frobisher, the Spaniards and a Sixteenth-Century Northern Spy," in Symons, *Meta Incognita*, 2:352–399, 575–588. Extracts from Nuño da Silva's depositions are in David B. Quinn et al., eds., *New American World: A Documentary History of North America to 1612*, 5 vols. (New York, 1979), 1:463. The Pacific coast was labeled the "backe side of America" in a marginal note to Richard Hakluyt's account of Drake's voyage in his *Principall Navigations, Voiages, Traffiques, and Discoveries of the English Nation* (London, 1589); see Quinn et al., *New American World*, 1:464.

19. Pedro Menéndez de Avilés to Philip II, December 12, 1565, in Quinn et al.,

New American World, 2:413–417, quote 415; see also Menéndez's letter of October 15, 1565, ibid., 398, 402. On the Pardo expedition, see Juan de la Bandera, "Relation" of the second expedition by Juan Pardo, September 1567–March 1568, trans. Paul E. Hoffman, in Charles Hudson, *The Juan Pardo Expeditions: Exploration of the Carolinas and Tennessee, 1566–1568* (Washington, D.C., 1990), 255–296. On Zacatecas, see Daniel T. Reff, *Plagues, Priests, and Demons: Sacred Narratives and the Rise of Christianity in the Old World and the New* (Cambridge, 2004), 157.

20. *The true and last discoverie of Florida made by Captaine John Ribault in the yeere 1562*, in Richard Hakluyt, *Divers Voyages touching the discoverie of America* (London, 1582), sig. F2v.

21. *The relation of David Ingram of Barking, in the Countie of Essex Sayler, of sundry things which he with others did see, in traveiling by land from the most Northerly partes of the Baie of Mexico (where he with many others were set on shoare by Master Hawkins) through a great part of America, untill he came within fiftie leagues or there abouts of Cape Britton*, in Hakluyt, *Principall Navigations*, 557–562. Hakluyt decided not to include Ingram's account in his second edition, and Samuel Purchas wrote that its exclusion was due to "some incredibilities of his reports"; see Samuel Purchas, *Hakluytus Posthumus or Purchas His Pilgrimes*, 5 vols. (London, 1625), 4:1179. For discussion of where on the east coast the three might have been picked up, see Cumming, Skelton, and Quinn, *Discovery of North America*, 98. On the Hawkins voyage, see Harry Kelsey, *Sir John Hawkins: Queen Elizabeth's Slave Trader* (New Haven, 2003).

22. Irene A. Wright, "Spanish Policy toward Virginia, 1606–1612," *American Historical Review* 25 (1920): 448–479, report 463–467.

23. "Relation of what Francis Magnel, an Irishman, learned in the land of Virginia during the eight months he was there," 1610, in Barbour, *Jamestown Voyages*, 1:151–157, quotes 155–156.

24. Report excerpted and translated in Hubert Howe Bancroft, *History of the Northwest Coast*, 2 vols. (San Francisco, 1884), 1:107. For discussion of the issues, see ibid., chap. 4.

25. Barthelemy Vimont, "Relation of occurrences in new France, in the year 1642 and 1643," in Reuben Gold Thwaites, ed., *The Jesuit Relations and Allied Documents*, 73 vols. (Cleveland, 1896–1901), 23:275–283, quotes 277–279. The account of this voyage was included in the relation for the year in which Nicolet died. On Nicolet's life, see C. W. Butterfield, *History of the Discovery of the Northwest by John Nicolet in 1634* (Cincinnati, 1881); and "Jean Nicolet, Interpreter and Voyageur in Canada, 1618–1642," first published in French by Henri Jouan in *Revue Manchoise* (1885), trans. Grace Clark, in *Collections of the State Historical Society of Wisconsin*, vol. 11 (1888), 1–25.

26. Paul LeJeune in Barthelemy Vimont, "Relation of what took place in New France, in the Year 1640," in Thwaites, *The Jesuit Relations*, 18:235–237.

27. Luca Codignola, "The Holy See and the Conversion of the Indians in French and British North America, 1486–1760," in Karen Ordahl Kupperman, ed., *America in European Consciousness* (Chapel Hill, 1995), 207–208.

28. Farrar's manuscript map is in the New York Public Library. A copy of it and the printed version can be seen in Cumming, Skelton, and Quinn, *Discovery of North America*, 268–269. John Lawson, *A New Voyage to Carolina* (1709), ed. Hugh Talmadge Lefler (Chapel Hill, 1967), 52–53.

29. His Majesties Counseil for Virginia, *A Declaration of the State of the Colonie and*

Affaires in Virginia (London, 1620), 3; John Smith, *New Englands Trials* (1620; rpt. London, 1622), in *Works*, 1:395.

30. Karen Ordahl Kupperman, "Apathy and Death in Early Jamestown," *Journal of American History* 66 (1979): 24–40.

31. Susan Myra Kingsbury, ed., *Records of the Virginia Company of London*, 4 vols. (Washington, D.C., 1906–1935), 3:15; Thomas Harriot, *A Briefe and True Report of the new found land of Virginia* (1588, 1590), in David Beers Quinn, ed., *The Roanoke Voyages, 1584–1590*, 2 vols. (London, 1955), 1:325–327.

32. For an extended discussion of this point, see Karen Ordahl Kupperman, "The Puzzle of the American Climate in the Early Colonial Period," *American Historical Review* 87 (1982): 1262–89.

33. George Best, *A true discourse of the late voyages of discouerie, for the finding of a passage to Cathaya, by the Northvveast, vnder the conduct of Martin Frobisher Generall . . . Also, there are annexed certayne reasons, to proue all partes of the worlde habitable* (London, 1578).

34. Pierre Biard, *A Relation of Occurrences in the Mission of New France during the years 1613 and 1614* (Lyons, 1618), in Thwaites, *Jesuit Relations*, 2:200; Pierre Biard, *Relation of New France, of its Lands, Nature of the Country, and of its Inhabitants* (Lyons, 1616), ibid., 3:33, 45.

35. Samuel Purchas, *Purchas His Pilgrimage*, 2nd ed. (London, 1614), 717–735, quotes 719, 720, 734.

36. Hayes, *Report*, 385–423, quotes 404–405.

37. Biard, *Relation of New France*, 3:33, 45.

38. Heylyn, *Cosmographie*, bk. 1, 262.

39. Biard, *Relation of New France*, 3:47–61.

40. Anthony Parkhurst, "A letter written to M. Richard Hakluyt of the middle Temple, conteining a report of the true state and commodities of Newfoundland, 1578," in E. G. R. Taylor, ed., *The Original Writings and Correspondence of the Two Richard Hakluyts*, 2 vols. (London, 1935), 1:131. On the climatic effects of forests and deforestation, see Thomas B. van Hoof et al., "Forest Regrowth on Medieval Farmland after the Black Death Pandemic: Implication for Atmospheric CO Levels," *Palaeogeography, Palaeoclimatology, Palaeoecology* 237 (2006): 369–409; and Betsy Mason, "The Hot Hand of History," *Nature* 427 (2004): 582–583.

41. For studies of the Little Ice Age, see Jean M. Grove, *The Little Ice Age* (London, 1988); Serena Ann Schwartz, "An Interdisciplinary Approach to the Little Ice Age and Its Implications for Global Change Research" (Ph.D. diss., University of Michigan, 1994); John Gribbin and H. H. Lamb, "Climatic Change in Historical Times," in John Gribbin, ed., *Climatic Change* (Cambridge, 1978), 68–82, esp. 74; Reid A. Bryson and Thomas J. Murray, *Climates of Hunger: Mankind and the World's Changing Weather* (Madison, 1977), 24–43; Brian Fagan, *The Little Ice Age: How Climate Made History, 1300–1850* (New York, 2000); Ray Bradley, "1000 Years of Climate Change," *Science* 288 (2000): 1353–55; Lloyd D. Keigwin, "The Little Ice Age and the Medieval Warm Period in the Sargasso Sea," *Science* 274 (1996): 1504–8.

42. H. H. Lamb, *Climate, History and the Modern World*, 2nd ed. (London, 1995), 74–76.

43. See James Anderson in *Harvard Gazette*, December 11, 1981, 3.

44. For a discussion of the different kinds of proxy data and their use, see Lamb, *Cli-*

mate, *History and the Modern World*, chap. 5. On the cod fisheries, see Hubert H. Lamb, "Climatic Variation and Changes in the Wind and Ocean Circulation: The Little Ice Age in the Northeast Atlantic," *Quaternary Research* 11 (1979): 1–20, esp. 11–15; and Grove, *Little Ice Age*, 391–392, 398–399.

45. B. H. Luckman, "The Little Ice Age in the Canadian Rockies," *Geomorphology* 32 (2000): 357–384, both presents the evidence and urges caution in its use.

46. On interpretation of this evidence, see Grove, *Little Ice Age*, 187–198.

47. P. D. Jones and M. E. Mann, "Climate over Past Millennia," *Reviews of Geophysics* 42 (2004), RG2002, doi:10.1029/2003RG00143.

48. For a discussion of possible causes and their interpretation, see ibid., and Grove, *Little Ice Age*, chap. 11.

49. Schwartz, "Interdisciplinary Approach to the Little Ice Age," chap. 1; Lamb, *Climate, History and the Modern World*, chap. 4; Harold C. Fritts, *Reconstructing Large-scale Climatic Patterns from Tree-Ring Data: A Diagnostic Analysis* (Tucson, 1991), 143–147; D. Dahl-Jensen et al., "Past Temperatures Directly from the Greenland Ice Sheet," *Science* 282 (1998): 269–271; Bradley, "1,000 Years of Climate Change"; Thomas J. Crowley, "Causes of Climate Change over the Past 1,000 Years," *Science* 289 (2000): 270–277; Richard A. Kerr, "Little Ice Age," *Science* 284 (1999): 2069; Michael E. Mann, Raymond S. Bradley, and Malcolm K. Hughes, "Global-Scale Temperature Patterns and Climate Forcing over the Past Six Centuries," *Nature* 392 (1998): 779–787; John F. Richards, *The Unending Frontier: An Environmental History of the Early Modern World* (Berkeley, 2003), 67; Brian Fagan, *The Little Ice Age: How Climate Made History, 1300–1850* (New York, 2000), 103–105, 143–147; *Volcanism and Climate Change: American Geophysical Union Special Report* (Washington, D.C., 1992). Because the prevailing winds carry dust and gases in the upper atmosphere toward the poles, eruptions at low latitudes have a greater effect on global weather than those at higher latitudes.

50. Richard Grove and John Chappell, "El Niño Chronology and the History of Global Crises during the Little Ice Age," in Grove and Chappell, *El Niño: History and Crisis* (Cambridge, 2000), 1–30. Grove and Chappell posit that repeated instances of extreme drought in the sixteenth and seventeenth centuries, confirmed by documentary evidence and correlated with El Niños, helped facilitate the European incursion into South Asia. On interconnected global weather systems, see William K. Stevens, *The Change in the Weather: People, Weather, and the Science of Climate* (New York, 1999), chap. 7.

51. For summaries of research, see Michael H. Glantz, *Currents of Change: El Niño's Impact on Climate and Society* (Cambridge, 1996), esp. secs. 1 and 2; Henry F. Diaz and Vera Markgraf, eds., *El Niño: Historical and Paleoclimatic Aspects of the Southern Oscillation* (Cambridge, 1992); Brian Fagan, *Floods, Famines, and Emperors: El Niño and the Fate of Civilizations* (New York, 1999), esp. chaps. 3, 4, 10; and William H. Quinn, "A Study of Southern Oscillation-Related Climatic Activity for A.D. 622–1900 Incorporating Nile River Flood Data," in Diaz and Markgraf, *El Niño*, 119–149, table 126.

52. Lamb, "Climatic Variation and Changes in the Wind and Ocean Circulation," 16–17; S. K. Douglas, H. H. Lamb, and C. Loader, "A Meteorological Study of July to October 1588: The Spanish Armada Storms," University of East Anglia, Climatic Research Unit Research Publications, Norwich, CRU RP6.

53. Rüdiger Glaser, Rudolf Brázdil, Christian Pfister et al., "Seasonal Temperature

and Precipitation Fluctuations in Selected Parts of Europe during the Sixteenth Century," *Climatic Change* 43 (1999): 169–200, esp. 188–197; Rüdiger Glaser, "On the Course of Temperature in Central Europe since the Year 1000 A.D.," *Historical Social Research* 22 (1997): 59–87; Keith R. Briffa et al., "Unusual Twentieth-Century Summer Warmth in a 1,000-Year Temperature Record from Siberia," *Nature* 376 (1995): 156–159.

54. Grove, *Little Ice Age*, 69–81, 113–120, 137–146.

55. Michael W. Flinn, ed., *Scottish Population History from the Seventeenth Century to the 1930s* (Cambridge, 1977), 116–126.

56. Hugo Beltrami and Jean-Claude Mareschal, "Ground Temperature Histories for Central and Eastern Canada from Geothermal Measurements: Little Ice Age Signature," *Geophysical Research Letters* 19 (1992): 689–692; William R. Baron, "Historical Climates of the Northeastern United States: Seventeenth through Nineteenth Centuries," in George P. Nicholas, ed., *Holocene Human Ecology in Northeastern North America* (New York, 1988), 29–46; Susan L. Swan, "Mexico in the Little Ice Age," *Journal of Interdisciplinary History* 11 (1981): 633–648; Grove, *Little Ice Age*, 237–239, 270–272.

57. David W. Stahle et al., "Tree-Ring Data Document 16th-Century Megadrought over North America," *Eos: Transactions, American Geophysical Union* 81 (2000): 121–125; Brian H. Luckman, "Little Ice Age in the Canadian Rockies," *Geomorphology* 32 (2000): esp. 368–370. On the changing species mix, see Grove, *Little Ice Age*, 390–391, and on the decade of the 1690s, 417–418.

58. Grove and Chappell, "El Niño Chronology."

59. Sir Ferdinando Gorges, *A briefe Relation of the Discovery and Plantation of New England*, 1622, reprinted in James Phinney Baxter, ed., *Sir Ferdinando Gorges and his Province of Maine*, 3 vols. (Boston, 1890), 1:206–207, and *A Briefe Narration of the Originall Undertakings of the Advancement of Plantations Into the Parts of America*, 1658, ibid., 2:16–17; Raleigh Gilbert, quoted in Purchas, *Purchas His Pilgrimes*, 1837; Francis Perkins to a Friend in England, March 28, 1608, in Barbour, *Jamestown Voyages*, 1:158–162, quote 160; Smith, *Map of Virginia*, 143–144; Captain John Smith, *Proceedings of the English Colony in Virginia*, in *Works*, 1:255; Smith, *The Generall Historie of Virginia, New-England and the Summer Isles* (London, 1624), in *Works*, 2:191, 194, 203, 205; William Strachey, *The Historie of Travell into Virginia Britania*, 1612, ed. Louis B. Wright and Virginia Freund (London, 1953), 173.

60. John Chamberlain to Dudley Carleton, December 30, 1607, January 5, 1608, and January 8, 1608, in *The Letters of John Chamberlain*, ed. Norman Egbert McClure, 2 vols. (Philadelphia, 1939), 1:248, 251, 253. On the ballad, see Hyder E. Rollins, "An Analytical Index to the Ballad-Entries in the Registers of the Company of Stationers of London," *Studies in Philology* 21 (1924): 129.

61. Lawson, *New Voyage to Carolina*, 181; Smith, *Proceedings of the English Colony in Virginia*, 245.

62. Biard, *Relation of New France*, 3:181; Marc Lescarbot, *Last Relation of what took place in the Voyage made by Sieur de Poutrincourt to New France* (Paris, 1612), in Thwaites, *Jesuit Relations*, 2:177. Biard's report of the priests numb with cold appears in an earlier account of the same voyage, "Letter From Father Biard, to Reverend Father Christopher Baltazar, Provincial of France, at Paris. June 10, 1611," ibid., 1:151.

63. Luckman, "Little Ice Age in the Canadian Rockies," 370; Fritts, *Reconstructing*

Large-Scale Climatic Patterns from Tree-Ring Data, 175–178, 192–198; K. R. Briffa, P. D. Jones, and F. H. Schweingruber, "Tree-Ring Density Reconstructions of Summer Temperature Patterns across Western North America since 1600," *Journal of Climate* 5 (1992): 735–754; Paul R. Fish et al., "Toward an Explanation for Southwestern 'Abandonments,'" in George J. Gumerman, ed., *Themes in Southwest Prehistory* (Santa Fe, 1994), 135–164; Jeffrey S. Dean, William H. Doelle, and Janet D. Orcutt, "Adaptive Stress, Environment, and Demography," in Gumerman, *Themes in Southwest Prehistory,* 53–86; Albert H. Schroeder, "Shifting for Survival in the Spanish Southwest," *New Mexico Historical Review* 43 (1968): 291–310; Elinore M. Barrett, *Conquest and Catastrophe: Changing Rio Grande Pueblo Settlement Patterns in the Sixteenth and Seventeenth Centuries* (Albuquerque, 2002); Andrew L. Knaut, *The Pueblo Revolt of 1680: Conquest and Resistance in Seventeenth-Century New Mexico* (Norman, 1995), 61; Swan, "Mexico in the Little Ice Age." Earlier drought and abandonment of settlements are analyzed in L. B. Jorde, "Precipitation Cycles and Cultural Buffering in the Prehistoric Southwest," in Lewis R. Binford, ed., *For Theory Building in Archaeology* (New York, 1977), 385–396.

64. Paul E. Hoffman, *Florida's Frontiers* (Bloomington, 2002), 15, 59, 77.

65. Gonzalo Solís de Merás, *Memorial of the Adelantado Pedro Menéndez de Avilés,* trans. and ed. Jeannette T. Connor (Gainesville, 1964), 170–171, 177–179, 181. In 1583 Pedro Menéndez Marqués offered a similar reason for that year's drought; see Hoffman, *Florida's Frontiers,* 69.

66. This account is from "Letter of Luís de Quirós and Juan Baptista de Segura to Juan de Hinistrosa, From Ajacán, September 12, 1570," in Clifford M. Lewis, S. J., and Albert J. Loomie, S. J., *The Spanish Jesuit Mission in Virginia, 1570–1572* (Chapel Hill, 1953), 89–90. See Charlotte Gradie, "The Powhatans in the Context of the Spanish Empire," in Helen C. Rountree, ed., *Powhatan Foreign Relations, 1500–1722* (Charlottesville, 1993), 154–172; and Gradie, "Spanish Jesuits in Virginia: The Mission That Failed," *Virginia Magazine of History and Biography* 96 (1988): 131–156.

67. Harriot, *Briefe and True Report,* 377.

68. John White, "The Fourth Voyage Made to Virginia," 1587, in Quinn, *Roanoke Voyages,* 2:526.

69. Pedro Menéndez Marqués, governor of Florida, to Philip II, July 17, 1588, *Historical Magazine* 3 (1859): 275–276. On repeated drought conditions in the Southeast in the latter part of the sixteenth century, see David G. Anderson, David W. Stahle, and Malcolm K. Cleaveland, "Paleoclimate and the Potential Food Reserves of Mississippian Societies: A Case Study from the Savannah River Valley," *American Antiquity* 60 (1995): 258–286.

70. David W. Stahle et al., "The Lost Colony and Jamestown Droughts," *Science* 280 (1998): 564–567.

71. Thomas Harriot, notes to John White's pictures, 1590, in Quinn, *Roanoke Voyages,* 1:434–435; Strachey, *Historie of Travell,* 75, 82; Ralph Lane, *An Account of the Particularities of the imployments of the English men left in Virginia,* 1586, in Quinn, *Roanoke Voyages,* 1:267–268, 272, 276, 282.

72. George Percy described Powhatan in this way in "A Trew Relacyon of the procedeinges and ocurrentes of momente which have hapned in Virginia from the Tyme Sir Thomas Gates was Shippwrackte uppon the Bermudes Anno 1609 untill my departure owtt of the Cowntry which was in Anno Domini

1612," in "George Percy's 'Trewe Relacyon': A Primary Source for the James-town Settlement," ed. Mark Nicholls, *Virginia Magazine of History and Biography* 113 (2005): 247. For a similar formulation from Smith, see *Proceedings of the English Colony in Virginia*, 246.

73. Henry Spelman, "Relation of Virginea," ca. 1613, in E. Arber and A. G. Bradley, eds., *Travels and Works of Captain John Smith*, 2 vols. (Edinburgh, 1910), 1:cv; Smith, *Proceedings of the English Colony in Virginia*, 266. On the Quiyoughcohannocks, whose capital town was across the river from Jamestown, see Helen C. Rountree, *The Powhatan Indians of Virginia: Their Traditional Culture* (Norman, Okla., 1989), 4, 9.

74. On conditions on the east coast, see Stahle et al., "The Lost Colony and James-town Droughts"; and Dennis B. Blanton, "Drought as a Factor in the Jamestown Colony, 1607–1612," *Historical Archaeology* 34 (2000): 84–81.

75. These are the words of the Geneva Bible, 1560.

76. Smith, *Map of Virginia*, 159, 168; *Proceedings of the English Colony in Virginia*, 212–213, 239, 255, 274; *Generall Historie*, 194.

77. Randy Showstack, "Natural Disasters Linked to Collapse of Some Indigenous Populations," *Eos* 82 (2001): 25–27; Hoffman, *Florida's Frontiers*, 77–78.

78. Nicolas Bownde, *The Doctrine of the Sabbath* (London, 1595), 230.

79. *A Commentarie of John Calvine, upon the first booke of Moses called Genesis*, trans. Thomas Tymme (London, 1578), 114. This was the first English translation of Calvin's commentary. Michael Wigglesworth experienced a personal interven-tion in which God changed snow to rain to allow him to travel; *The Diary of Michael Wigglesworth, 1653–1657: The Conscience of a Puritan*, ed. Edmund S. Morgan (New York, 1965), 51–52.

80. Richard Beacon, *Solon His Follie, or a Politique Discourse touching the Reformation of common-weales conquered, declined or corrupted*, 1594, ed. Vincent Carey and Clare Carroll (Binghamton, N.Y., 1996), 90–92; Andrew Hadfield, *Literature, Travel, and Colonial Writing in the English Renaissance, 1545–1625* (Oxford, 1998), 128.

81. William Jones, *Gods Warning to his people of England* (London, 1607), 3, 5–6.

82. George Percy, *Observations gathered out of a Discourse of the Plantation of the Southerne Colonie in Virginia by the English, 1606*, in Barbour, *Jamestown Voy-ages*, 1:129; Andrés Pérez de Ribas, *History of the Triumphs of our Holy Faith Amongst the Most Barbarous and Fierce Peoples of the New World*, ed. Daniel T. Reff (Tucson, 1999), 245–246, 675–677; see also Reff, *Plagues, Priests, and Demons: Sacred Narratives and the Rise of Christianity in the Old World and the New* (Cambridge, 2005), 175–177.

83. Harriot, *Briefe and True Report*, 380–381; Increase Mather, *Kometographia. Or a Discourse Concerning Comets* (Boston, 1682), 105, 107–108.

84. Patrick Copland, *Virginia's God be Thanked, or A Sermon of Thanksgiving for the Happie successe of the affayres in Virginia this last yeare* (London, 1622), 1 quoting Psalm 107:23–30, 3. See Richard Rath, *How Early America Sounded* (Ithaca, 2003), chap. 1, esp. 14–16.

85. Smith, *Generall Historie*, 137–138; Percy, *Observations gathered out of a Dis-course*, 129, 133.

86. Pedro Menendez de Aviles to Philip II, October 20, 1566, in Eugene Lyon, ed., *Pedro Menendez de Aviles*, Spanish Borderlands Sourcebooks, vol. 24 (New

York, 1995), 357–361, quote 358. The original is in the Archive of the Indies, Santo Domingo, 115.

87. Strachey, *Historie of Travell,* 98–100. Strachey here amplified an observation from Smith's *Map of Virginia,* 171. See also Henry Spelman, "Relation of Virginea," cv.

88. Alexander Whitaker to Mr. Crashaw, August 9, 1611, in Alexander Brown, ed., *The Genesis of the United States,* 2 vols. (New York, 1890), 497–500; Whitaker, *Good Newes from Virginia,* 26 (emphasis added); Percy, "Trew Relacyon," 259.

89. Cotton Mather, *Magnalia Christi Americana,* bks. 1 and 2, ed. Kenneth B. Murdock (Cambridge, Mass., 1977), 147.

6. A WELTER OF COLONIAL PROJECTS

1. P. E. H. Hair, ed., *Sierra Leone and the English in 1607: Extracts from the Unpublished Journals of the Keeling Voyage to the East Indies,* Institute of African Studies, University of Sierra Leone Occasional Paper no. 4 (1981), 25, 27, 30, 32; Hair and Robin Law, "The English in Western Africa to 1700," in *The Oxford History of the British Empire,* gen. ed. William Roger Louis, vol. 1, *The Origins of Empire: British Overseas Enterprise to the Close of the Seventeenth Century,* ed. Nicholas Canny (Oxford, 1998), 241–263; J. Theodore Bent, ed., *Early Voyages and Travels in the Levant* (London, 1893), xi.

2. *The True Travels, Adventures, and Observations of Captaine John Smith,* in Philip L. Barbour, ed., *The Complete Works of Captain John Smith,* 3 vols. (Chapel Hill, 1986), 3:224; Mark Nicholls, "George Percy," in *Oxford Dictionary of National Biography* (Oxford, 2004).

3. On the attempt to settle in the Magdalen Islands, see David Beers Quinn, "The First Pilgrims," in *England and the Discovery of America, 1481–1620* (London, 1974), 337–363; see also "England and the St. Lawrence, 1577–1602," ibid., 313–336.

4. Sir Walter Ralegh, *The Discoverie of the Large, Rich and Bewtiful Empyre of Guiana,* 1596, ed. Neil L. Whitehead (Norman, Okla., 1997), 133, 169, 185–186. On the number of Indians taken to England, see Alden T. Vaughan, "Powhatans Abroad: Virginia Indians in England," in Robert Appelbaum and John Wood Sweet, eds., *Envisioning an English Empire: Jamestown and the Making of the North Atlantic World* (Philadelphia, 2005), 51.

5. "The description of the Ile of Trinidad, the rich Countrie of Guiana, and mightie River of Orenoco, written by Francis Sparrey left there by Sir Walter Ralegh, 1595 and in the end taken by the Spaniards and sent prisoner into Spaine, and after long captivitie got into England by great sute. 1602," in Samuel Purchas, *Hakluytus Posthumus or Purchas His Pilgrimes,* 5 vols., (London, 1625), 4:1247–50; Neil L. Whitehead, intro. to Ralegh, *Discoverie of Guiana,* 30–31, 52, 66, and passim.

6. This book was redacted in 1625 by Purchas in *Purchas His Pilgrimes,* 4:1255–60, with the title "A true Relation of the traiterous massacre of the most part of threescore and seven English men, set on land out of a Ship of Sir Oliph Leagh, bound for Guiana, in Santa Lucia an Iland of the West Indie, the three and twentieth of August, written by John Nicol, 1605." It was registered with the Stationers Company in London in June 1607.

7. Ralegh, *Discoverie of Guiana*, 144–145. On these ventures, see Joyce Lorimer, ed., *English and Irish Settlement on the River Amazon, 1550–1646* (London, 1989), 9–44; D. W. Meinig, *The Shaping of America*, vol. 1, *Atlantic America, 1492–1800* (New Haven, 1986), pt. 1, chap. 6; David B. Quinn, *Ralegh and the British Empire* (Harmondsworth, 1973), chap. 6.

8. Alison M. Quinn and David B. Quinn, eds., *The English New England Voyages, 1602–1608* (London, 1983). On the plan to settle Irish and English Catholics, see ibid., 242–247; and David Quinn, *Ireland and America: Their Early Associations, 1500–1640* (Liverpool, 1991), and *England and the Discovery of America*, 383–386.

9. Quinn and Quinn, *English New England Voyages*, 74–75, 309. For the description of Challons's voyage by his pilot, John Stoneman, see ibid., 364–375.

10. Samuel Purchas, *Purchas His Pilgrimage*, 2nd ed. (London, 1614), 757; and *Purchas His Pilgrimes*, 4:1837; Captain John Smith, *The Generall Historie of Virginia, New-England and the Summer Isles* (London, 1624), in *Works*, 2:397–400, quote 399. For documents on Sagadahoc, see Quinn and Quinn, *English New England Voyages*.

11. David B. Quinn, *North America from Early Discovery to First Settlements: The Norse Voyages to 1612* (New York, 1977), 380–381, 410.

12. Peter E. Pope, *Fish into Wine: The Newfoundland Plantation in the Seventeenth Century* (Chapel Hill, 2004), esp. intro. and chap. 2; Gillian T. Cell, ed., *Newfoundland Discovered: English Attempts at Colonisation, 1610–1630* (London, 1982).

13. See Mark Nicholls, "Sir Walter Ralegh's Treason: A Prosecution Document," *English Historical Review* 110 (1995): 902–934.

14. Lorimer, *English and Irish Settlement on the River Amazon*, 36–37.

15. Smith, *Generall Historie*, 137.

16. Stuart Piggott, *Ancient Britons and the Antiquarian Imagination: Ideas from the Renaissance to the Regency* (London, 1989), chap. 3, esp. 60–61.

17. The discussion that follows draws heavily on Jane H. Ohlmeyer, "'Civilizinge of those rude partes': Colonization within Britain and Ireland," in Nicholas Canny, ed., *The Oxford History of the British Empire*, vol. 1, *The Origins of Empire: British Overseas Enterprise to the Close of the Seventeenth Century* (Oxford, 1998), 124–147; Canny, *Making Ireland British, 1580–1650* (Oxford, 2001), chaps. 1–3, and *Kingdom and Colony: Ireland in the Atlantic World, 1560–1800* (Baltimore, 1988), chaps. 1–4; Debora Shuger, "Irishmen, Aristocrats, and Other White Barbarians," *Renaissance Quarterly* 50 (1997): 494–525; and Quinn, *Ralegh and the British Empire*.

18. On Gilbert's career, see David B. Quinn, ed., *The Voyages and Colonising Enterprises of Sir Humphrey Gilbert*, 2 vols. (London, 1940), 1:1–104, quote 17.

19. Edmund Spenser, *A View of the State of Ireland*, ed. Andrew Hadfield and Willy Maley (Oxford, 1997), 101–102.

20. Sir Philip Sidney, *An Apology for Poetry (or The Defence of Poesy)*, ed. Geoffrey Shepherd and R. W. Maslen (Manchester, 2002), 83; Richard Eden, *The Decades of the newe worlde or West India* (London, 1555), title page, Decade 3, bk. 7, 125–126. On Peter Martyr and Eden's translation, see Andrew Hadfield, *Literature, Travel, and Colonial Writing in the English Renaissance, 1545–1625* (Oxford, 1998), 71–92.

21. Richard Beacon, *Solon His Follie, or a Politique Discourse touching the Reformation*

of common-weales conquered, declined or corrupted, 1594, ed. Vincent Carey and Clare Carroll (Binghamton, N.Y., 1996). On Beacon's argument, see Hadfield, *Literature, Travel, and Colonial Writing*, 126–131.

22. Spenser, *View of the State of Ireland*, 11, 12, 23, 27, 56–59, 62, 67–68, 71, 85, 103, 144.

23. See Ann Rosalind Jones and Peter Stallybrass, "Dismantling Irena: The Sexualizing of Ireland in Early Modern England," in Andrew Parker et al., eds., *Nationalisms and Sexualities* (London, 1992), 157–171. Jones and Stallybrass argue that English analysts saw Irish life as deficient in order because the mantle was worn by all classes and both genders (165–166).

24. Aileen Ribeiro, *Dress and Morality* (New York, 1986), chap. 4. On the evolution of thinking about Irish colonization during the sixteenth century, see Nicholas Canny, *The Elizabethan Conquest of Ireland: A Pattern Established, 1565–76* (New York, 1976), esp. chap. 4.

25. See Ohlmeyer, "'Civilizinge of those rude partes,'" 140–143.

26. John White to Richard Hakluyt, February 4, 1593, in David Beers Quinn, ed., *The Roanoke Voyages, 1584–1590*, 2 vols. (London, 1955), 2:712–716, quotes 715–716.

27. On Harriot and White in Ireland, see John W. Shirley, *Thomas Harriot: A Biography* (Oxford, 1983), 156–167.

28. Pauline Croft, *King James* (Basingstoke and New York, 2003), 143.

29. "A Letter from Sir John Davies, Knt. Attorney General of Ireland to Robert Earl of Salisbury," 1607, in Sir John Davies, *Historical Tracts* (Dublin, 1787), 217–721, quotes 219, 256–257, 269–270; "A Letter to the Earl of Salisbury, in 1610; giving an account of the Plantation in Ulster, Nov. 8 1610," ibid., 275–286, quotes 283–284.

30. Quinn, *Ireland and America*; John J. Silke, *Kinsale: The Spanish Intervention in Ireland at the End of the Elizabethan Wars* (New York, 1970); John McCavitt, *The Flight of the Earls* (Dublin, 2002); Croft, *King James*, 146.

31. Sir Francis Bacon, "Certain Considerations Touching the Plantation in Ireland. Presented to His Majesty, 1606," in *Works of Francis Bacon, Lord Chancellor of England*, ed. Basil Montague, 16 vols. (London, 1825–1834), 5:169–185, quote 171, 179, 181. The first part of *Don Quixote* was published in 1605; the first English translation appeared in 1612.

32. On the Nine Years' War and plans for the settlement of Ulster, see Ohlmeyer, "'Civilizinge of those rude partes'"; Canny, *Making Ireland British*, chaps. 3–4; Croft, *King James*, 143–154.

7. JAMESTOWN'S UNCERTAIN BEGINNINGS

1. William Camden, *The History of the Most Renowned and Victorious Princess Elizabeth Late Queen of England*, ed. Wallace T. MacCaffrey (Chicago, 1970), 161.

2. George Chapman, Ben Jonson, and John Marston, *Eastward Hoe* (London, 1605), 3.3. The Isle of Dogs was the point of embarkation for Virginia; see William M. Kelso and Beverly Straube, *Jamestown Rediscovery, 1994–2004* (Jamestown, 2004), 18.

3. Virginia Company, "Instructions given by way of advice," 1606, in Philip L. Barbour, ed., *The Jamestown Voyages Under the First Charter, 1606–1609*, 2 vols. (Cambridge, 1969), 49–54, quotes 51.

4. Robert Brenner, *Merchants and Revolution: Commercial Change, Political Conflict, and London's Overseas Traders, 1550–1653* (Princeton, 1993), chap. 1.

5. Gordon of Lochinvar, *Encouragements to Under-takers* (Edinburgh, 1625), sig. B3v, C2v.

6. Sir Francis Bacon, "Certain Considerations Touching the Plantation in Ireland, 1606," in *Works of Francis Bacon Lord Chancellor of England*, ed. Basil Montague, 16 vols. (London, 1825–39), 5:169–185, quote 179–181.

7. This point is made by Alden T. Vaughan, "Powhatans Abroad: Virginia Indians in England," in Robert Appelbaum and John Wood Sweet, eds., *Envisioning an English Empire: Jamestown and the Making of the North Atlantic World* (Philadelphia, 2005), 51.

8. For this discussion, see Virginia Company, "Instructions Given by way of Advice," 49–54.

9. George Percy, "Observations Gathered out of a Discourse of the Plantation of the Southerne Colonie in Virginia by the English, 1606," in Barbour, *Jamestown Voyages*, 1:138.

10. Captain John Smith, *A True Relation of such occurrences and accidents of noate, as hath hapned in Virginia, since the first planting of that Collony*, in *The Complete Works of Captain John Smith*, ed. Philip L. Barbour, 3 vols. (Chapel Hill, 1986), 1:29. On siting the colony, see Kelso and Straube, *Jamestown Rediscovery*, chap. 1.

11. Gabriel Archer, *A Relatyon of the Discovery of our River*, in Barbour, *Jamestown Voyages*, 1:96; Smith, *True Relation*, 33–35, and *The Proceedings of the English Colony in Virginia, 1612*, in *Works*, 1:229.

12. "Coppie of a letter from virginia dated 22th of June 1607 the Councell their, to the Councell of virginia here in England," in Barbour, *Jamestown Voyages*, 1:78–80.

13. George Percy included a summary of the almost daily deaths in late summer and early fall in his "Observations Gathered out of a Discourse," in Barbour, *Jamestown Voyages*, 1:143–145. A grave believed to be Gosnold's has been uncovered and excavated by the team headed by William Kelso at Jamestown Rediscovery; see Kelso and Straube, *Jamestown Rediscovery*, 120–125.

14. Percy, "Observations Gathered out of a Discourse," 144; Edward Maria Wingfield, "Discourse," 1608, in Barbour, *Jamestown Voyages*, 1:225.

15. "Relation of what Francis Magnel, an Irishman, learned in the land of Virginia during the eight months he was there," 1610, in Barbour, *Jamestown Voyages*, 1:156; Philip L. Barbour, "Captain George Kendall: Mutineer or Intelligencer?" *Virginia Magazine of History and Biography* 70 (1962): 297–313.

16. Archer, *Relatyon of the Discovery of our River*, 82–83, 84, 87–89; George Percy, fragment from Samuel Purchas, *Purchas His Pilgrimage*, 2nd ed. (London, 1614), 146–147.

17. Archer, *Relatyon of the Discovery of our River*, 97–98; Smith, *True Relation*, 31–33, and *Proceedings*, 209.

18. Captain John Smith, *A Map of Virginia*, 1612, in *Works*, 1:173–174.

19. William Strachey, *The Historie of Travell into Virginia Britania*, 1612, ed. Louis B. Wright and Virginia Freund (London, 1953), 60–61.

20. Captain John Smith, *The Generall Historie of Virginia, New-England and the Summer Isles* (London, 1624), in *Works*, 2:205; see also 259. Helen C. Rountree

has written extensively on women's roles in Chesapeake Algonquian societies and their ownership of food supplies.

21. Magnel, "Relation," 153–154. Magnel's deposition was part of a report sent home by the Spanish ambassador. See Kelso and Straube, *Jamestown Rediscovery,* 70.

22. Smith, *Generall Historie,* 189.

23. Frances Perkins to an unknown friend, March 28, 1608, in Barbour, *Jamestown Voyages,* 1:158–159.

24. Percy, "Observations gathered out of a Discourse," 144.

25. Smith, *True Relation,* 35, and *Generall Historie,* 259. On conditions in the colony, see Carville V. Earle, "Environment, Disease, and Mortality in Early Virginia," in Thad W. Tate and David L. Ammerman, eds., *The Chesapeake in the Seventeenth Century* (Chapel Hill, 1979), 96–125; Karen Ordahl Kupperman, "Apathy and Death in Early Jamestown," *Journal of American History* 66 (1979): 24–40.

26. Captain John Smith, *Advertisements For the unexperienced Planters of New-England, or any-where,* 1631, in *Works,* 3:272.

27. Smith, *Generall Historie,* 146–152, quotes 151. On interpretations of this event, see Frederic W. Gleach, *Powhatan's World and Colonial Virginia: A Conflict of Cultures* (Lincoln, Neb., 1997).

28. Smith, *Generall Historie,* 183–184; Virginia Company, *True Declaration of the Estate of the Colonie in Virginia,* 1610, in David B. Quinn et al., eds., *New American World: A Documentary History of North America to 1612,* 5 vols. (New York, 1979), 5:250.

29. Henry Spelman, "Relation of Virginea," in Edward Arber and A. G. Bradley, eds., *Travels and Works of Captain John Smith,* 2 vols. (Edinburgh, 1910), 1:cv, cxii; Helen C. Rountree, *The Powhatan Indians of Virginia: Their Traditional Culture* (Norman, Okla., 1989), 109–112.

30. Smith, *Generall Historie,* 196, 206.

31. Smith, *True Relation,* 67–69.

32. Smith, *Proceedings,* 244–245.

33. Ibid., 216; Ben Jonson, *Epicene,* 5.1.20.

34. Helen Rountree identifies Kemps and Tassore as Paspaheghans in *Pocahontas, Powhatan, Opechancanough: Three Indian Lives Changed by Jamestown* (Charlottesville, 2005), 136. On all these visitors, see Vaughan, "Powhatans Abroad," 58–60; Karen Ordahl Kupperman, *Indians and English: Facing Off in Early America* (Ithaca, N.Y., 2000), 49–67. One report held that Machumps murdered Namontack in Bermuda, but Vaughan presents reasons for doubting it (53–55).

35. Strachey, *Historie of Travell into Virginia Britania,* 72.

36. Smith, *True Relation,* 93, and *Generall Historie,* 198–199, 203, 259.

37. Smith, *True Relation,* 69, 91–93, and *Proceedings of the English Colony in Virginia,* 216.

38. Strachey, *Historie of Travell,* 85–86; Ralph Hamor, *A True Discourse of the Present Estate of Virginia* (London, 1615), 37–38; Dale to D. M., in Hamor, *True Discourse,* 53–54.

39. Spelman told his story in his "Relation of Virginea," quotes ciii, cviii; Smith, *Generall Historie,* 232.

40. "A Letter of Sir Samuell Argoll touching his Voyage to Virginia, and Actions

there: Written to Master Nicholas Hawes. June 1613," in Samuel Purchas, *Hakluytus Posthumus or Purchas His Pilgrimes*, 5 vols. (London, 1625), 4:1764–65.

41. Ralph Lane, *An Account of the Particularities of the imployments of the English men left in Virginia*, 1586, in David Beers Quinn, ed., *The Roanoke Voyages, 1584–1590*, 2 vols. (London, 1955), 1:273.

42. Smith, *Generall Historie*, 162, 181–190, quote 181, and *Map of Virginia*, 218–219.

43. On Ganz, see Quinn, *Roanoke Voyages*, 195–196; Ivor Noël Hume, *The Virginia Adventure, Roanoke to Jamestown: An Archaeological and Historical Odyssey* (New York, 1994), 76–81; Gary C. Grassl, "Joachim Gans of Prague and 'America's First Science Center,'" *The Web of Time* [Colonial Williamsburg's on-line magazine] 2, no. 3.

44. Edward Hayes, "A report of the voyage and successe thereof, attempted in the yeere of our Lord 1583 by sir Humfrey Gilbert knight," in David B. Quinn, ed., *The Voyages and Colonising Enterprises of Sir Humphrey Gilbert*, 2 vols. (London, 1940), 2:408, 413–414; James McDermott, ed., *The Third Voyage of Martin Frobisher to Baffin Island, 1578* (London, 2001); James Shapiro, *Shakespeare and the Jews* (New York: Columbia University Press, 1996), 74.

45. Smith, *Proceedings*, 234, 242–244, 246–247, 250, 256, 259, 266–267.

8. THE PROJECT REVISED

1. William Crashaw, *A Sermon Preached in London before the right honourable the Lord Lawarre . . . 1609* (London, 1610), sig. E4v; Virginia Company, *A True and Sincere Declaration of the Purpose and End of the Plantation Begun in Virginia* (London, 1610), 10.

2. *Advertisements For the unexperienced Planters of New-England, or any-where*, 1631, in Philip L. Barbour, ed., *The Complete Works of Captain John Smith*, 3 vols. (Chapel Hill, 1986), 3:271; Smith, *A Map of Virginia*, 1612, ibid., 1:175–176.

3. For Healey's preface to Smith's *True Relation of such occurrences and accidents of noate as hath hapned in Virginia*, 1608, see *Works*, 1:24–25.

4. See Wesley Frank Craven, *The Virginia Company of London, 1606–1624* (Charlottesville, 1957).

5. Chamberlain to Carleton, February 14, 1609, in Norman Egbert McClure, ed., *The Letters of John Chamberlain*, 2 vols. (Philadelphia, 1939), 1:283–284, quote 284; S. G. Culliford, *William Strachey, 1572–1621* (Charlottesville, 1965), 101–103.

6. William Symonds, *Virginia. A Sermon Preached at White-Chappell, In the Presence of the Adventurers and Planters for Virginia* (London, 1609), sig. A2v. On these sermons and English writing in the American colonies, see Andrew Fitzmaurice, *Humanism and America: An Intellectual History of English Colonisation, 1500–1625* (Cambridge, 2003).

7. Daniel Price, *Sauls Prohibition Staide* (London, 1609), sigs. E2v–E3, F, F3v; Crashaw, *Sermon Preached before the Lord Lawarre*, sig. C2; Robert Johnson, *The New Life of Virginea*, 1612, in Peter Force, comp., *Tracts and Other Papers, Relating Principally to the Origin, Settlement, and Progress of the Colonies in North America*, 4 vols. (Washington, D.C., 1844; rpt., 1963), 1:8. See also George

Benson, *A Sermon preached at Paules Crosse* (London, 1609); Richard Crakan-thorpe, *A Sermon at the Inauguration of King James* (London 1609); Robert Tynley, *Two Learned Sermons* (London, 1609); Robert Gray, *A Goodspeed to Virginia* (London, 1609); Robert Johnson, *Nova Brittania* (London, 1609).

8. Alexander Whitaker, *Good Newes from Virginia* (London, 1613), quotes 1, 11, 24, 27–28; William Crashaw, "Epistle Dedicatorie," ibid.; Alexander Whitaker, "To my verie deere and loving Cosen M. G. Minister of the B. F. in London," in Ralph Hamor, *A True Discourse of the Present Estate of Virginia* (London, 1615), 59–61. Whitaker's biblical text for *Good Newes* is Ecclesiastes 11:1.

9. John Rolfe, *A True Relation of the state of Virginia lefte by Sir Thomas Dale Knight in May last 1616* (Charlottesville, 1951), 4; Virginia Company, "Instruccions, orders and constitucions by way of advise sett downe, declared and propounded to Sir Thomas Gates, Knight, Governor of Virginia," in David B. Quinn et al., eds., *New American World: A Documentary History of North America to 1612,* 5 vols. (New York, 1979), 5:213.

10. Peter Winne to Sir John Egerton, November 26, 1608, in Philip L. Barbour, ed., *The Jamestown Voyages Under the First Charter, 1606–1609,* 2 vols. (Cambridge, 1969), 1:245–246; William Strachey, "A True Reportory of the Wreck and Redemption of Sir Thomas Gates, Knight," in Louis B. Wright, ed., *A Voyage to Virginia in 1609* (Charlottesville, 1964), 82–83; Virginia Company, "Instruccions to Gates," in Quinn et al., *New American World,* 5:214–215. On the corrupt water in the English fens, see I[ohn] L[ien], *A Discourse Concerning the Great Benefit of Drayning and imbanking, and of transportation by water within the Country* (London, 1641), 1. On projects to drain the English fens and their relationship to American ventures, see Karen Ordahl Kupperman, "Controlling Nature and Colonial Projects in Early America," in Hans-Jürgen Grabbe, ed., *Colonial Encounters: Essays in Early American History and Culture,* American Studies 109 (Ersch-Termin, 2003), 69–88.

11. Virginia Company, *True Declaration of the Estate of the Colonie in Virginia,* in Quinn et al., *New American World,* 5:252; Strachey, "True Reportory," 7.

12. Smith, *Map of Virginia,* 452; George Percy, "A Trewe Relacyon of the procedeings and ocurrentes of momente which have hapned in Virginia, from the Tyme Sir Thomas Gates was Shippwrackte uppon the Bermudes Anno 1609 untill my departure owtt of the Cowntry which was in Anno Domini 1612," in "George Percy's 'Trewe Relacyon': A Primary Source for the Jamestown Settlement," ed. Mark Nicholls, *Virginia Magazine of History and Biography* 113 (2004): 246; Virginia Company, *True and Sincere declaration,* 6–10, 13, 14–15.

13. William Bradford and Edward Winslow, *A Relation or Journall of the English Plantation setled at Plimoth in New England* (London, 1622), known as *Mourt's Relation,* 2–3; William Bradford, *Of Plymouth Plantation, 1620–1647,* ed. Samuel Eliot Morison (New York, 1952), 75–77, 442.

14. *The Tempest,* 2.2.186.

15. Virginia Company, *True and Sincere declaration,* 15, 17–19.

16. Ibid., 21.

17. Ibid., 11.

18. "A Letter of M. Gabriel Archer," August 31, 1609, in Barbour, *Jamestown Voyages,* 2:281–282.

19. Percy, "Trewe Relacyon," 244–247.

20. Strachey, "True Reportory," 63; Percy, "Trewe Relacyon," 251.

21. Percy, "Trewe Relacyon," 247–249; Virginia Company, *True Declaration of the Estate of the Colonie in Virginia*, 256. William Kelso's archaeological team at Jamestown Rediscovery has found bones of poisonous snakes, rats, and dogs from this period within the fort; William M. Kelso and Beverly Straube, *Jamestown Rediscovery, 1994–2004* (Jamestown, 2004), 63.

22. Strachey, "True Reportory," 63–77, quotes 63, 64; Governor and Council of Virginia to Virginia Company of London, July 7, 1610, in Alexander Brown, ed., *The Genesis of the United States*, 2 vols. (1890; rpt. Bowie, Md., 1994), 1:405

23. Strachey, "True Reportory," 84–87; Virginia Company, *True Declaration of the Estate of the Colonie in Virginia*, 257–258.

24. Strachey, "True Reportory," 65–70; Crashaw, *Sermon Preached before the Lord Lawarre*, sig. E4v; William Bullock, "To the Reader," in *Virginia Impartially examined, and left to publick view, to be considered by all Judicious and honest men* (London, 1649).

25. Virginia Company, *A True Declaration*, 5:248–262, quotes 248, 249, 251, 253, 255, 260.

26. *By the Counsell of Virginea* (London, 1611).

27. Sir Thomas Dale to the President and Counsell of the Companie of Adventurers and Planters in Virginia, May 25, 1611, in Brown, *Genesis of the United States*, 1:489–494; Dale to the earl of Salisbury, August 17, 1611, ibid., 501–508, quotes 503, 507.

28. Percy, "Trewe Relacyon," 261–262; William Strachey, *The Historie of Travell into Virginia Britania*, 1612, ed. Louis B. Wright and Virginia Freund (London, 1953), 61.

29. Hamor, *True Discourse of the Present Estate of Virginia*, 27–28; "A Letter of Sir Samuell Argoll touching his Voyage to Virginia, and Actions there: Written to Master Nicholas Hawes. June 1613," in Samuel Purchas, *Hakluytus Posthumus or Purchas His Pilgrimes*, 5 vols. (London, 1625) 4:1764–65.

30. Robert Johnson, *The New Life of Virginea* (London, 1612), in Force, *Tracts*, vol. 1, no. 6, 20–21; "London's Lotterie," *William and Mary Quarterly*, 3rd ser., 5 (1948): 258–264; Purchas, *Purchas His Pilgrimes*, 4:1773; Peter Walne, "The 'Running Lottery' of the Virginia Company," *Virginia Magazine of History and Biography* 70 (1962): 30–34.

31. Alden T. Vaughan, "Powhatans Abroad: Virginia Indians in England," in Robert Appelbaum and John Wood Sweet, eds., *Envisioning an English Empire: Jamestown and the Making of the North Atlantic World* (Philadelphia, 2005), 57–59.

32. Chamberlain to Sir Dudley Carleton, July 9, 1612, in *Letters of John Chamberlain*, 1:366–367.

33. Suits and replies to them are in Susan Myra Kingsbury, ed., *Records of the Virginia Company of London*, 4 vols. (Washington, D.C., 1906–1935), 3:34–58; Chamberlain to Sir Dudley Carleton, August 1, 1613, in *Letters of John Chamberlain*, 1:470.

34. This rendition of Jamestown is in "Anonymous Account of Virginia," in Barbour, *Jamestown Voyages*, 1:237.

35. "Relation of what Francis Magnel, an Irishman, learned in the land of Virginia during the eight months he was there," 1610, ibid., 151–157; David B. Quinn, *Ireland and America: Their Early Associations, 1500–1640* (Liverpool, 1991), 19.

36. Spanish investigations and correspondence can be followed through the docu-

ments in Quinn et al., *New American World*, 5:141–158; Irene A. Wright, "Spanish Policy toward Virginia, 1606–1612," *American Historical Review* 25 (1920): 448–479; and Brown, *Genesis of the United States*, passim. Diego's smuggled letter with its reference to the mysterious Venetian is in Brown, *Genesis of the United States*, 2:646–652, quote 650. George Percy's characterization of Limbreck is in his "Trewe Relacyon," 260, and Purchas's is in *Purchas His Pilgrimes*, 4:1773. On John Clark's voyage with the Pilgrims, see William Bradford, *Of Plymouth Plantation, 1620–1647*, ed. Samuel Eliot Morison (New York, 1952), 366.

37. "A Letter of Sir Samuell Argoll touching his Voyage to Virginia, and Actions there: Written to Master Nicholas Hawes. June 1613," in Purchas, *Purchas His Pilgrimes*, 4:1765; Hamor, *True Discourse of the Present Estate of Virginia*, 4–6, quote 4; Captain John Smith, *The Generall Historie of Virginia, New-England and the Summer Isles* (London, 1624), in *Works*, 2:243–244.

38. The story recounted here of Argall's raid and the providential storm was told many times by the Jesuits who were taken prisoner. This account is pieced together from *Records of New France, from the year 1607 to the year 1737*, in Reuben Gold Thwaites, ed., *The Jesuit Relations and Allied Documents*, 73 vols. (Cleveland, 1896–1901), 1:129–131; Joseph Jouvency, *An Account of the Canadian Mission From the year 1611 until the year 1613*, 1710, ibid., 229–235; *A Relation of Occurrences in the Mission of New France During the Years 1613 and 1614*, 1618, ibid., 2:251–275; Father Pierre Biard to the Very Reverend Father Claude Aquaviva, General of the Society of Jesus, at Rome, May 26, 1614, ibid., 3:7–18; and Father Pierre Biard, *Relation of New France* (Lyons, 1616), ibid., 3:275–83; quotes 1:129, 231, 131; 2:253, 265, 269; 3:279, 275. A pavesade is a canvas screen stretched around the ship to shield those on board from sight. On Argall and the situation in Jamestown, see Charles M. Andrews, *The Colonial Period of American History*, 4 vols. (New Haven, 1934), 1:114–115, 147–149.

39. Kelso and Straube, *Jamestown Rediscovery*, 30–31.

40. Smith, *Generall Historie*, 226; William Strachey also recorded Volday's death of a "burning-Fever" in *Historie of Travell*, 131; Dale to the President and Counsell of the Companie of Adventurers and Planters in Virginia, May 25, 1611, in Brown, *Genesis of the United States*, 1:490; Virginia Company, *True Declaration*, 258.

41. Kingsbury, *Records of the Virginia Company*, 1:633, 2:13–14, 3:423; Patrick Copland, *Virginia's God Be Thanked* (London, 1622), 14; Martha W. McCartney, "An Early Virginia Census Reprised," *Quarterly Bulletin of the Archaeological Society of Virginia* 54 (1999): 190.

42. Gondomar to Philip III, October 17, 1614, in Brown, *Genesis of the United States*, 2:740.

43. For this discussion, see Sir Thomas Dale "To the R. and my most esteemed friend, Mr. D. M.," in Hamor, *True Discourse of the Present Estate of Virginia*, 51–59, quotes 51, 55–56, 58; Whitaker "To my verie deere and loving Cosen M. G.," ibid., 59–61; John Rolfe, "The coppie of the Gentle-mans letters to sir Thomas Dale, that after maried Powhatans daughter, containing the reasons moving him thereunto," ibid., 61–68.

44. Sir Thomas Dale to Sir Ralph Winwood, June 3, 1616, in Brown, *Genesis of the United States*, 2:783.

45. Chamberlain to Sir Dudley Carleton, June 22, 1616, in *Letters of John Chamberlain*, 2:12.

46. Purchas, *Purchas His Pilgrimage*, 3rd ed. (London, 1617), 943; Ben Jonson, *The Staple of Newes*, ed. Anthony Parr (Manchester, 1988), 2.5.121–123, page 146; Smith, epistle dedicatory to the duchess of Richmond and Lennox, in *Generall Historie*, 42.

47. Purchas, *Purchas His Pilgrimage*, 954–955; Samuel Purchas, "Occurrents in Virginia, 1613–1619," in *Purchas His Pilgrimes*, 4:1773–74. Purchas said that his interpreter was "Sir Tho. Dales man." Helen Rountree has identified him as Spelman; see Rountree, *Pocahontas, Powhatan, Opechancanough: Three Indian Lives Changed by Jamestown* (Charlottesville, 2005), 179.

48. See Karen Robertson, "Pocahontas at the Masque," *Signs* 21 (1996): 551–583. The text of *The Vision of Delight* is in Stephen Orgel, ed., *Ben Jonson: Selected Masques*, (New Haven, 1970), 149–159; its presentation is discussed 21–22, 34–35.

49. Smith, *Generall Historie*, 258–262; David R. Ransome, "Pocahontas and the Mission to the Indians," *Virginia Magazine of History and Biography* 99 (1991): 81–94.

50. Rolfe to Sir Edwin Sandys, June 8, 1617, in Kingsbury, *Virginia Company Records*, 3:70–73.

51. George Thorpe et al. to Sir George Yeardley, February 18, 1619, ibid., 136.

52. Nathaniel Butler, *The Historye of the Bermudaes or Summer Islands*, ed. J. H. Lefroy (London, 1882), 271–272, 284; Ransome, "Pocahontas and the Mission to the Indians"; Vaughan, "Powhatans Abroad," 58–60; Karen Ordahl Kupperman, *Indians and English: Facing Off in Early America* (Ithaca, N.Y., 2000), 200.

53. Purchas, *Purchas His Pilgrimage*, 956. On Powhatan and the succession, see Rountree, *Pocahontas, Powhatan, Opechancanough*.

54. E. B. O'Callaghan, ed., *Documents Relative to the Colonial History of the State of New-York*, 15 vols. (Albany, 1856–1887), 1:2–3, 9–10, 16–21, quotes 16, 18. I thank Martha McCartney for calling this material to my attention. On Dutch involvement with Virginia, see Michael Jarvis and Jeroen van Driel, "The Vingboons Chart of the James River, Virginia, circa 1617," *William and Mary Quarterly*, 3rd ser., 54 (1997): 377–394, and April Lee Hatfield, *Atlantic Virginia: Intercolonial Relations in the Seventeenth Century* (Philadelphia, 2004). On the careers of Dale and Gates, see the *Oxford Dictionary of National Biography*.

55. Joyce Lorimer, ed., *English and Irish Settlement on the River Amazon, 1550–1646* (London, 1989), 47, 160.

56. Vincent T. Harlow, ed., *Ralegh's Last Voyage* (London, 1932), quote 243; Lorimer, *English and Irish Settlement on the River Amazon*; Chamberlain to Sir Dudley Carleton, December 4, 1618, in *Letters of John Chamberlain*, 2:191; John Pory to Carleton, October 31, 1618, in William S. Powell, *John Pory, 1572–1636* (Chapel Hill, 1977), 69–73, quote 73; Neil L. Whitehead, intro. to his edition of Ralegh's 1596 *Discoverie of the Large, Rich and Bewtiful Empyre of Guiana* (Norman, Okla., 1997), esp. n. 18, 56–57; David B. Quinn, *Ralegh and the British Empire* (Harmondsworth, 1973), chap. 8.

57. Captain John Smith, *A Description of New England* (London, 1616) in *Works*, 1:305–363, quote 351; Smith, *Generall Historie*, 428. In the *Generall Historie*, Smith wrote the Abenaki's name as "Dohoday."

58. "A Copie of the Articles which Master R. More, Governour Deputie of the Sommer Ilands, propounded to the Companie that were there with him to bee subscribed unto, which both hee and they subscribed the second of August, in his house, Anno 1612, which about the same time he sent into England to the worshipfull Companie of the Adventurers," in *A Plaine Description of the Barmudas, now called Sommer Ilands* (London, 1613), sig. G–G2; Chamberlain to Sir Dudley Carleton, October 27, 1613, in *Letters of John Chamberlain,* 1:482–483; Rolfe, *True Relation,* 11. On the early history of Bermuda, see Wesley Frank Craven, *An Introduction to the History of Bermuda* (Williamsburg, 1940); Neil Kennedy, "Anglo-Bermudian Society in the English Atlantic World, 1612 to 1701" (Ph.D. diss., University of Western Ontario, 2002); Michael J. Jarvis, "In the Eye of All Trade: Maritime Revolution and the Transformation of Bermudian Society, 1612–1800" (Ph.D. diss., College of William and Mary, 1998). Ambergris, a waxy substance excreted from the intestines of whales, was extremely valuable as an ingredient in perfumes.

59. Purchas, *Purchas His Pilgrimage,* 2nd ed. (London, 1614), 754 [misnumbered 748], 758.

9. JAMES CITTIE IN VIRGINIA

1. Chamberlain to Sir Dudley Carleton, June 22, 1616, in *The Letters of John Chamberlain,* ed. Norman Egbert McClure, 2 vols. (Philadelphia, 1939), 2:12.

2. Silvester Jourdain, *A Discovery of the Bermudas, Otherwise Called the Isle of Devils,* 1610, in Louis B. Wright, ed., *A Voyage to Virginia in 1609* (Charlottesville, 1964), 113; John Rolfe, *A True Relation of the state of Virginia lefte by Sir Thomas Dale Knight in May last 1616* (Charlottesville, 1951), 5, 8–11; Ralph Hamor, *A True Discourse of the Present Estate of Virginia* (London, 1615), 34–35; William M. Kelso and Beverly Straube, *Jamestown Rediscovery, 1994–2004* (Jamestown, 2004), 147, 156. I thank David Ransome for the suggestion that Bermuda may have been the source of Rolfe's good tobacco seed.

3. Ferrar Papers, Magdalene College, Cambridge, available on microfilm in *The Ferrar Papers, 1590–1790,* ed. David R. Ransome, 14 reels (Wakefield, West Yorkshire, 1992), reel 1, item 40. This letter is transcribed in Edward Wright Haile, ed., *Jamestown Narratives: Eyewitness Accounts of the Virginia Colony* (Champlain, Va., 1998), 761–775.

4. John Rolfe to Sir Edwin Sandys, June 8, 1617, in Susan Myra Kingsbury, ed., *Records of the Virginia Company of London,* 4 vols. (Washington, D.C., 1906–1935), 3:71; Rolfe, *True Relation,* 5, 7–8; Kelso and Straube, *Jamestown Rediscovery,* chap. 6.

5. Robert Brenner, *Merchants and Revolution: Commercial Change, Political Conflict, and London's Overseas Traders, 1550–1653* (Princeton, 1993), chaps. 3–4.

6. *A True Relation of such occurrences and accidents of noate, as hath hapned in Virginia, since the first planting of that Collony,* in *The Complete Works of Captain John Smith,* ed. Philip L. Barbour, 3 vols. (Chapel Hill, 1986), 1:29.

7. Carleton to John Chamberlain, August 18, 1607, in Philip L. Barbour, ed., *The Jamestown Voyages Under the First Charter, 1606–1609,* 2 vols. (Cambridge, 1969), 1:113–114; the city of Ralegh's grant of arms is in David Beers Quinn, ed., *The Roanoke Voyages, 1584–1590,* 2 vols. (London, 1955), 2:506–512.

8. Hamor, *True Discourse,* 30, 33.

9. On reports of Indian towns, see Karen Ordahl Kupperman, *Indians and English: Facing Off in Early America* (Ithaca, N.Y., 2000); on the baroque plan of St. Mary's City, see Henry M. Miller, "Colonies of Distinction: Maryland and New Netherland," *de Halve Maen* 78 (2005): 28–29.

10. Theodore K. Rabb, *Jacobean Gentleman: Sir Edwin Sandys, 1561–1629* (Princeton, 1998), pt. 3.

11. Rolfe, *True Relation*, 11.

12. *Virginia Company Records*, 1:256, 269, 391, 566; Virginia Company, "A Coppie of the Subscription for Maydes," July 16, 1621, Ferrar Papers, Magdalene College, Cambridge, partially reprinted in David R. Ransome, "Wives for Virginia, 1621," *William and Mary Quarterly*, 3rd ser., 48 (1991): 3–18, quote 7.

13. John Rolfe to Sir Edwin Sandys, in *Virginia Company Records*, 3:243; Engel Sluiter, "New Light on the '20. and Odd Negroes' Arriving in Virginia, August 1619," *William and Mary Quarterly*, 3rd ser., 54 (1997): 395–398; John Thornton, "The African Experience of the '20. and Odd Negroes' Arriving in Virginia in 1619," *William and Mary Quarterly*, 3rd ser., 55 (1998): 421–434.

14. "Coppie of the totall sums of the generall Muster of Virginia 1619," in *Ferrar Papers*, reel 1, 159. William Thorndale argued that the census was collected in March 1619, but Martha McCartney has since demonstrated conclusively that the date is Old Style, so the census was actually done in March 1620. See William Thorndale, "The Virginia Census of 1619," in *Magazine of Virginia Genealogy* 33 (1995): 60–161; and Martha W. McCartney, "An Early Virginia Census Reprised," *Quarterly Bulletin of the Archaeological Society of Virginia* 54 (1999): 178–196.

15. T. H. Breen and Stephen Innes, *"Myne Owne Ground": Race and Freedom on Virginia's Eastern Shore, 1640–1676* (New York, 1980).

16. Chamberlain to Carleton, November 23, 1616, and December 4, 1618, in *Letters of John Chamberlain*, 2:40, 190.

17. Pory's report of the assembly meeting is in *Virginia Company Records*, 3:153–177, quotes 174–175. Robert Poole's deposition, taken July 13, 1619, is in *Ferrar Papers*, reel 1, 113.

18. Rolfe to Sir Edwin Sandys, January 1620, in *Virginia Company Records*, 3:241–248, quotes 242, 244–245; Pory to Sandys, January 13, 1620, ibid., 249–253, quote 253.

19. Hamor, *True Discourse*, 44.

20. Pory to Chamberlain, September 30, 1619, in *Virginia Company Records*, 3:219–222, quotes 221–222; Pory to Sandys, January 16, 1620, ibid., 255–258, quote 256. On Pory's biography, see William S. Powell, *John Pory, 1572–1636* (Chapel Hill, 1977); for his reputed fondness for alcohol, see 60–61.

21. P. E. H. Hair and Robin Law, "The English in Western Africa to 1700," in Nicholas Canny, ed., *The Oxford History of the British Empire*, vol. 1, *The Origins of Empire: British Overseas Enterprise to the Close of the Seventeenth Century* (Oxford, 1998), 250–253.

22. John C. Appleby, "War, Politics, and Colonization, 1558–1625," ibid., 71; Joyce Lorimer, ed., *English and Irish Settlement on the River Amazon, 1550–1646* (London, 1989), chap. 3.

23. Increase Mather, *Kometographia. Or a Discourse Concerning Comets* (Boston, 1682), 108–111; Geoffrey Parker, *The Thirty Years' War* (New York, 1984);

W. B. Patterson, *King James VI and I and the Reunion of Christendom* (Cambridge, 1997), chap. 9; Pauline Croft, *King James* (Basingstoke and New York, 2003), 105–110.

24. Paul Slack, *The Impact of Plague in Tudor and Stuart England* (Oxford, 1985), 53–64, 144–151; Mary J. Dobson, *Contours of Death and Disease in Early Modern England* (Cambridge 1997), 371–372; Michael J. Braddick, *State Formation in Early Modern England, c. 1550–1700* (Cambridge, 2000), chap. 2; Keith Wrightson, *English Society, 1580–1680* (London, 1982), chap. 5.

25. Chamberlain to Sir Dudley Carleton, October 14, 1618, in *Letters of John Chamberlain*, 2:170; Patrick Copland, *Virginia's God Be Thanked* (London, 1622), 31–34.

26. Documents concerning the negotiations are in Edward D. Neill, *History of the Virginia Company of London* (1869; rpt., New York, 1968), chap. 8; and William Bradford, *Of Plymouth Plantation, 1620–1647*, ed. Samuel Eliot Morison (New York, 1952), 28–34. On puritan migration to the south, see Babette M. Levy, "Early Puritanism in the Southern and Island Colonies," *Proceedings of the American Antiquarian Society* 70 (1960): 69–348; John Bennet Boddie, *Seventeenth-Century Isle of Wight County Virginia* (Chicago, 1938), chaps. 2–5; James Horn, "To Parts Beyond the Seas," in Ida Altman and James Horn, "*To Make America,*" 86–87, 106–107; Horn, *Adapting to a New World: English Society in the Seventeenth-Century Chesapeake* (Chapel Hill, 1994), 55–57, 388–394; Rabb, *Jacobean Gentleman*, 330–331.

27. George Yeardley to Sir Edwin Sandys, June 7, 1620, in *Virginia Company Records*, 3:297–300.

28. Ibid.; John Pory to Sandys, June 12, 1620, ibid., 300–306.

29. Pory to Chamberlain, September 30, 1619, ibid., 219–222, quote 220; John Rolfe to Sir Edwin Sandys, January 1620, ibid., 241–248, quote 244.

30. *By the Treasuror, Councell, and Company for Virginia*, May 17, 1620, ibid., 275–280, quotes 275; Thorpe to John Smythe of Nibley, December 19, 1620, ibid., 417; "Notes from Lists showing total number of Emigrants to Virginia," ibid., 537; Rabb, *Jacobean Gentleman*, chap. 13; Karen Ordahl Kupperman, "Apathy and Death in Early Jamestown," *Journal of American History* 66 (1979): 24–40.

31. Rolfe, *True Relation*, 12.

32. John Pory to Sir Edwin Sandys, June 12, 1620, in *Virginia Company Records*, 3:305.

33. Virginia Company meeting, February 16, 1619, ibid., 309–312, quote 310–311; Virginia Company, *A Declaration of the State of the Colonie and Affaires in Virginia* (London, 1620), 6–8. On Thorpe and his mission, see Eric Gethyn-Jones, *George Thorpe and the Berkeley Company* (Gloucester, 1982); see also Peter Walne, "The Collections for Henrico College, 1616–1618," *Virginia Magazine of History and Biography* 80 (1972): 258–266.

34. George Thorpe to Sir Edwin Sandys, May 15 and 16, 1621, in *Virginia Company Records*, 3:446–447.

35. Robert Hunt Land, "Henrico and Its College," *William and Mary Quarterly*, 2nd ser., 18 (1938): 453–498.

36. The company announced this generous gift in a broadside published in May 1622; see *Virginia Company Records*, 3:642. On Copland, see Shona Vance, "Motifications (Bursaries and Endowments) for Education in Aberdeen, 1593–

1660 and Their Implementation in the Seventeenth Century" (Ph.D. diss., Aberdeen, 2000), 54–60; and Edward D. Neill, *Memoir of Rev. Patrick Copland, Rector Elect of the First Projected College in the United States* (New York, 1871).

37. Council in Virginia to Virginia Company, January 1622, in *Virginia Company Records*, 3:584.

38. Virginia Company meeting, January 16, 1622, ibid., 1:574; John Brinsley, *A Consolation for our Grammar Schooles* (London, 1622).

39. Virginia Company, *Declaration of the State of the Colonie and Affaires in Virginia*, 2; John Bonoeil, *Obseruations to be followed, for the making of fit roomes, to keepe silk-wormes in as also, for the best manner of planting of mulbery trees, to feed them. Published by authority for the benefit of the noble plantation in Virginia* (London, 1620). The list of products is 24–28.

40. George Yeardley to Sir Edwin Sandys, June 7, 1620, in *Virginia Company Records*, 3:298. A "stager" was an experienced hand.

41. Governor and Council in Virginia to Virginia Company, January 21, 1621, ibid., 424–425; William Strachey, *For the Colony in Virginea Britannia. Lawes Divine, Morall and Martiall, etc.* (London, 1612), in Peter Force, comp., *Tracts and Other Papers, Relating Principally to the Origin, Settlement, and Progress of the Colonies in North America*, 4 vols. (Washington, D.C., 1844; rpt., 1963), 67.

42. Virginia Company meeting, January 8, 1620, in *Virginia Company Records*, 1:290–291; Rabb, *Jacobean Gentleman*, 356–363; Charles M. Andrews, *The Colonial Period of American History*, 4 vols. (1934; rpt., New Haven, 1964), chap. 7.

43. Virginia Company, Instructions to Governor and Council in Virginia, July 24, 1621, in *Virginia Company Records*, 3:468–482, quotes 469, 473, 474. For the directions for glass beads, see Virginia Company to Governor and Council in Virginia, August 12, 1621, ibid., 495.

44. George Thorpe to Sir Edwin Sandys, May 15 and 16, 1621, ibid., 446–447; Thorpe to John Ferrar, May 15, 1621, ibid., 448–449; Nuce to Sir Edwin Sandys, May 27, 1621, ibid., 455–458; Virginia Company to Governor and Council in Virginia, July 25, 1621, ibid., 485–491, quote 486.

45. Yeardley to Sir Edwin Sandys, May 16, 1621, ibid., 452; Virginia Company to Governor and Council in Virginia, August 12, 1621, ibid., 496; George Thorpe to John Ferrar, May 15, 1621 ibid., 448.

46. Bonoeil, *Obseruations to be followed*, 19.

47. Dennis B. Blanton, "Drought as a Factor in the Jamestown Colony, 1607–1612," *Historical Archaeology* 34 (2000): 76.

48. Michael Drayton, "To Master George Sandys," in J. William Hebel, ed., *The Works of Michael Drayton*, 5 vols. (Oxford: Basil Blackwell, 1931–1941), 3:206–208, quote 207; Sandys to Samuel Wrote, March 23, 1623, in *Virginia Company Records*, 4:64–68, quote 66; G[eorge] S[andys], *Ovid's Metamorphoses Englished, Mythologiz'd, and Represented in Figures* (Oxford, 1632), 224, 330. Sandys's complete translation was first published in 1626; the 1632 edition added extensive commentaries and illustrations. See Raphael Lyne, *Ovid's Changing Worlds: English Metamorphoses, 1567–1632* (Oxford, 2001), 247–258; Deborah Rubin, *Ovid's Metamorphoses Englished: George Sandys as Translator and Mythographer* (New York, 1985), 151–177; Peter Hulme, *Colonial Encounters: Europe and the Native Caribbean, 1492–1797* (London, 1986), 154–155.

49. Two excellent accounts of this period are Helen C. Rountree, *Pocahontas, Powhatan, Opechancanough: Three Indian Lives Changed by Jamestown* (Charlottesville, 2005), and Frederic W. Gleach, *Powhatan's World and Colonial Virginia: A Conflict of Cultures* (Lincoln, 1997).

50. Council in Virginia to Virginia Company, January 1622, in *Virginia Company Records*, 3:584.

51. George Percy, "A Trewe Relacyon of the procedeings and ocurrentes of momente which have hapned in Virginia, from the Tyme Sir Thomas Gates was Shippwrackte uppon the Bermudes Anno 1609 untill my departure owtt of the Cowntry which was in Anno Domini 1612," in "George Percy's 'Trewe Relacyon': A Primary Source for the Jamestown Settlement," ed. Mark Nicholls, *Virginia Magazine of History and Biography* 115 (2005): 259, 261; Alexander Whitaker to Mr. Crashawe, August 9, 1911, in Alexander Brown, ed., *The Genesis of the United States*, 2 vols. (1890; rpt., Bowie Md., 1994), 1:497–499. For the conjecture that the fantasy may have been induced by ingestion of jimsonweed, see Ivor Noël Hume, *The Virginia Adventure* (New York, 1994), 301–303.

52. Governor and Council in Virginia, November 11, 1619, in *Virginia Company Records*, 3:228.

53. Captain John Smith, *The Generall Historie of Virginia, New-England and the Summer Isles* (1624), in *Works*, 2:293; "Voyage of Anthony Chester to Virginia, made in the year 1620" (Leyden, 1707), printed as "Two Tragical Events," *William and Mary Quarterly* 9 (1901): 213; Governor and Council in Virginia, January 20, 1623, in *Virginia Company Records*, 4:11.

54. Edward Waterhouse, *A Declaration of the State of the Colony and Affaires in Virginia* (London, 1622), quotes 15–17, 20. Captain John Smith reprinted Waterhouse's account with additional material in his *Generall Historie*, 293–305. Archaeological excavation of the plantation of Martin's Hundred has uncovered evidence that some victims may have been scalped; Ivor Noël Hume, *Martin's Hundred* (New York, 1982).

55. Virginia Council to Virginia Company, April 1620, in *Virginia Company Records*, 3:611–615, quote 612.

56. Extracts from the unpublished writings of D'Ewes and Mead are in notes by Robert C. Johnson in *Virginia Magazine of History and Biography* 68 (1960): 107 and 71, and (1963): 408–10; John Chamberlain to Sir Dudley Carleton, July 13, 1622, in *Letters of John Chamberlain*, 2:445–447, quote 446; Christopher Brooke, *A Poem on the Late Massacre in Virginia* (London, 1622), quotes sigs. A3v–A4, C. On *The Plantation in Virginia*, see Anthony Parr, ed., *Three Renaissance Travel Plays* (Manchester, 1995), 5.

57. For this account, see Virginia Company to Governor and Council in Virginia, August 1, 1622, in *Virginia Company Records*, 3:666–673, quotes 666, 667, 669, 672; Virginia Company to Governor and Council in Virginia, October 7, 1622, ibid., 683–90. The royal proclamation ending the lottery is 434–435.

58. *Virginia Company Records*, 3:536–537, 4:65.

59. Copland, *Virginia's God be Thanked*, 2, 9, 22, 24, 28.

60. Virginia Company, *A Note of the shipping men and provisions sent and provided for Virginia* (London, 1622), in *Virginia Company Records*, 3:639–643.

61. Waterhouse, *Declaration of the State of the Colony and Affaires in Virginia*, quotes 8, 22.

62. Governor and council in Virginia to Virginia Company, January 20, 1623, in *Virginia Company Records*, 4:9–17, quote 11.

63. George Sandys to Mr. Farrer, March 1623, ibid., 22–26, quotes 22, 23, 25; Sandys to Samuel Wrote, March 28, 1623, ibid., 64–68.

64. Sir Francis Wyatt to his father, ibid., 236–238.

65. Richard Frethorne to his Mother and Father, March 20, April 2 and 3, 1623, ibid., 58–62, quotes 58, 61. See "the names of the Dead" in John Camden Hotten, ed., *The Original Lists of Persons of Quality . . . Who went from Great Britain to the American Plantations* (London and New York, 1874), 93.

66. "Good Newes from Virginia, 1623," *William and Mary Quarterly*, 3rd ser., 5 (1948): 351–358.

67. John Donne, *A Sermon Preached to the Honourable Company of the Virginian Plantation*, November 13, 1622, in *The Sermons of John Donne*, ed. George R. Potter and Evelyn Simpson, 10 vols. (Berkeley, 1953–1962), 4:264–282, quotes 265, 272–273, 280.

68. J. Frederick Fausz and Jon Kukla, eds., "A Letter of Advice to the Governor of Virginia, 1624," *William and Mary Quarterly*, 3rd ser., 34 (1977): 104–129, quotes 116–117, 129.

69. Arundel to William Caninge, April 1623, in *Virginia Company Records*, 4:89.

70. Council in Virginia to Virginia Company, April 4, 1623, ibid., 98–99; "Notes taken from Letters which came from Virginia in the Abigail," June 19, 1623, ibid., 232, 238; Jane Dickenson, petition to the Governor and Council, March 30, 1624, ibid., 473.

71. Nicholas Canny, *Making Ireland British, 1580–1650* (Oxford, 2001), esp. 185–258.

72. Patterson, *King James and the Reunion of Christendom*, 314–338; Croft, *King James*, 107–122; Parker, *Thirty Years' War*, chap. 2. This point draws on the unpublished work of Emily Rose.

73. Virginia Company to Governor and Council in Virginia, October 7, 1622, in *Virginia Company Records*, 3:685–686; Edward L. Bond, Jan L. Perkowski, and Alison P. Weber, eds., "Father Gregorio Bolivar's 1625 Report: A Vatican Source for the History of Early Virginia," *Virginia Magazine of History and Biography* 110 (2002): 69–87, quote 80.

74. John Pory to the earl of Southampton, January 13, 1623, in Sidney V. James Jr., ed., *Three Visitors to Early Plymouth* (Plimoth Plantation, 1963), 5–13, quote 11; Pory to Sir Francis Wyatt, autumn 1622, ibid., 14–18; "Sir Francis Wiatt's Letter from Virginie whilst Governor," *William and Mary Quarterly*, ser. 2, 6 (1926): 114–121, quote 115.

75. John Chamberlain to Sir Dudley Carleton, July 13, 1622, in *Letters of John Chamberlain*, 2:445–447, quote 446; John Rawlins, *The Famous and Wonderfull Recoverie of a Ship of Bristoll, called the Exchange, from the Turkish Pirates of Argier* (London, 1622), sigs. C, D4–D4v.

76. *The Lamentable Cries of at Least 1500 Christians: Most of them Being English (Now Prisoners in Argiers Under the Turks)* (London, 1624), in Daniel J. Vitkus, ed., *Piracy, Slavery, and Redemption: Barbary Captivity Narratives from Early Modern England* (New York, 2001), 345–346; Robert Adams to his father, November 4, 1625, ibid., 349–350; Bradford, *Of Plymouth Plantation*, 176; Nabil Matar, *Islam in Britain, 1558–1685* (Cambridge, 1998), intro., chap. 1.

77. Henry Byam, *A Return from Argier. A Sermon Preached at Minhead in the County*

of Somerset the 16. of March, 1627, at the re-admission of a relapsed Christian in our Church (London, 1628). This publication also included the second sermon, by Edward Kellett.

78. H. R. McIlwaine, ed., *Minutes of the Council and General Court of Colonial Virginia*, 2nd ed. (Richmond, 1979), 128, 181.

79. Captain Nathaniel Butler, "The Unmasked Face of our Colony in Virginia," in *Virginia Company Records*, 2:374–376; replies from the colony are in H. R. McIlwaine, ed., *Journals of the House of Burgesses of Virginia, 1619–1658/59* (Richmond, 1915), 21–37, quote 21.

80. "Warrant to pay John Pory," in *Virginia Company Records*, 4:500 (Public Record Office, SP 39/16, no. 50); Virginia Council to Commissioners for Virginia, June 15, 1625, ibid., 563; Rabb, *Jacobean Gentleman*, 363–381; Powell, *John Pory*, 110–123.

81. See the chapters by Audrey Horning and Dennis Blanton in *Jamestown Archaeological Assessment* (Washington, D.C., n.d.).

82. See James R. Perry, *The Formation of a Society on Virginia's Eastern Shore, 1615–1655* (Chapel Hill, 1990); David R. Ransome, "Village Tensions in Early Virginia: Sex, Land, and Status at the Neck of Land in the 1620s," *Historical Journal* 43 (2000): 365–382; and Irene W. D. Hecht, "The Virginia Muster of 1624/5 as a Source for Demographic History," *William and Mary Quarterly*, 3rd ser., 30 (1973): 65–92.

83. Levy, "Early Puritanism," 108.

84. For this discussion, see Smith, *Generall Historie*, 33–478, quotes 462, 464, 474; *The True Travels, Adventures, and Observations of Captaine John Smith*, 1630, in *Works*, III:137–243; and *Advertisements For the unexperienced Planters of New-England, or any-where*, 1631, in *Works*, 3:287–302, quotes 287, 297.

85. On devolution, see David Thomas Konig, "Colonization and the Common Law in Ireland and Virginia, 1569–1634," in James A. Henretta, Michael Kammen, and Stanley N. Katz, eds., *The Transformation of Early American History: Society, Authority, and Ideology* (New York, 1991), 70–92.

Index